Intellectuals and the Articulation of the Nation

Intellectuals and
the Articulation of the Nation

Edited by
Ronald Grigor Suny
and
Michael D. Kennedy

Ann Arbor

THE UNIVERSITY OF MICHIGAN PRESS

Copyright © by the University of Michigan 1999
All rights reserved
Published in the United States of America by
The University of Michigan Press
Manufactured in the United States of America
⊗ Printed on acid-free paper

2002   2001   2000   1999   4   3   2   1

A CIP catalog record for this book is available from the British Library.

Library of Congress Cataloging-in-Publication Data

Intellectuals and the articulation of the nation / edited by Ronald
    Grigor Suny and Michael D. Kennedy.
        p.   cm.
    Includes bibliographical references and index.
    ISBN 0-472-10954-5 (acid-free paper)
        1. Intellectuals—Europe, Eastern.   2. Intellectuals—Eurasia.
    3. Nationalism—Europe, Eastern.   4. Nationalism—Eurasia.   I. Suny,
    Ronald Grigor.   II. Kennedy, Michael D.
    HM728   .I57   1999
    305.5'52'0947—dc21   99-6150
                                                                            CIP

Contents

Michael D. Kennedy and Ronald Grigor Suny

Introduction

Along with the rise of nationalism in the post–Cold War world has
come an explosion of interest in and study of what "makes" the nation.
Supplying their own answers to that difficult question, historians and
social scientists have arrived at a broad consensus on the modernity
and constructedness of nations, explicitly rejecting the concepts of
nationalists who argue for antique origins and long continuities of their
nations. Rather than the product of primitive or perennial cultural and
social forces, or the inevitable result of capitalist relations of production, or simply an expression of an innate ethnic or linguistic essence,
the nation has been reconceptualized as a community imagined by its
members and leaders to require their primary allegiance—within a
larger discourse in which nations, built on the people and a notion of
popular sovereignty, provide the justification of claims to national
rights, statehood, and territory.[1] The nation as representative of the
people has become in the twentieth century the principal form of legitimation of the state. However, "the fundamental problem," as Etienne
Balibar has pointed out,

> is therefore to produce the people. More exactly, it is to make the
> people *produce itself* continually as national community. Or again,
> it is to produce the effect of unity by virtue of which the people will
> appear, in everyone's eyes, "as a people," that is, as the basis and
> origin of political power.[2]

The production of the nation and its constituent people has been
variously elaborated in theoretical and macrohistorical accounts, but
increasingly the attempts to explain the emergence of the nation have
focused attention on the work of state and intellectual elites.[3] In her
work on South Africa, for example, Anne McClintock has emphasized

the inventedness of community in order more powerfully to demonstrate the "implications of labor and creative ingenuity, technology, and institutional power."

> Nations are elaborate social practices enacted through time, laboriously fabricated through the media and the printing press, in schools, churches, the myriad forms of popular culture, in trade unions and funerals, protest marches and uprisings.[4]

In this volume we focus on those who, in nationalism studies themselves, appear to have the greatest agency in the shaping of national understanding, propagating the values of the nation, disciplining the people internally, and enforcing the rules and boundaries of the constituent people. We focus on intellectuals. We do not agree that there has been "an excessive focus on the activities of nationalist intellectuals as opposed to what are arguably the two most important dramatis personae in any nationalist politics: state and society" (in the words of Mark Beissinger).[5] Although we do not disregard the broad structural and discursive frameworks and social dynamics that provided the context in which nations have been constructed or doubt that the popular exercise of nationalist visions and the utilization of national ideology by states have greater explicit social consequence, we are concerned here with the "quiet politics" (Beissinger's term) of nationalism that establishes the possibilities for what states and societies might do. In their contestation of the meaning of the nation intellectuals are disproportionately involved in such quiet politics. As individuals, and perhaps as a group, intellectuals, "those who create, distribute and apply culture," in Seymour Martin Lipset's phrase,[6] appear to have the greatest effect in their action, and the greatest autonomy in their actions. Intellectuals create different ideologies of national identity within a larger discursive universe of available materials. They do the imaginative ideological labor that brings together disparate cultural elements, selected historical memories, and interpretations of experiences, all the while silencing the inconvenient, the unheroic, and the anomalous.

Writers on nationalism have long appreciated the centrality of intellectuals to the emergence of national consciousness and political mobilization. For those who have thought of the nation as always with us, a real, natural given of social existence, intellectuals were those who articulated what was actually there but had remained hidden, the pervasive submerged presence of the national in conditions of unfreedom and unconsciousness. Intellectuals were enlighteners, liberators, the articulators of the national spirit that had to be revived, reborn, resurrected. For a more modernist group of theorists, like the influential Ernest Gellner, intellectuals were the articulators of necessary social processes without which industrial society was inconceivable. They were the clerks who carried out the functions of mass education and skilled labor needed by the modern world with its complex division of labor. Intellectuals helped to create the cultural homogeneity that industrialism required. Allied to this functionalist analysis, other modernists saw intellectuals as rational actors, even cynical instrumentalists, prepared to employ the rhetoric of nationalism for personal or political gains. Nationalism was available to outbid competitors in the political arena by appealing beyond the material to the affective. But more suggestive has been the work of those scholars who have seen intellectuals, not merely as reflective of what exists, but as constitutive of the nation itself, active agents providing new visions and languages that project a new set of social, cultural, and political possibilities. Intellectuals here are the creators, not only of nationalisms, but of the more universal discourse of the nation, of the very language and universe of meaning in which nations become possible. Our volume is interested in both the intellectual articulation of available materials and the creative construction of new visions and understandings. But it is also interested in something more. Our essays investigate the ways in which intellectuals as a category are provisionally constituted in the context of emerging nations. We are also interested in what happens to intellectuals once the nation exists, particularly in the conflicted relationship of intellectuals to power.

By focusing on the mutual articulation of national discourses and intellectuals, we shift the typical historical focus of sociological studies of intellectuals. Most such studies emphasize the significance of mass higher education and technocratic governance in late capitalism or postindustrial society for the production of intellectuals and their influence.[7] By focusing on the nation, we shift our historical eye to include the early industrial age and the beginnings of print capitalism, the moment when nations could become popular, and intellectuals might play a consequential role in refashioning the social imagination.

By focusing on the nation, we also diminish the salience of oppositions or tensions important in other studies of intellectuals. The tension between function and power in studies of professionals, so important for those who debate the relative value of expertise and its use in domination,[8] looms less large in discussions of nation making. Knowledge and power converge in studies of intellectuals and the nation. For nationalists the conquest of state power is motivated, at least in part, by a desire to create the conditions for the nation to know itself better. Similarly, the tension between expertise and criticality, so important for those who debate the political responsibility of intellectuals, is typically resolved in nationalism studies either by condemning nationalist intellectuals for generating dangerous products or celebrating those who elaborate the meaning of one's own nation.

When we put intellectuals in the center of attention, however, we are not treating nationalism as a simple instrumentalist practice in which elite interests, understood as relatively objective and timeless, determine action. In the era of nationalism, elite agents certainly operate within the discourse of the nation, utilizing national symbols and traditions, reinventing and redeploying them to realize their own desires and "interests," disguised as the "national interest." But a simple rational-choice argument could capture neither the complex construction of interests themselves nor the constitution of the subjects who become the interest-bearers. Without denying that elites try to achieve their material and nonmaterial "interests" in ways that can be formally modeled as a game, and acknowledging some sophisticated treatments of utility maximization in which both material and nonmaterial goals are included, we rather see how interests themselves are constituted by actors in changing historical and cultural contexts. It is not that nationalism is not "useful" or "rational" in certain circumstances, but that it is also much more than useful and rational; it is also irrational, excessive, even self-destructive. And it is even more than that. Nationalism is a complex cultural field that deserves as much explanation as do the actors who are caught up in it. It is especially complex if we take as subject formations both the nation and the intellectual.

Like Rogers Brubaker, we believe that decoupling the categories of the nation's practice and its analysis can facilitate the study of the nation in the variety of its formations.[9] For instance, we cannot accept at face value claims that nations are reawakened or that nations mature, and we would rather see such invocations as discursive strategies that elevate the nation's legitimacy into unassailable and teleological social formations. Such an approach also resonates with a familiar position within the normative politics of intellectual practice. For many analysts of intellectual practice, nationalism can destroy intellectuality. It is not, however, altogether clear that standing outside the streams of history, in an analytical position that claims to be divorced from practice, affords better tools for explaining social transformations.[10] We believe, in the end, that articulation offers us a way to study intellectuals and the nation simultaneously.

Articulation is our keyword, a word that is helpful precisely because it provides an important double meaning. A noun that implies expression, something intellectuals are obliged to do to fill their role, it also implies a measure of fit between a cultural product and the social environment that enables its production and makes that product consequential. We are focusing on intellectuals as actors, rather more than on their environment and the institutionalization of their ideas.[11] We also focus on that close articulation between intellectual and nation, and on the ways in which different kinds of intellectuals, and different kinds of nations, fit together. We have adopted a broad definition of intellectuals and explore the practices of intellectuals that are not so obviously "intellectual"—kitchen table talk or languishing in prison, for instance. We are also interested in people who may not be credentialed as intellectuals but whose practice has consequences normally reserved to intellectuals. Indeed, the politics of intellectual definition is nowhere more apparent than in the claim about the relationship between intellectuals and nation. Intellectuals face a double risk when enveloped by the nation. On the one hand, as patriots they lose their credentials as critical or independent. On the other hand, as critical intellectuals questioning the very "authenticity" of the nation, they are either ignored, marginalized, or cast out altogether. The very investigation in which our authors (as intellectuals) are engaged is likely to draw hostility from "true" nationalists, as Katherine Verdery's autobiography in this volume suggests.

This volume, then, is not only about the intellectual and the articulation of the nation, but also the articulation of two discursive fields of intellectual practice—around the responsibility of intellectuals and around the making of nations—that themselves have a limited fit with each other. The contest over what makes an intellectual is probably as vital as the dispute over the making of the nation, but those who have engaged in the discussion of the normative grounding of intellectual distinction have not usually investigated the nation. In this introductory chapter we begin by reviewing how intellectuals have posed intellectual responsibility yet have either marginalized or negatively valorized the nation in the discussion. We then turn to investigate one form of intellectual activity—active participation of the intellectual in emancipatory or oppositional politics, which has the effect not only of further reducing the nation's significance but of aspiring to minimize the distinction of the intellectual from the masses. This choice of identifying with popular elements, moreover, fails to engage seriously the notion that intellectuals might not only be distinct, but also occupy a location in power relations that produces privilege. In the next section, we consider the linkage of intellectuals to power, especially where some fraction of the intelligentsia has been defined as a "new class." The problem of intellectuals and the state, those within and without, was posed particularly harshly in the Soviet bloc, where intellectual distinction was framed by regimes that sought to monopolize all social discourse. We ask how intellectual authority expanded or was constrained, how visions became transformative or reproductive, how the intellectuals' lives, and not just their practices, resonated with the popular, and how the intellectual distinction itself was reduced or elevated in significance by movements of transformation. In the final section, we attempt to illustrate the ways in which intellectuals brought the nation into being and how intellectuals have been conceived in the making of nations.

The Normative Grounding of Intellectual Distinction

Intellectuals are their own harshest critics. Much of the literature on intellectuals (of course, written by intellectuals—who else?) is ruthlessly critical of their social effects,[12] but the normative grounding of that critique is not at all consistent. The foundational text is *La trahison des clercs* (1927) by Julien Benda (1867–1956), who argued that "thanks to the clerks"—those "whose activity essentially is *not* the pursuit of practical aims"—"humanity did evil for two thousand years, but honoured good."[13] At the end of the nineteenth century the clerks, "who had acted as a check on the realism of the people[,] began to act as its stimulators." Giving up their disinterested pursuits of knowledge, they "began to play the game of political passions," primarily adhering to nationalism, xenophobia, and racism, while favoring particularism over universalism, the practical over the spiritual, tradition and custom over reason, the strong state, the collective over the individual, action over knowledge, and political forms adapted to the unsocial and bloody nature of human beings.[14] Benda was writing at a time when he perceived the abandonment by intellectuals of dispassionate Reason and a willing acceptance of forms of irrationalism ranging from Bergsonism to fascism and bolshevism. He yearned for the critical free-thinking of such people as Socrates, Jesus, Spinoza, Voltaire, or his near contemporary Ernst Renan, "symbolic personages marked by their unyielding distance from practical concerns."[15]

In the next decade Karl Mannheim established the sociological foundations for this argument with his notion of intellectuals as socially unattached and relatively classless. They lose their "intellectuality," he wrote, when they suspend doubt, to become politically effective.[16] This general sociological turn was, of course, also inspired by political concerns. At about the same time Edward Shils, the Chicago sociologist of intellectuals and ideologies, was stimulated to undertake his lifelong studies by the negative example of American "fellow-travelers" and Communist intellectuals, as well as the "active mischief" of Weimar intellectuals, the "complaisant indifference or approval to ruin what might have been a decent society." Shils divided intellectuals into those who oppose prevailing norms and those who work to maintain "order and continuity in public life."[17] The latter clearly have a role in the formation of national communities. Shils argues that

> by means of preaching, teaching, and writing, intellectuals infuse into sections of the population which are intellectual neither by inner vocation nor by social role, a perceptiveness and an imagery which they would otherwise lack. By the provision of such techniques as reading and writing and calculation, they enable the laity to enter into a wider universe. The creation of nations out of tribes, in early modern times in Europe and in contemporary Asia and Africa, is the work of intellectuals, just as the formation of the American nation out of diverse ethnic groups is partly the work of teachers, clergymen, and journalists.[18]

From his very definition of intellectuals—as those distinct from the "laity" by their concern, not only with the immediate, but with more remote values—Shils appreciates that intellectuals can both elaborate and develop the potentialities inherent in a "system of cultural values" and reject "the inherited set of values."[19] While useful for elaborating how intellectuals work, his normative stance shapes profoundly how that work is to be evaluated. He is critical of their disruption of social solidarity, established tradition, and constituted authority and assumes a dedicated conservative opposition to the critical, oppositional intellectual.[20] Of course, normative politics can move in the opposite direction.

Alvin Gouldner finds precisely in the intellectuals' opposition to authority a normatively superior position. It is a universal class, if flawed, because "it subverts all establishments, social limits, and privileges, including its own . . . [and] bears a culture of critical and careful discourse which is an historically emancipatory rationality."[21] The critical intellectual gains authority by claiming it on the grounds of autonomous, ostensibly unself-interested rationality. The new intellectual class claims authority on the basis, not of force, violence, or even property, but of skill and science. The power of argument is juxtaposed to the argument from power. Nevertheless, in Gouldner's "new class" analysis, intellectuals remain a class whose interest disproportionately advantages them even as they seek knowledge.[22] In his words, they are "a cultural bourgeoisie who appropriates privately the advantages of an historically and collectively produced cultural capital."[23] Like any other class, its objective is "to increase its own share of the national product; to produce and reproduce the special social conditions enabling them to appropriate privately larger shares of the incomes produced by the special cultures they possess; to control their work and their work settings; and to increase their political power partly to achieve the foregoing."[24] These alternative normative positions embodied by Shils and Gouldner reflect the cultural politics of the American academy for the last thirty years, even if the tide has moved somewhat to the left over that time.

In the thoroughly politicized context in which they lived and worked, East European intellectuals could not have embraced such a Euro-American aversion to political engagement[25] in any other than a utopian way. Indeed, political engagement, especially over the national question, was the rule, rather than the exception, in Eastern Europe.[26]

Even the East European revisionist challenge to Stalinist rule, exhausted after the invasion of Czechoslovakia in 1968, might be understood as an attempt to transform Marxism and Communist rule into a more intellectually vital project.[27] In all of these efforts, intellectuality, of which reason is its prominent expression, was the primary challenge to crude political practice. It was a refuge from the pseudopolitics of a monopolistic regime, a sanctuary from which a new politics could be articulated even when actual political practice was precluded. As Kołakowski argued in 1972, when intellectuals fail to use reason to establish their political or moral position, they abandon their very identity as intellectuals.[28]

This normative position is applied not only to intellectuals and Communism but especially to the role played by intellectuals in the making of nationalism and anti-Semitism. Miklos Molnar finds that nationalism "paralyzed the minds of intellectuals[,] and . . . the political culture of the Hungarian elite which seemed so promising in the nineteenth century."[29] Leon Volovici demonstrates that the interwar Romanian intellectual, central to the nation's definition, became more and more invested in the irrationalism of nationalism and "the latent perception of Jew as alien; while few Romanian intellectuals were extremists in their antisemitism, few intellectuals would take a public stand against it.[30] In his analysis, there was a "replacement of thinking by commitment, the exchange of the criterion of truth—now in the service of mysticism and politics—for myth, the repudiation of the intellect and the praise of barbarism."[31]

This theme is quite common in the wars of Yugoslav succession, but the arguments for where intellectuality lies are less clear cut. Consider how one anthropologist refers to the hope for Western support: "[E]ven now some Croats are calling for a 'desert storm' operation to drive the occupiers from their soil, followed by the Bosnians who want air strikes on Serbian gunners and an end to the arms embargo that limits their capacity to fight Serbs. It is also not the first time that intellectuals have been vaporized, to be replaced by patriots. It is this sense of inevitability, of course, that politicians must have. They must create crisis so that the choice is to be loyal or disloyal, to be patriot or traitor, in order to achieve their own ends."[32] By contrast, Stjepan Mestrovic argues on behalf of political commitments; such a disengaged intellectuality before the wars of Yugoslav succession as proposed above is a kind of blasé voyeurism, based on Western naivete.[33]

In some circumstances, then, intellectual responsibility has demanded a political engagement infused with reason. Where Communism and Fascism have ruled, apolitical intellectual responsibility was harder to imagine, much less practice. To refuse to submit to Communist or Fascist ideological doctrine was obviously a political stance, and to submit was to refuse intellectual responsibility. But in the United States, intellectual responsibility could be constructed in opposition to political engagement entirely, based on ideologies of reason and science ostensibly devoid of politics.[34] To make these assessments of responsibility were obviously normative engagements themselves. But in the United States and other places where hegemony is articulated through political pluralism, to refuse to practice politics could more plausibly be constructed as apolitical. This commitment to an apolitical science in the context of political pluralism led Parsons and others to vaunt professionals as the intellectuals par excellence of modernity.[35]

In the construction of such an intellectual, "politics" in the national or class sense could disappear. At least those sociologists and others charged to explain the profession could miss its national and class bearings. The normative could slide into a narrowly conceived occupational code of ethics and miss the way in which the profession itself is national or embedded in class. The apolitical professional could be viewed in a mirror of the sociologist's own ostensibly apolitical gaze. While there has been an extensive critique of this political innocence by a long line of sociologists interested in the power and privilege of professions,[36] most of these sociologists have focused rather exclusively on the occupational politics of professionals. When they have gone beyond the profession to consider the political, they typically have done so to consider how national or class-based political conflicts affected the occupation's own professional projects.[37] Recently, however, the discursive link between professional identity and the making of nations and empires has been explored. Ming-cheng Lo has demonstrated that the internal contradictions of the professional project among Taiwanese physicians helps explain their trajectory from being the primary exponents of an independent Taiwanese nation in the 1920s to apolitical doctors during the 1930s to, finally, imperial physicians during World War II.[38] Indeed, it is one more reflection of the American national experience that intellectuals, or even professionals, could be theorized as somehow only occupational or class beings and not as themselves embedded in the nation.

While the relationship between the purely professional or scientific and the political has been increasingly problematized, the troubling relationship between the intellectual and the political remains. Professionals are, after all, manifestly political in their self-organization and reliance on the state for regulation.[39] Intellectuals, by contrast, are constructed as potentially above politics, allowing their intellectuality to construct their response to politics even as they engage it. Habermas and those inspired by him seem to hold onto the hope embodied in the example of Heinrich Heine, who simultaneously remained autonomous from the contemporary politics of critical intellectuals but nonetheless engaged the politics of the day. But Habermas mainly uses that example and his philosophical elaboration of it to provide a normative grounding for the critique he emphasizes: the segmentation between intellectuals who become expert but not public (professionals narrowly construed), and the masses who remain public but not critical.[40] This problem, however, should not be approached so readily as a general condition of modernity. There are several alternative relationships between intellectuals and power in modernity.

In China, intellectuals can draw on a tradition of "remonstration" to be simultaneously intellectual and political. Although the particular confrontation in Tiananmen Square led to an initially more egalitarian dialogue and subsequently greater "confrontation" than is traditional, its initial form was familiar. Intellectuals and students challenged the state and offered a different vision of what it meant to be Chinese in a familiar historical repertoire.[41] Remonstration is not an East European practice, but during late Communism intellectuals sought a new strategy for critique that embraced the distinction between intellectuals and politics.

While their Western critics were increasingly likely to be making the argument that intellectuals are always potentially political because they can understand fully neither the conditions nor the consequences of their actions, East Europeans sought to challenge the state-sponsored politicization of art and science by posing the distinction between knowledge and politics in a virtually utopian way. Jerzy Szacki, for instance, acknowledged the difficulty of being primarily responsible to one's own intellectual field and not to politics, but he nevertheless wished to consider just how the utopia of absolute cultural values could influence the cultivation of intellectual responsibility under Communism.[42] Communism collapsed before the full implications could be considered, but the volume in which Szacki's article appeared offered a remarkably interesting collection of views on how politics and intellectual responsibility should comingle.[43]

Of course, a substantial number of the authors in that collection followed Benda to argue that intellectuals must remain distinct and follow their own particular codes of responsibility. As Plato would have it, or as Benda argued, the treason of intellectuals is to abandon the commitment to a superior and ever more cultivated universalistic reason.[44] Others argued that an intellectual's primary responsibility is to the craft, a textual responsibility, and one abandons intellectual responsibility when one violates that code of textual responsibility.[45] Indeed, intellectual responsibility is most apparent when moral action is conducted through modes of intellectual practice, rather than in explicitly political engagement. But even with that intellectual craft, intellectuals cannot be relieved of political or moral responsibility since it can, and must, be practiced within their field.[46] For these authors, then, intellectuals have a different kind of political responsibility, perhaps even an elevated one, but one that is to be kept separate from popular politics. Ernest Gellner, however, offers caution by arguing that it is frankly difficult to recognize intellectual treason when any conclusion is reached by intellectual means; perhaps the greatest treason is to easily identify others who are guilty.[47]

On the other hand, several of the authors emphasized that one cannot separate very easily intellectual responsibility from a more general political responsibility. For instance, the defense of truth seeking cannot be limited to intellectual affairs, since the real world impinges on those intellectual affairs, and truth seeking is not only the province of intellectuals, but of all actors.[48] Indeed, intellectuals have more responsibility than ever before, given that technological prowess now threatens not only human communities but the biophysical world itself.[49] Another author, however, argues that to submerge one's intellectuality into a political position can be intellectually responsible if it is a strategy realized through intellectual means. Expertise cannot be neutral and is rather connected to the values one embraces, which might require political engagement.[50]

East Europeans were more likely to emphasize that intellectuality should be separated from power, and West Europeans were more likely to emphasize this impossibility. In part this was because Communism, as a system, sought to contain intellectuals, to co-opt them, and through that lead them to abandon intellectual responsibility.[51] To adopt the liberal position of intellectuals remaining apart from politics was a means of preserving that intellectual responsibility in late Communism. This tendency of emphasizing intellectual autonomy was, however, more difficult to maintain before the politics of the nation. Jerzy Jedlicki argued that despite the protests of liberal intellectuals, one cannot be responsible only for oneself. One must also address collective responsibility for a nation's past. As the nation is socially constructed, so is collective responsibility for its heritage. The obligation to assume that collective responsibility is as real as the nation.[52] In this regard, he says, historians have a special role. "The historian's conscious and subconscious choices of topics and interpretations may make people remember what ought to be remembered, or may help them to forget the events they do not like to think about."[53]

Although it is impossible to resolve these profound theoretical differences about intellectual responsibility, one point of departure for those interested in developing a normative theory of intellectual distinction would be to adopt a more Gramscian position. Here a normative theory of intellectual responsibility is replaced with a theory of intellectuals embedded in a larger account of social transformation. For Gramsci and those who follow him, the question then is how to become an effective oppositional intellectual.[54] Proximity to power is never a problem for Gramsci, for it is inevitable. The "taint" of power is not something to avoid, for far more relevant is where you stand.

Intellectuals and Opposition

If the institutions that authorize and empower intellectuals are relatively "legitimate" and present themselves as neutral and disinterested, like France's Ecole Nationale d'Administration, England's Oxford or Cambridge, America's Harvard or Yale, it is more likely that the politicized intellectual can be denied his or her status as intellectual. By contrast, where national liberation movements define the trajectory of younger generations, intellectuals are likely to move from movements to ministerial office after the revolution. They must be politicized. In Russia, China, Vietnam, and elsewhere, revolutionary movements have been an effective conduit from the margins of society into the state. Likewise, the social mobilizations that transformed Soviet-type societies in the late 1980s, notably in those places with developed civil societies, propelled intellectuals into explicitly political roles in post-Communist regimes,[55] with Václav Havel as the supreme exemplar. Clearly, then, the articulation of intellectuals and political engagement is shaped by the larger discursive field in which they are embedded, and the degree to which the dominant institutions are contested by those out of power.

In the intellectual politics of transformation, Gramsci is usually taken as the point of departure. Gramsci has most usefully distinguished between traditional intellectuals, "whose position in the interstices of society has a certain inter-class aura about it but derives ultimately from past and present class relations and conceals an attachment to various historical class formations," and organic intellectuals, who might serve any function and are "the thinking and organizing element of a particular fundamental social class."[56] As Geoff Eley reminds us of Gramsci's call for developing organic intellectuals of the Left: "Any social group that aspires to cast or recast society in its own image must be capable of generating its own organic intellectuals capable of exercising moral leadership and of winning over a significant proportion of existing traditional intellectuals; for otherwise the dominant meanings and understandings in society cannot be contested."[57]

Following in many ways both Benda and Gramsci, Edward Said has put forth his own program for the public role of the intellectual, that of the "outsider, 'amateur,' and disturber of the status quo."[58] For Said, intellectuals are "precisely those figures whose public performances can neither be predicted nor compelled into some slogan, orthodox party line, or fixed dogma." "Nothing disfigures the intellectual's public performance as much as trimming, careful silence, patriotic bluster, and retrospective and self-dramatizing apostasy."[59] Said distinguishes, then, between intellectuals as critical, subversive outsiders who "speak the truth to power," and supportive insiders who promote special interests, "patriotic nationalism, corporate thinking, and a sense of class, racial or gender privilege."[60]

Said defines an intellectual as "an individual endowed with a faculty for representing, embodying, articulating a message, a view, an attitude, philosophy or opinion to, as well as for, a public."[61] This definition works for the academic as well as the president of the republic. The intellectual is more than a thinker—all human beings think. Intellectuals have an essentially public role in which they use their intellect and intellectual skills to some public end. Some engage in the unmasking of oppression and exploitation; others generate the mystifications that allow existing power relations to flourish.

This approach, however, assumes away the challenge of recognizing what is public and what is not and also takes for granted that the products are intellectual if they are produced by those who are credentialed so. It does not question how the credentialing takes place. Moreover, it takes a profoundly intellectual location to be able to recognize which products are intellectual and which are not and which products are contributing to the masking of power and which are unmasking it. In short, even in this self-evident definition, the power and limitations of intellectuals radiate: their power to define distinction, including their own,[62] but only at the expense of hiding other problems. And very often, although not always, these accounts underplay the problem of the nation.

All intellectuals, given the fatality of language and the necessity of citizenship in the modern world, are "nationed." Contingently, at least, they have a national identity, and their practices may have important consequences for the nation. Intellectuals sometimes take up the most fundamental roles in the definition of the nation, being charged with "building" the nation, or perhaps even "destroying" it. Said clearly has a preferred role: "With regard to the consensus on group or national identity it is the intellectual's task to show how the group is not a natural or God-given entity but is a constructed, manufactured, even in some cases invented object, with a history of struggle and conquest behind it, that it is sometimes important to represent." The dilemma for this approach, of course, is to challenge one of the most important resources of a national identity: the power that comes from claims of antique origins or divine fates. Speaking truth to power may involve challenging the power of the community one seeks to empower.

One need not begin from a Marxist or post-Marxist foundation to adopt a similar position on a politicized intellectual's responsibility for speaking truth to power and practicing a national politics that is inclusive or expansive. One of the most potent examples of a theorist of, and practitioner in, a politics that emphasizes the engaged role of intellectuals is Václav Havel. Although all individuals are enjoined to develop their own personal morality and responsibility to resist ideology's destruction of both life and environment, in Havel's view intellectuals, as those leading in the elaboration of human consciousness, have a spe-

cial role. As he argued to the U.S. Congress shortly after the East European revolutions of 1989, "If the hope of the world lies in human consciousness, then it is obvious that intellectuals cannot go on forever
avoiding their share of responsibility for the world, hiding their distaste for politics under the alleged need to be independent."[63] Unlike
Gramsci and Said, Havel begins from a much more individualist and
spiritual normative foundation. Personal reason, humility, and dignity
are the basis for resistance to Communism and other ideologically
dominated forms of life.[64] Without defining a set of power relations in
which some individuals or groups are clearly aligned with power and
others clearly aligned with emancipation, Havel's theory of intellectual
politics rests more comfortably with traditional approaches to intellectuals and their normative distinction. If intellectuals are only obliged to
articulate "truth" and not to empower collectivities, Havel does not
face the same dilemmas as Gramsci and Said. He need not question
whether he must compromise his intellectuality for its social effect.
Ethics are his principal guide, not social change.

     Havel, Said, and Gramsci, all exemplary intellectuals, illustrate a
similar resolution of the relationship between the politics of intellectual
responsibility and of the nation. While embracing their nation, they do
so on grounds that are more "universal," whether in an embrace of liberal respect for human rights, or in a philosophy of history committed
to general emancipation. The nation is not foregrounded in their philosophy.

     In general, nationalism is presented as the intellectual's nemesis.
Indeed, it is relatively rare to find those who would write first about
intellectual responsibility to then go on and engage the nation positively and prominently. Of course, within national historiographies
intellectuals are lauded because they struggle to release and elaborate
their nation. But here the narrative of intellectual responsibility is subordinated to the narrative of the nation's trajectory. With this collection,
we hope to stimulate more discussion about the politics of intellectual
responsibility that neither distances the nation nor is subordinated to it.
We can suggest this direction of discussion by identifying one recent,
and exemplary, effort within this problematic.

     The celebrated Hungarian theorist of antipolitics, György Konrad,
has recently fixed his gaze on the nation in fear of the growth of anti-
Communist fascism. Rather than condemn nationalism as inherently
exclusive, Konrad recommends to his fellow nationals that the Hun-

garian nation be reconceived as a project rather than an identity, and as one that is open to external influences, rather than closed off from them. He writes:

> The self-shrinking national strategy takes what it considers non-national and delights in condemning it. The self-expanding national strategy takes anything from the outside world that can be fruitfully related to what was previously considered national and delights in integrating the two.[65]

As he proposes a reconception of the nation, he also writes from a remarkably confident position, eager to see the expansion of the nation's meaning, rather than its consolidation. That is certainly a strategy for articulating the making of nations and of intellectual practice, but it also has the potential for reinforcing the gap between those globally oriented citizens and those unable to partake, for whatever reason, of this international access. It opens the door for the critique, once again, of intellectual privilege and, dare we say it, cosmopolitanism. And it also treats the global as rather benign, or at least subject to intellectually responsible selection, rather than to the nation's subversion.

For most postcolonial accounts, the global is by no means so benign. In his accounts of India's nationalism, for instance, Partha Chatterjee explores how even nationalism, that which is supposed to be the property of a nation, is conceived within a global framework that undermines the indigenousness of Indian expression.[66] How can one articulate an emancipatory politics in the frame of one's own community when that frame, the nation, is not an indigenous cultural form but one gradually appropriated from the colonizers by Indian intellectuals and leaders? Part of the problem for India, he argues, is that one is resisting the domination of Europeans within the problematic of European creation. Part of the solution is to develop a different kind of methodology that searches for the community that a European imperialism has destroyed. East Europeans, by contrast, rarely find such a dilemma or need to unpack European imperialism from their own national projects. They have another kind of imperialism in the forefront of their mind.

Those escaping Communism are also likely to see their movement as one away from empire, from a kind of imperialism that many East European liberals and/or nationalists see as far more destructive of community than global capitalism. In radical distinction from many postcolonial positions like that of Chatterjee, community might be found alongside global capital. Konrad's own fusion of liberalism and nationalism suggests just such an emancipatory hope.

The comparison between such different kinds of postcolonial expressions as Konrad's and Chatterjee's suggests just how powerfully Soviet imperialism, as much as global capitalism, has shaped the construction of the nation and global capitalism. The differences are profound, but the similarities are intriguing too. In both cases, the nation is being reconceived as something that must be constructed and made along lines that are not already given. And here, the intellectual becomes absolutely central, whether in facilitating a nation's adaptation to an external world, or in search of that which global forces have destroyed.

These various examples—from Benda to Gramsci and Said to Havel—make it clear that any account of the relationship of intellectuals to power, to the nation, to the state, or to society is implicated in a complicated cultural politics informed by the case at hand. In some cases, the independence of intellectuals from politics is celebrated, while in others it is identified as irresponsibility. Sometimes, intellectuals are praised for their devotion to the nation, while in other cases, their devotion is devalued as irrational mysticism. If the politics are shared, whether revolutionary Marxist, nationalist, or liberal democratic, the analyst is likely to celebrate the responsibility of political intellectuals; if the politics are opposed, he/she is likely to identify intellectuals as having lost their identity. Regardless, the Gramscian point is fundamental: intellectuals are invaluable in the refashioning of a nation, especially when that goes beyond rearticulating existing forms, as Konrad and Chatterjee recommend. Equally fundamental, however, is that intellectual indispensability and the political definition of responsibility cannot address that basic sociological question of the relationship between intellectuals and power.

Intellectuals and Power

This transformation of intellectual roles—from leaders or advisers of social movements to those with state authority and power—invites consideration of intellectuals as a separate class or social group. Nationalist ideology makes little room for this kind of question, but certainly Marxism and populism have long made this a central object of inquiry, especially around the question of whether intellectuals form a "new class." To see intellectuals as a new class, seeking or achieving power, is to ask whether their particular "interests," either in terms of the valuation of intellectual labor over manual labor[67] or in terms of alternative discursive frames—the culture of critical discourse[68] or the culture of rational discourse[69]—privilege intellectuals over others. This problematic is commonly pursued in class analysis but relatively rarely in studies of social movements or nationalism. Here we explore how theories of nation formation might be affected by a new-class approach, and how the new-class approach might be transformed if we consider how the articulation of the nation is connected to intellectual privilege.

Michel Foucault, in his many essays linking knowledge and power, most notably "Truth and Power," questions the role of intellectuals by laying out the limiting and particular claims of putatively general or universal intellectuals.[70] "For a long period," he writes, "the 'left' intellectual spoke and was acknowledged the right of speaking in the capacity of master of truth and justice. He was heard, or purported to make himself heard, as the spokesman of the universal. To be an intellectual meant something like being the consciousness/conscience of us all."[71] He finds that over time, such general intellectuals become less capable of claiming universal consequence. With the development of science and its extension to all domains of material and social life, the "specific intellectual" with a particular rather than general expertise eventually eliminates the general intellectual's claims to relevance. At the same time, the specific intellectual becomes closer to the masses, as they are both confronted by the same adversaries and have the same material concerns. Although Foucault does not say it, the main domain left for general intellectuals could be in articulating the nation. But following Foucault, this remaining general ambition might be analyzed with attention to very specific lineages and circuits of power.[72]

Pierre Bourdieu also has analyzed intellectuals in terms of his more general theory of fields, where each set of engagements is constituted by particular forms of capital and strategies of action. In this approach, rather than being obliged to define intellectuals in terms of some familiar theory of class, one considers each site of activity in terms of the relationship between the specific forms of capital circulating in a particular field of activity that is mediated by particular forms of habitus. He claims that intellectuals, and sociologists in particular, typically

focus on their relationship to politics and power but outside the particular kinds of power relations that constitute their own field of activity.
So, instead of beginning an analysis of intellectuals and movements by
assessing their relationship, one should begin with the field of power
relations in which intellectuals are operating and ask how the "aesthetic dimension of political conduct matters to intellectuals" or how
the university or a discipline is connected to the political fields existing
outside of it.[73] Indeed, in his call for a reflexive sociology, one of the
first objects of scrutiny should be one's own field of action. This means,
then, that we must be far more specific about the category of intellectuals we invoke: clearly historians are different from physicians who are
different from engineers in their relation to the nation. This, then, is a
different picture of intellectuals: rather than begin their analysis once
they hit the political field, Bourdieu suggests we begin their political
analysis within the field of relations with specific forms of capital that
are appropriate to their own stakes of advance and loss.

One of the more thorough applications and elaborations of Bourdieu's theory is found in Katherine Verdery's work.[74] Verdery portrays
in exquisite detail why national discourse becomes so central in the cultural productions of Romanian state socialism, and why intellectuals
are so important. She argues that national identity's meaning, so
important in Romanian discourse for a long time before Communist
rule, becomes even more significant in Romania when the Communist
Party opted to control society through coercive and symbolic/ideolog-
ical controls more than remunerative ones. Intellectuals become significant because the invisible forms of domination Western societies manage through surveillance, manipulation, and disciplining are radically
underdeveloped in Communist-led societies, and thus the more
explicit control over what is said by whom makes intellectuals crucial
as both propagandists and threats.[75] The intellectuals' own milieu,
Verdery argues, also contributes to making the nation ever more significant. In their own contest for resources, intellectuals use various
images of the nation to situate themselves and their particular claims
for the allocation of resources from the center. In this process, entirely
derived from the rules and resources of their own intellectual fields,
intellectuals elevate the overall centrality of the nation in public discourse. The West also elevated the nation in Romania and among its
intellectuals.

The West's emphasis on Ceauşescu's "maverick" status among

Communist authorities encouraged this national discourse. The West simply did not support an internal opposition, as they did in "entrepreneurial" Hungary or "brave" Poland.[76] The Western articulation of the meaning of Hungarian, Polish, and Romanian nations shaped profoundly how the state, nation, and civil society would be understood under Communism and after. Even with Communism's collapse and a wish to return to Europe, the possibility for democracy and pluralism to replace the discourse of the Romanian nation appeared slim in the first half of the 1990s. That changed in 1996, but Western definitions of the Romanian nation remain profoundly important in shaping its own internal discourse, as promises of inclusion in NATO and the European Union shape the liberal hope.

To be sure intellectuals are not the *only* ones that shape the nation. We do find, however, that Verdery's work is exemplary: to understand the intellectual articulation of the nation, one must examine particular fields of action within which specific intellectuals work, as well as those more global conditions that shape how that work is to be received. Beginning with an intellectual field, however, skips over one of the most profound implications of Gramsci's work.

Gramsci argued that intellectuals have no particular distinction, and that all people are intellectuals, though they do not always have that function.[77] Defining intellectuals by existing fields of social relations overlooks how intellectuals might be made in milieus defined as anti-intellectual or nonintellectual by those who rule. One of the best illustrations of this problem of identifying who is, and who is not, an intellectual can be found in the 1980–81 Solidarity movement. In that movement, the intellectual role was "crystallized" in the form of the "expert." But many activists were as "intellectual," in terms of degrees of education or social imagination, as the experts themselves; intellectuals had adopted both roles as suitable to their own influence. Coauthors of the famous "Open Letter to the Party," Jacek Kuroń and Karol Modzelewski[78] were on opposite sides of the role divide, with the former serving as adviser and expert, the latter as political activist. Where was the intellectual operating?[79]

More generally, the creation of women's[80] and new social movements[81] illustrates that distinguishing the "intellectual" is anachronistic in postmodern cultural politics.[82] As activists become more informed and educated, and as activists emphasize everyday life, as opposed to the grander claims of history and culture in most nationalist movements,[83] traditional claims to intellectual distinction diminish. Access to "meaning," whether in consumption or production, is not so difficult to reach. At least the traditional credentials of recognizing the "intellectual" are not so essential.[84] The primary intellectual challenge in postmodern movement politics is to "identify the discursive conditions for the emergence of a collective action" and then "identify the conditions in which a relation of subordination becomes a relation of oppression, and therefore constitutes itself into the site of an antagonism."[85] The task of the intellectual in such movements is to rely on everyday life and a deep, "organic," understanding of the popular classes. Here the distinctions among intellectual, activist, and participant can become difficult indeed to draw.

Claims to intellectual authority in one domain are also difficult to transfer to another. Some kinds of knowledge are restricted to the area of a particular intellectual's claims to authority. For instance, physicians are permitted to make claims about the health of a body but may not be authorized to speak about the health of a nation.[86] Or even more profoundly, when can those without any particular credentials challenge those with ultimate credentials, as when peace activists challenge those with military power over the definition of national security?[87] Political sympathies obviously influence the accreditation of expertise too. During the Cold War leftist intellectuals critical of various aspects of American foreign policy were completely marginalized, excluded from decision-making circles, ostensibly because they were "committed" politically or even "disloyal," at a time when their ideological opponents on the right were acceptable as value-free, or perhaps uncritically loyal, intellectual "experts." Suny was made particularly aware of this exclusion by his subsequent inclusion in such discussions at the time of the Soviet collapse, when ideological confusion and shaken confidence in ruling circles created an ecumenical opening. That opening, however, may not last, as ideological forces realign and reconstruct new barriers to influence.

Challenges to the articulation of the nation come not only in conflicts between movements and state, but within social movements too. Janet Hart, for instance, has introduced a powerful argument about the elaboration of a national movement in Greece and its transformation by women into a movement whose nation had new voices.[88] World War II provided the political opportunity for women in the left-wing EAM (Ethniko Apeleftherotiko Metopo) to transform gender regimes. The

EAM was not, however, a feminist movement, though a women's movement existed within the larger movement, reconstructing gender relations in the EAM and in the broader imagination of how the nation was gendered.

The transformation of gender relations fits with modernist narratives on progressiveness in education and a belief in personal autonomy or self-improvement, but it gained its power by becoming embedded within a kind of Greek nationalism, articulated before the Axis invasion by a series of progressive intellectuals, beginning with those in the demotic movement aiming to popularize Greek language. This emphasis continued later with Dimitris Glinos and others who sought to link education and the women question. Hart argues that without this opening by intellectuals, pressure from women for the transformation of gender relations could neither have been made nor have been as successful as it was. The defensive nationalism that was developed to resist the Axis, then, not only drew upon the need for women to forget their "proper" gender roles and defend the nation but was merged with a political nationalism that extended citizenship rights and equality to the subaltern, to women. Although this ideology and praxis were still rooted in masculinist narratives, women's subsequent mobilization in the EAM transformed these activists' sense of themselves and enabled them to resist the postwar Greek authorities' attempts at forced confessions in the prisons of Averoff and elsewhere. While intellectuals provided the opening, women activists on the ground completed the translation and transformed their own sense of women's rights and responsibilities. While we can easily attribute great intellectual innovation and consequence to those with authorial recognition and power, like Glinos, we must recognize the qualities of intellectuality in those, like the women whose histories Hart depicts, whose voices are hard to hear. In theorizing intellectuals it is essential to move beyond the matter of what elite intellectuals write and consider the institutional spaces available in any society for "free intellectual activity" and the particular products associated with that work.[89]

In addition to seeking intellectual activity among those deemed nonintellectual, it is also important to consider the mundane worlds of intellectuals themselves in order to consider how their distinction articulates with their commonality. Indeed, it seems that to consider that world of the everyday, we might more clearly identify the conditions under which intellectuals become organic. Even while the Russian *intelligenty* have never failed to speak on the nation's behalf, Jane Burbank has argued that their historic connections to autocracy and elitism led to their failure during perestroika and after to generate the popular counterculture Gramscians would advise. Their culture of entitlement, their confidence in commitments rather than pragmatic politics, and their inattention to the public itself were the source, she believes, for their failure as organic intellectuals.[90] A view from the kitchen table suggests a different account.

Nancy Ries argues that Moscow intellectuals in their publicly prominent role could articulate the liminality of opposition to perestroika but could not transform politics more fundamentally because of their real link to society. By examining their informal talk and everyday life, she identifies the commonality of genres between talk at the kitchen table and in the public sphere. Both tended to invoke litanies of what was wrong with everyday life and the entire system. Both tended to portray the problem in moral, folkloric terms—the inadequacy of superiors and the victim's moral superiority in suffering—rather than in terms of systemic organization and rational political change. Solutions also were posed in these mythical/moral terms, dependent either on the saint for breaking out of the cycle of absurdities and resistance through victimhood's validation, or absolutely utopian demands unrelated to what might be realized.[91] Kitchen table talk was transported into politics, which in turn assured the reproduction of old forms of power.[92]

Organic intellectuals ought therefore to be considered not only in terms of their intellectual articulation with the subaltern, but also in the ways their mundane lives articulate with the popular and their visions articulate with the transformative. One ought to consider where their intellectuality is consequential and how new engagements with the popular transform intellectual articulations, as Hart's work has suggested. One ought also to consider how intellectuals transfer their claims to competence beyond the spheres in which authorities credential their expertise, as Kennedy has suggested, and examine the conditions under which those authorities exclude claims to competence, as Suny's experience with American foreign policy has suggested. One ought to consider how intellectuals' fields of action articulate with larger political fields, as Verdery has elaborated, but also consider how intellectuals are in fact identified as such and distinguished from others, as Kurczewski's work on Solidarity and those involved in contemporary identity politics illustrate.

Intellectuals and Nation Making

We have tried to suggest that intellectuals are best defined, not by their intrinsic qualities or self-defined role (which can be supportive or subversive or power), but by their social position, their relationship to most people, the nonintellectuals, from whom they would distinguish themselves. As Zygmunt Bauman reconstructs their early history, these heirs of *les philosophes* of the eighteenth-century Enlightenment played a key role in the transference of the pastoral role of the Church to the secular, tutelary state.[93] With the emergence of the modern state, Bauman goes on, legislators, including intellectuals, carried out the functions of disciplining, repressing, educating, and training the people. Bauman's negative valence here is reminiscent of Foucault. Intellectuals "inherited the image of 'the people' as it had been construed by the political action of the absolutist state. It had been constructed as a problem for, simultaneously, repressive measures and social policy."[94] With the constitution of "the people," it was but a short step to link that community with aspects of culture, language, shared religion, "customs," or myths, to create that most "invented" of communities, the nation.

The thrust of much recent scholarship on nation-formation has stressed how nationalism preceded the nation. In Eric J. Hobsbawm's succinct formulation: "[N]ationalism comes before nations. Nations do not make states and nationalisms but the other way round."[95] This scholarly turn in the work of such theorists as Elie Kedourie, Ernest Gellner, Hobsbawm, Miroslav Hroch, and Benedict Anderson has had the effect of confirming the role of intellectuals. "One factor," writes Anthony D. Smith succinctly, "*does* appear to be a necessary condition of all nationalist movements . . . the role of the intelligentsia.[96] Particularly in the work of modernization theorists, like Gellner and Karl Deutsch, nationalism is seen to arise from a new form of education or technology that creates both the intelligentsia and the media through which intellectuals are able to reach a newly literate mass audience.

Gellner argues that modernization, which for him subsumes industrialization, erodes traditional agrarian societies and replaces "structure," the older system of role relationships, with "culture," a new form of identity that becomes equivalent to nationality. To be a member of the new community requires literacy and a minimal technical competence. This in turn demands a mass educational system that integrates subgroups into a single national community. But because this occurs unevenly across the globe and through society, modernization leads to class competition and the exclusion of some from the community. Nationalist intellectuals lead movements of national secession with the support of the excluded lower classes. For Gellner the nation, though constructed, is not a subjective choice but a matter of "genuine, objective, practical necessity, however obscurely recognised."[97] Unlike agrarian society, Gellner argues, industrial society requires a national educational and communications system, a state, and "the kind of cultural homogeneity demanded by nationalism."[98] As we noted above, for all his apparent emphasis on intellectuals, Gellner's argument is properly criticized for its functionalism, in which nationalism is made to play an essential role in the making of industrial society, and its lack of agency in the synthesis of the discourse of the nation. As must already be clear, our volume seeks to bring the creative, constitutive role of intellectuals, the key agents in generating and propagating nationalism and the discourse of the nation, back to the center of the nation-making effort.

The first and most successful ideas that nationalist intellectuals expounded were that nations were the natural units into which humanity is divided and that these units were culturally unique. From these "facts" followed a series of political claims: that the nation is the highest loyalty of "man," a clear challenge to earlier God-centered political legitimations; that political power ought to reside in "the people" constituted as "the nation"; that nations have primary claims over the piece of territory, that is, their "homeland"; and that nations must be recognized and institutionalized in their own states. In this discourse of the nation, it was only in the nation-state, the highest stage of history, that the essence of humans was restored and allowed to develop in freedom. As Smith summarizes the "core doctrine," "[N]ationalism fuses three ideals: collective self-determination of the people, the expression of national character and individuality, and finally the vertical division of the world into unique nations each contributing its special genius to the common fund of humanity."[99] Left unspecified, however, are all the important matters of what constitutes the nation, its character and qualities, its boundaries and membership. That selection and privileging of the elements by which a given nation will be known—and know itself—has historically been the foundational role of patriotic and nationalist intellectuals. As Smith explains,

> Nationalists aim to construct nations out of populations that lack, in varying degrees, a sense of identity and purpose, or are ethnically heterogeneous, economically backward and socially divided. They provide often elaborate and sophisticated analyses and programmes for communal regeneration and collective decision-making. They must often build up from nothing the whole apparatus of the sovereign state and instill a sense of group dignity through the creation of an autonomous system of education and culture. . . . Turning a social grouping into a "nation" exercising sovereignty in its own "nation-state" is a taxing and agonising task; but it is also a positive and constructive one, a challenge to man.[100]

Theorists and historians of nationalism have often noted that nationalism has been most powerful as a mobilizing ideology at moments of revolutionary instability, often during or following wars, as in the French revolutionary era (1789–1815), the revolutions of 1848–52, the aftermath of the two world wars, and the revolutionary transformations of statist "socialist" regimes at the end of the Cold War. It is then argued that in a context of instability, insecurity, and unpredictability, intellectuals and politicians search for or choose the available forms of community to recreate a degree of stability and certainty.[101] But here too an overly simple functionalist explanation loses the complex sense of creativity that comes together in generating nationalisms. The initial generation of the nationalist synthesis came from Enlightenment intellectuals, like the Germans Fichte and Herder, who married an affection for ethnic culture and tradition with a project of progress and enlightenment and in the process transformed the understanding of the solidarities that made up the community.

Perhaps the quintessential early national patriot, or "historicist intellectual" (in Smith's phrasing), was Johann Gottfried von Herder (1744–1803), the Baltic German literary scholar who inspired generations of his countrymen and others to investigate the creative function of language. In praise of Homer and Shakespeare, Herder proclaimed, "A poet is the creator of the nation around him, he gives them a world to see and has their souls in his hand to lead them to that world." In search of the soul of the nation, Herder collected his people's folk songs, read Norse poetry and mythology, and analyzed the prose of Martin Luther. Language was for Herder intimately connected to culture and community, the medium through which humans understood and thought, were conscious and able to express their inner selves. "Language expresses the collective experience of the group," he wrote.[102] Through language people understand that they share a culture and historical tradition and therefore form a people *(Volk)*. Rather than biological or racial unity, the nation for Herder was a matter of shared awareness of the social milieu into which one is born. This shared culture is, in the words of his translator, the "proper foundation for a sense of collective political identity."[103]

Herder contrasted the particularity of the nation and its *Volkgeist* to the universalistic rationality of the French Enlightenment. Yet, as Isaiah Berlin has noted, he was at the same time a creature of the Enlightenment, explaining his own philosophy of history in naturalistic and scientific terms. Nature (or God) created the plurality of languages and cultures, or, as Berlin puts it, "A nation is made what it is by 'climate,' education, relations with its neighbours, and other changeable and empirical factors, and not by an impalpable inner essence or an unalterable factor such as race or colour."[104] At the same time Herder's love of nations did not extend to the state. He despised government and power, the great absolutist monarchs of his time, and celebrated the cleansing force of the French Revolution. His *Nationalismus,* a word he apparently created, was cultural rather than political, and Berlin claims Herder as the ancestor, not of political or statist nationalism, but of all forms of populism. However he might be characterized, Herder, like his contemporary and successive historicist intellectuals, was a unique, often isolated figure, who pioneered the "recovery" of the cultural and national past.

An East European pioneer in theorizing the link between the intellectual and labor, Stanisław Brzozowski (1878–1911), brought a more "nationed" argument to a subsequently elaborated "Gramscian" position from which intellectuals are seen as central in the class struggle against those who rule. In his "Marxist" phase, Brzozowski argued that the working class ought to lead the national struggle; when they did not, it was a sign of social disintegration. The intelligentsia, he argued, should facilitate the development of the intellectual life of the working class "by creating a culture which would express and develop the potential spiritual richness inherent in the 'life-world' (*Lebenswelt*) of the workers." The intelligentsia, according to Brzozowski, fulfills its mission only in alliance with the working class, as this proletariat realizes its conscious and purposeful control over labor.[105]

Brzozowski subsequently abandoned his anthropocentric theory of labor for a more nationalist and spiritualist position, one that finds the deepest source of the collective subconscious in the fatherland (*ojczyzna*), by which he understood family structure, material production, and statehood with military organization as the "material" side, with language and the nation as the subjective dimension of this fatherland.[106] While Brzozowski never entirely abandoned the working class as the agent of Poland's future, he believed in this last phase that the intelligentsia had to return to the Catholic Church, which he thought potentially could be transformed into the "organ of will of working people, while preserving its historical continuity."[107] Nations become the "deepest reality" for humanity and a "necessary form of truth," while labor, even if humanity's universal experience, could not be its ultimate foundation.[108]

The social role of nationalist intellectuals was codified by Miroslav Hroch in his very useful periodization of nationalism. Phase A begins when patriotic scholars, like Herder, initiate the search for a usable national past and a language through which it might be expressed. In the succeeding generation individual patriotic intellectuals fuse into a collective social stratum, the intelligentsia, and in phase B they turn nationalist ideas into a social force through their writings, editing newspapers, organizing clubs, leading marches, and teaching, as Brzozowski did.

As an example of the extraordinary effect of Herder's and other early patriots' ideas on intellectuals in various parts of Europe, it is worthwhile examining the case of Finland. Early in the nineteenth century the "Turku Romantics" collected Finnish songs and stories, and even though they were themselves Swedish-speakers they promoted the language of Finnish-speaking Finns. One of them, Elias Lönnrot, published in 1835 a collection of tales he had collected from rural Finns, the *Kalevala*, which was seen as the epic expression of the early Finns. The *Kalevala* gave the Finns an heroic past and identity and inspired the Fennomania movement that pushed for recovery of Finnish culture and language. Fennomen intellectuals organized clubs to speak Finnish and study the national epic.[109] The Russian imperial government, which ruled Finland, also encouraged Finnish-language schooling in order to reduce the influence of the Swedish elite in Finland, and in 1863 Finnish was made an official language of the grand duchy equal to Swedish. A sense of Finnish nation liberated from Swedish cultural superiority developed in the conjuncture of three factors: Russian state interests, intellectual activity in forging a sense of Finnish identity, and the receptivity of the Finnish-speaking rural population.[110] Empowered by a new positive identity, the Finnish-speaking Finns became more active politically in the late nineteenth century, ultimately forming a mass Social Democratic Party alongside smaller, less powerful nationalist and conservative parties. In Finland Hroch's phase C, the stage at which the broad masses become involved in nationalist politics, involved not so much a unified all-class national movement but a broad national consensus in favor of autonomy (and later independence) for Finland that fractured socially along class lines. Finnish identity over time became increasingly anti-Russian, anti-imperial, and in favor of an independent Finnish state, but that independence was achieved only after a brief and bloody civil war between Finns of different social classes.[111]

Hroch's historiographical treatment of intellectuals in small European nations fits reasonably well with a more general historical sociological theory of intellectuals as a social stratum initially produced by, and then rendered redundant by, a colonial power. Imperial rule both creates the conditions for the education of a native intelligentsia and then makes impossible its full development into the effective elite of its own society. This is a familiar story that has been told about many places. Benedict Anderson indeed begins his tale of modular nationalisms with a similar story of the "Creole pioneers" of South and North America. Local elites, frustrated by their stunted "pilgrimages" into the ruling strata of the empire, developed national independence movements based, not on ethnicity and culture (which they shared with the metropole), but on borrowed Enlightenment principles and on the territoriality that their "pilgrimages" marked out. These American Creoles "constituted simultaneously a colonial community and an upper class," "economically subjected and exploited" to be sure, but able to read the writings of Rousseau and Herder and interpret their existence as essentially separate from the metropolitans by virtue of their different climate and "ecology" that they believed "had a constitutive impact on culture and character."[112] Summing up his approach, which has moved the discussion of nationalism from social determination to the complexities of cultural construction, and providing an explanation for the particular multiple nationalisms based on imperial administrative units, Anderson writes:

> Liberalism and the Enlightenment clearly had a powerful impact, above all in providing an arsenal of ideological criticisms of imperial and *anciens regimes.* What I am proposing is that neither economic interest, Liberalism, nor Enlightenment could, or did, create *in themselves* the *kind,* or shape, of imagined community to be defended from these regimes' depredations; to put it another way, none provided the framework of a new consciousness—the scarcely-seen periphery of its vision—as opposed to centre-field objects of its admiration or disgust. In accomplishing *this* specific task, pilgrim creole functionaries and provincial creole printmen played the decisive historic role.[113]

In a later chapter Anderson continues the story into the period of twentieth-century anticolonial nationalism, where once again the administrative unit "came to acquire a national meaning in part because it circumscribed the ascent of creole functionaries."[114] Here the vanguard role of intelligentsias "derived from their bilingual literacy, or rather literacy and bilingualism. Print-literacy already made possible the imagined community floating in homogeneous, empty time. . . . Bilingualism meant access, through the European language-of-state, to modern Western culture in the broadest sense, and, in particular, to the models of nationalism, nation-ness, and nation-state produced elsewhere in the course of the nineteenth century."[115] Similarly, just as frustrated westernized intellectuals tended to be the primary movers in the decolonization efforts that ended overseas European empires and created new states in Asia and Africa, in the last years of the Soviet empire Soviet-trained intellectuals were the catalysts in a series of anticentrist movements for greater autonomy, cultural rights, and ultimately independence. Intellectuals in Armenia, Georgia, and the Baltic republics eventually came to power in relatively free elections, while in other republics, notably Central Asia and Azerbaijan, established political elites managed to crush the fledgling nationalist groupings and transform themselves into the ostensible leaders of the nation. Borrowing from the universal discourse of the nation, both anticolonialist intellectuals and state elites attempted to make the case for their peoples' right to exist as nations and states, weakening the will of the colonizers to maintain the former empires, and enhancing their own claim as the leaders of newly independent states.

Nationalist intellectuals beyond Europe and the Americas introduced the idea of the modern and allied the local to the global within their societies. Though they began as relatively isolated groups of intellectuals, nationalist movements were able to translate into mass movements with the participation of charismatics like Gandhi or in alliance with the military. Intellectual nationalism thus preceded a sense of nationality among the population. By articulating forcefully the distinction between the colonized and the colonizer, they fostered a sense of the "people-nation." Colonial nationalists rejected the imperial rulers, while in admiration of their technology and statecraft they adopted their Western ways to build a new postcolonial state.[116] Just as in the earlier Russian Revolution, so in the anticolonial revolutions and the post-Soviet transformations, wherever the transition was revolutionary and the former imperial elite was swept aside, intellectuals made their way into the seats of power. With power, however, their identity as intellectuals becomes ever more difficult to maintain; at least it becomes increasingly contentious. State power is not, however, the only threat to intellectual distinction.

Intellectual Challenges

Commodification is another threat to intellectuals, especially in advanced capitalist societies. In such societies, celebrity can overwhelm intellectual work and notoriety can replace the acclaim of the scholarly community. To become a "public intellectual" requires some engagement with commodified media, and in so doing, the public intellectual risks becoming the media pundit. Intellectuals can themselves be claimed by consumer culture. Zygmunt Bauman writes,

> Consumer culture creates its own, self-sustained and self-sufficient world, complete with its own heroes and pace-setters. . . . Tightly squeezed by the consumer heroes, politicians must behave like them—or perish. . . . "[N]ews" is mostly a tool of forgetting, a way of crowding out yesterday's headlines from the audience con-

sciousness. . . . [W]ithin the context of consumer culture no room has been left for the intellectual as legislator.[117]

Even in France, a society that accords intellectuals greater distinction than most other advanced capitalist societies, intellectual prestige has become increasingly the consequence of media access, which is in turn determined by the ease with which their products are commodified and circulated through media.[118] Under these circumstances, then, intellectuals and the articulation of the nation change. That articulation becomes more difficult to consider without considering its increasingly commodified media.

Intellectual distinction has also receded with the displacement of the general intellectual. Bauman has argued that the rationalizing intrusive state of modernity, the nation-state, created the space for modern intellectuals by inviting them to provide a culture that legitimates that state's intervention into new spheres of social life.[119] Once state and culture are so constructed, the general intellectual recedes in importance. Simply put, intellectuals retreat to a relatively privileged life of autonomy (the independent intellectual), become the interpreter for cultures not represented by the logic of state power (the organic intellectual), or become a servant of bureaucratic power (a professional or technocrat). This shift, however, has not made intellectuals irrelevant.

As Foucault notes, the displacement of the "universal" intellectual, the writer as figurehead, by the "specific" intellectual, the specialist, the expert, since World War II has not lessened the interest of power in the intellectual. With J. Robert Oppenheimer, the atomic scientist who headed the Manhattan Project, Foucault writes, "For the first time, the intellectual was hounded by political powers, no longer on account of the general discourse which he conducted, but because of the knowledge at his disposal: it was at this level that he constituted a political threat."[120] The specific intellectual is "no longer he who bears the values of all, opposes the unjust sovereign or his ministers and makes his cry resound even beyond the grave. It is rather he who, along with a handful of others, has at his disposal, whether in the service of the State or against it, powers which can either benefit or irrevocably destroy life. He is no longer the rhapsodist of the eternal, but the strategist of life and death."[121]

Although intellectuals do own certain kinds of knowledge that are variably powerful, they continue to be made themselves by social forces beyond their jurisdiction, and their effect is magnified or diminished by institutions and cultural projects in which they are embedded. The state, after all, was the principal agent behind the making of intellectuals like Oppenheimer. It also produced the bounty of elementary-particle physicists in 1980s America, whose overproduction was a consequence of state investments in higher education and research. This in turn, however, was a consequence of an ideology of the nation: the national interest in the Cold War, in which particle physics was deemed essential to national security to stay ahead of the Soviet Union's own imagined military prowess. And now, without the link to the Cold War and national security, this intellectual specialization has lost its clout and its Texas supercollider.[122]

Universities are the most immediate institution that simultaneously produces intellectuals and serves as their sanctuary. This institution can provide its resident and incipient intellectuals with the autonomy to define their mission and preserve their distinction from a more "interested" pursuit of knowledge stimulated by profit or power. This autonomy can be defended on its own grounds, but it also contributes to the public welfare by providing an institution from which truth can be spoken to power. Such an institution is important for all democratic societies, but it is increasingly difficult to preserve in post-Communist societies where universities and other institutions of research and higher education fail to provide the material conditions that enable intellectuals to choose "truth" over professional or bureaucratic service. Market research and governmental consulting become increasingly lucrative substitutes for intellectual practice.

In general, universities also are national institutions in which national historiographies and historians are produced, and entire specializations or disciplines are cast within a national frame. Within the United States, for instance, whole departments of sociology can focus only on its own nation, as if the study of one society were enough to produce expertise on societies in general. Departments of political science identify American politics as a specialty entirely apart from comparative politics in which the rest of the world is studied. Of course, this kind of ethnocentrism is unlikely to be viewed by most Americans as a reflection of the nation's ideological centrality, much less as an expression of nationalism. That is partly because nationalism in the

United States specifically, and in the advanced capitalist world generally, tends to be less obvious because it is both more deeply insinuated in the reproduction of power, rather than its transformation, and more directly attached to those ideologies that claim the universality of being on top, rather than in the particularities of resistance. This, however, may be in the process of deep transformation. As the power of the nation-state recedes and as capital and other social relations become more global,[123] the university itself is likely to be transformed. With the globalization of scholarship, scholars and students within leading universities of the advanced countries challenge the ways in which these institutions generate national visions and national intellectuals. The more immediate challenge to that national formation of intellectuality, however, comes from the proliferation of contests over claims to competence.

In the United States, cultural wars over the canon of the humanities, over the appropriateness of weapons research on university campuses, over affirmative action, and over freedom of speech are not just isolated academic arguments, but contests that are redefining the relationship between intellectuals, universities, and the nation. These contests are demonstrating the importance and profundity of a university life guided by academic ideals. The losers in these contests are, however, likely to contribute to the delegitimation of the university as intellectual sanctuary by claiming that ideology, rather than intellectuality, rules. Familiar epithets like "tenured radical" or "racist administration" and charges of duplicity on all sides help to undermine the notion that intellectuals of various inclinations can belong to the same communities of discourse, and that intellectuals can share a culture of critical discourse.

From without, these contests may appear to make intellectuals no different from others motivated by ideology, profit, or power. It can lead some, nostalgic for mythological days of a single canon and uncontested claims to competence, to question why intellectuals need a different kind of institution to articulate the truth when the intellectual distinction is so dubious. Ironically, or perhaps tragically, at the very moment when intellectual debate becomes ever more important for rearticulating the nation in the United States, the institution and its defining qualities, like tenure, itself are being doubted. And in such times, the challenge to intellectuals may be terrific; for in the contest over truth, the very importance of preserving and strengthening such a site may become increasingly important. Not only need its autonomy be preserved, for the development of intellectuality as such. It also must find a way to extend its influence when commodified media and corporate- or state-sponsored knowledge overwhelms the public sphere. The university, in these circumstances, becomes an especially important place to cultivate the general intellectual as a transnational community, if not as an individual. If that discourse cannot be generated within the university, then it is unlikely to be generated anywhere.

Intellectuals are significant in the articulation of nations. This is relatively obvious in the modern world of newly emerging states and postcolonial nations, where new states attempt to nationalize themselves and embryonic nations seek full statehood. There, intellectuals find familiar and obvious work in the codification of more pure languages, in the production of histories and future scenaria. Although postmodern conditions in the developed capitalist world might reduce the prominence of traditional intellectuals, intellectual powers remain potentially quite significant. In order to recognize their powers, however, new theoretical tools must be developed to recognize the distinction of a dispersed intellectuality and its potential organization within university settings only partially insulated from the circuits of capital, power, and ideology that characterize public discourse beyond its walls. And as the nation is transformed through processes of globalization, the analysis of this intellectual articulation becomes ever more critical.

We hope this book inspires many more works on intellectuals in the articulation of the nation, for much needs to be done. First of all, the variety of ways in which different kinds of intellectuals articulate the nation ought to be studied. These articulations need be assessed in different circumstances, in times of rapid social transformation, explicit social struggle, quiet resistance, and apparent social reproduction. We need not only study how intellectuals articulate the nation, but also how the nation articulates intellectuals, as well as how intellectuals are embedded in everyday life, institutional arrangements, power relations, and above all, the discourse of the nation. If nationalism remains the most powerful of the world's explicit ideologies, then the functions and distinctions of intellectuals will be transformed as the nation itself moves from its initial consolidations, to the contest over its expression, to its potential transformation by globalization. These questions might be approached anywhere, of course, but we focus here on the distinction of Eastern Europe and Eurasia.

The Distinction of Eastern Europe and Eurasia

We have this geographical focus not only because the two of us have been specialists in this world region and associates of the University of Michigan Center for Russian and East European Studies. It is also because Eastern Europe provides a fertile empirical ground for examples of nationalism and has been disproportionately influential in generating theories of both the nation and the intelligentsia. Consider, for instance, Jeromy Karabel's sociological attempt to develop a theory of intellectuals and politics. The following conditions make radical intellectual politics more likely:

> 1) the presence of well-organized and politically radical subordinate social groups; 2) the absence of a strong business class; 3) a high ratio of "relatively unattached" intellectuals to those employed by large scale organizations; 4) the presence of a moderately repressive regime that lacks the means and or the will to stamp out dissent; 5) weakness or divisions within the ruling group; 6) when the state is unable to protect the "people" or the "nation" from economic, political, or military encroachments from other states that occupy more powerful positions in the world system; 7) the presence of sharp boundaries between social groups, including the boundary separating intellectuals from non-intellectuals (i.e. the people); 8) the existence of historically grounded cultural repertoires of resistance to authority.[124]

There are few places in the world that have such a concentration of these conditions as in Eastern Europe and the lands comprising the former Soviet Union. And it is in radical politics that the most powerful linkages between intellectuals and transformative practices can be found. By using these more dramatic moments as a lens, or as a comparative base, theories of intellectuals and politics are typically built, but not without their limitations.

The relationship between the East European intelligentsia and Communist regimes and progressive social movements has been the typical focus of sociologists like Karabel and Kennedy who focus on intellectuals and power. In this collection we seek to go beyond the particularly problematic relationships between Communism and intellectuals, and rather focus on what likely complicates that relationship between intellectuals and radical politics in Eastern Europe, Russia, and the Caucasus: the relation between intellectuals and the nation. Indeed, and especially for those scholars who have long focused on the relationship between intellectuals and left politics, we find another of Geoff Eley's recent reminders quite useful: that national politics has shaped left politics profoundly and not always in such obvious ways that one can leave the relationship unstated. In particular, at the turn of the century, it was difficult to say what nation the intellectuals of the German labor movement were articulating, given the "cosmopolitan messiness" of the period.[125] Part of our effort in this volume is to show how the nation is indeed "messy" and, where it is not, how intellectuals have contributed to fixing its clarity. Indeed, in each of the articles, the "fixing" of the nation—whether in more familiar terms as in defining its membership or claims to a state, or in less commonly discussed terms, as in relation to matters of democracy, gender, and business—is the object of intellectual labor. Thus, one virtue of this region has been that it has several of modernity's powerful ideologies—liberalism, communism, and nationalism—well articulated in opposition to, and in conjunction with, each other, making the significance of intellectual labor in reformulating them more obvious than it might be in other sites.[126]

We are not only, however, focusing on these ideological labilities. By studying the agents themselves, their own social production, we can also explore the making of this intellectual power. We are considering, therefore, not just the fixing of messy nations in periods of dramatic social transformation. We also seek those more mundane moments, where the "quiet" politics of nation making are being conducted through intellectual labor. Thus, we consider how the social conditions and national discourses that envelope intellectuals shape their own work and establish the conditions at least of the production of intellectuals, their articulation, if not also their influence.

Finally, this collection is an attempt to introduce a more nuanced approach to intellectuals and the articulation of the nation by considering how the relationship is itself influenced by the gaze of the theorists themselves. We wish to suggest the importance of the analyst's conditions of scholarly production in accounts of intellectuals and power.

Simply put, the power relations in which an analyst is embedded inflect the story of intellectuals and power that is told. The story of Emilia Plater in this case can then become exemplary.

In 1830, Emilia Plater, subsequently elevated to the pantheon of Polish national heroes, led a regiment of men to storm the fortress of Dynaburg. Halina Filipowicz compares various ways in which Plater's life was used by different intellectuals at different times to emphasize different themes.[127] While some have noted that Plater was elevated to that pantheon because Adam Mickiewicz, in his poem "The Death of a Colonel," found the literary device that could install her as hero at a moment of need, Filipowicz writes that Plater's elevation was more deeply implicated in a complex politics of class, nation, and gender. Her Lithuanian aristocratic status meant her sacrifice was all the greater; her wealthy relatives promoted her cause; and her virginity, implied but underplayed in all texts, was absolutely central, especially for those of the old Polish-Lithuanian Commonwealth, in which "her inviolate body is a metaphor of moral good as well as an urgent political symbol of national integrity, a projection of future restoration and unity."[128] Underlying all of these portraits, however, was an emphasis on her patriotism, rather than her challenge to gender hierarchies.[129]

Because we wish to highlight the importance of the conditions of scholarly production on the products of intellectuals, we have included autobiographical essays of our volume's contributors in this collection. If the social production of intellectuals is so important for the articulation of nations, the authors represented in this collection are themselves "nationed" and imprinted with a particular life experience that enables, and constrains, them to make the arguments that they do. While short autobiographical statements are hardly adequate to explaining the articles written here, they suggest the directions of research we find essential to a theory of "national intellectual practice." We shall let these autobiographical statements more or less represent themselves. In the conclusion, however, we shall discuss the essays in order to construct a more positive direction for the analysis of intellectuals in the articulation of the nation. We provide only a brief introduction below.

Contributions

In the opening essay Alexander J. Motyl challenges the now widely accepted constructivist view on nation making. Constructivists or modernists, including the editors of this volume, have argued that nations are neither primordial, perennial, nor natural divisions of humanity but rather the historically contingent and relatively recent product of imagination and invention. Without returning to primordialism, Motyl questions the role of elites in the "invention of tradition" and the generation of national identity and emphasizes the collective undertakings of ordinary people, those who orally transmit myths and epics, poems and songs, and live the lives that contribute the raw material for national identification.

Khachig Tololyan employs his skills as a literary scholar to illuminate a key early-nineteenth-century Armenian poem that stands at the point of transition from the self-conception of the Armenian community as religious, oppressed, and dispersed, to a protonational discourse of return, liberation, and restoration. Tololyan's story is of a nationalist intelligentsia that operated outside of Ottoman Armenia in the dispersed communities of India, Venice, Moscow, Tbilisi, and Constantinople, where "a distant diaspora reinvented, reimagined, reconceived the homeland." Patriotic intellectuals and self-proclaimed liberators constructed a national tradition, linking discrete events in the past into a continuous narrative of the nation subject (the subjugated nation) moving through history toward emancipation.

John-Paul Himka enthusiastically embraces the new theoretical openings of the recent nationalism literature to examine the contest of identities that Galician Rusyns held in the nineteenth century and explain why some identities resonated while others were silenced. Among a people that called themselves "Rus," Galician nobles were polonized, both linguistically and religiously, long before the nineteenth century, and even the first generation of "nationalists," the patriotic clerics, had adopted Polish culture. But from Poland they had a template of national culture available for application to their own experience. A Russophilic orientation competed with a weak Belorussian alternative, but religion prevented full merger with the Catholic Poles or the Orthodox Russians. Himka's explanation for the potency of a Ukrainian identity by the early twentieth century is historically contextualized in the politics of the Austrian state, the preferences of the local church, and the intense competition between Ukrainophile and Russophile intellectuals.

Yuri Slezkine uses the figure of Nikolai Marr, the dean of early Soviet linguists, to show how a powerfully placed intellectual not only established a unique pedigree for his mother language but more grandly attempted to solve the "Ethnological Predicament" (the missing symmetry among language, nation, state, and territory) with an elaborate classificatory system. Here authority was conferred by a discourse of science and the imprimatur of the Soviet state, possessor of or at least arbiter of truth. Marr's work began in czarist Russia, but it was with the empowerment of loyal intellectuals by the Soviets and in the context of the collaboration of intellectuals in the generation of a particular Soviet Marxism that Marr's linguistics took its final shape. But Marr's "final solution of the Great Ethnological Predicament proved temporary." Scholars and state officials picked away at his theories until in 1950 the question of the relation of language to social base was "resolved" by Stalin himself.

While Marr was the quintessential establishment intellectual during his later life, Antonio Gramsci and Dimitris Glinos were, in Janet Hart's phrase "civil intellectuals" who combined critical thinking with political activity, like the Russian *intelligenty* of the nineteenth century, to save their nations from perceived disaster. Reading closely their letters and articles, Hart explores the "paralanguage" of the nation that lies behind the more explicit expression of politics. Deeply imbedded in the work of these revolutionary intellectuals was a commitment to "generativity," the inspiration and education of young people to carry on the national revolutionary cause.

Andrzej Walicki is critical of the rush by scholars to imagination and invention as the primary forms of nation making. His own historical narrative proposes an alternation between moments of ethnic consolidation, as in medieval Poland, and intellectual reconceptualization, as in the Polish-Lithuanian Commonwealth. Contests over conceptions of the nation marked the politics and high culture of Poland through the eighteenth and nineteenth centuries, but, he maintains, ultimately intellectuals only can imagine a nation on "a firm ethnic basis."

Katherine Verdery explores a dynamic moment just after the fall of the Communist regime in Romania when politicians, dissidents, and other intellectuals competed over definitions of the nation and its connection to Europe. Focusing on the "political economy of symbolism," she weighs the relative power of different conceptualizations and finds that more inclusive, multinational models or borrowed notions of "civil society" fail to resonate as loudly as the master symbol of "the nation" conceived more ethnically. But the opposition of the nation to notions of a liberal civil society does not exhaust the complex interrelationship of liberalism and nationalism.

As Michael D. Kennedy shows, both liberalism and nationalism are labile ideologies, internally discordant discourses in which the very understanding of liberalism requires the understanding of the nation and vice versa. Kennedy extends the category of intellectual to include articulate Polish businessmen who self-consciously cultivate images of, and play the functional role of, more traditionally conceived intellectuals. Their business activity is involved in the articulation of a new Polish nation, now imbricated in the global networks of liberalism, democracy, and capitalism.

NOTES

Originating in a lecture series on Ethnopolitics and Culture proposed by Ron Suny, this volume reflects the theme developed by him, Michael Kennedy, and Zvi Gitelman at the Center for Russian and East European Studies at the University of Michigan in 1993 and 1994. Funded by the University of Michigan's Council on International Academic Affairs, the series was administered by Donna Parmelee, whose contribution was invaluable. The editors are grateful to the University, the Center, their colleagues, the University of Michigan Press, its external reviewers, and our editor Susan Whitlock, not to mention the series' participants, for all their work and advice. Without their effort and help, this volume would not have come together. We also wish to thank Liz, Emma, Lucas, Armena, Sevan, and Anoush, for without their support, we could never find the spirit and time to complete this volume. Thank you.

From the beginning, this volume, the introduction, and conclusion have been the result of the collaborative work of the coeditors, with the invaluable input of the paper writers. As we wrote, rewrote, discussed, argued with, and learned from each other, we lost a sense of who had originated or developed an idea or line of argument. This process has given us a greater appreciation of the value of collaborative work, especially since many of the conventions and rewards in the academy encourage more solipsistic practices of research and writing.

1. Among the most influential works that have developed and synthesized these ideas are Ernest Gellner, *Nations and Nationalism* (Ithaca, N.Y.: Cornell University Press, 1983); Benedict Anderson, *Imagined Communities: Reflections on the Origin and Spread of Nationalism*, 2d ed. (London: Verso, 1991); Miroslav Hroch, *Social Preconditions of National Revival in Europe: A Comparative Analysis of the Social Composition of Patriotic Groups among the Smaller European Nations*, trans. Ben Fowkes (Cambridge: Cambridge University Press, 1985); and E. J. Hobsbawm, *Nations and Nationalism since 1780: Programme, Myth, Reality* (Cambridge: Cambridge University Press, 1990).

2. Etienne Balibar, "The Nation Form, History, and Ideology," *Review* 13, no. 3 (1990): 346.

3. See, for example, Michael Keren, *The Pen and the Sword: Israeli Intellectuals and the Making of the Nation-State* (Boulder, Colo.: Westview, 1989).

4. Anne McClintock, "'No Longer in a Future Heaven': Women and Nationalism in South Africa," *Transition* 51 (1991): 104.

5. Mark Beissinger, "How Nationalisms Spread: Eastern Europe Adrift the Tides and Cycles of Nationalist Contention," *Social Research* 59, no. 1 (1996): 98.

6. Seymour Martin Lipset, *Political Man: The Social Bases of Politics* (Garden City, N.Y.: Doubleday, 1963), 333.

7. With Daniel Bell, *The Coming of Post-Industrial Society* (New York: Basic Books, 1973), as the central text in this validation of the "information age." See Mayer N. Zald and John D. McCarthy, "Organizational Intellectuals and the Criticism of Society," in *Social Movements in an Organizational Society* (New Brunswick, N.J.: Transaction, 1987), 97–121, for an application of these ideas to the study of social movements.

8. See, for example, Stephen T. Leonard, "Introduction: A Genealogy of the Politicized Intellectual," in *Intellectuals and Public Life: Between Radicalism and Reform,* ed. Leon Fink, Stephen T. Leonard, and Donald M. Reid (Ithaca, N.Y.: Cornell University Press, 1996).

9. Rogers Brubaker, *Nationalism Reframed: Nationhood and the National Question in the New Europe* (Cambridge: Cambridge University Press, 1996).

10. Michael Burawoy, "Two Methods in Search of Science: Skocpol vs. Trotsky," *Theory and Society* 18 (1989): 759–805.

11. Robert Wuthnow, *Communities of Discourse: Ideology and Social Structure in the Reformation, the Enlightenment, and European Socialism* (Cambridge, Mass.: Harvard University Press, 1989), likewise makes articulation his central concept for exploring the relationship between ideology and social structure, but focuses on the environment and the institutionalization of ideas.

12. Consider, for example, the Russian intelligentsia's self-critique in *Vekhi, Sbornik statei o russkoi intelligentsiia* (Moscow: N. Khushnerev, 1909); the work of the Polish critic of the Russian intelligentsia, Jan Wacław Machajski (1866–1926); Raymond Aron, *The Opium of the Intellectuals,* trans. Terence Kilmartin (Garden City, N.Y.: Doubleday, 1957); Milovan Djilas, *The New Class: An Analysis of the Communist System* (New York: Frederick A. Praeger, 1957); George Konrad and Ivan Szelenyi, *The Intellectuals on the Road to Class Power: A Sociological Study of the Intelligentsia in Socialism,* trans. Andrew Arato and Richard E. Allen (New York: Harcourt Brace Jovanovich, 1979); and Russell Jacoby, *The Last Intellectuals: American Culture in the Age of Academe* (New York: Basic Books, 1987).

13. Julien Benda, *The Great Betrayal (La Trahison des Clercs),* trans. Richard Aldington (London: George Rutledge and Sons, 1928), 30, 31.

14. Benda, *The Great Betrayal,* 31.

15. Edward W. Said, *Representations of the Intellectual: The 1993 Reith Lectures* (New York: Vintage, 1994), 5–6.

16. Karl Mannheim, *Ideology and Utopia* (New York: Harcourt Brace Jovanovich, 1936).

17. Edward Shils, "The Intellectuals and the Powers: Some Perspectives for Comparative Analysis," *Comparative Studies in Society and History* 1, no. 1 (1958): 5–22, reprinted in Shils, *The Intellectuals and the Powers and Other Essays* (Chicago: University of Chicago Press, 1972), 3–22.

18. Shils, *Intellectuals and Powers*, 5.

19. Shils, *Intellectuals and Powers*, 7.

20. For a more recent statement, see also Edward Shils, "Intellectuals and Responsibility," in *The Political Responsibility of Intellectuals*, ed. Ian Maclean, Alan Montefiore, and Peter Winch (Cambridge: Cambridge University Press, 1990), 257–306.

21. Alvin W. Gouldner, *The Future of Intellectuals and the Rise of the New Class* (New York: Seabury, 1979), 83–85.

22. Gouldner, *Future of Intellectuals*, 32–35.

23. Gouldner, *Future of Intellectuals*, 19.

24. Gouldner, *Future of Intellectuals*, 19–20.

25. The significance of African Americans' political engagement, from W. E. B. Du Bois to Cornel West, illustrates the limits of such easy summary stances on intellectuals and politics in the United States. See Alford Young Jr., "The 'Negro Problem' and the Social Character of the Black Community: Charles S. Johnson, E. Franklin Frazier, and the Constitution of a Black Sociological Tradition, 1920–1935," *National Journal of Sociology* 7, no. 1 (1993): 95–133, and his "Political Engagement and African American Scholars in the Age of the African American Intellectual Celebrity," in *The Black Intellectuals: Research in Race and Ethnic Relations*, ed. Rutledge Dennis, vol. 10 (JAI Press, 1997), 117–46.

26. Zygmunt Bauman, "Intellectuals in East Central Europe," *East European Politics and Societies* 1, no. 2 (1987): 162–86.

27. Leszek Kołakowski, "Intellectuals and the Communist Movement," in *Toward a Marxist Humanism* (New York: Grove, 1968). For elaboration, see Michael D. Kennedy, "Eastern Europe's Lessons for Critical Intellectuals," in *Intellectuals and Politics: Social Theory in a Changing World*, ed. Charles Lemert, Key Issues in Sociological Theory, vol. 5 (Boulder, Colo.: Sage, 1991), 94–112.

28. Leszek Kołakowski, "Intellectuals against Intellect," *Daedalus* 101, no. 3 (1972): 1–16.

29. Miklos Molnar, "The Hungarian Intellectual and the Choice of Commitment or Neutrality," in Maclean, Montefiore and Winch, *Political Responsibility of Intellectuals*, 189–200.

30. Leon Volovici, *Nationalist Ideology and Anti-Semitism: The Case of Romanian Intellectuals in the 1930s* (Oxford: Pergamon Press, 1991), 194.

31. Volovici, *Nationalist Ideology and Anti-Semitism*, 77. In this, Volovici is explicitly invoking Kołakowski's 1972 essay.

32. E. A. Hammel, "The Yugoslav Labyrinth," *Anthropology of East Europe Review* 11, nos. 1–2 (1993): 44.

33. Stjepan Mestrovic, *The Balkanization of the West: The Confluence of Post-modernism and Postcommunism* (London: Routledge, 1994), 83, 149.

34. Shils, Talcott Parsons, and others worked in this mode that charged certain politically engaged intellectuals with the loss of their identity; but by political they meant those whom they perceived as ideological or dogmatic, whose reason or science they could not appreciate. Such critics, of course, spoke from a politics of their own that largely went unacknowledged. See Talcott Parsons, "The Intellectual: A Social Role Category," in *On Intellectuals: Theoretical Studies and Case Studies*, ed. Philip Rieff (Garden City, N.Y.: Doubleday, 1969), especially 23–26. An excellent survey of this trajectory can be found in Leonard, "Introduction."

35. Talcott Parsons, "Professions and Social Structure," *Social Forces* 17 (1939): 457–67.

36. See, for example, Magali Sarfatti Larson, *The Rise of Professionalism* (Berkeley and Los Angeles: University of California Press, 1977); Andrew Abbott, *The System of Professions* (Chicago: University of Chicago Press, 1988).

37. Lily M. Hoffman, *The Politics of Knowledge: Activist Movements in Medicine and Planning* (Albany: State University of New York Press , 1989); Michael D. Kennedy, *Professionals, Power, and Solidarity in Poland: A Critical Sociology of Soviet-Type Society* (Cambridge: Cambridge University Press, 1991); Duujian Tsai, "Transformations of Physicians' Public Identities in Taiwan and the United States: A Comparative and Historical Study of Ambivalence, Public Policy, and Civil Society," Ph.D. diss., University of Michigan, 1996.

38. Ming-cheng Lo, "From National Physicians to Medical Modernists: Taiwanese Doctors under Japanese Rule," Ph.D. diss., University of Michigan, 1996.

39. See Elliott A. Krause, "Professions and the State in the Soviet Union and Eastern Europe: Theoretical Issues," and Michael D. Kennedy and Konrad Sadkowski, "Constraints on Professional Power in Soviet-Type Society: Insights from the 1980–81 Solidarity Period in Poland," in *Professions and the State: Expertise and Autonomy in the Soviet Union and Eastern Europe*, ed. Anthony Jones (Philadelphia: Temple University Press, 1991), 3–42 and 167–206.

40. Jürgen Habermas, *The Philosophical Discourses of Modernity: Twelve Lectures*, trans. Thomas A. McCarthy (Cambridge, Mass.: MIT Press, 1987), 203. This is discussed most eloquently alongside a discussion of Foucault in Lloyd Kramer, "Habermas, Foucault, and the Legacy of Enlightenment Intellectuals," in Fink, Leonard, and Reid, *Intellectuals and Public Life*, 29–50. Jeromy Karabel continues this "realist" approach to the sociology of intellectuals, but in a way much more sympathetic to the politics of both the East European intelligentsia whom he has studied and the American progressive politics in which he is a practitioner. See "Towards a Theory of Intellectuals and Politics," *Theory and Society* 25, no. 2 (1996): 205–33.

41. Craig Calhoun, "The Ideology of Intellectuals and the Chinese Student Protest Movement of 1989," in Lemert, *Intellectuals and Politics*, 113–42, "The Beijing Spring, 1989: Notes on the Making of a Protest," *Dissent* 36, no. 4

(1989): 435–47, *Neither Gods Nor Emperors: Students and the Struggle for Democracy in China* (Berkeley and Los Angeles: University of California Press, 1994), and "Elites and Democracy: The Ideology of Intellectuals and the Chinese Student Protest Movement of 1989," in Fink, Leonard, and Reid, *Intellectuals and Public Life*, 285–318.

42. Jerzy Szacki, "Intellectuals between Politics and Culture," in Maclean, Montefiore, and Winch, *Political Responsibility of Intellectuals*, 229–46.

43. Maclean, Montefiore, and Winch, *Political Responsibility of Intellectuals*.

44. Grahame Lock, "The Intellectual and the Imitation of the Masses," in Maclean, Montefiore, and Winch, *Political Responsibility of Intellectuals*, 143–60.

45. J. J. LeCercle, "Textual Responsibility," in Maclean, Montefiore, and Winch, *Political Responsibility of Intellectuals*, 101–21.

46. Molnar, "Hungarian Intellectual." See also G. M. Tamas, "The Political Irresponsibility of Intellectuals," in Maclean, Montefiore, and Winch, *Political Responsibility of Intellectuals*, 247–56.

47. Ernest Gellner, "La trahison de la trahison des clercs," in Maclean, Montefiore, Winch, *Political Responsibility of Intellectuals*, 17–27.

48. Alan Montefiore, "The Political Responsibility of Intellectuals," in Maclean, Montefiore, and Winch, *Political Responsibility of Intellectuals*, 201–28.

49. David J. Levy, "Politics, Technology, and the Responsibility of Intellectuals," in Maclean, Montefiore, and Winch, *Political Responsibility of Intellectuals*, 123–42.

50. Jacek Kurczewski, "Power and Wisdom: The Expert as Mediating Figure in Contemporary Polish History," in Maclean, Montefiore, and Winch, *Political Responsibility of Intellectuals*, 77–100.

51. Elemer Hankiss, "The Loss of Responsibility," in Maclean, Montefiore, and Winch, *Political Responsibility of Intellectuals*, 29–52.

52. Jerzy Jedlicki, "Heritage and Collective Responsibility," in Maclean, Montefiore, and Winch, *Political Responsibility of Intellectuals*, 53–76.

53. Jedlicki, "Heritage and Collective Responsibility," 76.

54. R. Radhakrishnan, "Toward an Effective Intellectual: Foucault or Gramsci?" in *Intellectuals: Aesthetics, Politics, Academics*, ed. Bruce Robbins (Minneapolis: University of Minnesota Press, 1990), 57–100.

55. The meaning and reasons for this are contested. For a "new class" interpretation, see Ivan Szelenyi and Bill Martin, "The Three Waves of New Class Theories and a Postscript," in Lemert, *Intellectuals and Politics*, 19–30. For an alternative, more historically and culturally embedded account, see Michael D. Kennedy, "The Intelligentsia in the Constitution of Civil Societies and Post-Communist Regimes in Hungary and Poland," *Theory and Society* 21, no. 1 (1992): 129–76.

56. Editors' introduction to Antonio Gramsci, "The Intellectuals," in *Selections from the Prison Notebooks*, ed. and trans. Quintin Hoare and Geoffrey Nowell Smith (London: Lawrence and Wishart, 1971), 3.

57. Geoff Eley, "Intellectuals and the German Labor Movement," in Fink, Leonard, and Reid, *Intellectuals and Public Life*, 75.

58. Said, *Representations of the Intellectual*, x.

59. Said, *Representations of the Intellectual*, xi.

60. Said, *Representations of the Intellectual*, xii.

61. Said, *Representations of the Intellectual*, 9.

62. For this distinction, see Kennedy, "Eastern Europe's Lessons."

63. Václav Havel, "Address to the Joint Session of the US Congress, February 21, 1990," in *Without Force of Lies: Voices from the Revolution of Central Europe, 1989–90*, ed. William M. Brinton and Alan Rinzler (San Francisco: Mercury House, 1990).

64. Václav Havel, "The Power of the Powerless," in *Living in Truth*, trans. Paul Wilson (London: Faber and Faber, 1986); for reflections on this role since becoming president of Czechoslovakia, see his *Summer Meditations*, trans. Paul Wilson (New York: Vintage Press, 1992). Note that he tends too to subordinate the "nation" and his own "Czechness" to more universal references. See Václav Havel, *Disturbing the Peace: A Conversation with Karel Hvizdala*, trans. Paul Wilson (New York: Knopf, 1990), 178–80.

65. György Konrad, "What Is a Hungarian?" in *The Melancholy of Rebirth: Essays from Postcommunist Central Europe* (San Diego: Harcourt Brace Jovanovich, 1995), 67–68.

66. Partha Chatterjee, *Nationalist Thought and the Colonial World* (London: Zed Press, 1986), and *The Nation and Its Fragments* (Princeton, N.J.: Princeton University Press, 1993).

67. Marshall S. Shatz, *Jan Wacław Machajski: A Radical Critic of the Russian Intelligentsia and Socialism* (Pittsburgh: University of Pittsburgh Press, 1989); Michael D. Kennedy, "The Alternative in Eastern Europe at Century's Start: Brzozowski and Machajski on Intellectuals and Socialism," *Theory and Society* 21, no. 4 (1992): 735–53; also Konrad and Szelenyi, *Intellectuals on the Road;* and Szelenyi and Martin, "Three Waves."

68. Gouldner, *Future of Intellectuals*.

69. Charles Derber, William A. Schwartz, and Yale Magrass, *Power in the Highest Degree: Professionals and Rise of a New Mandarin Order* (New York: Oxford University Press, 1990). The culture of rational discourse includes these elements: *(a)* a claim to scientific method and detachment; or to be rational and objective; *(b)* anonymity and an impersonal relationship to clients; *(c)* reification of the object of inquiry; *(d)* abstraction and an emphasis on measurement, which allows for that absence of morality from the questions professionals investigate, and for a distinction from "craftsmen." This rational discourse is the dominant ideology of professionalism: critical discourse is at best a rival flower, and one that focuses more on the importance of making any assumption subject to critique.

70. Michel Foucault, "Truth and Power," in *Power/Knowledge: Selected Interviews and Other Writings, 1972–1977*, ed. Colin Gordon (New York: Pantheon, 1980).

71. Foucault, "Truth and Power," 126.

72. Ironically, some argue that while Foucault emphasizes the constitution of subjectivity, even of intellectual subjectivity, his own writing implies a

kind of traditional intellectual disposition, in which he "'chooses freely and joyously to be a specific, deglobalized, local and countermnemonic intellectual" (Radhakrishnan, "Toward an Effective Intellectual," 70).

73. Pierre Bourdieu, "For a Socio-Analysis of Intellectuals: On Homo Academicus," interview, *Berkeley Journal of Sociology* 34 (1989): 25. See Pierre Bourdieu, *Homo Academicus,* trans. Peter Collier (Stanford, Calif.: Stanford University Press, 1988) for the application of this approach to the assessment of the May 1968 conflicts.

74. Katherine Verdery, *National Ideology under Socialism: Identity and Cultural Politics in Ceauşescu's Romania* (Berkeley and Los Angeles: University of California Press, 1991).

75. See also Jeffery Goldfarb, *On Cultural Freedom* (New York: Oxford University Press, 1982).

76. Verdery, *National Ideology under Socialism,* 311.

77. Gramsci, "The Intellectuals," 9.

78. Jacek Kuroń and Karol Modzelewski, "An Open Letter to the Party," *New Politics* 5, no. 2 (1966): 5–46.

79. Kurczewski, "Power and Wisdom."

80. Roslyn Wallach Bologh, "Learning from Feminism: Social Theory and Intellectual Vitality, " in Lemert, *Intellectuals and Politics,* 31–46.

81. Especially if one reframes the question of the locus of "reflexivity" from intellectual to movement. See Joseph R. Gusfield, "The Reflexivity of Social Movements: Collective Behavior and Mass Society Theory Revisited," in *New Social Movements: From Ideology to Identity,* ed. Enrique Larana, Han Johnston, and Joseph R. Gusfield (Philadelphia: Temple University Press, 1994), 58–78.

82. Richard Rorty, "Intellectuals in Politics: Too Far In? Too Far Out?" *Dissent* 38, no. 4 (1991): 483–90. See also Michael D. Kennedy, "Intellectuals, Intellectuality, and the Restructuring of Power after Modernity and Communism," Program for the Comparative Study of Social Transformations, University of Michigan Working Paper no. 80, May 1992.

83. Hank Johnston, "New Social Movements and Old Regional Nationalisms," in Larana, Johnston, and Gusfield, *New Social Movements,* 267–86.

84. The difficulty of recognizing intellectual distinction is not only a postmodern condition, but might also be recognized as a postmodern disposition in viewing earlier periods. Richard Carlile and his zetetic movement in nineteenth-century England are not typically thought of in terms of "intellectual" politics, but once put into a Gramscian frame suggest one of the challenges of radical intellectuals in an inhospitable popular culture. See James Epstein, "Bred as a Mechanic: Plebian Intellectuals and Popular Politics in Nineteenth Century England," in Fink, Leonard, and Reid, *Intellectuals and Public Life,* 53–73.

85. Ernesto Laclau and Chantal Mouffe, *Hegemony and Socialist Strategy: Towards a Radical Democratic Politics* (London: Verso, 1985), 153.

86. Michael D. Kennedy, "The Constitution of Critical Intellectuals: Polish

Physicians, Peace Activists, and Democratic Civil Society," *Studies in Comparative Communism* 23, nos. 3–4 (1990): 281–304.

87. Kennedy, "Constitutions of Critical Intellectuals."

88. Janet Hart, *New Voices in the Nation: Women and the Greek Resistance, 1941–1964* (Ithaca, N.Y.: Cornell University Press, 1996). Beyond demonstrating how the movement transformed the lives of women, Hart also has to argue against the dominant historigraphical literature on the EAM as a Communist and antinational movement. By comparing the EAM to the Yugoslav partisans, whose odes to Stalin were extreme but did not last, the Greek movement was far more inclusive and populist in its mobilization narrative.

89. Eley, "Intellectuals and German Labor," uses these points to consider intellectuals and the German labor movement (see especially 75).

90. Jane Burbank, "Were the Russian *Intelligenty* Organic Intellectuals?" in Fink, Leonard, and Reid, *Intellectuals and Public Life*, especially 120. For background, see Jane Burbank, *Intelligentsia and Revolution: Russian Views of Bolshevism, 1917–1922* (New York: Oxford, 1986).

91. Nancy Ries, *Russian Talk: Culture and Conversation during Perestroika* (Ithaca, N.Y.: Cornell University Press, 1997).

92. Much as Jadwiga Staniszkis charged Solidarity of 1980–81 with a kind of moral rebelliousness that appeared oppositional but was only a pseudoradicalism that promised no systemic transformation because of its reproduction of the redistributive, not rational, economy. See *Poland's Self-Limiting Revolution: Solidarity* (Princeton, N.J.: Princeton University Press, 1984).

93. This formulation comes from Zygmunt Bauman, *Legislators and Interpreters: On Modernity, Post-Modernity, and Intellectuals* (Ithaca, N.Y.: Cornell University Press, 1987).

94. Bauman, *Legislators and Interpreters*, 77.

95. Hobsbawm, *Nations and Nationalism*, 10.

96. Anthony D. Smith, *Theories of Nationalism* (London: Duckworth, 1971), 87. Florian Znaniecki also emphasized this in an earlier age of scholarship.

97. Ernest Gellner, *Thought and Change* (Chicago: University of Chicago Press, 1964), 160.

98. Gellner, *Nations and Nationalism*, 39.

99. Smith, *Theories of Nationalism*, 23.

100. Smith, *Theories of Nationalism*, 106.

101. See Ernest Gellner, "Nationalism in the Vacuum," in *Thinking Theoretically about Soviet Nationalities*, ed. Alexander J. Motyl (New York: Columbia University Press, 1992), for an illustration of that point of view for the end of Communism.

102. Herder, as cited by Isaiah Berlin, *Vico and Herder: Two Studies in the History of Ideas* (New York: Viking Press, 1976), 169.

103. F. M. Barnard, trans. and ed., *J. G. Herder on Social and Political Culture* (Cambridge: Cambridge University Press, 1969), 7.

104. Berlin, *Vico and Herder*, 163.

105. Andrzej Walicki, *Stanislaw Brzozowski and the Polish Beginnings of*

Western Marxism (Cambridge: Oxford University Press, 1989), 187–95, 194. See also Kennedy, "Alternative in Eastern Europe."

106. Walicki, *Stanislaw Brzozowski*, 162–65, 275–314.

107. Walicki, *Stanislaw Brzozowski*, 298.

108. Walicki, *Stanislaw Brzozowski*, 301–9.

109. Tracy X. Karner, "Ideology and Nationalism: The Finnish Move to Independence, 1809–1918," *Ethnic and Racial Studies* 14, no. 2 (1991): 152–69.

110. For the significance of other factors beyond intellectual labor, see Chris Hann, "Intellectuals, Ethnic Groups, and Nations," in *Notions of Nationalism*, ed. Sukumar Periwal (Budapest: Central European University Press, 1995), 106–28.

111. Risto Alapuro, *State and Revolution in Finland* (Berkeley and Los Angeles: University of California Press, 1988); Anthony F. Upton, *The Finnish Revolution, 1917–1918* (Minneapolis: University of Minnesota Press, 1980); and for a briefer treatment, Ronald Grigor Suny, *The Revenge of the Past: Nationalism, Revolution, and the Collapse of the Soviet Union* (Stanford, Calif.: Stanford University Press, 1993), 64–72.

112. Anderson, *Imagined Communities*, 58, 60.

113. Anderson, *Imagined Communities*, 65.

114. Anderson, *Imagined Communities*, 114.

115. Anderson, *Imagined Communities*, 116.

116. This is one of the themes in Chatterjee, *Nation and Its Fragments.*

117. Bauman, *Legislators and Interpreters*, 167.

118. Regis Debray emphasizes this mediological approach; see his *Teachers, Writers, Celebrities*, trans. David Macey (London, 1981), cited in Donald M. Reid, "Regis Debray: Republican in a Democratic Age" in Fink, Leonard, and Reid, *Intellectuals and Public Life*, 121–44.

119. See Bauman, *Legislators and Interpreters*, and "Legislators and Interpreters: Culture as Ideology of Intellectuals," in *Social Structure and Culture*, ed. Hans Haferkamp (Berlin: Walter de Gruyter, 1989), 313–32.

120. Foucault, "Truth and Power," 128.

121. Foucault, "Truth and Power," 129.

122. Cited in Daniel Kevles, "The Death of the Superconducting Supercollider: The End of the Cold War and Particle Physics," paper presented to "Beyond the Wall," conference at the Advanced Study Center, International Institute, University of Michigan, March 24–26, 1995.

123. David Held, "The Decline of the Nation State," in *Becoming National: A Reader*, ed. Geoff Eley and Ronald Grigor Suny (New York: Oxford University Press, 1996), 407–16.

124. Karabel, "Towards a Theory," 211–14.

125. Eley, "Intellectuals and German Labor."

126. Nicolae Harsanyi and Michael D. Kennedy, "Between Utopia and Dystopia: The Labilities of Nationalism in Eastern Europe," in *Envisioning Eastern Europe: Postcommunist Cultural Studies*, ed. Kennedy (Ann Arbor: University of Michigan Press, 1994).

127. Halina Filipowicz, "The Daughters of Emilia Plater," in *Engendering Slavic Literatures*, ed. Pamela Chester and Sibelan Forrester (Bloomington: Indiana University Press, 1996), 34–58.

128. Filipowicz, "Daughters of Emila Plater," 45.

129. She was celebrated in an American feminist's text but was apparently not so well received by many readers of that volume. Filipowicz, "Daughters of Emila Plater," 37–38.

Confessions

I was born in Philadelphia of Armenian parents, my mother American-born, my father born "on the other side." From my father I heard stories of his boyhood in Tiflis (now the capital of Georgia), his memories of the revolution and the coming of the Bolsheviks. But the most constant theme through his tales was the enormous affection and respect for his father, the ethnomusicologist and composer, Grikor Mirzaian Suni. This fascinating, contradictory "maestro" combined high culture with an un-Armenian bohemianism and a dedication to revolution, Marxism, and Soviet Armenia. "Suni," as he was always called, had died the year before I was born, but his legacy was stamped on me early in the 1950s when, provoked by my father, I gave a report to my seventh-grade class on the achievements of the Soviet Union. The teacher in those frigid days of the Cold War was shocked and wanted to know where I had come up with such ideas. My classmates rewarded me with the epithet "Comrade Suny" for the bulk of my high school years.

A skinny, shy kid, I now had a kind of identity that I wore (and defended) proudly. For me and my father (but not in the same way for my mother and sister), the Soviet Union was an ideal against which the inadequacies of capitalist America, into which I seemed not to fit particularly well, were judged. Part of that misfit came as well from the other side of my family, the side we socialized with almost exclusively. My mother's mother was a woman of saintly simplicity and kindness, whose world was bounded by the Armenian community in Philadelphia, and her love for her people and a land from which her family had been driven was simply part of her nature, unconscious, assumed, unquestioned. She told me of the death of her sister, whose throat had been cut during the 1894 massacres of Armenians in the Ottoman Empire. But much more impressive was her confidence that we Armenians were a special people, privileged to speak a language that had not only been the first language of human beings, spoken before the Tower of Babel, but was still the lingua franca of heaven. Thus began my lifelong struggle with the intricacies of a language that was assumed to be my "mother tongue"! Grandma always insisted that my sister and I "marry Armenian," and she made it clear that "menk hai enk" (we are Armenian), but "anonk amerikatsi en" (they are American). The Americans, it was understood, were odar *(foreign). Here we were in America, and we considered the Americans, at least those who were not Armenian, to be foreigners! Thus, from an early age I had a double sense of distance from the society and the nation in which I actually lived, as an Armenian and a person of the Left.*

Armenians, whose self-representation is often that of the victim and mar-tyr, in the United States were an "invisible diaspora," not particularly perse-cuted and often not seen at all. There was always great delight when someone notable turned out to be Armenian or something Armenian was recognized by others. I felt no essential conflict between an Armenian and American identity. They were simply available for use in different situations and complemented each other almost everywhere with no need to choose between them. It was not until my freshman year in college that I first heard an odar *refer to me, the son of an immigrant, as a "foreigner"!*

For most of my growing-up years the opportunity to be a part of, and yet stand apart from, either of my "national" identities gave me a freedom from unquestioning American patriotism—particularly during the Cold War and Vietnam War—and the narrowing nationalism of the Armenian community. My parents gave my sister and me wide choice in defining ourselves, never forcing on us the stamp of ethnicity. Eventually Linda married a Greek, learned modern Greek, and distanced herself from things Armenian. Within the family being different was something worth preserving, even celebrating. Outside there were limits, of course. When as an idealistic seventeen-year-old I wrote a commencement speech about the need for nonconformity, it was gently rejected as "too controversial."

When it came time to make the decisive choice of what career to choose—in my case between theater and the academy—the decision to go to graduate school in history was deeply shaped by the need to know more about the Soviet Union. Socialism remained in my young adulthood a utopia that firsthand knowledge of the actualities of the Soviet system did not tarnish. For me, as for many who drifted from Old to New Left, the USSR was no longer the model of socialism but a distorted or degenerate failure to realize the emancipatory promise of Marxism. Still, when I finally arrived in the Soviet Union in 1964, I was extraordinarily happy with what I found, particularly the people I met. I experienced no disillusionment, only a concrete confirmation that socialism lay in the future. The people I met seemed to live a more authentic life than my compatriots back home, struggling, to be sure, with the material poverty of the early Brezhnev years, but at the same time maneuvering through the restrictions on public life and preserving a rich interior, private life marked by a deep humanism, a sense of social justice, and faith in a better future. That mid-1960s moment, living with students at Moscow and Erevan Universities, was my first and most durable experience of a noncapitalist world, a place free of commercialism, concern for money, and marked by a rough equality. Much of that immediate post-Khrushchevian affection for the system on the part of those I knew would soon disappear. Inequities and corruption grew in the next decades, along with social pessimism and inertia. Still, my own take was that the USSR was fundamentally a healthy society, but one that required radical reform to open its constricted public sphere. My very first published article (in a New Left journal published by Oberlin College students) was about the need for a "bourgeois democratic revolution" in the USSR. Paradoxically, the greatest sense of distance I felt in the Soviet Union was in Armenia itself, where I was received as a long-lost relative but was immediately aware of how different I was from the "we" that insisted I was one of them.

At Oberlin in the late 1960s and through the 1970s, I was the young firebrand professor, the "Red-in-Residence" on that isolated Ohio campus, a self-proclaimed "Marxist" (who was just beginning to struggle through Capital, *the* Economic and Philosophical Manuscripts, *and the* Grundrisse*). Though the Marxism of that time was that of the young Marx and the socialist humanism of Fromm, Marcuse, Lukács, and Kołakowski, it provided a compelling theoretical tradition that informed my work on Soviet history. Intellectually the most innovative writing was by the new social historians, particularly British Marxist labor historians, and again I found a standpoint outside the society in which I lived from which to observe, analyze, and advocate. Teaching and scholarship, even in northeastern Ohio, was, I believed, a kind of political activity that required the most meticulous scholarly engagement. "Truth was revolutionary" (in Regis Debray's phrase), and honest scholarship on the USSR was essential for the Left, which all too often was too apologetic or content to be just plain ignorant. The student movement, with its sense that antiwar agitation was merely the first step toward a more radical restructuring of American society, was infectious, and I was an active participant, even from the precarious perch of an untenured assistant professor. The Department of History slapped my wrists firmly when they refused to put me up for tenure, but in the best traditions of that liberal college the faculty pressured reconsideration.*

Without much self-reflection I wrote about class and nationality, which now seems to have come out of my own life experience as a leftist Armenian in America. After more than a decade as a Soviet historian at Oberlin, I moved to the University of Michigan, where I became a "professional Armenian," that is, I taught Armenian history largely to Armenian students, lectured to the Armenian community, and tried to elevate a rather parochial subdiscipline to the standards of the discipline. My interests in Transcaucasia and nationality problems in the Soviet Union continued to be marginal among mainline "Russianists" until the explosion of national resistance in 1988. Suddenly, I was given my "fifteen minutes of fame," as I glided from radio to television to appearances in Washington as the "expert on the Caucasus."

The promise presented by Gorbachev was extraordinarily consequential for those of us in Soviet studies who had argued against the demonization of the Soviet Union and for a more "détentist" approach in foreign policy. At that effervescent moment of the late 1980s, "actually existing socialism" seemed about to become modern and humane, against the pessimistic predictions of most of the Sovietological community that was convinced either of the permanence of the Stalinist infrastructure or the inevitability of collapse. Gorbachev's failure, in part because of the emergence of separatist nationalisms, had a catastrophic effect on the identities that I had formed over much of my life. The Soviet Union disappeared; Armenia became independent; socialism was (at least temporarily) thrown on the trashheap of history. When someone innocently congratulated me that now I had a country, I told him coldly, no, I have lost my country. I remember with sadness my father's query to me shortly before his death, would socialism come back again? I told him, not in the short run, though as long as there was capitalism there would be some kind of socialist opposition.

But just as the reality of the Soviet Union did not diminish the ideal of a more egalitarian, socially just, and participatory social order beyond "actually existing democracy," so its disappearance did not scour the political landscape of alternatives or bring history to an end. America had not changed as we had wanted in the 1960s, and the Soviet Union had metamorphosed into something more like what we hoped to avoid. But the optimism and security that my family had given prevented political despair. Indeed, marriage to Armena (an Armenian to be sure!) and a new family kept me afloat, even when tragedy—the death of our first child, Grikor—nearly drowned the two of us. Now having shifted identities slightly, from Soviet and Armenian historian to Soviet and post-Soviet political scientist interested in nations and nationalisms, I

continue to search for new places from which to observe. I remain a foreigner,
an odar, *in my native land, but that, it seems to me, is perhaps the best place*
to try to look beyond the political limits that the present offers us.

Ronald Grigor Suny
The University of Chicago

Alexander J. Motyl

Inventing Invention: The Limits of National Identity Formation

Loose lips sink ships.

According to Eric Hobsbawm, Benedict Anderson, and the "constructivist" school they have inspired, national identity, like the nation claiming it, is invented or imagined.[1] As a construct, it is neither natural or given—adjectives that might be favored by such currently unfashionable "primordialists" as Harold Isaacs and Clifford Geertz[2]—nor mythic or rooted, designations central to the "perennialist" thought of Anthony Smith and John Armstrong.[3] As I argue in this essay, the constructivists are persuasive only if invention and imagination are not taken seriously as concepts.[4] If they are, the constructivists are either trivial or unpersuasive. The problem with constructivism, therefore, is both self-imposed and conceptual. It follows that the constructivist project might be salvaged if the language of invention and imagination is modified or abandoned.

My discussion of the constructivist approach to national identity formation consists of four parts. The first unpacks the concepts of invention and imagination. The second examines what a nontrivial constructivist approach to national identity formation must entail. The third argues that the only conceptually consistent form of constructivism, one that sees national identity formation as the product of conscious elite invention and imagination, collapses under closer scrutiny. I conclude the essay with an alternative approach that retains many of constructivism's insights, while avoiding, I trust successfully, its mistakes. In particular, I decouple national identity formation from elites

57

engaged in conscious inventing and imagining and argue that national identity can emerge under conditions that, while more prevalent in modern times, could have existed in the distant past and can exist in the future. Nations, therefore, while historical and contingent, are not uniquely modern or, for that matter, necessarily transient.

Constructivism's Concepts

Hobsbawm suggests that the scope of invention "includes both 'traditions' actually invented, constructed and formally instituted and those emerging in a less easily traceable manner within a brief and dateable period."[5] He also notes that invention is the "attempt to structure at least some parts of social life . . . as unchanging and invariant."[6] Anderson claims that the nation is "*imagined* because the members of even the smallest nation will never know most of their fellow-members, meet them, or even hear of them, yet in the minds of each lives the image of their communion."[7]

Hobsbawm's elaborations are confusing. Some reflection shows that construction, institution, emergence, and structuring are quite different concepts. Construction and structuring imply conscious activity of a directed and innovative kind; emergence suggests unwilled occurrences or processes; and institution implies an interaction between individual and mass human behavior. Anderson is closer to the mark in arguing that imagination involves not just an image, but an image of a nonexistent thing, the *communion* of the members of the nation. Yet he, too, leaves us without a clear sense of what imagination entails.

A closer look at invention and imagination might start with dictionary definitions: to imagine is "to form a mental image of (something not present)," and to invent is "to think up or imagine," "to create or produce for the first time."[8] Regardless of what they denote, inventing and imagining clearly connote a bringing into being of something previously absent. But what, and how?

Consider the act of invention. Whatever its form and whatever the context, invention—or, more precisely, the inventor performing it—transforms the materials at hand into something qualitatively different and new. The invented thing is a novel entity, neither an agglomeration of previously given materials and, hence, merely the sum of its parts, nor something hidden in these materials, something waiting for the inventor to set it free. Thus, a hammer is neither a piece of wood and a piece of metal nor the external manifestation of the "hammerness" they embody, but a thing that, while consisting of wood and metal, represents an ontological reality different from theirs.

Imagination—or, again, the imaginer—works in the same way, juxtaposing or combining elements in novel ways that produce qualitatively new, because otherwise nonexistent, things or situations. I do not imagine the horse outside my window or the horns on the bull in my barn. But I do imagine a being that represents an amalgam of both—a unicorn. Likewise, I do not imagine the homeless in New York City—after all, I see them every day—but I might imagine a city without any poverty whatsoever. I imagine Utopia, Schlaraffenland, and many other such *imaginary* situations, just as I imagine similarly nonexistent entities, such as phoenixes, trolls, and fairies, although I can see their component parts—wings, fangs, and wands—in everyday life.

The point is that both invention and imagination presuppose preexisting building blocks on the one hand and their combination and subsequent transformation by inventors or imaginers into a novel end-product on the other. We cannot invent or imagine ex nihilo. Such an act should be called *creation.* Nor do we invent or imagine already existing things. Here, *remembrance* might be the more appropriate term. Nor, finally, can invention or imagination occur without conscious inventors and imaginers. It is not enough for images passively to "live," as Anderson puts it, in people's minds. Imagination, like invention, requires *active* imaginers and inventors. In sum, invention and imagination have three defining characteristics: building blocks, conscious human agency, and novelty. If any characteristic is absent, then invention or imagination cannot be said to have taken place.

This, I suggest, is a sensible way for the invention and imagination of national identity to be understood. If traditions are *not* invented and if communities are *not* imagined in such a precise manner, then invention and imagination are only metaphors of marginal relevance to rigorous social scientific enquiry. As metaphors, both terms might signify that something *like* actual invention and imagination is taking place. That something may involve active people or new things, but inasmuch as just about everything involves people or things, we are left with fuzzy variables that encompass most of life.

Hard and Soft Constructivism

As with all schools of thought, constructivism is a nuanced intellectual undertaking. While all constructivists would agree that identity is the product of social and historical developments, they disagree, implicitly if not explicitly, on the manner in which construction takes place. "Hard" constructivists, such as Hobsbawm wants to be, emphasize conscious elite activity; "soft" constructivists, such as Anderson actually is, focus on mere human agency. In the first instance, elites rooted in concrete social and historical situations purposefully create identity; in the second, identity is created, emerging almost as an unintended consequence of the actions of human beings rooted in concrete social and historical situations.

Hobsbawm, typically, peppers his writings with examples of conscious activity, such as that of the "Hindu zealots [who] destroyed a mosque in Ayodhya, ostensibly on the grounds that the mosque had been imposed by the Muslim Moghul conqueror Babur on the Hindus in a particularly sacred location which marked the birthplace of the god Rama." And yet, as Hobsbawm notes, "nobody until the nineteenth century suggested that Ayodhya was the birthplace of Rama" and "the mosque was almost certainly not built in the time of Babur."[9] In contrast, Anderson locates national identity within a swirl of such grand historical forces as the rise of print capitalism and the threefold decline of a "particular script-language," Latin, of the "belief that society was naturally organised around and under high centres," and a "conception of temporality in which cosmology and history were indistinguishable."[10]

I suggest that the only conceptually consistent and theoretically coherent form of constructivism is, and must be, hard. If constructivism does *not* argue that elites create national identity consciously, if the nationalists of whom Ernest Gellner writes as the "historic agents" of nationalism "know not what they do,"[11] then we are, at best, left with the trivial conclusion that, since "men make their own history," as they obviously must for history to be more than the recording of natural events, everything in history is in some sense "made"—constructed— by men and women. At worst, we descend into self-contradiction and subvert invention and imagination semantically by depriving both of one of their defining characteristics: active inventors and imaginers. Constructivism, then, *must* argue that national identity can arise only if elites consciously take preexisting building blocks and transform them into national identity.

Let us unpack this proposition by examining, first, the elites. As noted above, the logic of invention and imagination as concepts implies only that they be self-consciously acting inventors and imaginers. No other characteristics are essential. Thus, elites may or may not be rich or poor, powerful or powerless, with or without status and influence. Inasmuch as they must be *self-consciously* involved in inventing and imagining, however, it is clear that elites will be a select, and probably fairly small, group of people with unusual cognitive and/or affective capacities. Intellectuals, writers, and political activists, precisely those individuals discussed by Miroslav Hroch, come to mind.[12]

Inventors and imaginers act on the preexisting materials or building blocks of national identity. What these building blocks are will depend on what national identity is or, more precisely, on how it is defined, and the definition, clearly, may not logically entail either a confirmation or a refutation of constructivism's claims. Defining national identity as a set of beliefs—about the nation, its nationness, and so on—meets this condition. As such a set, national identity consists of *propositions* about life, statements of the "This is that" variety.[13] It follows that identity construction must be a form of belief construction and that a nation, a group of people with national identity, holds certain propositions about itself to be true. Hard constructivists must therefore claim that elites consciously attempt to persuade a population that a set of propositions—each of the form $A' = B'$, $A'' = B''$, . . . , $A^n = B^n$—is true. These propositions need not actually *be* true: they need not correspond to empirical reality and therefore qualify as facts. Indeed, contrary to the view of national identity as irremediably bogus and backward, national propositions by their very nature as propositions need be neither more nor less true than nonnational propositions.

One logical consequence of defining national identity as a belief system is that the entity we call a nation need not call itself that as well. The term may be absent from the language of the people concerned—the Inuit are a case in point—and even if it were present, it might have a thoroughly different meaning from that we use or from those other nations use. For instance, Americans use the word *nation*—as in "this nation's capital"—to mean "country." There is, thus, no logical reason for nations not to have existed before the word *nation* or the doctrine of nationalism entered politics and the social-science discourse.[14] To suppose otherwise is either to conflate the etymology of the word *nation* with the origins of the phenomenon, as does Liah Greenfeld, or to reduce the phenomenon to a word or words, or a "stance," as does Rogers Brubaker.[15] In either case, the implicit—and, to my mind, unwarranted—assumption is that language constitutes all of reality.

National Identity and Lifeworld

If national identity consists of knowledge claims, then the preexisting materials, the building blocks that comprise national identity, must also consist of knowledge claims. What can they be? Consider first that national identity draws on only some materials from within a larger array of building blocks. Consider also that all of these materials have in common their potential utility as building blocks of national identity. It seems fair to conclude that preexisting materials form a coherent set and are not a mere agglomeration of randomly aligned elements. For the sake of convenience, let us call this set of propositional building blocks a "lifeworld"—the intersubjectively held knowledge claims that a group—*any* group—presumably takes for granted and that enables its members to communicate with one another. It is irrelevant for our purposes whether or not what I designate a lifeworld is identical with, or has all the theoretical overtones of, the concept discussed by Jürgen Habermas and other philosophers.[16]

National identity and lifeworld are distinct concepts with distinct referents. While national identity refers to a particular way in which people see themselves, lifeworld refers to the ontological and epistemological claims they share in order to contemplate seeing themselves in a particular way, say, as having an identity. To ask about the origins of national identity is, thus, not to ask about the origins of lifeworlds. Human beings have been constructing ontologies and epistemologies since time immemorial, and although the question of why they do so is interesting, it is not one that we have to answer in order to get at the problem of national identity. We expect lifeworlds to occur, perhaps as a result of some inner need on the part of men and women to deal with the existential frailty of the human condition, to give shape to shapelessness in an effort to overcome, as Peter Berger and Thomas Luckmann put it, "chaos."[17] The search for meaning may therefore be immanent in the human condition; national identity, at least according to nonprimordialist assumptions, obviously is not.

We can express the relationship between national identity and life-world in the following manner, where N stands for national identity proposition and L for lifeworld proposition:

Na   Nb   Nc   . . .
        .   .   .
    .   .   .   .   .   .
.   .   .   .   .   .
La   Lb   Lc   Ld   Le   Lf   . . .

Each N represents a novel amalgam of at least two L's. The diagram notwithstanding, it is not necessary that N propositions consist only of separate L pairs or that there be fewer N propositions than L propositions.

A closer look at the relationship between the set of L propositions and the set of N propositions leads to several important conclusions. First, and most obviously, we see that would-be inventors and imaginers are actually under severe constraints in their ability to invent and imagine. They may and do combine L propositions in novel ways to produce N, but they are confined to drawing on L and only on L. They cannot invent and imagine anything they wish; the sky, evidently, is not the limit.

Second, inventors and imaginers are constrained by more than just the field of L. Although there is no reason why N propositions cannot be constructed so as to contradict individual L propositions, it is unlikely that the "nation" intended to entertain contradictory propositions will be able to maintain such a balancing act for any meaningful length of time. We therefore expect the set of N propositions to be consistent with the set of L propositions, at least over time. By the same token, N propositions should be equally consistent with one another as well.

Third, the elites transforming L propositions into N propositions must be intimately familiar with the lifeworld. If they are not, they would be incapable of identifying its propositions and combining them in noncontradictory ways. But this requirement leads to a paradox. For if the elites *are* ensconced in the lifeworld, how could they, and why should they, invent or imagine N? *Pre*national elites have no reason even to suspect that L propositions could produce distinctly national N propositions. And even if they did, it is unclear why they should care.

Inventions are useful things, but elites cannot know that N is useful before nations exist. Circularity seems to be unavoidable.

Fourth, even if elites could create N, how and why do these propositions come to be accepted by the target audience? We have no reason to think that people at large share elite preferences; indeed, if they did, elites would be irrelevant to national identity formation. If, alternatively, the people are assumed to be indifferent to, or ignorant of, elite preferences, then there is no reason to expect them to accept the veracity of propositions that represent novel additions to already functioning lifeworlds. Of course, elites might force these ideas on the masses, but such behavior decidedly is not what constructivists mean by construction.

In the final analysis, there appears to be no logically persuasive reason for national identity formation to occur as a result of conscious elite activity. Without introducing exogenous conditions into the argument, we cannot explain why elites should invent N or why masses should accept N. If some nations or a discourse of nationalism are assumed already to exist, then we might be able to provide nonnational elites with a motive to invent their own N propositions and masses with a reason to believe them, but this "solution" of the problem is, of course, merely a restatement of the problem.

The Irrelevance of Elites

While accepting the logic of hard constructivism, the above analysis revealed that the centerpiece of that approach—the proposition that national identity is constructed by elites acting in a self-consciously constructivist manner—is problematic. It will be worthwhile to pursue this point by examining whether all instances of the construction of N really require conscious elites. If even some N propositions can and do emerge without elites, then it logically follows that elites are not a necessary condition of their emergence.

The simplest way of addressing this issue is by identifying the kind of truth claims that can pass for national propositions. These may, of course, be abstract philosophical statements that would seem to require the creative intervention of intellectuals. More likely than not, however, national propositions will take the form of the myths, traditions, rites, and rituals that Hobsbawm carelessly dismisses as mere "custom."[18] Clearly, if national propositions can legitimately encompass so many disparate truth claims—and familiarity with any nation suggests that they surely can—then the view of national identity as an elite construct only is manifestly false.

Orally transmitted myths, such as epics, poems, and songs, are collective undertakings as much as they are the creations of a Homer or the preserve only of the actual storytellers. Their collective telling and retelling—and the listening to their telling and retelling—translate into a continual process of textual creation and recreation within which authors and readers are more or less equally implicated. The following passage, narrated by the young Muslim protagonist of Kurban Said's remarkable novel, *Ali and Nino*, illustrates the point:

> It really was amazing, what wonderful liars these people were. There is no story they would not invent to glorify their country. Only yesterday a fat Armenian tried to tell me that the Christian Maras Church in Shusha was five thousand years old. "Don't tell such tall stories," I told him. "The Christian Faith is not yet two thousand years old. They can't have built a Christian church before Christianity was even thought of." The fat man was very hurt and said reproachfully: "You are, of course, an educated man. But let an old man tell you: The Christian Faith may be only two thousand years old in other countries. But to us, the people of Karabagh, the Saviour showed the light three thousand years before the others. That's how it is." Five minutes later the same man went on to tell me without batting an eyelid that the French General Murat had been an Armenian from Shusha. He had gone to France as a child to make Karabagh's name famous there as well. Even when I was just on the way to Shusha the driver of my coach pointed at the little stone bridge we were about to cross and said proudly: "This bridge was built by Alexander the Great when he went forth to immortal victories in Persia!" "1897" was chiseled in big figures on the parapet. I pointed this out to the coachman, but he only waved his hand: "Och, sir, the Russians put that in later, because they were jealous of our glory!"[19]

Like national myths, national traditions can also emerge without elites. Thus, some customary ways of doing things appear to be rooted in their functionality within a given material context, and what is functional—such as cattle grazing in a flatland or wine growing on a mountainside—then "becomes," for reasons that anthropologists may be better equipped to answer, natural, meaningful, symbolically inevitable, and profoundly national without the necessary intervention of elites. Other ways of doing things may appear to be, and may indeed be, materially dysfunctional, but can make perfect sense within a cultural matrix that well-nigh demands such traditions for the sake of internal consistency and coherence. Human sacrifice may seem to be an odd way of overcoming droughts or economic distress, until it is recognized that appeasing angry gods who brought about the calamity requires an especially precious offering. Ritual sacrifice may be a logical consequence of a worldview whose assumptions are that emotional deities run the world and are wont to wreak havoc upon it.

Finally, some rites—such as church rites—may be dated to the creative intervention of a St. Basil, but we should beware of falling into the genetic fallacy by assuming that Basil the Great is the cause of the continued maintenance of currently existing rites among, say, Orthodox Serbs or Ukrainian Uniates. He may have institutionalized the rites, but he is not responsible for the existence of the institution. Who or what, then, is? Religious elites foster rites, but so do churchgoers who partake of the rituals. But—and, I know, this verges on circularity—so does the institution. Patterned behavior assumes a life of its own, independent of the volition of the individuals involved in its structures. Put another way, institutions, as types of structures, involve people in predetermined relations that, in turn, determine the overall pattern of their behavior.[20]

Evidently, there can be national propositions without elites. And if elites are not a necessary condition of national identity formation, then their being or not being conscious of identity construction is obviously a moot issue. Equally important, however, the above examples suggest that even generalized consciousness of construction may not be necessary for construction to occur. Many established elites, the officeholders, construct identity simply by "doing their job," by "mindlessly" following the rules, patterns, habits, and procedures prescribed by institutions. By the same logic, ordinary people may also have an incremental impact on national identity formation. We do not suppose that the development of agriculture or art required premeditated invention; so, too, it should be possible for national "self-awareness," although admittedly different from agriculture and art, to be generated "unconsciously," by the force of numerous cumulative acts with unintended consequences.

In light of these conclusions, the appropriate research question is neither, as hard constructivism would have it, "Why and how do elites construct national identity?" nor, as soft constructivism would ask, "Is national identity constructed historically?" but, "Why and how can the construction of national identity take place?" In other words, what are the conditions that make national identity possible?

Conditions of National Identity Formation

To ask such a question is to embark on a *conditional* argument. That is to say, we want to isolate the necessary, facilitating, and sufficient conditions of national identity formation. Without necessary conditions, national identity formation cannot occur. With facilitating conditions, it is more likely to occur. And with sufficient conditions, it must occur—but only if necessary conditions are present as well.

Conditional arguments resemble, but emphatically are not, soft constructivist or "conjunctural" in nature.[21] Conditional arguments do not merely assert that things happen in history because people act; nor do they claim that the chance coming together of certain things brings about other things. Rather, conditional arguments claim to be able to illuminate the logic or pattern underlying the occurrence of phenomena. They do this by rigorously isolating not concrete, and hence unique, historical phenomena, but abstract causal variables, or conditions, that must be present and related to one another in a specific way, as necessary, sufficient, and facilitating.[22]

This essay has gone to some pains to point out that one condition of national identity formation is unnecessary—elites—and one necessary—a lifeworld. If there is no lifeworld at hand, there can be no national identity, regardless of whether or not inventive or imaginative elites are present. Unpacking national identity will help us isolate additional conditions, including the elusive sufficient condition.

Regardless of its particular relationship with a lifeworld, a distinctly *national* belief system has to be a special kind of set of intersubjectively held propositions. Otherwise, classes and other kinds of identity groups could also be nations, and we do not want to say that. Rather than filling the notion of nation with positive content, however, and thereby suggesting that nations have essences, I propose that national identity be seen as a coherent package of propositions relating to origins and boundaries. Origins provide a nation with historical authenticity, while boundaries grant it present-day distinctiveness. The inspiration is, of course, Anthony Smith and Fredrik Barth. The former's focus on *mythomoteurs* alerts us to the importance of a nation's having a place in time, while the latter's discussion of boundaries underscores a nation's difference from "the other" and hence its place in space.[23]

At the very least, therefore, nations are groups of people who believe in two things: that their group, as a group, comes from somewhere, and that their group differs from other groups in other ways besides origins as well. A nation's claims to origins and otherness may be "objectively" false, although there is no reason to think they must be so. Nor is there any reason to insist that such claims must be made in the modern language of the nation: clearly, one can believe in origins and otherness without resorting to a nationalist discourse.

The existence of two sets of propositions, one relating to a group's origins, another to its otherness, is another necessary condition of national identity formation, and not an exhaustive list of the defining characteristics of a nation. A complete definition would entail more particulars about origins and otherness. Even so, this protodefinition has its uses. In particular, it permits us to differentiate nations from classes, as well as to underscore the former's kinship with religious and ethnic groups. The propositions characteristic of classes distinguish them from other classes but, as a rule, do not root them in originary myths. In contrast, religious identity shares both characteristics with national identity, and it is, as a result, no surprise that the overlap between religious groups and nations is and has been historically great.[24] Positioned in between classes and religious groups are ethnic and kinship groups, which generally possess a weaker sense of the other and a vague sense of origins.

If a national identity must consist of both sets of propositions, it can do so if and only if they fit together in a single propositional package. If propositional sets are at odds with each other, then, as I argued above, the proto-nation will be unable to sustain both for any meaningful length of time. Sooner or later, one set will have to be abandoned or modified. The sufficient condition of national identity formation, therefore, must be the logical *compatibility* or *complementarity* of propositions regarding a nation's historical origins on the one hand and its relationship with "the other" on the other hand. Thus, national identity is possible if a lifeworld is present and if there exist propositions relating to a group's place in time and space. National identity is inevitable if both sets of propositions are complementary. A nation, then, exists, or comes into being, when people sharing a lifeworld believe in a set of logically complementary propositions regarding origins and otherness.

Consider the following example. Contemporary Ukrainians trace their origins as a nation to the state of Kievan Rus', founded some one thousand years ago. They also define themselves in contrast to their quintessential version of "the other," the Russians. Both propositional sets complement each other perfectly. By claiming Rus' and Kiev for themselves, Ukrainians challenge the prevailing Russian originary myth and exclude the Russian other from their past and from their present. By differentiating themselves from the Russians, they perforce reject the Russian rejection of Ukrainian historicity and thereby claim historical legitimacy for themselves. Inasmuch as these two complementary propositional sets exist in contemporary Ukraine and are believed by its inhabitants, they make of their believers a nation even if, as is indeed the case, many "Ukrainians" might dispute their own nationhood or prefer the term *narod* to *natsiia*.[25]

Explaining (Sort of) National Identity

National identity exists wherever and whenever such compatible propositions arise and are believed in. To some degree, complementarity, like spontaneous combustion, may be serendipitous. But inasmuch as we expect N propositions to be as consistent with one another as with L propositions, the process by which N propositions are constructed "naturally" facilitates national identity formation. There is, thus, a self-propelling dynamic built into propositional construction, one that pushes N propositions toward complementarity. *Attaining* complementarity, however, is an entirely different matter, one that is not a logically necessary consequence of this dynamic.

What, then, is? *I do not know.* As I have argued in this essay, however, I do claim to know that complementarity can come about as a result of elites *and* nonelites, acting and speaking as nationalists *and* as nonnationalists. The construction of national identity cannot therefore be confined to some historical period or to certain social actors. While this insight does not permit us to predict instances of national identity formation, it does lead us to conclude that national identity is, ceteris paribus, always and everywhere possible. This, I submit, is a truly radical claim of the historicity and contingency of nations, one that goes far further than Anderson and Hobsbawm can go because of their insistence on imagination and invention.

There is, as a result, no reason to expect national identity formation not to have taken place before, say, 1789. The ancient Israelites, whose national belief system provided them with a distinct place in time and space, were as much of a nation as most contemporary nations. The Romans, especially during the republic, appear to have fit the definitional requirements as well. So too did the Greeks, whose myths provided them with origins and whose distaste for "barbarians" testified to their refined sense of "the other." These examples notwithstanding, it goes without saying that nations have been far more common in recent centuries than in the distant past. But to put the issue in this manner is to embark on a search for those conditions that *facilitate*— that is to say, make more likely—national identity formation. Two such conditions come to mind.

Modernity—by which I mean both the secular and rationalist ethos of the Enlightenment and the material trappings of the modern world—facilitates the emergence of national identities in two ways that directly address the question of origins and place. First, as a set of ideas regarding the worldly rootedness of humanity and its ability to determine its own destiny according to this-worldly needs, modernity translates into a sense of history, of human historicity, and thus encourages a concern with secular origins. To understand better where we are and where we are going, we want also to understand where we came from.[26] And second, technology, urbanization, communications, "print capitalism," and industrialization bring disparate peoples together, compel them to interact and communicate with one another, and thereby enhance awareness of "the other" and, possibly, the creation of boundaries.[27]

Modernity has also produced an ideology—nationalism—that explicitly argues for the complementarity of these two propositional sets and proposes that the existential needs of nations demand their conjunction with states.[28] More exactly, not modernity per se, but modern-day intellectual, cultural, and political elites invented and imagined nationalism—and *not*, as I have argued, tradition or communities.

While nationalism's emergence as a zeitgeist clearly facilitates national identity formation, the two phenomena are, no less clearly, ontologically independent of each other. There can be nationalism without nations and nations without nationalism—a proposition that rests on a crucial distinction between identity and ideology that constructivism has failed to appreciate.

Finally, there is the state. By its very existence, a territorially defined state "imposes," though not in any remotely constructivist sense, physical unity—that is, both territorial and conceptual boundaries—on a population. A modern bureaucratic state goes even further and imposes administrative unity on some territorially bounded population. If complex, such a population would, as Gellner notes, interact more effectively and efficiently if united in a belief system endowing it with an overarching identity.[29] Where a complex (i.e., modern) population exists within a unified political-spatial setting, such as that which the state defines, a national identity functions to overcome the cleavages dividing the population and to provide it with the ability to communicate more effectively, to act more efficiently, to *live* more meaningfully and easily. At the very least, shared beliefs facilitate cooperation by reducing, if not eliminating, the "free rider" problem and associated transaction costs.[30] The resulting identification of the nation with the state also contributes to originary enquiries hoping to root the latter, and hence also the former, in a historical past connoting naturalness and legitimacy.

These reflections suggest an interesting corollary. We know that people can attain a sense of overarching groupness and share in its propositions by means of the actions of a charismatic warrior, a priestly caste, a "barbarian" invader, itinerant bards and poets, or, even, themselves. Naturally, there are physical limits to how many people can be brought together under an overarching identity in ancient or premodern times. In contrast, modernity and the state increase exponentially the number of people that national identity can encompass. As a result, we correctly expect the communities sharing a national identity to have been, in general, substantially smaller in the past than in the present. Inasmuch as largeness is not a defining characteristic of nations, however, there is, *pace* Anderson, no reason why the "members of even the smallest nation" could *not* know "most of their fellow-members, meet them, or even hear of them." Such familiarity may be unlikely, but it is not impossible.

Rights and Wrongs

Not accidentally, constructivism's current popularity is a reflection of primordialism's unpopularity. Despite their having become thoroughly unfashionable in most academic circles, however, primordialist views are not as unreflective as their unquestioning supporters, most run-of-the-mill nationalists, frequently are. Sophisticated nationalist thinkers, such as Maurice Barrès and Dmytro Dontsov, understood that their ontological assumptions reflected such philosophical currents as essentialism and realism.[31] Nationalists and primordialists can, without too much difficulty, claim continuity with the ideas of, among many other philosophers, Plato, Kant, and Hegel. Forms, the Truth, and the Spirit all reflect the belief that appearances are only surface phenomena and that the reality lies somewhere below, in the essence or essences that presumably encapsulate it. How one approaches the question of national identity—construction versus presence—is not, thus, really an empirical issue that more research, or less nationalism, can resolve. Bridging so deep a philosophical divide may be impossible.

Sharing the assumptions of postmodernism, much contemporary social science concludes that nonessentialist and nominalist perspectives are singularly correct. Such a view is not unpersuasive, but the very spirit of postmodernism also cautions us against being too dogmatic in our judgments. After all, the relativism underlying postmodernism must grant essences a hearing as well. George Steiner, for instance, accepts the ultimate validity of the deconstructionist message but still believes it possible to insist that an appreciation of art, a genuine understanding of the creative act itself, necessitates some belief in a "real presence"—a God—that our postmodern convictions actively strive to deny.[32] In similar fashion Charles Taylor argues that the modern search for personal authenticity must presuppose some standards to be meaningful.[33]

My point is as little that primordialism is *right* and constructivism *wrong* as that constructivism is *right* and primordialism is *wrong*. Here, as elsewhere, it all depends. As Arthur Danto reminds us, good arguments are good, not because they alone are in possession of the truth, but because they are crafted well.[34] And a well-crafted argument is one that, at a minimum, is sensitive to conceptual clarity and rigor. Constructivism can be persuasive if it abandons the language of invention and imagination and the unwarranted theoretical claims they imply.

Like any set of propositions, constructivism fails when it ignores the building blocks of its own knowledge claims.

NOTES

I thank Ron Suny, Michael Kennedy, Mark von Hagen, Jack Snyder, Stefan Cornelis, and Karen Ballentine for their criticism and comments.

1. Eric Hobsbawm, *Nations and Nationalism since 1780: Programme, Myth, Reality* (Cambridge: Cambridge University Press, 1990); Eric Hobsbawm and Terence Ranger, eds., *The Invention of Tradition* (Cambridge: Cambridge University Press, 1992); Benedict Anderson, *Imagined Communities* (London: Verso, 1983).

2. Harold R. Isaacs, "Basic Group Identity: The Idols of the Tribe," in *Ethnicity*, ed. Nathan Glazer and Daniel P. Moynihan (Cambridge, Mass.: Harvard University Press, 1975), 29–52; Clifford Geertz, "The Integrative Revolution: Primordial Sentiments and Civil Politics in the New States," in *Political Development and Social Change*, ed. Jason L. Finkle and Richard W. Gable (New York: John Wiley and Sons, 1966), 655–69. Donald Horowitz, *Ethnic Groups in Conflict* (Berkeley and Los Angeles: University of California Press, 1985), also comes close to making a primordialist case. Consider Jürgen Habermas's neoprimordialist explanation of recent events in West Germany: "[W]hat happened was that the floodgates of public opinion must have opened and changed the general climate to the point where stereotypes and opinions that had lurked beneath the surface . . . now suddenly burst forth." "'More Humility, Fewer Illusions'—a Talk between Adam Michnik and Jürgen Habermas," *New York Review of Books*, March 24, 1994, 24.

3. Anthony Smith, *The Ethnic Origins of Nations* (Oxford: Basil Blackwell, 1986), and "The Nation: Invented, Imagined, Reconstructed?" *Millennium* 20, no. 3 (winter 1991): 353–68; John A. Armstrong, *Nations before Nationalism* (Chapel Hill: University of North Carolina Press, 1982), and "The Autonomy of Ethnic Identity: Historic Cleavages and Nationality Relations in the USSR," in *Thinking Theoretically about Soviet Nationalities*, ed. Alexander J. Motyl (New York: Columbia University Press, 1992), 23–43.

4. Much of my thinking about concepts is drawn from Giovanni Sartori, "Guidelines for Concept Analysis," in *Social Science Concepts*, ed. Sartori (Beverly Hills, Calif.: Sage, 1984), 15–85.

5. Eric Hobsbawm, "Introduction: Inventing Traditions," in Hobsbawm and Ranger, *The Invention of Tradition*, 1.

6. Hobsbawm, "Introduction," 2.

7. Anderson, *Imagined Communities*, 15.

8. *Webster's Seventh New Collegiate Dictionary* (Springfield: G. and C. Merriam, 1963), 445, 416.

9. Eric Hobsbawm, "The New Threat to History," *New York Review of Books*, December 16, 1993, 63.

10. Anderson, *Imagined Communities*, 40.

11. Ernest Gellner, *Nations and Nationalism* (Ithaca, N.Y.: Cornell University Press, 1983), 49.

12. Miroslav Hroch, *Social Preconditions of National Revival in Europe* (Cambridge: Cambridge University Press, 1985).

13. See Sartori, "Guidelines for Concept Analysis," 81–82; Kenneth Russell Olson, *An Essay on Facts* (Stanford, Calif.: Center for the Study of Language and Information, 1987).

14. Many historians would of course strenuously disagree. See Hobsbawm, *Nations and Nationalism*, 14.

15. Liah Greenfeld, *Nationalism: Five Roads to Modernity* (Cambridge, Mass.: Harvard University Press, 1992), 4–8; Rogers Brubaker, "Rethinking Nationhood," *Contention* 4 (fall 1994): 3–14.

16. On the concept of lifeworld, see Donald M. Lowe, "Intentionality and the Method of History," in *Phenomenology and the Social Sciences*, ed. Maurice Natanson (Evanston, Ill.: Northwestern University Press, 1973), 2:103–30; Aron Gurwitsch, *Phenomenology and the Theory of Science* (Evanston, Ill.: Northwestern University Press, 1974), 3–32; Jürgen Habermas, *Legitimation Crisis*, trans. Thomas McCarthy (Boston: Beacon Press, 1975), 10–11.

17. Peter L. Berger and Thomas Luckmann, *The Social Construction of Reality: A Treatise in the Sociology of Knowledge* (Garden City, N.Y.: Doubleday, 1966).

18. Hobsbawm, "Introduction," 2.

19. Kurban Said, *Ali and Nino* (New York: Random House, 1970), 43–44. I am grateful to John A. Armstrong for bringing to my attention information that identified Kurban Said as one Essad Bey, an Azerbaijani Jew who converted to Islam and dropped his family name, Nussinbaum. After the Soviet takeover of Azerbaijan, he fled to Berlin, where he began his career as a writer. He moved to Vienna in 1933, where he stayed until 1938, emigrating after the Anschluss to Italy, where he died.

20. The "new institutionalist" literature is enormous. For a summary of its basic arguments, see Douglass North, *Institutions, Institutional Change, and Economic Performance* (Cambridge: Cambridge University Press, 1990).

21. Note Theda Skocpol's definition of conjuncture as the "coming together of separately determined and not consciously coordinated . . . processes and group efforts." *States and Social Revolutions* (Cambridge: Cambridge University Press, 1979), 298.

22. See Ernest Sosa and Michael Tooley, introduction to *Causation*, ed. Sosa and Tooley (Oxford: Oxford University Press, 1993), 5–8.

23. Smith, *Ethnic Origins of Nations*; Fredrik Barth, *Ethnic Groups and Boundaries* (Boston: Little, Brown, 1969). See also Crawford Young, *The Politics of Cultural Pluralism* (Madison: University of Wisconsin Press, 1976), 41–44.

24. See Pedro Ramet, ed., *Religion and Nationalism in Soviet and East European Politics* (Durham, N.C.: Duke University Press, 1989).

25. Alexander J. Motyl, *Dilemmas of Independence: Ukraine after Totalitarianism* (New York: Council on Foreign Relations, 1993), 76–103.

26. For a fascinating discussion of these issues, see Zygmunt Bauman, "Soil, Blood, and Identity," *Sociological Review* 40, no. 4 (November 1992): 675–701.

27. Joseph Rothschild discusses these points in *Ethnopolitics* (New York: Columbia University Press, 1981).

28. On the connection between nationalism and modernity, see Greenfeld, *Nationalism;* and Alexander J. Motyl, "The Modernity of Nationalism," *Journal of International Affairs* 45 (winter 1992): 307–23.

29. Gellner, *Nations and Nationalism,* 19–52.

30. For a "soft" rational-choice interpretation of nationalism, see Alexander J. Motyl, *Sovietology, Rationality, Nationality: Coming to Grips with Nationalism in the USSR* (New York: Columbia University Press, 1990).

31. John A. Armstrong, "Collaborationism in World War II: The Integral Nationalist Variant in Eastern Europe," *Journal of Modern History* 40 (1968): 396–410; Alexander J. Motyl, *The Turn to the Right: The Ideological Origins and Development of Ukrainian Nationalism, 1919–1929* (Boulder, Colo.: East European Monographs, 1980); J. S. McClelland, ed., *The French Right* (New York: Harper and Row, 1970), 143–211.

32. George Steiner, *Real Presences* (Chicago: University of Chicago Press, 1989).

33. Charles Taylor, *The Ethics of Authenticity* (Cambridge, Mass.: Harvard University Press, 1992).

34. Arthur C. Danto, *Narration and Knowledge* (New York: Columbia University Press, 1985).

Getting Here

When asked about my nationality, I usually respond that I'm a New Yorker. The answer is evasive, but not quite incorrect.

I was born and raised in the Ukrainian ghetto on New York City's Lower East Side. The bathtub was in the kitchen, the toilet was in the hallway, and the telephone was eight years away. I remember the ragman's horse-drawn cart on East Tenth Street, the bums who lined the Bowery, the shouts of "mira, mira" in Tompkins Square Park, and St. Mark's Place when it was just an ordinary street.

The pharmacist was a Galician Jew, Pan Guzman, but everything else—school, church, doctor, shoe store, youth club, soda fountain, and grocery—was Ukrainian. My friends and I spoke English with one another and Ukrainian in the presence of Americans. The natives, as my parents' generation used to call them, were "the foreigners."

High school marked my exit from the ghetto. My new friends were Italian and Irish Catholic boys with names like Emil and Mike. I learned to pray in English and to distinguish between pickles and cucumbers. My Jesuit teachers also taught me how to ask questions and when to believe answers.

Naturally, I questioned my ethnicity. I rejected things Ukrainian with a vengeance. But I could not embrace things American. The Yankees were fun, but the Hardy Boys were no match for the Three Musketeers, flag-waving failed to resonate, and popular representations of Ukrainians as primordial anti-Semites seemed overstated, especially to a teen-ager immersed in Virgil, calculus, and Cream. I came to occupy a middle ground, a kind of no-man's-land, that I have never left.

Life in the no-man's-land forces you to look both ways, to be on guard, to walk through smoke, to negotiate shadows, to dodge bombs, to avoid searchlights. Equidistance easily translates into detachment, and that, in turn, cultivates an appreciation of the absurd. After Dido and Aeneas, I discovered Dada and Ada. It was hard to keep a straight face while reading between the front lines.

Two developments undermined my cynicism about things Ukrainian. One was the obligatory trip through Europe at the age of twenty-three. Traveling from capital to capital for six months opened my eyes to the provincialism of being American and the cosmopolitanism of being Ukrainian. Americans wore bright orange ski jackets and sneakers and complained about the French and their food. The Ukrainian language enabled me to eat snails and drink Weizenbier with the unimagined communities of Paris and Munich. I embraced Europe, as Vienna eventually came to embrace me.

The other development had more of an intellectual nature. Growing up in an intensely nationalist, and just as intensely anti-Soviet, community—America? the Lower East Side?—whetted my interest in Ukrainian nationalism and anti-Sovietism. I studied the former, reading memoirs, interviewing members of the nationalist underground, visiting cemeteries, and delving into archives. Dmytro Dontsov's description of nationalists as people who "know what they want and want it very much" sticks in my memory.

I also observed the ingenuity of anti-Soviet émigrés dedicated to subverting the USSR from Second Avenue bars and New Jersey basements. Fascinated with ideological struggles, propaganda, and counterpropaganda, I learned much about the KGB, both through books and through a series of personal encounters ranging from indiscreet tailings to discreet interrogations to overt attempts at recruitment. Soviet prefects and Stalin's successors seemed infinitely less interesting than Smiley's people.

I was intrigued, not by Russia, Ukraine, or the Soviet Union, but the means by which the Soviet system kept itself intact. Graduate school told me that these means were largely consensual and that only Cold Warriors mistrusted the USSR. Having been raised on stories of the Stalinist terror—a woodcut of a loutish commissar beating a poor Ukrainian peasant greatly impressed me as a child—and knowing that close relatives had spent time in the Gulag or been killed, I had fewer illusions about the Soviets. But, like other students exposed to the dark side of academic life, I ritualistically denounced totalitarianism. In rehabilitating the concept while damning the term in my dissertation I unwittingly stumbled upon theory.

My interest in Ukrainian nationalism led to an interest in the Soviet "national question." The jump from there to nationalism in general, to theorizing about nationalism, and finally to a self-reflective theorizing about theorizing about nationalism was small. The process was hardly linear, however. I had studied mathematics, nineteenth-century West European intellectual history, painting, and journalism, and nothing could have been further from my mind than a scholarly career devoted to, of all things, Eastern Europe. I recall distinctly the nausea I felt when walking through the stacks and viewing the sad rows of dust-covered books.

Life between the fronts may have made me especially sensitive to language. I learned to see through nationalist propaganda and Soviet diatribes, while thoroughly enjoying both sides' skill at weaving such marvelous stories. I think I also learned to see through scholarly cant. Decidedly less cheery was the epiphany—lightning can strike slowly, says my friend John—that most academic verities were fashionable dogmas and that theoretical breakthroughs usually rested on conceptual breakdowns. Recent revelations about exterminationist Germans and clashing civilizations have not disconfirmed that hypothesis.

No less distrustful of social scientists than of nationalists and communists, I have become as interested in how scholars think and talk about things as in the things they think and talk about. For a while I thought it might be possible to find a solid foundation for thinking theoretically, but, after learning that the philosophers knew only how to ask good questions and when to disbelieve bad answers, I realized that, at best, we can make either more sense or less. Sadly, it seems to me, much of what we do and say makes rather less sense than more.

Alexander J. Motyl
New York City
January 13, 1997

Khachig Tololyan

Textual Nation: Poetry and Nationalism in Armenian Political Culture

In the late eighteenth century, a Georgian chronicler named Meskhiia denounced the advancement of Armenians in the service of Georgian rulers, claiming that his countrymen should not favor a people punished by God. As evidence of God's wrath, he pointed out that "Armenians . . . have been dispersed by God," then asked: "Is it in man's power to reunite them?"[1] At just about the same time, in 1792, Joseph Emin, an Armenian activist who set out single-handedly and quixotically to obtain European support for the liberation of his countrymen from Muslim rulers, wrote in his memoirs: "I grieved . . . for my religion and my country, that we were in slavery and ignorance like Jews, vagabonds upon the Earth."[2] Dispersion and "vagabondage," analogous to that of the Jewish diaspora, are the shared figures and common themes that run through both denunciation and lamentation; their authors allude to the biblical tradition in which God ordains punitive expulsions (e.g. Adam and Eve from Paradise and the Jews from Judaea) followed by sustained dispersion.[3]

Soon after these statements were made, in the first third of the nineteenth century, Armenian intellectuals living in diaspora developed a new discourse marked by its focus on dispersion as an exceptionally important feature of *collective* misfortune, even though it was by no means the only difficulty that afflicted the Armenians. In fact, the Muslim overlords of the homeland made life more difficult than it was in diaspora, by misgovernment, excessive taxation, and wars in which Armenian peasants were always the chief victims and their monasteries the target of looting. The frequent protests and lamentations arising from such conditions in the homeland remained localist, respectful of hierarchy, and couched in the traditional rhetoric of a suffering religious community. By contrast, the new diasporan discourse of dispersion envisaged the Armenians not simply as a series of religious communities but as a collectivity that could become a nation.

I will exemplify the emergence of this new discourse of dispersion with a key poem that imagines the reversal of dispersion in a language still precariously balanced between its religious and secular sources. I will argue that this mixture of languages provides a freeze-frame, a snapshot of the few brief decades during which the religious discourse with which Armenians expressed their collective consciousness was transformed and displaced by a discourse that was largely, though never wholly, secular and national.[4] Finally, I will engage and critique theories of the emergence of nationalism that polarize causative factors of that emergence as subjective or objective, discursive or material, and emphasize one role at the expense of the other.

For reasons that will become clear, my discussion begins with a literary-historical analysis of the linked questions of who wrote the poem in question, and when. It was originally untitled and was variously known to the energetic but untidy advocates of modern Armenian literature as the "Ter Getzo" or as "Ter Getzo Doo 'Zhyes" ("Lord, Sustain" or "Lord, Sustain the Armenian People"), and also as the "Orhnerkootyun Azkayin" ("Song of National Benediction"). It is widely attributed to Mesrop Daviti Taghiatiantz[5] (1803–1858) and is best known from the version published in 1847 in a periodical named *Azkaser* ("Patriot"), which he edited in Calcutta for distribution to the Armenian merchant-diaspora of India.[6] Though numerically small, the Armenian-Indian community, which was concentrated in Madras, Calcutta, and Surat, was for some time of considerable economic and cultural importance to Armenians everywhere; its publications circulated to other diasporan centers of intellectual activity, such as Moscow, Tbilisi, Istanbul, Smyrna, and Venice. In 1847, Armenians existed as a transnation,[7] a partially diasporized entity. More than half lived in a divided homeland ruled by the Ottoman, Persian, and Russian empires; most of the rest lived in intrastate diasporas (that is, in communities ruled by the same imperial states that ruled the portion of the homeland from which they originated, and with which they could maintain relatively easy contact);[8] and the remaining small but influential fraction lived in interstate or transnational diasporas that stretched from Manchester and Venice to Singapore and Batavia.

The "Ter Getzo" poem was circulated among the elites of this transnation, until an event occurred a dozen years later that transformed it into a cultural icon for a wider audience that had never been in contact with Calcutta. In the mid–nineteenth century, the Moscow-based periodical *Hyusisapyle* ("Northern Lights") played a major role as both a forum and shaper of progressive thought in the Romanovs' empire and beyond. In this journal, the revolutionary intellectual Mikayel Nalpantian(tz)[9] published *Merelahartzoug* ("Necromancy," 1859), fragments of a fiction whose narrator refers to the "Ter Getzo" poem, attributes it to Taghiatiantz, and praises it lavishly: "If I could, I would make it a sacred duty for every Armenian to memorize this poem. Hitherto I have never seen or heard another song like it, a true national *(azgayin)* song."[10] In mid-nineteenth-century Armenian, "song" is used to mean either "music," or "lyrics," or both. The reference to memorization implies that the poem was not yet set to music in 1859. Who set it to music is not known, but apparently this was done soon after, because in 1868, Miansarian's songbook, *Knar Hygagan* ("Armenian Lyre"), published both verse and lyrics, further facilitating their circulation. It's worth noting that Nalpantian uses the adjective *azgayin* to mean "national," though the term was then most commonly applied to the Armenian Church, the one institution recognized by the vast majority of the Armenian people.

The popularity of the poem/song is significant because, in the Armenian case, there was as yet no nation-state or state-supervised pedagogic institution that might dictate or effect such popularity. Its circulation can plausibly be taken as an index of the appeal that the subsequently much-quoted *words* of the song held for the mass of people, about whose state of mind we often do not have other indications, of the sort that the constant polling of our own time, say, claims to provide. The poem/song remained popular for a century, waning only after World War II,[11] and it has been known as Taghiatiantz's throughout that time. But as Alboyajian (see note 10) showed conclusively, Taghiatiantz found the poem in an earlier periodical and never claimed authorship. Its 1847 publication in Calcutta was "signed" by the initials "H.C.,"[12] and to it Taghiatiantz had attached a footnote, which Nalpantian failed to mention and subsequent editors neglected or never knew. The footnote says nothing about the original author's identity but states that the poem was originally published in 1820, in an ephemeral publication of the Armenian community of Calcutta, *Hyeli Calcatian* ("The Mirror of Calcutta," whose Armenian initials are H.C.). Since Taghiatiantz was seventeen in 1820, and living in Russian Armenia, Alboyajian thinks it highly unlikely that he was the author of the poem. Neither he nor anyone else can establish who the author was; for the vast majority of Armenians who have lived since Nalpantian's 1859 essay, Taghiatiantz is that author.

These details matter insofar as my argument has a quasi-biographical component: "quasi-" because the unknown author shared with Taghiatiantz a social milieu, a vocabulary, and a protonationalist discourse of dispersion and its reversal. My interpretation depends on the resemblances between the language of the poem and of later work indisputably attributed to Taghiatiantz but does not demonstrate that resemblance here; such work would require at least a separate philological essay.[13] My contention is that Taghiatiantz republished the poem because it echoed his own strongly held convictions; and that Nalpantian misconstrued its authorship, despite the evidence of "H.C.," in part because of the similarity between Taghiatiantz's discourse and the poems, and in part, perhaps, because he wrote in journalistic haste.

The poem is in five stanzas of seven lines each. It is written in a late and "corrupt" form of *grabar*, the classical Armenian that stopped being the daily language of Armenian life before the end of the eleventh century but remained the language of the liturgy (to this day), and dominated the writing of theology and some belles lettres until the mid–nineteenth century. The poem was written at a historical moment in which two important transitional events of Armenian life intersected and overlapped: the passage of territory from Persian to Russian rule; and the move from undisputed clerical and merchant-prince domination of diasporan institutions to a contentious struggle with the emerging middle class for control of those institutions.

I have translated the poem for fidelity to the original, which inevitably creates a somewhat stilted English version:

[1.1]   Lord, sustain the Armenians,
        make them resplendent.

Support them.
Your higher mercy
be pleased to bestow,
enable them to live
in this place below.

[2.1]　O Lord, make haste
to save all our people
from their enemies.
Close the foe's eyes,
Sever them root and stalk
and make strong
our weary nation.

[3.1]　Where you descended to earth
there the throne of our patriarch
establish again.
Long life
to our God-vested Father give,
grant it to this leader of our fathers
that he may shepherd us.

[4.1]　With your all-encompassing right hand,
with caring speed
our expelled nation
gather together
in the land of Ararat,
the place of our birth
which alien nations now hold.

[5.1]　From on high send
a coherence of will
to our compatriots.
From among them raise up
a shepherd for our people
and give him a mighty staff,
that he may shepherd us.
Lord, sustain the Armenians.

The poem ends with the phrase with which it begins, but this formal circularity is deceptive. In fact, it develops in remarkable fashion, asking for the restoration of a religion-dominated prenationalist past in the first three stanzas, then for the installation of a more secular and protonationalist future in the last two. It does so through a set of allusions to Armenian history and through particular word choices that require careful unpacking by a combination of literary and historical interpretation.

The poet begins by using a generally shared Christian vocabulary to ask for support and sustenance (1.1), then increases the stakes: in 2.1, he asks the Lord to "save," to act once again as a Savior,[14] this time not of mankind in general but of the Armenian faithful in particular. He specifies the form of "saving" he requests: not that of the soul, but one that involves making the Armenians strong (2.6) while striking at their enemies "root and stalk" (2.5). He then refers to the place where "you" [God as Christ] descended to earth (3.1). This requires some background for the non-Armenian reader, but none for Armenians, who understand the allusion through a legend they encounter very early, soon after they learn the Lord's Prayer: Armenian tradition narrates that the choice of Echmiadzin,[15] the site where "the throne of the patriarch [now called the catholicos]"[16] (3.2) is situated, was dictated in a vision granted to the founding father of the Armenian Apostolic Church, some time around 301 C.E. Thus, an invocation of the site is also a reference to a time when God favored the Armenians as a people worthy of his attention and assistance in selecting the site.

Still, though the first three stanzas begin with the memory of that original divine favor, they seem to end in a slight anticlimax. The Lord's intervention is asked to restore the Armenian Church to its glory: a traditional sentiment, however unexpectedly conjoined with sentiments about "severing the enemy root and stalk." But then the last two stanzas of the poem move definitively beyond tradition as they ask God for much more than religious restoration; such restoration, in the vision of this poem, is not sufficient to save the Armenian people. It asks also for an ingathering of the nation, to which it refers as "expelled" (ardahaladz). The root word, haladz-el, means "to drive out," and in the mid–nineteenth century, it was also beginning to acquire a secondary, now common and often explicitly political meaning, "to persecute." The vocabulary of Armenian is so marked by the discourse of dispersion that the words "to be persecuted" and "to be driven out of the homeland" are the same. Such political nuances become more explicit with every further line of the poem: "which alien nations now hold" (4.7), "send a coherence of will" (5.2), and so on.

It's worth noting that though the poem moves from religious restoration to political innovation, the religious and secular dimensions never become altogether distinct. The last and most political stanzas open and close with a religious phrase, "that he may shepherd us" (3.7, 5.6). The word used for "staff" (*tzoub*, 5.5) in Armenian, as in English, has a Judeo-Christian connotation (specifically, the staff of the shepherd-leader from Moses on). The word for "scepter" (*makan*), an icon of secular power, which might have been used in its place, is avoided. In effect, the poem deploys the religious vocabulary of divinely approved legitimate clerical leadership ("throne," 3.2; "God-vested Father," 3.5) and then asks that such authority either be supplemented or replaced—the text simply does not make that clear—by a political authority "raised up" by the will of God and the Armenian people on the territory of the homeland, to which the dispersed must return. Its vision of an ideal polity is still hierarchical, not democratic, but the "coherent will of compatriots" is an indication that the consent of the nation must somehow be involved in the elevation of new leadership, and what is more, that such coherence will have sacred legitimacy.

Here, the unknown poet and Taghiatiantz are astute about the religiopolitical in a way that Armenian and other political nationalists of later generations have failed to be. As Pierre Taminiaux has claimed, even the most sophisticated and rational arguments for the nation (by which he means his own French nation) depend on a "discourse of the sacred," a discourse that understands what "our secular political systems and institutions have become incapable of representing for themselves, [namely, that] irrational forces bind a community beyond abstract principles and conceptual models."[17] Of course there are substantial dangers in such religion-based views of the collectivity, recognized from Durkheim on, but the dangers of sacralizing the nation are part and parcel of a functioning nationalism, not dispensable elements of it, as the form of this poem affirms.

A sense of urgency attends the poem that the English-speaking reader may discern in its sheer presumption, in its use of the imperative as it asks God to reverse a dispersion. The Armenian text makes the urgency even stronger, marking the occasion as one of crisis, by its use two versions of a particular word: *poota* (2.1) and *pooyt* (4.2), which I have translated as "make haste" and "with caring speed." Originally, *pooyt* and *pootal* meant "haste" and "to make haste," respectively, but they acquired additional meaning in a complex semantic domain. Metaphorically, *anpooyt* came to mean "inattentive" or "careless," in the sense of not making haste to look after what needed care. In a related and now archaic usage, *pooyt anel* came to mean "to make an effort," while in modern Armenian *pootgod* becomes an adjective to describe efforts that combine precisely the terms of my analysis, "care" and "urgency." The poet asks God not just to care, but to hurry up and care: the dispersion has acquired a new quality of urgency, so much so that the poet must risk impertinence by asking God for more than mercy for and salvation of his and the nation's soul: those pleas are routine in the discourse of its time. Instead, in the last stanza he asks God "to send" *(arakya)* a coherence of will and "to raise up" a shepherd, and does so in the core vocabulary of religious discourse. *Arakya* is not the colloquial and expected word for "to send," but the elevated choice: the Armenian word for "apostle" or "emissary" is *arakyal*, "he who is sent from on high." Similarly, the poem uses *haro* for "to raise up" (5.4), the verb whose noun form, *harootyun*, means the resurrection or raising/rising of Lazarus and Christ, which together prefigure the possibility of resurrection for the devout at the end of time and, here in the poem, of the metaphorically dead, because dispersed, Armenian nation. In fact, without quite approaching apocalyptic tones, the poet conveys a secular urgency to the divinity in his request that God end dispersion, gather the people on the homeland, and give it new leadership.

A final textual caveat is in order here. Decisions about translation are rarely purely linguistic; they also involve historical, indeed often political, assumptions. In this case, my translation of the word *azg* requires particular attention. The poem uses *azg* five times. I have translated it as "people" in 2.2 and 5.5, and as "nation" in 2.7, 4.3, and 4.7. The warrant for this inconsistency is the ambiguity inherent in the Armenian word. Classical Armenian uses *azg* to signify several things. It can refer to a large kinship group; this meaning is retained in the modern *azgakan*, a blood relative. But *azg* can also mean a "people" or an "ethnie"; such groupings usually imagine themselves as sharing blood kinship. Finally, the polyvalent word can also denote "nation" in the same loose way that the King James Bible speaks of the "nations of the earth" to encompass a great civilization like the Babylonian, along with minor desert tribes, neither of which were nation(-state)s in the contemporary sense. Thus, from the fifth to the nineteenth century, *azg* could mean kinship group, ethnos, people, and nation in the prenationalist sense of the word, in which Latin *natio*, birth, still has a central place. This sense is evoked by the poem in line 4.6, where the concept of the homeland as "the place of our *birth*" is emphasized. That notion of birthplace is of course metaphor, not fact, since most of the Armenians of Calcutta, say, were born in India or Iran, not the homeland. Characteristically, in many diasporan literatures, the loss of the sense that one is "at home" in the place of one's birth begets a yearning for another "home" that can take many forms, some of them nationalistic.

One way of describing the project of nationalism is to say that it proposes to turn a people into a nation. From this perspective, my translation of *azg* as both people and nation may seem opportunistic, because it can lead to the implication that the anonymous author had both of the current meanings of the word in mind, as well as the transformation of one into the other. I do, in fact, believe that the language of this particular poem, written in a moment of discursive transformation to which it substantially contributes, does use *azg* to mean "nation" not just in the loose King James Bible sense, or as "the religious community of Apostolic Armenians," but in a protomodern sense. I base that conclusion on two kinds of evidence. The first is that by the early decades of the nineteenth century, Armenian writers had begun to shake off the classical form of the language and used *azg* to refer to European nations endowed with states at the same time that they continued to use it for the stateless Armenian transnation. The second evidence is inherent in the poem itself, in its imagined move from a stateless, leaderless dispersal to its antithesis: a territorialized nation with leaders raised up by popular will and divine favor.

Poetry does more with less. It is an art of compactness. The words of poems are selected to make a coherent aesthetic object with its own internal logic, and simultaneously to draw into the constrained space of the poem relevant meanings from other texts and discourses, from the institutions and experiences of "real life." Successful poems are verbal sites where the emotions, thoughts, and discourses of past and present generations are made to intersect and sometimes to invoke a future. By that definition, "Ter Getzo" is an extraordinarily successful poem. It draws both upon the Armenian past and upon emerging contemporary values; it deploys religious and other discourses to represent the redemption of dispersion, projecting an Armenian future sensitively and shrewdly. In this section, I want to explicate the process by which the poem situates itself in history and makes itself an agent of history.

The unknown author and Taghiatiantz were both clearly immersed in the history, language, claims, and even pretensions of the Armenian Church. Furthermore, writing in 1820, the author hopes for a future for his church's leader, the "patriarch"-catholicos, that had already become a reality by the time Taghiatiantz republished his poem in 1847. It may well be that the latter, struck by the success of the "prophetic" elements of the first three stanzas, hoped that the rest, too, would become a reality. At any rate, the poem's enthroned patriarch in the Armenian heartland not only invokes the prosperity and glory of the church in general terms, it also explicitly alludes to the political role of that church before 1820 and projects a greater role, which was realized in 1827–28 (see below).

Since we do not know the author's identity, we have no way of knowing just how much he knew, beyond generalities that were public knowledge, about the past political activity of catholicoses. On the other hand, Taghiatiantz was educated in Echmiadzin's seminary (in 1816–21) and knew a great deal about the recent past and something of the more remote past of ecclesiastical intervention in protonational affairs. It is difficult to ascertain, but reasonable to speculate, that much of his knowledge was acquired through oral tradition in the seminary rather than through the perusal of histories and documents. Ecclesiastical scholarship in areas beyond theology and the teaching of the classical language was notoriously slack in his time, and records of secretive political activity would have been inaccessible to a mere seminarian.

In 1847, when Taghiatiantz reprinted the poem, the catholicos at Echmiadzin was Nerses Ashtaraketzi (r. 1843–57), who had played a vital and not merely symbolic role at a crucial moment in recent Armenian history. In 1826–27, as a bishop, he had helped to raise, had blessed, and then accompanied a column of ten thousand Armenians who fought with the czar's troops against the Persians during the Russian conquest of the Transcaucasus. Ashtaraketzi never completely fulfilled the dream that had motivated him and a number of other Armenian bishops in 1827,[18] of bringing even more Armenian land under the dominion of the Christian czar and (it was futilely hoped) of Armenian notables who would become the local agents of his rule. But one result of his tenure at Echmiadzin was the perpetuation of the institutional memory of the largely failed prenationalist activism of even earlier catholicoses.

In this memory, rumors about the Armenian catholicos's participation in efforts "to liberate" Armenia allege that the first political move was made in 1547, when Catholicos Stepanos Salmasdetsi sought relief from Persian rule at a moment of crisis in that empire. Emboldened by a civil war that strained Shah Tahmasp's power even as it brought misery to Armenians, Salmasdetsi is said to have consulted with clerical and lay notables—all "the coherence of will" needed in that still-feudal society—before setting out with his retinue on a difficult journey to the European West and the Armenian diaspora there. He met with Pope Julius III in Rome, visited the court of the Habsburg emperor, dealt at length with representatives of the Venetian republic, and finally went to meet King Sigismund II of Poland in Lviv (now a Ukrainian city), where there was an influential community of Armenian merchants. This diplomatic journey brought no visible results, but in 1562 the next catholicos, Mikayel Sebastatsi, convened a secret gathering of clerical and lay notables in Sebastia, now Sivas, his hometown in the Ottoman Empire. After eliciting an invitation to travel to Venice, he declined to go and instead sent a spokesman, Apkar Tokatetsi, who died in Venice before he could report any results. Subsequently, in 1575, the catholicos Tadeos visited the prosperous diaspora in Lviv, probably to raise funds, but also to interest the Poles in military intervention. No action followed. Nearly a century later, in 1677, Catholicos Hakob Jughayetsi arranged still another secret conclave of clergymen and landed gentry and led another delegation to Europe.[19] This mission, too, proved unproductive, never getting beyond Istanbul. Because these missions would have been regarded as treason by the Persian and Ottoman authorities, and because they failed, they were not boasted of, but their memory was kept alive in Echmiadzin. The motives for these actions were primarily the preservation of some of the powers and privileges of the Christian church and the surviving Armenian feudal gentry, and the restoration of others. The sovereignty of a feudal Christian Armenia that they hoped to rule again would not automatically result in the inclusion of the diasporic merchant-princes, who as yet had no role to play in the homeland aside from the auxiliary and philanthropic. For the very few who might be considered the intellectuals of that diaspora, who were both financially dependent on the merchant princes and were more radical in pursuit of their objectives, no role at all could be envisaged.

Though we have no sure way of knowing to what extent and in what detail this ecclesiastical pursuit of Armenian sovereignty was known to the nameless poet, or to Taghiatiantz, the possibility that both authors entertained in their writings, that religious leaders (and, in the case of this poem, God), might again intervene in political life, was more than an abstract idea in Echmiadzin or in India. Furthermore, India was (in the language of current cultural theory) the "margin," the periphery, the site in which a distant diaspora reinvented, reimagined, reconceived the homeland "center" in terms that included the ecclesiastical but went beyond it, just as the poem does. This transformative effort came about because the Armenian diaspora met the most advanced elements of the West, the British bourgeoisie, in India even before it encountered them later on their home territory of Britain.

By the late 1770s, while the still-devout yet increasingly "politicized" Armenian merchant-intellectuals of Madras were formulating ideas of what an Armenian constitutional monarchy might be, in the homeland a reactionary catholicos, Simeon Yerevantsi (d. 1780) was formulating new arguments for what can only be called the divine right of catholicoses. He reasoned that as Christ was the sole intercessor between man and God, so the first Armenian catholicos, Gregory the Illuminator, was the first intercessor between Armenians and Christ; consequently, his successors were also the only proper intermediaries between Armenians and God, the master of their political fate.[20] Though such arguments seemed old-fashioned to Indian-Armenians after their long and agonizing encounter with the East India Company, clerical intercession and intervention were both institutionalized traditions in Armenian life.[21] Thus, asking God, who was himself something of an absent foreign power in Armenian history, to intervene in Armenian life was not simply a product of the unknown poet's or Taghiatiantz's personal nationalism, religiosity, subjectivity, or imagination. By 1820/1847, requests for such intervention were a form embedded in discourse, had a history,[22] indeed had become a secular agent of history.

Of course, poetry differs from historiography. It draws on more than the record of clerical diplomatic activism and does so with a different sense of order and development. The linear order of the poem—

from clerical to secular leadership of the restored nation—does not draw on actual events or on a linear development then available in discourse; it *constructs* that linearity. For the poet, earlier and more recent events, as well as the narrative discourses that grew up around them and came to represent them to later generations, are not more or less remotely arranged in a fixed and receding linearity. They are equally and simultaneously available to him, as he writes: Moses' staff and Catholicos Ashtaraketsi, so to speak, are coevals. It is best to think of the discursive resources available to the early-nineteenth-century pro-tonationalist as being residual in some cases and emergent in others. Sometimes intentionally and at other times quite inadvertently, the poetic use of these discourses recruits people to ideas, behaviors, and loyalties that intersect and are superimposed upon each other, creating the subject position of the nationalist, waiting in the antechamber of history.

What is the model of the mighty shepherd who takes form in Judeo-Christian discourse but is by the end of this poem a political leader of the Armenians? Is there a text, a discursive resource in Armenian history on which the unknown poet was drawing in the secular moment of his poem? Of course there need have been no such moment: after George Washington and Napoleon Bonaparte, the idea of state-fathering leadership was widespread in the anglophone Indian-Armenian community, which knew of both of these figures who fought the British (who were fast becoming the unwelcome masters of India), discussing them in early newspapers from 1794 on. But Armenian history had also provided such a figure fairly recently. We do not know whether the unknown author spent much of his life, as Taghia-tiantz did, traveling along the diaspora-homeland circuit (as failed businessman, teacher, emissary, clerk, and intellectual), moving between the Transcaucasus, the Ottoman Empire, Persia, and India. On these journeys, Taghiatiantz came to know, and his poet-predecessor would have come to learn, the story of the two leading actors of non-ecclesiastical Armenian struggle for sovereignty, Israel Ori and Davit Beg, descendants of the minor landowning gentry of Karabagh and neighboring Syunik.

The rebellion led by Davit Beg in the years 1722–28 is an event that was made into text soon after his death, between 1733 and 1736. In that time period, a minor leader and survivor of the rebellion, Stepanos Shahumian of Ghapan, traveled to Venice to live with his diasporan

merchant relatives. There, one vector of protonationalist struggle met
another that had until then been wholly independent of it. The island of
San Lazzaro in Venice had been granted to the Mekhitarian monastic
Catholic brotherhood in 1717, and this order of extraordinarily diligent
and productive scholars had already launched the projects that led the
historian Leo to call the eighteenth century "the Mekhitarian century"
of Armenian history. Of all the institutional actors and individual
agents in my account, the Mekhitarians are the only ones of whom it
could be said that at least the design of their institution was culturally
nationalist at the outset, even though that design was articulated in
Catholic vocabulary and modeled as a Catholic brotherhood combining monastic and missionary-pedagogic work.

Shahumian told his eyewitness account of the Davit Beg rebellion
to the monk Ghougas Sebastatzi.[23] By 1759, there were two copies of his
tale, amended by other eyewitness accounts, in San Lazzaro, and
another version traveled to Smyrna, then Amsterdam, then Echmiadzin, where it was recopied in 1847, the same year in which Taghiatiantz reprinted the "Ter Getzo." In 1871, the account was edited and
published in Echmiadzin by A. Gulamiriants.[24] If there is a historical
model of the strong shepherd, the figure of Davit Beg is the most probable candidate for the role. In the regions of Ghapan and Karabagh, the
material effects of Davit Beg's memory continue to ripple in the fabric
of politics down to the present day; memory was and remains a powerful preserving yet fictionalizing force in those regions.

What is more nearly certain is the link between a third element of
our poem, the reversal of dispersion, and the diasporan bourgeois
dream of collective return to the homeland, a product of the third phase
of Armenian protonationalism. The unknown poet of *The Mirror of Calcutta* and Taghiatiantz were both participants in a Calcuttan culture
that had only very recently replaced Madras as the center of the intellectual life of the Indian-Armenian community. Calcutta was the inheritor of the Madras tradition of the 1770s and 1780s. There, Armenian
merchants from Persia had grown wealthy after the mid–seventeenth
century, thanks to their role as intermediaries between the realms of the
czar, the shah, the Ottoman sultan, and various rajahs, as well as (after
1688) the British East India Company. A century later, these merchants
began to lose their capital in competition against the better-capitalized
and England-backed company, which did not hesitate to press local
rulers to act against its Armenian competitors, withdrawing their favor

and contracts. Gerard Libaridian, who has a brief but astute analysis of this diasporan community, writes that "the involvement of these merchants in political action on behalf of Armenians must be understood in terms of their constant search for a social base as a counterweight to the power of protector states."[25] Relatively educated, prosperous, yet haunted by the precariousness of its fortunes, this Indian-Armenian community produced Joseph Emin, who quixotically sought to become a new Israel Ori or Davit Beg, a leader of a military expeditions to and in Armenia. The same community published in 1794–95 the first Armenian newspaper in the world (*Aztarar*, edited by the priest Harootyun Shemavonian), after it had already published in 1773 the first Armenian political program, written by Emin's friend Movses Baghramian, *Nor tetrak vor kochi hortorak* ("A New Pamphlet Called Exhortation"). This advocated an Armenian force to liberate Armenia, and a constitutional monarchy with senatorial government. In 1788, Shahamir Shahamirian published, also in Madras, *Girk Anvanyal Vorokayt Parats* ("Book Named the Snare of Glory"), which advocated a mercantilist Armenian republic governed by merchants and productive artisans rather than the old nobility and the clergy. Five years earlier, in 1783, Shahamirian had published *Nshavak* ("The Roadsign" or "Guideline"), which advocated a temporary Armenian settlement in South Russia to serve as a base for a return to Armenia. Two thousand copies of the *Vorokayt* were published in Russia and distributed to Armenians there. Hundreds were sent to Armenia, but Catholicos Erevantsi had all the copies burned; his medieval belief in his exclusive position as intercessor between Armenians, God, and their political fate could hardly coexist with Shahamirian's vision.

As members of the Indian-Armenian diaspora and a generally loyal devotee of Echmiadzin, then, the unknown poet and Taghiatiantz wrote as the heirs of both the Indian-Armenian authors of the manifesto and of the catholicos who burned copies of it. In this position as the inheritor of conflict and contradiction, Taghiatiantz himself was an exemplary figure, for the history of the Armenian nationalist intelligentsia combines dependence on necessary yet contradictory institutions until at least the 1880s, when they established political parties in alliance with workers and peasants, basically bypassing the church and the bourgeoisie, with mixed success. The poet and Taghiatiantz are silent about these tensions. I have tried to show, in this symptomatic reading that tries to unpack the poem's silences as well as its explicit appeal, that words, images, and figures drawn from diverse discourses (folk, ecclesiastical, gentry-related, or bourgeois) are not just the "context" of the text; discussion of them as "historical background" is neither optional nor sufficient. They are what the poet draws upon: though autonomously and discontinuously produced in history from 1547 on, and though residual in one case and emergent in another, as far as the society of 1820/1847 was concerned, they are coeval and simultaneous discursive resources in the poem, which arranges them as a progression of its own making, a progression that invokes and projects a national future.[26]

How does this discussion engage the vigorous current debates concerning nations and nationalism? Anthony D. Smith, who provides an account of nationalism that is noteworthy for its accommodation of the Armenian and Jewish diasporan variants of the phenomenon, writes that "only the domination of the 'organic' version of nationalism in nineteenth-century Europe has obscured the doctrinal possibility of nationalism inventing nations."[27] He is well aware of the potential charge that his statement may be taken to reflect a "subjectivist bias";[28] like "life imitates art," "nationalism invents nations" is a potentially disturbing statement.[29] The scholarship on nations and nationalism that had dominated in Britain from 1964[30] until 1983 (when Smith's work was reissued and Anderson's first published) not unreasonably argued that dynastic states and the administrative entities of their republican successor states (e.g. ministries of education) had invented nationalism and had used it to construct, out of their subject populations, homogeneous nations that could be mobilized to serve state and social elites. Modernization both enabled this kind of nationalist nation-building project and was accelerated by it. The standardized schooling required equally by modernized nations and their industry became an essential part of this nationalizing project, which concentrates on mass populations and not on the subjectivity of small, elite intellectuals living, in the Armenian case, some thousands of miles away from the homeland.

Smith (like Anderson) does not reject such a view, which holds true for parts of western Europe. Instead, he argues that whereas the nation, when achieved, is not merely a subjective entity but a territory and a state, nationalism may well be defined by "subjective attributes—

will, sentiment, aspiration." He is cautious enough to add that "the distinction between 'objective' characteristics, like economy, geography or history, and subjective ones, is at best dubious" and concludes that a proper definition of nationalism must "contain elements all along the so-called 'subjective-objective' continuum."[31] He acknowledges that such a procedure can lead to a definition of " 'nationalism' (and to some extent 'nation') in terms of individual perceptions—usually those of a tiny minority of the given unit of a population. At the same time," he adds, "those perceptions do refer to independently verifiable characteristics or processes."[32]

This essay has focused on discourse precisely because discourse is situated midway in the subjective-objective continuum. Discourse originates in real events—the rebellion of Davit Beg, the missions of the catholicoses—and is perpetuated and made accessible by material and social practices (manuscript copying, printing, seminaries supported by the taxes the church levied on the Armenian peasantry, and the gifts offered by the gentry and bourgeoisie). Yet both poetry and the discourses on which it draws speak to the subjectivity of individuals and slightly larger audiences and constituencies—in Smith's words, to "the will, sentiment, and aspiration of a tiny minority of the population." Poised between materialism and subjectivist idealism, the poetic text of the "Ter Getzo" draws on events and on institutional and discursive resources, to initiate not just emotions but a new consciousness (cf. Hroch)—an entity best reached by a combination of intellect and emotion—that in turn produces new texts and eventually (not always, as Hroch reminds us) leads to a new politics; a politics that the earlier events described in texts could not initiate by themselves, once faded into history.

This, after all, is what distinguishes the material world from the human. In the former, physical events—the motion of billiard balls, the growth of an embryo—are caused solely by prior physical conditions and events. In the human world, mediation—through language, other sign-systems, and by the mind and the emotions—is the inevitable intermediary between material events and conditions: high taxes do not always lead to revolt, and ecclesiastical missions pleading for western help do not in themselves lead to nationalism, because such material events must undergo two further steps before they can initiate new action: they must be formulated as meaningful in some text, whether as ephemeral as a politician's speech or as enduring as the "Ter Getzo," and then they must be interpreted as meaningful by those to whom they are disseminated.

The "subjectivist" focus on texts, artists, and intellectuals is happily unavoidable in the responsible study of nationalism, as we can see in a discussion of the role played by pilgrimage in the construction of medieval Christianity and the Muslim *umma* by Benedict Anderson. He writes: "The Berber encountering the Malay before the Ka'bah must, as it were, ask himself: 'Why is this man doing what I am doing, uttering the same words that I am uttering, even though we cannot talk to one another? There is only one answer . . . Because *we* are Muslims.'"[33] The plausibility of this analysis depends entirely upon a subjective notion of consciousness that is tautologically taken for granted: the pilgrims come because they are Muslims and in coming discover they are Muslims like other Muslims, which is to say that they share not just an institutionalized set of ritual behaviors but also an invisible, immaterial consciousness with others. Anderson could have described the cause of the pilgrimage in social and material terms: he might have spoken of the built-in coercion and incentive that push/pull a Muslim who can afford the pilgrimage to make the pilgrimage. But in describing how people come to imagine a religious community that is like a *nation,* Anderson lapses into subjectivism, the default position of analyses of nationalism, which should not be thought wrong just because so many lapse into it so easily. But it is a move of whose dangers we must be aware.

A similar confusion of material events and immaterial consciousness, of effects with causes, is discussed by Gayatri Spivak in a sympathetic critique of the Subaltern Studies School of Indian historiography. She quotes a passage in which a historian of the subaltern writes that what he has to work with are documents expressing the fear and rage of "policemen, bureaucrats, landlords, usurers [who] register their sentiments [in documents which] amount to a representation of their will. But these documents . . . [are] predicated on another will—that of the insurgent. It should be possible therefore to read the presence of a rebel consciousness as a necessary and pervasive element within that body of evidence."[34] Like historians of nationalism working backward from texts to consciousness, the historian of the subaltern discovers and identifies an insurgent consciousness as a cause, and an insurgency as its effect. Spivak points out that the actual *cause* that launches this process of identification is itself an effect. From the historian's view, the texts recording the rage of the oppressors are an effect of insurgency; in turn, it is theorized that the insurgency is the result, or effect, of the insurgent's rage; and, crucially, that rage is not theorized as merely the result/effect of material conditions, but as the manifestation of insurgent consciousness, of subaltern consciousness. This may actually be right, or seem plausible, Spivak points out, but in fact the only concrete cause she sees operating is the existence of the texts recording the landlords' rage, which the historian of the subaltern interprets. They cause the historian to read in a way that leads him or her to posit a subaltern consciousness. In this scheme, all roles are reversed, and what the subaltern historians think is the prime mover is a final effect.

Spivak thinks that even the historians whose motives are pure and with whom she is in political solidarity are nevertheless in danger of positing a "sovereign" and "determining" subject or consciousness that is the moving cause and hero of a "continuist" version of history. The investigator of Armenian nationalism must be wary of the same danger of positing a subjectivist continuum where none exists—or of doing the opposite.

Both dangers are real. Many Armenian historiographers of the late medieval and modern periods, deprived of even a weak nation-state to occupy them, have instead concentrated on looking for and fashioning a continuist narrative of the development of nationalist consciousness and the nation. They have based their work on texts and events that can lend themselves to another argument, to the counterclaim that where they, eager to establish the pedigree of Armenian nationalism, see continuity, there may only be discontinuity, that each act that is placed in a linear narrative of developing nationalism was in fact a discrete response to a different situation.

To illustrate these positions by their extremes, one can look at Ashot Hovhannissian's *Drvagner Hye Azatagrakan Mtki Patmootyunits* ("Episodes from the History of Armenian Liberation Thought"), volume 1,[35] which, despite its title's reference to the episodic and therefore discontinuous, links the episodes it identifies and explores into a slowly emerging, disembodied subjective entity, *the* thought of Armenian liberation. At the other extreme, Gerard Libaridian argues that the history of Armenian "liberation" is radically discontinuous. In his analysis, each figure, institution, elite, or class acts in response to its perception of its own interests in various times and places and is repeatedly defeated or co-opted, producing no political or intellectual progeny. "Efforts of liberation," Libaridian writes, "do not constitute a continuous chain of events. . . . they succeed each other but are not related. It is the historian's conceptualization . . . that brings them together. These initiatives on the part of particular individuals or groups responded not to any mandate or obligation but to a void. . . . Changes in Armenian political thought were similarly disjointed."[36]

The choice Libaridian and Hovhannisian present is helpful because it is stark. On the one hand there is a void of discontinuity, and on the other the synthesis of a fiction of continuity, attributed to a dis-embodied subject, a collective mind seeking liberation or a sovereign nation. Of course it is possible to modulate (though not to reconcile) their positions by a closer reading of their claims, but I will not attempt that here. Instead, what this essay has offered, through its reading of the "Ter Getzo" and the discourses that made its production and recep-tion possible, is a third way. I have argued that in Armenian history, from that first, rumored mission to the West of 1547, to the point, exactly three hundred years later, when Taghiatiantz reprinted the "Ter Getzo," there is neither a void of discontinuity in the matter of nation-alism, nor its opposite, the embryonic form of a nation moving slowly but continuously toward its "birth." There is, rather, a set of events and interests that (as Libaridian argues) do not stem from a continuity in consciousness or fall naturally in a constellation that we could identify as truly collective, let alone as national. But these material events are narrated, and these interests posited, in words and discourses that then are brought into proximity, and connected, by intellectuals and artists. The Mekhitarist historians, the poet of the "Ter Getzo," Taghiatiantz, and the almost exactly contemporaneous homeland intellectual Khachadoor Abovian (each and every one of them dead before national political parties were created by Armenians in the 1880s) gave the Armenian people the luxury of a textual continuity and connection where the material events of history could offer little or nothing of that kind. That is what the "Ter Getzo" does, and other texts did with vary-ing degrees of success. Using texts and discourses, attentive to the ways in which they invoke and reshape events, it *is* possible and defensible to write a history of the emergence of Armenian nationalism as a cumu-lative phenomenon, one that could plausibly represent (re-present) a discontinuity of causes as a convergence of effects. It is not so much the

cunning of history as of literature and historiography that wrote
Armenian nationalism into being.

NOTES

I am indebted to Kevork Bardakjian, Alex and Marie Manoogian Professor
of Armenian Literature at the University of Michigan, for information and
advice concerning the authorship of the poem discussed in this essay, and for
helping me to establish the archaic meanings of certain key words. I thank Professor Ronald Suny for inviting me to present a shorter version of this paper at
the Center for Russian and East European Studies in Ann Arbor, on March 11,
1993. And I am grateful to Professor Ellen Rooney of Brown University for her
careful reading of early drafts.

1. Ronald G. Suny, *Looking toward Ararat: Armenia in Modern History*
(Bloomington: Indiana University Press, 1993), 38.

2. Suny, *Looking toward Ararat*, 55.

3. Ever since the fifth century C.E., when the Bible was translated and
Armenian historiography launched, Armenians have narrated and understood
some important features of their history in biblical terms. For example, Robert
Thomson has argued that a key episode of early Armenian historiography is
modeled on the biblical narrative of the Maccabees. While details of his argument need revision, his basic claim remains plausible. Cf. Yeghishe, *History of
Vartan and the Armenian War*, translated with a commentary by Robert Thomson (Cambridge, Mass.: Harvard University Press, 1982).

4. This aspect of my argument is indebted to Miroslav Hroch's description of phases in the emergence of Central European nationalisms, in which a
"collective consciousness" forms, becomes specifically "national consciousness," then develops into a "national movement," which in turn aspires to create a nation-state. Hroch's great contribution is that, having specified this trajectory, he emphatically insists that there is no automatic momentum built into
it, that each phase can stop without developing further. Only under conditions
that are specific to each site can this development pass through every stage.
Miroslav Hroch, "From National Movement to the Fully-Formed Nation," *New
Left Review* 198 (1993): 3–20, in particular 4 and 6–7.

5. In his own day, the author was Taghiatiantz. Armenian last names
ended with various suffixes, but by the nineteenth century -*ian* was becoming
the most standard ending. "Eastern" Armenians (those living under Persian
and Russian rule) standardized more slowly, in a process not completed until
the Soviet period imposed the -*ian* ending universally. In scholarly essays that
cite both the author and his later commentators faithfully, it is not uncommon
to find two versions of the name. I shall use *Taghiatiantz* throughout.

6. The term "merchant-diaspora" was popularized by the historian Philip
Curtin in work on Africa. It has been appropriately applied to some Armenian
communities of the Middle East, especially in Aleppo, Syria, by Bruce Masters,

The Origins of Western Economic Dominance in the Middle East (New York: NYU Press, 1988). There were in fact many such Armenian communities, which often contained a few professionals, many artisans, and others of more modest occupation, but whose internal organization and social profile were dominated by the merchant princes and their clerical allies.

7. In dispersion studies, *transnation* is applied to the totality of a people that exists simultaneously in a homeland and across the borders of many nation-states, in diaspora. The term is a way of including the diaspora in the nation while detaching the notion of nation from exclusive association with homeland and state. Influenced by the increasing use of the adjective *transnational* since the early 1970s, the noun *transnation* has more recently come to refer to dispersions that are not isolated communities, but rather circulate ideas and cultural productions such as literature and music with the homeland and each other. For a paradigmatic use of the term, see Gage Averill, "Musical Constructions of the Haitian Transnation," *Diaspora* 3, no. 3 (1994): 253–72.

8. For a discussion of intrastate diasporas, see Khachig Tololyan, "Exile Governments in the Armenian Polity," in *Governments-in-Exile in Contemporary World Politics,* ed. Yossi Shain (New York: Routledge, 1991), 166–87, esp. 170–71.

9. Author of the poem "Mer Hyrenik" (Our Fatherland), which, set to music, became the quasi anthem of Armenian nationalism and which, in 1991, was slightly modified and adopted as the anthem of the new Republic of Armenia.

10. Cited in A[rshag] Alboyajian, "Grgnvadz Skhalner: Der Getzo Du Zhyes Yerkin Heghinage" (Iterated errors: The author of the song "Der Getzo Du Zhyes"), *Armaveni* (Annual of the Union of Alumni of the Kaloosdian National School of Egypt), Cairo, 1937–38, 118.

11. For example, my eighty-three-year-old father has sung it since his teens. I have known the verse but not the song.

12. The Armenian letters *Ho* and *Ken.*

13. To reassure the reader that mine is not an idiosyncratic claim, I refer to the *Soviet Armenian Encyclopedia* (Yerevan: Academy of Sciences of the Armenian SSR, 1978), 4:131, in whose entry on Taghiatiantz we read that "he was the first to link nostalgia for the homeland with the idea of a return to the homeland, and to see in such a return the possibility of Armenia's development.... Taghiatiantz refused to accept the finality of Armenian diasporization as a final stage of Armenian history." The *Encyclopedia* does not mention the "Ter Getzo" poem, which was probably too religious for Soviet-era approval. Its reference is to the meditative travel essays Taghiatiantz wrote about his voyages through India, Iran, the Transcaucasus, and the Ottoman Empire. As in European romanticism, so in nineteenth-century Armenian literature, the travel essay (of Abovian, Taghiatiantz, Raffi) is a protonationalist genre.

14. The Armenian word is *Prgya,* the imperative form of *Prgel,* to save, as in *Prgich,* Savior and Christ.

15. *Ech-mi-a-dzin,* a compound word made up of three roots: *Ech* = descent; *mi* = one, the only; *dzin* = born, begotten. The *-a-* joins the root-words to mean "where the only-begotten descended to Earth."

16. Literally, "zator hyrabedi." Because the discourse of the church is linguistically conservative, the term has been used throughout its existence and is understood by Armenian readers today, as in Taghiatiantz's time.

Confusingly, there are two Armenian catholicoses today, one based in Armenia and the other in Lebanon. There have been others throughout history. The jurisdictional disputes are intricate, powered both by Armenian and non-Armenian state politics and by a clerical desire to administer autonomous fiefdoms. Tradition favors the catholicos in Echmiadzin, Armenia, as a first among equals.

17. Pierre Taminiaux, "Sacred Text, Sacred Nation," in *Text and Nation*, ed. Peter C. Pfeiffer and Laura Garcia-Moreno (Camden House, S.C.: Published for the Symposium "Text and Nation," Georgetown University, April 19–21, 1995), 97, 102.

18. Robert H. Hewsen, "Russian-Armenian Relations, 1700–1828," Occasional Paper no. 4 of the Society for Armenian Studies, Cambridge, Mass., 1984, 30, lists five other bishops and archbishops who joined Ashtaraketsi in favoring the Russian invasion: John, Simeon, Seraphim, Stephen, and Karapet.

19. Gerard J. Libaridian, "The Ideology of Armenian Liberation: The Development of Armenian Political Thought before the Revolutionary Movement, 1639–1885," Ph.D. diss., UCLA, 1987, 25, takes the position that Jughayetsi was impelled by financial motives. Not only was Echmiadzin in danger of losing mortgaged lands, but the catholicos was personally indebted, due to speculation, and (Libaridian argues) he sought to change the political situation as a way out of economic malaise.

20. The matter is discussed by G. H. Grigorian, *Hye arajabah hasarakakan-kaghakakan mtki patmootyunits* (From the history of progressive Armenian sociopolitical thought) (Yerevan: Haikakan SSR Kitakan Akademia, 1957), 153–55.

21. Leaders of other Armenian religious centers have their own record of such attempts, but it is unlikely that Taghiatiantz would have known any but the last of them. In 1575, Khachatur Zeytuntsi, catholicos of Cilicia, had appealed to the pope for help. In 1662 and 1663, Khachatur Gaghadatsi had joined other prelates of Eastern Christianity (Syriac and Greek) in an appeal to Louis XIV. Most importantly, Catholicos Petros of Gantsasar had appealed to St. Petersburg for help in 1670, soon after Armenian merchants began to trade in Russia with the official approval of the Persian and Russian courts. The institutional memory of this appeal, along with the imperatives of the situation, led to a similar appeal of Catholicos Yesayi of Gantsasar to Russia in 1724, which was public and significant enough in the Armenian rebellion of 1722–30 to be known to Echmiadzin. For details of Yesayi's role, see Father Samuel Aramian, *Davit Beg Gam Badmootyun Ghapanetsvots* (Davit Beg; or, the history of the people of Ghapan), an edition of two versions of the manuscript of that title (Venice: San Lazzaro, 1978), 48–55.

22. To the best of my knowledge, there is no thorough study of the reasons why the illusion of a "Crusade" from the West had such a grip on the minds of Armenians, and some other eastern Christians, for seven centuries after the original crusades temporarily defeated an Islam weakened by internal crises.

Of course, as a disparity of strength developed between industrialized Europe, on the one hand, and the Persian and Ottoman empires, on the other, Western intervention "on behalf" of Armenians and Maronites was forthcoming from time to time, but in the case of the Armenians it rarely did much good, and it eventually caused harm. Yet the dream persisted.

23. See Aramian, *Davit Beg*, for further details.

24. Aramian, *Davit Beg*, 72–74. Once published, the Davit Beg story became the center of more historiographic research, and more importantly of novelistic effort that led to Raffi's novel, *Davit Beg* (1881–82) and study, *Khamsayi Melikootyunner* (1882–83). Published serially and then in volumes in Tbilisi, they were immensely influential in the decade that followed, when the Armenian liberation organizations were established. Raffi's historical sources have been studied, as Taghiatiantz's have not. See N. Adonts, *Davit Beg Vepi Patmakan Hime yev Gaghaparakhosagan Arzheke* (The historical foundation and ideological value of *Davit Beg*) (Paris: Kh. Matevosian, 1937), 122–48, part of a memorial volume commemorating the centenary of Raffi's birth.

25. Libaridian, "Ideology of Armenian Liberation," 50.

26. I have not mentioned one other possible model for the poem, discussion of which would take us in a new direction. Alboyajian believes that the "Ter Getzo" may be an attempt to create a sort of national anthem for the Armenians, on the model of "God Save the King." He offers no argument for what I consider an implausible claim.

27. Anthony D. Smith, *Theories of Nationalism*, 2d ed. (New York: Holmes and Meier, 1983), 173.

28. Smith, *Theories of Nationalism*.

29. It is interesting to note that Smith's and Benedict Anderson's landmark texts on nationalism were published within months of each other, in 1983. In general, the decade was one in which it became steadily easier, and eventually too easy, to speak of "inventing" and "imagining" nationalisms, communities, and traditions.

30. Exemplified by two books also published within months of each other: Ernest Gellner, *Thought and Change* (London: Weidenfeld and Nicholson, 1964) and Benjamin Akzin, *State and Nation* (London: Hutchinson University Library, 1964).

31. Smith, *Theories of Nationalism*, 173.

32. Smith, *Theories of Nationalism*.

33. Benedict Anderson, *Imagined Communities: Reflections on the Origin and Spread of Nationalism*, 2d ed. (London: Verso, 1991), 55.

34. Gayatri Chakravorty Spivak, "Subaltern Studies: Deconstructing Historiography," *In Other Worlds* (New York: Methuen, 1987), 204–5.

35. Ashot Hovhannissian, *Drvagner Hye Azatagrakan Mtki Patmootyunits* (Episodes from the history of Armenian liberation thought), vol. 1 (Yerevan: Haikakan SSR Kitakan Akademia, 1957).

36. Libaridian, "Ideology of Armenian Liberation," 13.

Memoirs of a
Diasporan Nationalist

Seven years ago, when I began the planning that culminated in Diaspora: A Journal of Transnational Studies, *which I still edit, I had a moment of particularly intense self-doubt. I communicated it to Ellen, my partner. She reassured me by saying that everything she knew about me suggested that my entire life had been an unplanned but thorough preparation for editing such a multidisciplinary journal, among whose topics nationalism—of the sort that sustains and motivates some diasporas—looms large.*

To believe in such "unplanned but thorough preparation" is to believe that any intellectual trajectory I discern in my life is not entirely a retrospective construct imposed upon the past fifty-two years. I am devoted to narrative: within comparative literature, I was trained in the theory of narrative, and by far the most successful article I've written is titled "Cultural Narrative and the Motivation of the Terrorist." But I remain an agnostic about the possibility of avoiding the fictive as one constructs narrative out of memories and projects it upon them. Yet that is what the contributors to this volume are asked to do. A story, then.

I was born in 1944 in the Armenian diasporan community of Aleppo, Syria, the child of refugees from Turkey. Almost everyone I knew over the age of thirty-five was a genocide survivor. Most belonged to a community in which the dominant political and cultural institution was the Tashnag Party: the ARF, or Federation of Armenian Revolutionaries, that, between 1890 and 1920, had been the equivalent of a National Liberation Front, and since the victory of Turkish genocide and Soviet Communism had become a diasporan, transnational organization that ran, with an efficacy I admire to this day, schools, newspapers, parish councils, athletic unions, and the like. I attended its schools, read the books it favored (among others), and imbibed its view of recent Armenian history. My father was a party member, my mother a sympathizer. Like the party, both were nationalists and socialists, but the socialism owed more to Jean Jaurès than Karl Marx and amounted to a belief that the citizens of a nation are responsible for their fellow citizens; that the state is the repository of that responsibility, so must be empowered to counterbalance private property; and that fairness and justice were supreme values, to be accomplished by democracy whenever possible. Both my parents taught Armenian literature, among other topics; both wrote in Armenian, my father with prodigious productivity: some poems, countless essays and editorials, several books. Mine was an environment saturated with the memory of the collective tragedy of the genocide and of the failed yet enduring diasporized national vision of the ARF. When, in the mid-1960s, I saw La Guerre est Finie, *Alain Resnais and Jorge Semprun's extraordinary film about Spanish Communists in French exile, I was overwhelmed to the point of tears by the familiarity of the atmosphere, of the way in which Yves Montand captured the gallant futility and shameless hope of the exiled.*

The Tashnags' was not the only national vision I imbibed and had to contend with. Arab nationalism was a powerful force; it and I grew up together. Furthermore, Syria was still a French colony when I was born. For at least a decade after independence, France was both the colonialist enemy and the admired model of a nation-state and culture. In addition, living a hundred miles south of the Turkish border, we Armenian children learned Turkish and led a polyglot life dominated by four nationalist visions of collectivity: Danton, Ataturk, Antoine Sa'adeh of the Syrian Q'awmi Party (my godfather was a member, later jailed by the Ba'ath), and General Andranik of the Tashnag Party could be reconciled in nothing else but their nationalism.

These intense public nationalisms—cultural as well as political, diasporic dreams as well as statist agendas—were mediated by the fact that I was almost constantly ill between the ages of four and twelve and kept safe in a familial world. There was no television; the radio was on for only an hour a day; we had no car, no phone, and no record player. There were books and people, stories and lessons. My mother taught me to read Armenian and French when I was four, from an illustrated dictionary of science and an even more excitingly illustrated zoology textbook, both published by the Armenian Catholic Mekhitarist monks of Venice: the perfect diasporan, multidisciplinary texts. She began to teach me the elements of anatomy and dissection at five, on chickens and fish. Arabic I began to learn at six. Mine was largely an indoor and sickly life of reading, punctuated by periods of relative robustness, dominated by soccer and occasional hunting. At twelve, we moved to Egypt, where I began to learn English, and at thirteen, went on to Beirut and the International "Col-

lege," a high school attached to the American University of Beirut. Fluency in English opened up to me a world of new genres—detective novels, science fiction, pornography, comic books—but also a world where nationalism was not worn on the sleeve. Financial motives, romance, and codes of gunfighter honor all loomed large in a whole new world, more brave than not, albeit sadly lacking in Tintin or Alixe L'Intrepide.

When my father survived the first Lebanese civil war of 1958 and the two attempts to kill him, we emigrated to the United States, arriving in 1960. I was sixteen; the emotional and intellectual loyalties, interests and tensions that have since molded my life were scripted and already in place. The next thirty-six years have been postscript, a playing out of reaction and counterreaction.

I lived the immigrant dream: at eighteen, I began to attend Harvard with a scholarship, an oddly educated teenager, shaky in math, good at chemistry and biology, well read in literature and history, both ancient and modern, and knowledgeable about European and Middle Eastern politics. The only continuities in my education were of my own devising, though enabled by environment, accident and curiosity. For example, I learned by age nine who Lucullus and Pompey were (they conquered Armenia in the first century B.C.) and went on to read about the Gracchi and Marius and Sulla and Caesar, Rome's republic and empire. I was urged along by Hollywood's Quo Vadis, *the movie, which led me to its Polish author's, Henryk Sienkiewicz's, other books, all translated to Armenian, which led me to Mazuria and Tannenberg and Bogdan Khmelnitsky and a knowledge of the geography of medieval Lithuania and the Ukraine, because I liked looking up battle and campaign maps, and then, circuitously, to the Armenian diaspora in Poland. I was the sort who took nerdy pleasure in knowing at twelve, as Armenian neighbors from Germanic (Turkish Marash) did not know, that Germanicus had founded their city circa A.D. 8. I possessed a fussy sort of extensive and superficial knowledge, whose only virtue was that I liked both the broad sweep of narrative and the detail— facts and metaphors, the grain and texture of both history and literature.*

Perhaps predictably, I reacted against all that at Harvard, set them entirely aside, and did my B.A. in molecular biology, at a time when that field's excitement was infectious, when it brought together concreteness and speculation, and Nobel Prize winners taught sophomores. It was exhilarating, yet I decided to pursue a Ph.D. not at the level of the subcellular but in another biological scale: that of ichthyology, marine biology, and oceanography, which I studied at the University of Rhode Island for three more years. The sixties and the great national struggles of Vietnam and the United States were happening, and I finally admitted to myself that I did not want to live in the laboratory. In

1969 I switched from URI's well-known marine biology program to do my M.A. in the supportive obscurity of its English department, reading voraciously and, through Roman Jakobson and Lévi-Strauss, "finding" theory and myself. In 1970 I went to the Department of Comparative Literature at Brown, where I wrote my dissertation on "cosmographic narrative": epic narratives that try to give cultural confusion a shape. Homer, Virgil, Joyce, and Faulkner provided my texts, to which I later added Thomas Pynchon.

I came to teach at Wesleyan in 1974, and here I have stayed, in a college-university of extraordinary liveliness, endowed with a Center for the Humanities that has been the axis of my continuing education in cultural theory and social history. I wrote a series of articles on modern literature and founded a small journal (Pynchon Notes, 1979-)*—barely enough for tenure—and also wrote polemical columns and cultural essays in Armenian for* Haratch, *Paris's and indeed the diaspora's paper of record. Some of these were collected as* Spurki Mech *("In the Diaspora," 1980), which remains my only book.*

Since 1975, I have been trying to balance my life as a professional, academic, and scholar with my life as an Armenian intellectual. I wanted neither to give up those first sixteen years nor to belong to them: the choice between communal deprivation and communal suffocation was clear to me by the time I was thirty, and I have reacted to it by negotiating a zigzag path between the two. This negotiation has been the motive force of my intellectual and personal life.

After tenure, during the 1980s, I found the liberal piety that in reaction to Reaganite America morphed into political correctness and came to dominate literature and literary theory as suffocating as the laboratory and the diasporan enclave had become earlier. The new discourse demanded loyalty oaths I could not give and did not want what I could give. Chance interceded in the form of an invitation to write on the new transnational Armenian terrorism (against Turkish diplomats) for journals of political science; linguistic and historical knowledge were my passport to the thriving circuit of terrorism studies. Once there, I realized how much the transnational features of that terrorism were connected not just to Armenian life but to the diasporization that is an intrinsic part of globalization in general. I went on to found Diaspora. *This I could do only because of my involvement with the Zoryan Institute for Armenian Documentation and Research, which nurtured and funded the concept.*

Since 1990, comparative and multidisciplinary diaspora studies has been the focus of my work. Because many kinds of dispersions—of exiles, overseas communities, refugees, and immigrants—have been renamed "diasporas," the field has grown, as has the number of key terms and concepts used to think about it: diaspora, nationalism, transnationalism, ethnicity, globalization, postcolonialism *all circulate. Literature and the newer media—film, TV, the endless fictive elaborations camouflaged by the notion of "communication" on the Internet—are important features of the diasporan cultural and social phenomena I am concerned with. At the moment, I think about diasporas as the exemplary instantiations of the globalizing moment, and about the transformations of nationalism in that context. The article I have contributed to this book is about an earlier transformation that created modern nationalism in the Armenian diaspora.*

Khachig Tololyan

John-Paul Himka

The Construction of Nationality in Galician Rus': Icarian Flights in Almost All Directions

E. J. Hobsbawm argues that the literature on nations and nationalism entered a particularly fruitful phase in the late 1960s, a phase that marks a turning point in our understanding of the subject.[1] One might make the case that the 1980s marked even more of a turning point, since at this time the emphasis in the literature shifted to the problem of the social construction of nationality and national cultures. The purpose of this essay is to apply the framework of cultural construction developed in the newer literature to the particular case of the Ukrainians of Eastern Galicia. It is hoped that this confrontation of the general theoretical literature with a concrete case study will serve both to explore the utility and the limitations of the new thinking on nationalism and to generate fresh formulations and questions with regard to the history of the Ukrainian national movement in Galicia. After sketching the general thrust of the newer literature, the essay that follows will look at different "constructions" that competed or could have competed for the cultural loyalties of the inhabitants of the easternmost extension of the Habsburg monarchy. The people under consideration call themselves Ukrainians in the twentieth century, but in the nineteenth they called themselves *rusyny*, usually rendered in English as Ruthenians. For reasons that will become obvious, I will use the historical name in this essay; I will also make use of their traditional name for their own territory: Galician Rus'.

The Cultural Work of Nationalism

One of the most striking features of the new literature (especially Hobsbawm, Emil Niederhauser,[2] and Ernest Gellner)[3] is a major displacement of emphasis with regard to the so-called national characteristics. The nationalists themselves and much of the older literature on nationalism emphasized that certain characteristics—particularly language, but also others, including religion, historical experience, and territory—created nations.[4] The emphasis of the new literature is rather that nations create these characteristics. In particular, it has focused on "the invention of tradition" and the *questione della lingua,* that is, on the active role national awakeners played in constructing a version of the past and a standard literary language. Where the awakeners themselves thought they were only reviving an existing national culture,[5] their most recent analysts think rather that they were creating a new culture.[6] The fullest theoretical development of this view is by Gellner.

Gellner divides the whole of world history into three phases— hunting-gathering, agrarian, and industrial—and postulates that nationalism is a form of politics appropriate to the transition between the second and third phase; in fact, it creates the cultural-political conditions in which industrial society can function. Although Gellner's framework of industrialism does not seem directly relevant to persistently agrarian Galicia, his view on the cultural work of nationalism certainly is. He postulates that the nationalists create a new cultural amalgam that, on the one hand, contains enough elements of the traditional culture of a particular ethnic community to be accessible to and function as a source of identification for its members, but that, on the other hand, also contains the essential elements of the new universalist culture appropriate to the industrial age. Nationalism thus uses elements of traditional culture to create a new cultural unit that can participate in a larger modern society based on a shared cognitive base and a global economy.[7]

Whether one prefers Gellner's "industrial culture" or Benedict Anderson's "print culture"[8] or even the loaded older terms used with regard to a similar conceptualization (e.g., *high culture, civilization, history*), it is clear that many East Central European peoples developed one of these cultural systems as part of their national awakening. The case of the Ruthenians of Galicia is not untypical in this regard. Before the national awakening, they lacked, for example, their own professional theater and composers in the classical style—these did not constitute components of the authentic culture of Galician Rus'; but by the 1860s they had both a national theater company and a number of orchestral works with national themes. Such examples of the introduction of new cultural pursuits following models from the general European high culture, but with a national twist, could constitute a long list. Perhaps heading such a list would be the creation, through translation, imitation, and original composition, of a literary medium capable of expressing all the concepts contained in other European literary mediums.

Elements of the traditional culture were incorporated into the new culture, but this was a very selective process.[9] Selectivity is most obvious in the case of language (since, of course, not all dialectical features could be absorbed into a single literary standard), but the principle extends to every one of the national characteristics. Not all customs, for example, found a place in the new national culture. The Ukrainian national culture readily incorporated painted Easter eggs *(pysanky)*, which could be taken as an expression of the high aesthetic demands of the folk culture, but the tradition of night courting *(dosvitky, vechornytsi)*,[10] which seemed to suggest savagery and immorality, was rejected.

A number of features of the Galician Ruthenian case are particularly interesting.

For example, almost totally neglected or misunderstood by the new literature,[11] but extremely important in the Galician Ruthenian (and, for that matter, the Galician Jewish) case, was what might be termed a "larval stage." Before the creation of the new Ruthenian national culture came a stage in which educated Ruthenians assimilated to Polish culture, that is, into an alien "high" culture. Whether it would have been possible for the Ruthenians of Galicia to have proceeded directly from their traditional cultural environment to the task of creating the new national culture is an open question, but there can be little doubt that this larval stage accelerated the process. The same applies to the creation of a modern Jewish culture on the territory of Galicia at the end of the nineteenth century; until then the Jewish elite had tended to assimilate to German and, later, Polish culture. The Czech national revival also began from a situation in which the better-educated classes were acculturated or at least deeply steeped in German culture. It is within the framework of the recent emphasis on nationalism's creation of a new high culture that the function of this

acculturation becomes clear, even if this point has not been brought
out: the very earliest "awakeners," and their predecessors, entered a
foreign high culture, which provided them with a model upon which to
base a new, national high culture.

Also, in Galician Rus' there was not only an acute *questione della
lingua* and fashioning/refashioning of a national language, but a
prominent *questione della religione* and fashioning/refashioning of a
national religion, that is, a modification of the traditional Greek
Catholicism (movements for ritual purification to shed Latin-Polish
accretions) or abandonment of it for "the faith of the forefathers"
(Orthodoxy). Although there are many other cases in which nationalism has introduced considerable modification into traditional religious
practices and allegiances (e.g., the *Los von Rom* movement in Austria,
the creation of the Ukrainian Autocephalous Orthodox Church, the
establishment of national patriarchates in the Balkans), this is a topic
that has not received the attention it deserves in the literature.

But perhaps of greatest interest in the case of the Galician Ruthenians, at least from the perspective of the national-construction literature,
is that in the nineteenth century the Galician Ruthenians elaborated
two very distinct and mutually exclusive constructions of their nationality (Ukrainian and Russian), could well have been drawn into a third
(Polish), exhibited tendencies toward a fourth (Rusyn), and had at least
the theoretical possibility of formulating a fifth (a hypothetical nationality, with serious historical underpinnings, that would have included
the peoples now called Ukrainians and Belarusians). This proliferation
of real and hypothetical constructions on the basis of a single, socially
and culturally rather homogeneous, and territorially quite compact
ethnic group would seem to confirm the validity of the new approach
to the study of nationality. It would also, however, seem to raise a new
question, which can be formulated in different ways: why did some
constructions fail and some succeed? how free was the emergent
national intelligentsia in its creative work of national-cultural construction? to what degree did the national characteristics after all determine
the viability of the national construction plans? The case of Galician
Rus' offers unusually rich material for the exploration of this theme. In
the remainder of this essay, I will begin the exploration and suggest
questions and directions for further research. As an organizing framework, I will examine each of the constructions in terms of the cultural,

political, religious, and social factors influencing its development or lack of development.

Natione Polonus, Gente Ruthenus

The most important question to ask initially is why the Galician Ruthenians did not simply assimilate to the Polish nationality.[12] In the past, the acquisition of a high culture had often been synonymous with adopting Polish culture, not developing Ruthenian culture to a higher level. Thus in the late sixteenth and early seventeenth centuries, the Ruthenian nobility became polonized, abandoning its ancestral religion and adopting the Polish language;[13] the assimilation of the traditional elite created the situation of the early nineteenth century in which the Ruthenians constituted a largely plebeian people with only a thin stratum of clergy at the (rather low) summit. In the eighteenth century, after Galician Ruthenians accepted the church union with Roman Catholicism, the clergy of the Ruthenian church consisted of an elite of Basilian monks who monopolized episcopal office, received the most lucrative benefices, and acquired a formal education, and also of parish priests who were poor, informally and imperfectly educated, and of such low social prestige that their sons could be enserfed; the former were largely Polish by culture, the latter Ruthenian.[14] Ruthenians who migrated to Galicia's largest city, Lviv, were steadily assimilated to Polish culture until at least some time in the late nineteenth or early twentieth century.[15]

When an entire generation of candidates for the Ruthenian priesthood acquired a higher seminary education as a result of the Austrian reforms of the late eighteenth century, the immediate result was linguistic and cultural polonization. A polonized Ruthenian described the situation in the first half of the nineteenth century:

> The education of the Ruthenian clergy . . . acquainted it with the civilized world, showed it various needs and paths. . . . You wouldn't say his wife was the spouse of a Ruthenian priest, because she began to dress up like some countess in hats, scarves, and fashionable dresses; guests from the manor came over frequently, and the reception was lavish.
>
> But if one of the parishioners had need to come over, he did not dare to go right into the chamber, because the floor was washed

and covered with a canvas; instead he went to the kitchen or vestibule and waited as long as it took for the good reverend to come out to him. . . .

The conversation in the house was in Polish, the upbringing and conduct of the children in the house was also Polish.[16]

The polonization attendant upon social and cultural advancement in the early nineteenth century was partly due to the absence of a Ruthenian high culture that could meet the newly created needs of an educated Ruthenian elite; thus a priest of the 1820s who maintained an interest in books perforce read in Polish and other languages, but little in Ruthenian or in the Ruthenian liturgical language.[17]

It seemed, from the vantage point of the early nineteenth century, that there was something like a mathematical formula in operation.

Ruthenian + higher education = Pole

This was certainly how most educated Poles understood the situation. Józef Supiński, for example, writing for *Dziennik Narodowy* in 1848, claimed that Ruthenian was but a dialect of Polish, fine for addressing the common people, but unsuitable for higher purposes. To have access to "all the branches of national knowledge" and to "general European culture," it was necessary to use the standard literary language, that is, Polish. Another author writing in the same newspaper at roughly the same time, Leon Korecki, put it even more simply: "Every Ruthenian is a Pole, since every enlightened Ruthenian to this day uses Polish as his customary language."[18] Also in 1848, the radical democrat Kasper Cięglewicz, himself a polonized Ruthenian, argued that the Ruthenian language was a mere dialect, unsuited to be the vehicle of a higher culture, incapable of expressing the needs of an educated community; the vehicle to meet the needs of educated Galician Ruthenians was, naturally, Polish.[19] Again in the same year, Polish democrats appealing to Emperor Ferdinand I not to partition Galicia into separate Polish and Ruthenian provinces explained to the monarch that

the entire literature of this crownland has developed in the Polish language and exclusively in the Polish language. . . . This language is the binding element of all the educated strata of the population;

this language is used by all Ruthenians insofar as they do not belong to the agricultural class.[20]

To rephrase all this: had things run their "natural" course, all Galicians, even those who were Greek Catholic and spoke various Ruthenian dialects, would have adopted "industrial culture" in its Polish form.

They did not, of course, and the reasons behind this unexpected result form the intellectual problem that awaits exploration and, to the extent possible, resolution.

It will be useful, however, before turning to an exploration of the reasons why Ruthenians did not simply become Poles, to sketch the chronology of the differentiation process. The great caesura was undoubtedly the revolutionary years 1848–49. There were, however, educated Ruthenians who sought to develop an independent national culture before those years. The main examples are Viennese seminarians from the 1820s on[21] and a group of Lviv seminarians in the 1830s and 1840s, the so-called Ruthenian Triad. However, their views did not become hegemonic in educated Ruthenian circles (mainly composed of clergymen) until the revolution of 1848 and its aftermath. There were still *gente Rutheni, natione Poloni* in existence after 1848, but they were small in number by the late 1860s and dropped from sight altogether by the late 1880s.[22]

Students of Ukrainian history have assumed that it was only natural that the Ruthenians did not become Poles, so they have never posed the question of why precisely this did not happen. Thus the present essay is not able to build on the insights of a previous literature that has engaged this question directly, and it cannot do much more than offer a few preliminary observations. We will proceed through our four broad categories: the religious, cultural, political, and social.

When confronted with the emergence of an unexpectedly strong political and cultural movement among the hitherto rather dormant Ruthenians in 1848, Polish publicists attempting to explain this anomaly tended to give a great deal of weight to religious factors. Since, as they conceived it, Ruthenian was but a dialect of Polish and since all educated Ruthenians spoke standard Polish, the emphasis of a national difference between Ruthenians and Poles was clearly an emphasis of the religious difference between the Greek and Roman rite. This view seemed confirmed by the prominence of churchmen in the Supreme Ruthenian Council. Thus Cięglewicz wrote that the attempt of the

Ruthenians to divide Galicia was an attempt to institute "rule by priests," to restore "the times of Moses."[23] The Poles addressing Ferdinand I also explained that the troubles in Galicia were the result of "religious sectarianism" and specifically the ambitions of the Greek Catholic church hierarchy.[24]

Even allowing that such publicists were conjuring up the religious factor to discredit the Ruthenian movement in the eyes of mid-nineteenth-century liberals, they certainly seem to have had a point. The religious division between Poles and Ruthenians was one of the most salient in East Central Europe. Although both Poles and Ruthenians were Catholic, they belonged to different rites, and this latter division—the division between Western and Eastern Christians—constituted a deep cultural cleavage. Single nationalities could be composed of both Catholic and Orthodox, providing they were united by the same Eastern rite (aside from the Ukrainians, the Romanians are an example); they could also be both Catholic and Protestant, since both came out of the same Western tradition (the Germans constitute the classic example, but there are others, including the Slovaks). On the other hand, the differentiation between the Western and Eastern Christian heritage sometimes figured crucially as the fundamental division between nationalities: it marked off Croats from Serbs and East Slavs from West Slavs. Cases in which one nationality incorporated both the Western and Eastern Christian traditions are such singular exceptions as prove the rule.[25] In sum, the divide between Western and Eastern Christianity was one of those religio-civilizational divides difficult to cross, like the divides between Islam, Judaism, and Christianity. It is true that many individuals over the course of history have crossed these divides, especially within the context of intermarriage, but seen in the larger context these have proven rather to be lasting, formative barriers.

Let us add a few more considerations to this: With one exception, all the Ruthenian awakeners before 1848 were priests or seminarians. The Ruthenian leadership in the revolutionary years also consisted largely of priests. Priests continued to dominate the Ruthenian national movement until the 1860s, when the secular intelligentsia (in large part, the sons of priests) took the helm; even then, however, priests served as the most important activists of the movement on the local, village level. Given, then, the unusually strong influence of the clergy in the Ruthenian national movement, perhaps the religious difference between Poles and Ruthenians took on a greater significance than it would have otherwise. Linguistic obstacles could have been overcome, and perhaps the religious one could have as well, had not priests played so prominent a part in the development of the Galician Ruthenians' national culture. This, of course, brings us back to the view of the Polish contemporaries who saw precisely clerical interests behind the emergence of the Ruthenian movement in 1848.

But we need not single out the relationship between the clergy and the national movement, which sets up the problem somewhat tautologically. We can start instead from a consideration of the weight of the clergy in Ruthenian educated society. Until probably the 1860s priests constituted the majority of all Ruthenians who had acquired any centralized higher education.[26] At least into midcentury they were linguistically polonized. Why did they not then polonize completely? Was it because complete polonization entailed or seemed to entail a change to the Latin from the Greek rite? This was a change that was difficult both psychologically and canonically. In addition, it was a much more impracticable change for clergymen than for laymen: the Greek Catholic clergy was married and could not simply transfer to the Latin rite, which did not accept married clergy; thus even if a Greek Catholic priest somehow managed to overcome the canonical hurdles involved in a change of rite, he would have to abandon his living as a clergyman and enter some new profession.[27] In short, for the vast majority of educated Ruthenians, in the historical period in which the decision was made, total entrance into the Polish national culture was not a real option; running up against the religious barrier to entry, they turned their attention instead to elaborating a separate Ruthenian high culture.

Although the arguments for the impact of religion as the crucial differentiating factor seem fairly strong, there is also something weighty to be laid against them: evidence from three closely related cases suggests that the Eastern rite did not necessarily stand in the way of cultural assimilation to a nationality in which the Western rite predominated. The first case is that of the Greek-rite clergy of the Chełm eparchy, the last surviving Uniate diocese in the Russian empire. The Chełm region was not unlike Galicia: the landlords were Polish-speaking and Roman Catholic, the peasants were Ruthenian-speaking and Greek Catholic. By the 1860s and up until the abolition of the church union and forced conversion to Russian Orthodoxy in 1875, the native Greek Catholic clergy of Chełm eparchy was largely polonized, both linguistically and politically (even to the extent of supporting Polish insurrectionary activity against the czarist regime). Beginning in the 1860s the Russian government imported Greek Catholic seminarians and clergy from Galicia to serve as a counterweight to the polonized and polonophile native clergy. Relations between the Galicians and the natives were hostile, even though both were clergymen of the same religion and both considered themselves Ruthenians; but the native priests of Chełm also considered themselves, in some way at least, Poles and regularly used the Polish language, while the Galician priests were fanatically anti-Polish. As their confrontation demonstrated, the Galician outcome—that is, the development of a separate, indeed anti-Polish, Ruthenian nationality—was not the only possible outcome of a similar religio-historical starting-point. It should be noted, however, that the situation in the Chełm eparchy was exceptional in some ways; the Chełm region was one of the Ruthenian-inhabited territories most exposed to Polish influence (unlike other Ruthenian/Ukrainian territories in the Russian empire, it had been included in the Congress Kingdom) and the strong attraction of Polish culture evident in the 1860s may have represented a temporary waxing of pro-Polish sympathies connected with the patriotic wave that swept most of the former Polish territories at that time.[28]

The second relevant counterexample is that of the Armenians of Galicia, mainly concentrated in the crownland capital, Lviv. The Galician Armenians, like the Galician Ruthenians, were Uniates, that is, Catholics of the Eastern tradition. They, however, unlike the Ruthenians, were polonized in the nineteenth century and indeed became very prominent representatives of the Polish establishment in Galicia. For example, in the late nineteenth and early twentieth centuries the head of the influential Podolian party—the most conservative political grouping in the crownland, anti-Ruthenian and anti-Jewish—was the Armenian Dawid Abrahamowicz. Also, the principal spokesman of the Polish episcopate on social and political issues in the early twentieth century was the Armenian Catholic archbishop of Lviv (and conservative Polish nationalist), Józef Teodorowicz. Again, belonging to the Eastern Christian tradition did not prevent assimilation to a Polish cultural and political identity. However, it should be pointed out that the Armenian community in Galicia was miniscule: Galicia had a total population of over seven million in 1900, of whom a mere 1,532 were

Armenian Catholics.[29] In the mid–seventeenth century, Armenians in Lviv alone had numbered twenty-five hundred, accounting for a tenth of the city's total population;[30] evidently by the end of the nineteenth century many had assimilated so completely to Polish culture that they abandoned their traditional rite and embraced the Latin. It is also well to remember that the Armenians, who came to Galicia as merchants, were concentrated in a Polish urban environment, that is, they were much more exposed to the assimilative forces of the city than were the primarily agrarian Ruthenians.

The third example is that of the Ruthenians of Sub- or Transcarpathia in historical Hungary. Through judicious episcopal appointments, through careful control of the seminaries and the rest of the educational system, and through far-reaching limitations on voluntary associations, the press, and political participation, the Magyar gentry succeeded in fostering a strong Magyarone element in the Greek Catholic clergy of this region. By the early twentieth century most newly ordained priests here seem to have thought of themselves as Hungarian patriots and of their Ruthenianism as a clearly subordinate local identity.[31] Again, however, this is a case that differs substantially from the Galician Ruthenian one, since the Hungarian Ruthenians were a small population exposed to very strong, state-directed assimilatory pressures.

In sum, at least given certain conditions, it was possible for Eastern-rite Christians to assimilate to a cultural identity infused with the Western-Christian tradition. Thus, whatever role religion played in the failure of a Polish construction of Ruthenian nationality, it is difficult to argue that it served as the overriding factor.

The other factors—cultural, political, and social—do not require as detailed treatment as the religious one. By the cultural factor I mean the cultural environment in which the decision not to be Polish was made. The Greek Catholic seminarians and clergymen of the second quarter of the nineteenth century, the "national awakeners" who undertook the construction of a new Ruthenian culture at once national and universal, were exposed to certain intellectual influences and cultural attitudes that did not exist when the old Ruthenian nobility assimilated to Polish culture and that did not, until carefully packaged and delivered, reach the Ruthenian children who came to the city to learn a trade. I mean, of course, the idea of nationality, the vision that every folk should aspire to its place in the sun and that every son of the people should devote himself to finding (less consciously: creating) that place. To a certain extent at least, I find that the problem of why the Ruthenians did not become Polish is solved when I consult the reading list of the archetypical awakeners, the "Ruthenian Triad" of the 1830s (Iakiv Holovatsky, Markiian Shashkevych, Ivan Vahylevych). When they were between the ages of eighteen and twenty-four they read the Kralovédvorský manuscript, *Časopis ceského musea*, Karadžić, Kopitar, Šafarik, Kollar, Dobrovský, Schlözer, Herder, the Lay of Igor's Campaign, the Polish romantic poets, Russian, Ukrainian, and Polish history, and Ukrainian ethnography.[32] The zeitgeist that drove these young men to such books, and then these books themselves, would seem sufficient to explain the motivation of the work of Ruthenian "awakening" they undertook. They were aware that Ruthenians differed from Poles in a number of respects—religion, alphabet, language, folk customs—and their research indicated the historical basis of these divergences. How—in the early nineteenth century, in this part of Europe, with the education they received and the aspirations they absorbed—how could they not help but *make* something of those differences?

The third factor to be considered is the political one. Of course, it could not be mere coincidence that the revolution of 1848 marked the point of no return on the journey toward the construction of a completely separate national culture. The revolution witnessed not only the first political actions of the Ruthenians—the formation of the Supreme Ruthenian Council, the petition to partition Galicia, participation in parliament—but major milestones in their cultural development: the publication of their first newspapers, the establishment of the Galician-Ruthenian *Matytsia* (an educational-literary association modeled on similar *matice* of other "awakening" Slav nations), the first congress of Ruthenian scholars.

In 1848 the Ruthenians became involved in a process that John Breuilly has described thus:

> There is a general tendency for the initial nationalist response to come from culturally dominant groups. The nationalist movements express their case in historic territorial terms. They tend to promote, as a reaction, nationalist movements among culturally subordinate groups which express their case in ethnic and linguistic terms.[33]

In this scenario, the Poles were the culturally dominant group, the Ruthenians the subordinate one. What happened at the outset of the revolution was that the Poles formed their national council with the intention that it serve as the political representative of the entire population of Galicia. The Ruthenians were thus forced into making a choice in a way that they had not been even a few years earlier: would the national council represent their interests? were they Poles too? The revolution was giving a political weight to nationality—for Italians, Germans, Croats, Poles, and many others; it perforce raised the question: did the Ruthenians constitute a nationality too? and if so, what were the implications for them in terms of the development of a national culture?

The question is, then: did national *politics* generate the impetus to the construction of a national culture? Its contributory and accelerative role in the period from 1848 on can hardly be questioned, but what about prior to 1848, when, after all, the national awakening began? There has been solid research demonstrating the pervasive influence of the Polish democratic revolutionary movement of the 1830s on Ruthenian seminarians in Lviv.[34] Some Ruthenians joined underground Polish groups like the Association of the Polish People and became completely polonized; Kasper Cięglewicz is a prominent example. Others joined that same organization and left it after the Poles refused to add the words "and Ruthenian" to its title.[35] Others remained aloof, such as the members of the Ruthenian Triad, but they could not help but be aware of the Polish conspiratorial movement and assess their relation to it. The point is this: in Galicia nationality was formulated within a political framework from the very inception of the Ruthenian awakening. There is, however, a caveat to be registered: the first stirrings associated with the national awakening can be dated to the 1820s, before the Poles undertook large-scale conspiratorial activity, and located in Vienna, where the Polish presence was minimal and the cultural context more important than the strictly political one.

A final point about Polish politics and Ruthenian culture: during the course of the revolution of 1848–49 there crystallized a very small group of Ruthenians—organized in the Ruthenian Assembly—who supported the anti-imperial, revolutionary politics of the Poles yet also championed the retention and development of a separate Ruthenian cultural identity. The group could not play an important role during the revolution because it lacked the support of either the Ruthenians or the Poles. The mass of Ruthenians held that their political interests were separate from, indeed opposed to, those of the Poles, and they regarded the Ruthenian Assembly as an instrument devised by their foes in order to divide Ruthenian ranks. As for the Poles, many of them did not care for an organization that promoted Ruthenian cultural separatism. Cięglewicz expressed the view of many Polish democrats when he insisted that Ruthenians retain Polish as the language of cultural interchange; otherwise an effective link binding Poles and Ruthenians into a single political nation would be broken.[36] In sum, the Ruthenian Assembly tried to separate the political from the cultural strand during the revolution; its isolation and irrelevance seem to confirm that the development of a Ruthenian national culture cannot be understood apart from the political dynamics of Polish-Ruthenian relations.

In a recent article, Roman Szporluk argues against Miroslav Hroch's model of a progression of national movements from a cultural to a political stage. Szporluk stresses instead that the development of Ukrainian nationalism in the nineteenth century was preeminently and from the first a political, not a cultural, question and that it was closely linked with the development of two other political questions, the Russian question and the Polish question. The thrust of his argument is not, on the whole, belied by the evidence of the Galician Ruthenian case.[37]

The last factor to be discussed is the social factor, which overlaps to some degree with the previous, political factor. In its starkest form it is this: almost all landlords in Galicia were Polish, almost all Ruthenians were peasants. This had immense political ramifications. In 1848, when the questions of emancipation and terms of emancipation appeared on the political agenda, it determined that the interests of educated Poles and most Ruthenians would be diametrically opposed. It meant that the peasantry, who took an active part in the revolution, opposed the landlord-dominated Polish National Council and supported the Supreme Ruthenian Assembly, in which their pastors took an active part. This in turn made the Ruthenian entrance into politics all the more forceful, since it brought to the revolutionary situation the energy and political clout of the popular masses. While it was easy to dismiss the political opinions of a group composed largely of priests, it was much harder to do so when hundreds of thousands of peasants stood behind them (moreover, these were Galician peasants, infamous throughout the empire for slaughtering their landlords two years earlier). The continuing antagonism between Polish landlords and Ruthenian peasants in the decades after emancipation was to ensure that the Ruthenian national movement always enjoyed a large popular base.

The social difference between Poles and Ruthenians also had immense cultural implications. The Polish gentry had developed a "high" culture that was linked with the "high" culture of the rest of Europe. This lay at the root of the claim that Polish culture was the natural vehicle for all Galicians who wished to be connected to the achievements of universal culture (European culture, "industrial" culture). The Poles enjoyed a language with words for every item and every concept that existed in contemporary Europe. The Ruthenians had a traditional, "low" culture, a folk culture, and a (intellectually underdeveloped) religious culture that was primitive by the standards of, and incapable of communicating with, Europe. Their language had separate words for branches that had fallen off a tree and branches that were broken but were still attached, since these words came in very handy when gathering fuel in the strictly regulated Galician forests, but it did not have words to express the scientific, technological, and political advances that had been made in Europe and almost no vocabulary for philosophy, philology, and other branches of scholarship. Poles played the piano, Ruthenians the handmade hurdy-gurdy. In short, the social differences between Poles and Ruthenians established the situation that is being explored here: to join the rest of the world culturally, Ruthenians either had to adopt Polish culture or else fashion a culture of their own that could perform the same functions.

But did the social differences not only set up the terms of the problem, but also influence the way in which it was eventually to be solved? I think so. The variant of high culture that the Poles offered was one that had been developed in an aristocratic and gentry context and necessarily incorporated elements from this formative social milieu. This was evidenced in certain linguistic formulations of the standardized language (*Pan mówi*—"You say," but literally "The squire says") and permeated the national historical mythos. It is certainly conceivable that a largely peasant people like the Ruthenians could have assimilated to such a culture, since after all the Polish peasantry eventually did. Yet the national acculturation of the Polish peasantry was a slow process and entailed, perhaps as a necessary condition, the positing of a mediating identity (articulated by Polish populism or *ludowstwo*). It is probable that the social origins of modern Polish culture had a repellent rather than attractive effect on the Ruthenians.

The Ukrainian and All-Russian Ideas

From the 1830s through World War I two different constructions of nationality existed and competed in Galician Rus'—the Ukrainian and the all-Russian. Adherents of the Ukrainian orientation maintained that they were of the same nationality as the Ukrainians or Little Russians across the river Zbruch in the Russian empire. Adherents of the all-Russian orientation, or Russophiles (as they are more frequently called in the literature), did not deny this, but they minimized the differences between Little Russians and Great Russians and saw all East Slavs, including the Ruthenians of Austria-Hungary, as part of a single Russian nationality.

The two orientations elaborated different versions of the primary national characteristics. The literary language of the Ukrainophiles, for all purposes, was a mixture of local Galician vernaculars and the emerging standard Ukrainian as represented in the works of Ivan Kotliarevsky, Hryhorii Kvita-Osnovianenko, Taras Shevchenko, and other exponents of the Ukrainian literary revival in Russia. The Russophiles also made use of a Ukrainianized Galician vernacular when they wrote for the peasantry, especially before the turn of the twentieth century, but when writing for the intelligentsia they used either a literary language that approximated Russian (with some concessions to the local vernacular and some homage to the church-Slavonic-based literary language used in Galician Rus' prior to the era of national awakening) or else, particularly in the twentieth century, standard literary Russian.[38] One could quickly glance at a newspaper and know to which orientation it belonged, because Ukrainophile publications generally used the phonetic orthography developed by the Ukrainian writer Panteleimon Kulish, while Russophile publications used the etymological orthography; letters like ï and r were present in Ukrainophile publications and absent in Russophile ones, while letters like ъ and ѣ could only be found in Russophile publications. In the center of the Ukrainophiles' historical myth stood the Cossack period; even though Galician Rus' had not been Cossack territory, the myth was important because it both expressed solidarity with the Ukrainian nation of the Left and Right Banks and served to fuel the ongoing struggle with the Poles. For the Russophiles the central historical experience was the existence of Kyivan Rus', which united all East Slavs and in which the Galician principality played a prominent role.[39] With regard to religion, the Ukrainophiles sought the preservation of their Greek Catholic church, which distinguished them from both Poles and Russians; the Russophiles gravitated, with varying degrees of consistency, toward Russian Orthodoxy. The two camps developed different names for the people of Galician Rus'. By the latter half of the nineteenth century, they had generated different spellings for the adjectival form "Ruthenian": the Ukrainophiles wrote *rus'kyi*, the Russophiles wrote *russkii*. In the early twentieth century the Ukrainophiles fairly consistently referred to the people of Galician Rus' as *ukraintsi*, the Russophiles referred to them as *russkie*. Thus two fully elaborated conceptions of nationality vied with each other for the loyalties of the Galician Ruthenians.

Before attempting an analysis of the political, cultural, religious, and social factors underlying the formation and determining the fate of the two conceptions, it will be useful to survey their historic fortunes over the course of the nineteenth and twentieth centuries. It is difficult to speak of either a Ukrainian or all-Russian orientation before the 1830s. The vast majority of the population of Galician Rus' were enserfed peasants who did not think in categories of nationality. Although the peasants were aware that they were not Poles, or Jews, or Germans—peoples whom they knew from their encounters in Galicia—they would have had no (or at least little) idea of whether they were the same as the people who lived on the banks of the Dnieper or the Volga. The small, mainly clerical elite that had been formed as a result of the educational reforms of the end of the eighteenth century was heavily influenced by Polish culture. Those who had a clear idea that they were not Poles, but Ruthenians, did not yet express this in terms that fit either the Ukrainian or all-Russian conception cleanly. The traditional, preawakening attitude of the Ruthenian elite seems to have been that the Ruthenians of Galicia and the population of Right and Left Bank Ukraine were essentially the same people, different from both the Poles to the west and the Russians to the east. But this traditional, "protonational" sense of community (which was often enough blurry around the eastern edges) was not the same thing as the Ukrainian conception that surfaced in the 1830s, even though it undoubtedly did much to prepare the ground for its reception.

Both the Ukrainian idea and the all-Russian idea were imported into Austrian Galicia from the Russian empire, and representatives of both conceptions can be identified by the 1830s. At this time, and through the revolution of 1848–49, the Ukrainophile current was stronger and more clearly defined than the Russophile current. The chief representatives of the Ukrainian idea before the revolution were the Ruthenian Triad and their associates at the Lviv seminary as well as the grammarians Iosyf Levytsky and Iosyf Lozynsky. The Ruthenian Triad consciously linked themselves with the Ukrainian literary and folkloric movement in Russian-ruled Ukraine. The Triad's greatest literary talent, Markiian Shashkevych, wrote verse in a language heavily influenced by his reading of Left Bank poets and ethnographers, verse about Cossacks, the steppe, and "native Ukraine" (ridna Ukraina). In their famous miscellany Rusalka dnistrovaia the Triad included a bibliography of the Ukrainian cultural revival in the Russian empire.[40] As to the grammarians, the titles of their major works identified the language they were codifying as both "Ruthenian" and "Little Russian."[41] During the revolution, the Supreme Ruthenian Council proclaimed that the Ruthenians of Galicia belonged "to a large nation of 15 million,"[42] that is, to a nation including the Ukrainians of the Russian empire, but excluding the Russians. However, this statement should not simply be interpreted as an expression of a full-fledged Ukrainophile framework, since the council in its activities focused almost exclusively on local Galician affairs, did not otherwise discuss the Ukrainian movement in the Russian empire, and did not appeal in its manifestos to the touchstone Cossack heritage. The statement could be understood as an expression of the traditional, protonational sense of "Ukrainian" community that was evident before the 1830s, albeit informed by the work of the Ukrainophile activists of the 1830s and 1840s; the statement was also, as we shall see in a moment, compatible with early expressions of Russophilism. Although some Ruthenian activists took advantage of the revolutionary possibilities to republish some of the works of the Ukrainian literary revival in Russian Ukraine, this was done on a surprisingly small scale.[43]

The all-Russian conception was introduced to Galicia by the Russian pan-Slavist Mikhail Pogodin, who visited Lviv in 1835 and

1839–40 and thereafter carried on an active correspondence with Ruthenian intellectuals. The main proponent of his views in Galicia was the historian Denys Zubrytsky, who became a corresponding member of the St. Petersburg Archaeographic Commission in 1842 and published, in the Russian language, a three-volume history of the Principality of Galicia-Volhynia in the 1850s. Although the all-Russian conception was weak in Galician Rus' prior to the 1850s, it seems to have had more currency than is generally admitted in Ukrainian historiography. The Austrian government, the Greek Catholic church authorities, and Polish political activists sometimes suspected or maintained that the Ruthenian national movement in Galicia was pro-Russian; some of these suspicions and claims were laughably specious,[44] but Ukrainian historiography has not searched very hard to see if there was indeed some fire behind the smoke.[45] During the revolution, some Ruthenian activists published a leaflet addressed to their "German brothers" that was quite Russophile in conception. It declared that "the Russians are ethnically related to us *(uns stammverwandt)*; the same Slavic blood flows in our veins; a common history in earlier times, almost the same language, customs, etc., make our Russian brothers dear to our hearts." The leaflet threatened the Austrian Germans that if they continued to leave the Ruthenians at the mercy of their "mortal enemies" the Poles, the Ruthenians would "seek their fortune under Russia's scepter" and work to unite with their "less oppressed brothers in Russia." Interestingly, in spite of its Russophile sentiments, the leaflet declared that "we Ruthenians [are] an as yet unrecognized people of 15 million."[46]

In the decade of reaction that followed the revolution, the all-Russian conception made important advances in Galician Rus'. Many of the former associates of the Ruthenian Triad abandoned their previous views in favor of the vernacular language and Ukrainian identity and instead began to promote a literary language closer to Russian and an all-Russian national identity. Among the new Russophiles were some of Galician Rus's most prominent intellectuals—the poets Ivan Hushalevych and Nykolai Ustyianovych, the future journalist Bohdan Didytsky, and the future historian Antonii Petrushevych.[47] But undoubtedly the most important defector from the Ukrainophile position was an original member of the Ruthenian Triad, Iakiv Holovatsky. With Shashkevych dead and Vahylevych compromised by his cooperation with the Poles during the revolution, Holovatsky was the sole heir to the Triad's legacy, which he used after 1851 to promote his newly adopted, Russophile view. Moreover, as professor of Ruthenian language and literature at Lviv University, Holovatsky was well placed to influence the younger generation of the Ruthenian intelligentsia (until 1867 when he was dismissed from the university and emigrated to Russia). During this same period, the 1850s, proponents of the Russophile conception, including the very talented Didytsky, dominated the editorial offices of the Ruthenian periodical press. The Ukrainian conception had by no means died, but it did not exhibit the same dynamism that Russophilism did in the 1850s.

In the next period, from 1860 to 1882, the two conceptions waged open intellectual war, and the Russophiles clearly constituted the stronger camp. The Ukrainophiles had regrouped in the early 1860s around a series of short-lived but explicitly Ukrainian periodicals. They consolidated their forces beginning in the late 1860s, after the introduction of the Austrian constitution: in 1867 they established the journal *Pravda*, in 1868 the adult-education society Prosvita, and in 1880 the newspaper *Dilo*. They made steady progress from the late 1860s on but did not begin to outpace the Russophiles until the mid-1880s at the earliest. The Russophiles also laid institutional foundations in this period, establishing the newspaper *Slovo* (1861), the Kachkovsky Society to promote adult education (1874),[48] and the Society of Russian Ladies (1879).[49] The popularity of the Russophile conception increased in the 1860s as a result of the constitutional rearrangements in the Habsburg monarchy, which left the Polish nobility in control of Galicia; the loyalty of the Galician Ruthenian intelligentsia to the Habsburg dynasty was firmly shaken by this disposition, and the notion of Russian irredentism began to look more attractive.[50]

From 1882 until the turn of the twentieth century Russophilism waned in popularity, while Ukrainophilism made rapid and irreversible progress. The turn in the fortunes of the Russophile camp came in 1882 when one of the leading Russophile propagandists, the priest Ioann (Ivan) Naumovych, encouraged the inhabitants of the village of Hnylychky to petition the government that they be allowed to change their religion from Greek Catholicism to Orthodoxy. Both the Austrian government and the Vatican had been concerned about the spread of Russophilism for some time, but the Hnylychky incident was to prove the straw that broke the camel's back. Working together, the state and ecclesiastical authorities mounted an energetic campaign to combat Russophilism among the Greek Catholic clergy and among the intelligentsia at large. Measures included the forced resignation of the reigning metropolitan of Halych, a purge of his consistory, a Jesuit-led reformation of the Greek Catholic monastic order, a public trial of leading Russophiles on charges of high treason, the excommunication of Father Naumovych, the reorganization of ecclesiastical boundaries, the selection of politically reliable bishops, a closer surveillance of the movement of people and literature across the Russian-Austrian border, and the hounding of the Russophile press. The result was the creation of a climate in which Russophilism found it difficult to flourish. It is perhaps impossible to assess how much the decline of Russophilism in the late nineteenth century was specifically the result of the interventions of the Austrian state and the Vatican and not the culmination of a natural process of expansion on the part of the Ukrainophile movement. Russophilism did not, of course, disappear, but it was weaker in the late nineteenth century than it had been earlier, more localized (particularly in the westernmost Ruthenian settlements, i.e., in the Lemko region), and more of an old man's party. By contrast, the Ruthenian national movement connected with the Ukrainian orientation grew by leaps and bounds in this period, covering the countryside with a network of reading clubs and other voluntary associations,[51] politically differentiating into four camps (national democratic, radical, social democratic, and Christian social), establishing an academy of sciences (the Shevchenko Scientific Society), and formulating the goal of erecting an independent Ukrainian state.[52]

The turn of the twentieth century saw a number of changes in the situation of the Russophiles. Losing support in Galician Ruthenian society, the Russophiles began to depend much more on outside patronage. From 1898 until 1908 they enjoyed the support of two Galician lieutenants (namisnyky) associated with the conservative Polish Podolian party, namely Counts Leon Piniński (1898–1903) and Andrzej Potocki (1903–8). How the curious alliance between the Polish-chauvinist Podolians and the Russophiles came to be is a somewhat more complicated story, but the main point is that the Podolians had come to the conclusion that the Russophiles made a useful counterweight to the much more dynamic and socially more radical Ukrainian movement. The alliance ended when a Ukrainian student assassinated Lieutenant Potocki and Vienna decided to take the lieutenancy out of the Podolians' hands and give the post to someone who could come to an understanding with the Ukrainians. It was fortunate for the

Russophiles that the assassination of Potocki and the loss of the lieu-tenancy's patronage occurred in 1908, the year of Austria's annexation of Bosnia. As a result of that incident, the Russian government, which had always given clandestine material support to the Galician Rus-sophiles, redoubled its efforts. It launched a major campaign to propa-gate Russian Orthodoxy in Galicia (unsuccessfully) and among Gali-cian immigrants in North America (in part successfully). It also planted articles in the British press to suggest that Galicia was *Russia irredenta*.[53] In this situation the Russophiles became more distinctly than ever before foreign agents of Russian czardom. Facing persecution, a num-ber of Russophile leaders fled to Kyiv in Russian-ruled Ukraine. There they established the Carpatho-Russian Liberation Committee in August 1914. A month later the committee found itself in Lviv, where it assisted the Russian occupation authorities. The Russians held Galicia until June 1915 and returned to its easternmost portion for a year in 1916–17. Particularly during the first occupation, the Russian civil and ecclesiastical authorities attempted to suppress the Ukrainian move-ment and convert the population to Russian Orthodoxy. They were not very successful in accomplishing these aims, although they would have achieved more had the Habsburg government and military not under-taken preventive incarcerations and executions of thousands of real and suspected Russophiles on the eve of the Russian invasion. The main Austrian internment camp for Galician Russophiles was located in the Styrian village of Thalerhof, which became for the postwar Rus-sophiles an important symbol of the sacrifices they had made for their cause and of the perfidy of the Habsburg government and its Ukrainian collaborators.[54]

Also since the turn of the century the Russophiles underwent ide-ological differentiation. The movement split between the youth and their elders, the so-called *novokursnyky* and *starokursnyky*, respectively. The new tendency, formalized in the establishment of the Russian National Party in Lviv in 1900, was more consistently Russian than the older Russophilism. The *novokursnyky* used Russian, unadulterated by Galicianisms and Old Church Slavonicisms, as their literary language. They openly championed Russian Orthodoxy and often converted to that faith. They traveled to Russia frequently and met with government agents there. They were the ones who founded the Carpatho-Russian Liberation Committee and placed themselves at the service of the

Russian occupation regime, which they, of course, regarded as a regime of national emancipation.

By this time, however, the Russophiles were already marginalized in Galicia and the Ukrainian conception was hegemonic. In the 1907 elections, for example, the Ukrainophiles sent twenty-two deputies to parliament (seventeen national democrats, three radicals, two social democrats); the Russophiles sent five.[55] The strength of the Ukrainian movement is perhaps best indicated by the political success it enjoyed in its struggle with the Poles. By the eve of World War I it had won major concessions from the Polish ruling elite: significantly increased representation in the Galician Diet and a Ukrainian university in Lviv. (The outbreak of world war and the collapse of Austria-Hungary, however, prevented these concessions from being implemented.) When the Habsburg monarchy disintegrated, the Ukrainians of Galicia proclaimed the Western Ukrainian National Republic in November 1918. After being driven from Galicia by Haller's army in the summer of 1919, the Ukrainian Galician Army joined the struggle for national independence in the formerly Russian Ukraine. At its maximum strength the Ukrainian Galician Army numbered seventy to seventy-five thousand men, including reserves. Although the Ukrainians failed to achieve independence in the aftermath of World War I, the experience of proclaiming a Ukrainian state and of waging war to retain it established the Ukrainian idea in the Galician population even more deeply and extensively than before.

There is little point in outlining the history of the Ukrainian conception after World War I, since the story is well known: Galicia became the major center of Ukrainian nationalism in the interwar era, retained its Ukrainian consciousness through the Soviet period,[56] and has emerged today as the greatest stronghold of nationalism in independent Ukraine.

Russophilism survived the world war, but barely. The struggle for Ukrainian independence brought youth and peasants into the Ukrainian movement who might otherwise have replenished the ranks of the Russophiles. The collapse of czarist Russia and its replacement by Bolshevik Russia was also a severe blow. There was a segment of the Russophiles, however, who were left-leaning and Sovietophile. Although they formally abjured their Russophilism to enter the Communist Party of Western Ukraine, they soon came into conflict with the Ukrainian national Communists in the party.[57] Other Russophiles managed to hang on owing to the support given to Russophile institutions by the Polish government in the interwar era. Taking their example from the Podolian tactics of the early twentieth century, Polish governments deliberately fostered Russophilism in hopes of dividing the loyalties of the Galician population. This tactic had little success, however; apart from adherents in the Lemko region in the extreme west, the Russophiles in Galicia were few and aging. The Russophile movement in Galicia did not survive World War II and the Soviet period, although there was one curious attempt to rehabilitate the Russophile legacy during the years of the Thaw.[58]

Let us turn now to a consideration of our four factors and begin with the political, since its salience, particularly with regard to the all-Russian idea, is so evident from the foregoing sketch. With the possible exception of their emergence in the 1830s, every major turning point in the Russophiles' fortunes was connected with a political event: the failure of the revolution of 1848–49, the constitutional reorganization of the Habsburg monarchy in the 1860s, the purge of 1882, the aggravation of Austro-Russian tensions in the early twentieth century, World War I, the Russian Revolution, the Soviet annexation of Galicia. The moment of its emergence constitutes only a possible exception, since it did coincide with the decade in which Polish conspiratorial activity in Galicia was at its height.

Russophilism was also an expression of the most elementary political logic, clearly formulated, for example, in the leaflet addressed to the "German brothers" in 1848. The exact same political logic led Kyiv Metropolitan Iov Boretsky to appeal to the Russian czar in 1624 to protect the Orthodox faith in Ukraine against Polish persecution, led the leader of the anti-Polish rebellion, Hetman Bohdan Khmelnytsky, to swear loyalty to the czar at Pereislav in 1654, and brought together Russian agents and Ukrainian peasants and Cossacks in the anti-Polish *haidamaka* rebellions of the eighteenth century. (This logic also, of course, worked the other way around: in 1658, after falling out with Muscovy, Hetman Ivan Vyhovsky signed the Hadiach treaty with Poland, in 1708 Hetman Ivan Mazepa concluded an alliance against Czar Peter I with King Stanisław Leszczyński of Poland, and in 1920 the Ukrainian National Republic renounced its claims to Galicia in order to make an alliance with Poland against their common enemy, Soviet Russia.)

The political logic involved in Russophilism was so elementary and compelling that it found its counterparts even outside the Ruthenian intelligentsia, among peasants of the 1860s to 1880s who hoped that the White Czar would come to Galicia and slaughter the Polish landlords and the Jews,[59] and even outside Galicia, Czech Russophilism being perhaps the best-known example, although directed against the Germans rather than the Poles.

But did a political alliance with the Russians against the Poles necessarily entail the adoption of a conception of all-Russian nationality? Could the Ruthenians of Galicia have followed, say, the Czech pattern of Russophilism, that is, political orientation on Russia without submerging their own specific nationality?[60] Since the terms of an alliance are set by the stronger partner, in this case Russia, the same questions might be reformulated as follows: Would Russia have been interested in a pro-Russian political orientation in Galician Rus' that did not involve a sense of unity that was more than the general Slavic unity expressed in Czech Russophilism?

On the whole, it is unlikely: for most of the nineteenth and twentieth centuries, the political and intellectual climate in Russia was not conducive to the view that Ruthenians—who worshipped in the same tongue and manner as the Russians, who made use of the same alphabet, who sprang from the same cradle of Kyivan Rus'—stood in the same relation to the Russians as the Slovaks or Czechs. Russia did find tolerable a local, Galician or Carpathian, distinctiveness; in fact the interchange of cadres between various local (Rusyn, Lemko) orientations and the Russophile orientation in Transcarpathia and the Lemko region has demonstrated historically the fundamental compatibility of a strictly local identity and an all-Russian identity. In fact, even a certain (but limited) recognition of a general "Ukrainian" distinctiveness has been acceptable even to extreme Russian chauvinists.[61] The development of the Ukrainian movement in Dnieper Ukraine, for example, owed much to the Russian government's russifying policies in Right Bank Ukraine in the 1830s and most of the 1840s; the government gave support to the Ukrainian movement in an effort to eradicate Polish influence in the "Southwestern Land" after the November insurrection. However, when the Ukrainian movement turned overtly political, with the establishment of the Cyril and Methodius Brotherhood in 1845, the government changed its attitude completely, arresting the brotherhood's members in 1847 and persecuting their successors over the next seventy years. To make what could be a long story short: from 1850 until 1917, when Russophilism was most evident in Galicia, the dominant partner in the political alliance, Russia, could work with a pro-Russian political orientation that admitted of a certain local distinctiveness; it was absolutely not, however, prepared to make common cause with a political orientation that included an emphasis on Ukrainian distinctiveness as part of its program. Or to put it another way: generally, neither Russia nor its clients in Galicia denied the ethnographic and linguistic evidence and the historical record that pointed to both Ruthenian distinctiveness from the Russians and Ruthenian traits shared with the Little Russians of the Russian empire, but they denied and opposed the view that this distinctiveness and these shared traits had political meaning or could form the basis for a separate national culture of the "industrial" variety (the latter point will be discussed below).

To understand the appeal of Russophilism, it is important to be clear about the political advantages the Ruthenian Russophiles gained from their orientation on Russia. There were, as I see it, three. First, the Russophiles had the backing of a Great Power. Although converting the political prestige this brought into concrete advantages was not a straightforward matter, it could be done. Certainly the Austrian government had to proceed more gingerly with its Ruthenian population than it would have, had its huge neighbor not been looking over its shoulder. Feeling the power of Russia behind them also, of course, had an effect on the Russophiles' political psychology, imbuing them with confidence. Second, and much more concretely, the backing of Russia translated into considerable material support for the Russophile movement. Already in the 1850s the Russian government and Pogodin had sent money to Zubrytsky, who was old and infirm.[62] In the 1860s and early 1870s Russia needed the Galician Russophiles to help them depolonize, russify (and eventually convert to Russian Orthodoxy) the Uniate church in the Chełm region; in consequence of this action close to 150 Galicians settled in the Chełm region and occupied well-paying positions that would not have been available to them otherwise. In the late 1870s and 1880s, in the context of Austro-Russian tensions over the Balkans, the Russian government gave huge subsidies to the Galician Russophile press.[63] After Naumovych was deprived of his parish, Czar Alexander III sent him a thousand rubles.[64] And, of course, after Austria annexed Bosnia in 1908 the material support from Russia increased even more. Third, the Russophiles, especially in the early twentieth

century, looked to Russia to liberate the Ruthenians from Polish domination by annexing Galicia to Russia, a dream that came to fruition for
some months during World War I.

So much for the political aspects of the all-Russian idea. What
about the politics of the Ukrainian idea? Certainly at first glance and
seen through the prism of the Russophile situation, the idea of constructing a separate Ukrainian nationality seemed politically ludicrous.
Who were the Galician Ukrainophiles' allies? One might answer: a
small, politically persecuted group in another country, with few material resources at its disposal and absolutely no clout. But this answer is
not quite correct. For all their weakness, the Ukrainophiles of the Russian empire were not an entirely negligible ally. By social origin they
were mostly descendents of the Cossack *starshyna* or officer class, and
hence of gentry status, and hence also by and large of greater wealth
and higher social prestige than their Galician counterparts, who were
priests and priests' sons. Someone someday should make a detailed list
of all the material aid that Ukrainophiles from Russia gave the Galician
movement. They contributed money to publish *Pravda*, they were the
main benefactors of the Shevchenko Society, they were the primary
source of income of the press associated with the Ukrainophile radical
current. I would not be surprised to learn that the sum total of their contributions approached that of Russia's investment in the Russophiles.
As to political clout, there were those who had it. The great intellectual
patron of the Galician radicals, Mykhailo Drahomanov, enjoyed some
prestige in left-wing and scholarly circles throughout Europe and was
able to plead the Galician Ukrainophiles' case in the Russian and European press. Volodymyr Antonovych had connections among the Polish
aristocracy that he was able to use to facilitate the establishment of a
chair of Ukrainian history at Lviv University, filled by his student
Mykhailo Hrushevsky.

Moreover, the Ukrainophiles of Dnieper Ukraine proved to have
certain advantages as allies that Russia lacked. When Russians in Russia had something important to say, they published either in their own
excellent journals in Russia or, if the content would be too irritating to
the czarist censorship, in equally excellent Russian-language journals
published in London, Geneva, or elsewhere in Western Europe. They
do not seem ever to have considered Lviv's *Slovo* or Kolomyia's *Nauka*.
By contrast, the Ukrainophiles of Russia, suffering under an intermit-
tent, but constraining, publication ban for most of the period after 1863,

frequently published their works, including some of their best works, in Galician Ukrainophile periodicals and printing establishments. Already by the 1870s this difference in the amount of exported intellectual capital had produced the paradox that Drahomanov was fond of pointing to: for all their love of Russia, the Russophiles knew the least about it and were the least influenced by its cultural-intellectual life, which was generally on a much higher plane than Galicia's; the Ukrainophiles, on the other hand, were, through the mediation of modern Ukrainian literature, au courant with all the latest Russian trends.[65] Related to this is the fact that the "brain drain" phenomenon worked to the advantage of the Ukrainophiles and to the disadvantage of the Russophiles. Many talented Ukrainophiles, fleeing persecution or for other reasons, emigrated from the Russian empire to Galicia; examples include Paulin Święcicki and other Ukrainophiles who participated in the Polish insurrection and settled in Galicia in the 1860s, the abovementioned Hrushevsky, the future ideologue of Ukrainian integral nationalism Dmytro Dontsov, and many others. There were enough political émigrés in Lviv in 1914 to form the Union for the Liberation of Ukraine (the pro-Austrian Ukrainophile equivalent of the Carpatho-Russian Liberation Committee). By contrast, I cannot name a single Russian of note who settled in Galicia and put his or her talents at the disposal of the local Russophile movement. I can, however, name hundreds of Galician Russophiles who left Galicia for non-Carpathian Russia, including some of the movement's most prominent leaders, such as Holovatsky and Naumovych.[66] In sum, the Ukrainophiles of Russia made better political allies than might at first sight appear to have been the case.

Furthermore, just as the all-Russian idea found favorable conditions for development in the complicated geopolitical constellation of the later nineteenth and early twentieth centuries, so too did Ukrainophilism. It took some time, but the Austrian state eventually came to realize that the Ukrainian movement could serve as an ally in the struggle with Russia and its supporters among the Ruthenians. One might distinguish three phases in the Austrian state's support of the Ukrainian movement. In the first phase, Austria had no particular intention of promoting the Ukrainian idea as such, of which it remained suspicious; it was only interested in stifling Russophilism. The persecution of the Russophiles, however, worked to the advantage of the Ukrainophiles.

The clearest moment of this phase came in 1882. In the second phase, Austria made the conscious choice to favor the Ukrainians over the all-Russians; this was unambiguous by 1908. In the third phase, Austria supported the Ukrainian movement also with a view to partitioning the Russian empire; this phase came, of course, in 1914. In the first phase, then, Austria's attitude to the Ukrainian movement ranged from hostile to indifferent, but its actions favored it; in the second phase Ukrainophilism was viewed as at least the lesser of two evils, and in the third phase as a useful instrument.

During most of the late nineteenth and early twentieth centuries, the Ukrainophiles themselves did not see Austria as much more than a lesser evil. They did not have for it the enthusiasm that the Russophiles had for Russia. They made formal declarations of loyalty, but they had already lost in the 1860s the devotion to the Austrian state and Habsburg dynasty that had marked the Ruthenians in 1848–49. Only in 1912–14, when the smell of war was in the air, did they develop a strongly pro-Austrian position, in the formulation of which political émigrés from Russian-ruled Ukraine, notably the young Dmytro Dontsov, played a prominent part.[67] Although subjective relations between Austria and the Ukrainian movement in Galicia were tepid until the eve of the Great War, although Russian nationalists' assertions that Austria instigated the Ukrainian movement there cannot be taken seriously,[68] it is nonetheless clear that the objective relation of Austria to the Ukrainian movement created a political environment in which it could flourish.

There is a subtler and more complicated point to make about a political constellation favoring the development of the Ukrainian idea in Galicia. It has gone virtually unnoticed in the literature, unless one counts the Russian nationalist assertion that the Ukrainian movement was both an Austrian and a Polish intrigue. We might introduce the point by recalling what Ivan L. Rudnytsky had to say about Russophilism as a renunciation of Polonism: "The rupture with Polish society was so difficult that the generation of Ruthenian intellectuals which had effected the break tended to lean to the opposite direction."[69] Indeed, many of the Russophile leaders had been Polish patriots in their youth, including Naumovych and even Zubrytsky, who served as a secretary to the pro-Napoleonic Polish forces that occupied Lviv in 1809.[70] Russophilism was a complete, radical break with the Polish past; it was, in fact, the conclusion of an anti-Polish alliance with the Poles' most powerful and ruthless enemy. Ukrainophilism did not go this far.

The Russophiles always maintained that their Ukrainian rivals were covertly sympathetic to the Poles and that they themselves were the "hard Ruthenians" *(tverdi rusyny)*, uncompromising in their anti-Polish politics. Although this posture became a bit embarrassing for the Russophiles by the late 1890s, when they found themselves under the patronage of the Podolians, it was based on authentic historical experience, primarily of the 1860s. During the Polish insurrection of 1863–64 in Russia, many Galician Ukrainophiles sympathized with the insurgents, while all Russophiles sympathized with the Russian government and its military. Not long thereafter, in 1869–70, some liberal Ukrainophile leaders, notably Iuliian Lavrivsky and others associated with the periodical *Osnova,* tried to reach a compromise with the Poles and end the Polish-Ruthenian struggle in Galicia.[71] I would identify, further, one more decade in which Ukrainophilism's anti-Polish edge was rather blunted: the 1830s. The Ruthenian Triad asserted its own cultural distinctiveness, but it did not make an issue of opposition to the Poles. Indeed, the members of the Triad relied on a Polish library for information about the Little Russian and all-Slavic world, Shashkevych penned the odd verse in Polish, and, when the moment for political action arrived, Vahylevych cooperated with the Polish camp.

If we consider the pressures of public opinion in 1830s Galicia, we might have a better understanding of why the construction of Ruthenian nationality took the Ukrainian form instead of the all-Russian form at that time. The number of intelligentsia of Ruthenian origin was still small in the 1830s and, of course, almost exclusively clerical. The tone in polite society, to which these members of the new Ruthenian intelligentsia aspired, was set by the Polish gentry. The decade opened with the Polish insurrection of 1830–31 against Russia and its brutal suppression. The climate of public opinion in Galicia was therefore strongly anti-Russian, and Polish national sensitivities were enflamed. It would have been very difficult at that time for members of the fledgling Ruthenian revival to have embraced a pro-Russian, anti-Polish program. Ukrainophilism was a form of Ruthenian nationality construction that was psychologically easier to embrace. Furthermore, in the 1830s there existed a tendency in Polish political and cultural life that allotted space for the Ukrainophile construction; this tendency was

articulated in the emergence of "the Ukrainian school in Polish literature."

In fact, a very similar situation recurred in the 1860s, the second
epiphany of a relatively Polonophile Ruthenian Ukrainophilism.
Again, the Poles in the Russian empire rose in revolt and were brutally
crushed, and Polish patriotic feeling in Galicia ran high. By now, it is
true, the Ruthenian movement had acquired a critical enough mass of
adherents and had gone through enough political wrangling with the
Poles during the revolution so that there were many, indeed the majority of the Ruthenian intelligentsia, who accepted the Russophile program. There were also, however, those Ruthenians who considered
such a political stance indecent. And again, as in the 1830s, the Ukrainophile Ruthenians could find sympathizers in the Polish camp, since
the 1860s produced the Ukrainophile *chłopomani*, primarily Poles of
Right Bank Ukraine, some of whom, such as Paulin Święcicki, settled in
Galicia and took an active part in the revived Ruthenian Ukrainophile
movement.

The point, then, is that links with the Poles worked to promote the
Ruthenian Ukrainophile construction in two of its most crucial
decades, the decade of emergence (1830s) and the decade of revival
(1860s).

There is one final aspect of the politics of Ukrainophilism versus
Russophilism that deserves attention. Ukrainophilism was a more
democratically oriented movement than Russophilism. Ukrainophilism took a positive view of the peasant vernacular and supported the
liberal, democratic Ukrainophile opposition in the Russian empire. As
Ivan Holovatsky wrote (disapprovingly) to his brother Iakiv in 1852,
"These Ukrainians are ready for anything—for the sake of love of the
people" [khakhly na vse gotovy—radi narodoliubiia].[72] Russophilism
also had some democratic tendencies (for example, the activities of
Father Naumovych as publisher of popular literature for the peasantry
and founder of the adult-education Kachkovsky Society). But, ultimately, it both denied that the peasant speech could form the basis of a
legitimate literary language and allied itself with the most reactionary
power in Europe. The founder of the movement, Zubrytsky, was so
reactionary that he defended the institution of serfdom both before and
after its abolition in Galicia in 1848.[73] From the viewpoint of midcentury, it was perhaps not clear whether Europe would evolve in the
direction of democracy or not. By the turn of the century, however, the

victory of the democratic conception seemed assured. Less than two decades later the Russian autocracy would fall. Ukrainophilism was, in short, better situated to ride the wave of all-European political developments than was Russophilism.

We turn now to an exploration of the cultural dimension of the Ukrainian and all-Russian constructions. As generally presented in the Ukrainian historiography, the Ruthenians' cultural choice of a Ukrainian identity was a fully natural choice, in fact, not even a choice, but merely the expression of the preexisting cultural identity. In language, religion, folkways, historical consciousness, the Ruthenians of Galicia were basically the same as other Ukrainians, albeit with certain local variations. This is a viewpoint that cannot withstand sustained criticism, either from the theoretical side (if we accept the theoretical framework of the construction of a new "industrial" national culture) or even from the empirical side (who determines whether Lemko or Ukrainian is a dialect or a language? is the religious difference between Galician Greek Catholicism and Dnieper-Ukrainian Russian Orthodoxy so minimal as to be discounted? are not agricultural settlement patterns radically different in Galicia and Left Bank Ukraine? how common were Cossack *dumy* in Galicia?). Yet, when all is said and done, there is something to the standard Ukrainian argument, particularly with regard to the issue that the national revivals seemed to have cared most about—language. Literary Ukrainian, as it was first formulated by the writers of the Ukrainophile movement in Russian-ruled Ukraine, was almost perfectly intelligible to Galician Ruthenians, educated or not. As the Ukrainophile movement in Galicia itself developed, it contributed to the further refinement of literary Ukrainian, bringing it even closer to the vernaculars spoken in Galicia.[74] Russian was more distant, intelligible to those Ruthenians who had had a higher education, difficult for the rest. A similar case, although not quite as strong, could be made about the correspondence of folkways and historical consciousness (shared Polish past with the Ukrainians of the Russian empire, shared absence of old Muscovite cultural roots), and an only somewhat weaker case could be made with regard to religion (Uniatism and other westernizing tendencies within Orthodoxy as a phenomenon historically shared by Ruthenians and Ukrainians of the Russian empire, absent among the Russians). To put this all more precisely: the Ukrainian construction could accommodate more elements of the preexisting culture(s) of Ruthenian Galicia than could the all-Russian construction.

But there is a rich paradox concealed here. It can be argued that in fact the Ukrainophiles made a much more radical break with linguistic tradition than did the Russophiles, that the Russophiles were truer both to the linguistic traditions of the Ruthenian/Little Russian/Ukrainian people and to the contemporary linguistic practice of the autochthonous population of Dnieper Ukraine. For the fact of the matter is that the Rus' of Galicia and Ukraine traditionally, historically, did not use their vernacular language as a high-cultural, great-traditional linguistic vehicle. For the latter purpose the Rus' of the old Kyivan polity used Church Slavonic in the Bulgarian recension; it was adapted, of course, to the local vernacular, but this vernacular did not figure independently at that time as a written language. After the Polish and Lithuanian conquest of Galicia, Volhynia, Kyiv, and other Ukrainian territories, one finds the Rus' here using Latin, a new (Euthymian) version of Church Slavonic purified of vernacularisms, and Chancery Ruthenian, that is, a form of Belarusian.[75] From the mid–sixteenth century to the end of the eighteenth, the chief literary languages in use on Galician and Ukrainian territory were Latin, Polish, (Meletian) Church Slavonic, and Russian. There was some, very limited use of the written vernacular, the so-called *prostaia mova* ("simple/vulgar language"), but the overwhelming number of texts produced in this region were written in one (and often a mixture of two) of the foreign literary languages. In 1798, the year when the Ukrainian vernacular literary revival began with the publication of Ivan Kotliarevsky's *Eneida,* most Ruthenians in Galicia who had something to write did so in Polish, while their counterparts in the Left Bank did so in Russian. In short, it was traditional for the Ruthenians-Ukrainians to write in a foreign, usually related, literary language and to allot a completely subsidiary role, if any, to the vernacular as a written language. The practice of the Russophiles, who wrote for the educated either in a Russian- and Church Slavonic–influenced, highly "constructed" literary language or else in Russian pure and simple and who only wrote in the vernacular when addressing peasants, was perfectly consonant with the long-established Ruthenian-Ukrainian tradition.[76]

Not only were the Russophiles more consistent continuers of the cultural past than the Ukrainophiles, they were also more "Ukrainian" in their linguistic practices and attitudes. After all, as the Ukrainian historian Mykhailo Maksymovych explained to Zubrytsky in 1840, Russian is the language "in which we speak, write and think, the universal language used in Ukraine among the educated class of the nation."[77] The "industrial" culture of Ukraine, with the partial exception of a small circle of Ukrainophile intellectuals, was Russian. The Galician Russophiles were thus culturally in tune with the Dnieper Ukrainian reality,[78] the Galician Ukrainophiles lived in a dreamworld.[79]

There is another, at first glance quite distinct, point to be made about the cultural, and specifically linguistic, factor in the Ukrainian/all-Russian divide. In the Russophile armament of arguments, there was one that appears quite compelling: namely, that to transform a peasant vernacular into a literary language capable of fulfilling all the functions appropriate to an "industrial" culture was an extremely difficult (in their mind: impossible) task.[80] Undoubtedly, this difficulty had indeed inhibited the emergence and use of the Ruthenian-Ukrainian vernacular as a literary language in centuries past. By adopting (or— outside Galicia in Dnieper Ukraine: retaining) Russian as a literary language, the difficulty disappeared entirely. Of course, the problem with this argument was that, if easier solutions were optimal, then the Galician Ruthenians should really just have continued to use Polish as a higher literary vehicle. In fact, the cultural choice here was a political choice. The Ukrainophiles chose the harder road, the transformation of the vernacular, but it was a road that most European nations had already traversed and it was a road already made straight by the Dnieper Ukrainophiles. The transformation process for the Ukrainian language was unusually encumbered by political obstacles and is still not complete, but I think it is correct to state that, at least as far as Galicia is concerned, the job had in essentials been done by the late 1880s or early 1890s. Certainly the many excellent publications of the Shevchenko Scientific Society in Lviv from the mid-1890s on testify to the elaboration of a language fully suited for modern, "industrial" usage.

We turn now to religion. In the period when the all-Russian and Ukrainian ideas clashed in Galicia, Galicia was Greek Catholic, while both Dnieper Ukraine and Russia were Russian Orthodox. The Russophile movement was, as mentioned earlier, in favor of cleansing the Greek Catholic church of Latin practices, bringing the Greek Catholic ritual as close to Russian Orthodox ritual as possible, and, often ideally and sometimes in practice, converting from Greek Catholicism to Orthodoxy, preferably to Russian Orthodoxy. (In Austria, however, Russian Orthodoxy was not recognized as a legal religion; converts to Orthodoxy generally had to convert to the officially recognized "Greek Oriental" church, administered out of Bukovina and limited to Austria.)

The Russophiles often had important links to the Russian Orthodox clergy and hierarchy; for instance, the chaplain of the Russian embassy in Vienna, Father Mikhail Raevsky, was the main intermediary between Russian pan-Slavists and government circles, on the one hand, and Galician Russophiles, on the other, in the 1840s to 1880s,[81] and the Russian Orthodox bishops of Volhynia and Chełm and the archimandrite of the Pochaiv monastery were deeply involved in supporting Russophile agitation in Galicia in the several years preceding World War I.[82] The Galician Ukrainophiles had no links to speak of with clerics in Dnieper Ukraine or Russia. The Dnieper Ukrainophiles did not, by and large, have much of an interest in religion, and relations between the official church and the Ukrainian movement in the Russian empire were cool. The most prominent representatives of the Dnieper Ukrainian movement were either anti-Catholic and heterodox (Taras Shevchenko) or anti-Catholic, anticlerical, and agnostic (Mykhailo Drahomanov). Some of the Dnieper Ukrainophiles' anticlericalism rubbed off on their Galician counterparts (especially on the radicals). The religious program of the Galician Ukrainophiles was the development of the Greek Catholic church as a national church, free of both Polish and Russian influence.[83]

Since I have presented the argument in so much detail elsewhere,[84] here I will restrict myself to a brief conceptual summary of why the Greek Catholic church eventually became the patron of the Ukrainophile orientation. The key to this lay in Rome, which succeeded in reasserting more direct control over the Greek Catholic church in the period 1882–99. Rome's viewpoint was very similar to that of Vienna's, with which it cooperated closely in regard to Ruthenian affairs. Like Vienna, Rome was generally cool to Ukrainophilism, but it considered Russophilism the greater evil. Both tendencies, in the assessment of the Vatican and its closest collaborators and supporters among the Galician clergy and hierarchy, suffered from the error of viewing a divine institution, the Church, instrumentally, as a national institution. They put the interests of the nation before those of God's Church. Russophilism, moreover, exposed the Ruthenians to the dangers of schism, Ukrainophilism exposed them to religious indifference and even agnosticism. In Rome's judgment, the former danger seemed greater, probably because of the conjuncture (Rome was moved to intervene at a time when Russophilism was the dominant orientation), strategic consider-ations (agnostics and their children could be won back to the church more easily than defectors who ended up in a different confessional structure), and the calculation that pro-Orthodox sympathies were more inherent in Russophilism than religious indifference was in Ukrainophilism. Very telling was the position of the reformed Basilian order, which was instituted to promote the Vatican line in Galician Rus'; although it shunned demonstrations of Ukrainian patriotism and stayed away from Ukrainophile politics, it consistently employed the Ukrainian language and in other ways was culturally close to the Ukrainophile orientation.

The social differences between adherents of the all-Russian idea and adherents of the Ukrainian idea were not substantial, nothing on the order of the social difference that separated the Polish gentry and burghers from the Ruthenian clergy and peasants. Both movements consisted of a leadership of clerical and secular intelligentsia and a mass following of peasantry. However, there may have been important nuances of difference that only detailed prosopographic analysis of lists (membership in representative organizations, subscribers to peri-odicals) would reveal.[85]

As to larger social factors influencing the outcome of the struggle between Russophilism and Ukrainophilism, I would single out as pre-eminent the emancipation of the peasantry in 1848 and its subsequent transformation (particularly its adoption of an "operational" cognitive style).[86] This certainly aided the Ukrainophile movement, which relied heavily on developing a mass base of support in the countryside, but was less important for the irredentist, and socially more conservative, Russophiles.

It is appropriate to conclude this survey of the rivalry between the two most viable constructions of nationality in Galician Rus' by offer-ing some larger, if somewhat speculative, perspectives on the issue. The exploration undertaken above suggests that there was no inevitability in the victory of the Ukrainophile orientation in Galicia and, in particular, that there was no inevitability based simply on the preexisting culture of Galician Rus', that is, that this particular ethnie had to develop into this particular nation. Rather, many contingencies were at work, although some loomed larger than others. Elsewhere I have played with historical might-have-beens and suggested that had

Russia occupied Galicia in 1878 (in connection with the international crisis over the Balkans) the Ukrainian game would have been over not only for Galician Rus' but for Dnieper Ukraine as well.[87] Here I will suggest what I think is an even more compelling scenario: imagine if, as a result of the territorial reshuffling in eastern Europe between 1772 and 1815, Russia had ended up not with the Congress Kingdom of Poland, but with Eastern Galicia. This is not such a far-fetched idea, since Russia did acquire southeastern Eastern Galicia (Ternopil circle) temporarily during the Napoleonic period (1809–15). What would have happened then? We can surmise much of it: no enlightened-absolutist-sponsored centralized education to create a national intelligentsia rapidly, the abolition of the Greek Catholic church and its integration into Russian Orthodoxy, an extra decade of serfdom, the prohibition of the Ukrainian vernacular with no "Galician Piedmont" to help save the day, less primary education and that strictly in Russian, no constitutional framework and civil liberties, effective Russian state support in the struggle against the local Polish gentry, no distant Vienna or Rome to rule occasionally in favor of the Ukrainian orientation—the list could go on. I find it difficult to imagine that the innate Ukrainian spirit of the Galician Ruthenians was so irrepressible that Ukrainophilism would have been able in such conditions to carry the day. Ultimately, I think, the crucial factor in the victory of Ukrainophilism in Galician Rus' was the Austrian state. In other words, a major determinant in the cultural choice of national identity emanated from the political sphere.

Hypothetical Constructions: "Rusynism" and "Ruthenianism"

The final section of this study concerns two hypothetical constructions of nationality for Galician Rus', one actually more hypothetical than the other, which I will call Rusynism and Ruthenianism. By Rusynism[88] I mean a conception of Galician Rus' nationality that was narrowly local, either limited to Galicia alone or to Galicia and the other Ruthenian-inhabited territories of the Habsburg monarchy (Bukovina and Transcarpathia/Subcarpathia/Hungarian Rus'). By Ruthenianism I mean a construction that would include Galician Ruthenians in a nationality composed of those Eastern Slavs who had lived in the Polish-Lithuanian Commonwealth in the early modern period, that is, today's Ukrainians and Belarusians (the Russians would be excluded). We will examine the two constructs in turn, again filing our observations under categories labeled political, cultural, religious, and social.

The less hypothetical of the two is Rusynism, which has existed and indeed has received a new lease on life since 1989 in Transcarpathia and (to a lesser extent) in the western, Lemko regions of Galicia.[89] In Eastern Galicia Rusynophilism never crystallized into an orientation *für sich*, although certain Rusynophile tendencies in the Galician-Ruthenian national movement emerged from time to time. One might, for instance, characterize the behavior of the Ruthenian national leadership in 1848–49 as Rusynophile *an sich*. After the revolution, highly placed clerics within that national leadership formed a loose grouping known as the Old Ruthenian or St. George party.[90] The Old Ruthenians were, in some respects, analogous to the Rusynophiles of Transcarpathia, although they were not very locally oriented; for example, they were vague about the ultimate national allegiance of the Galician Ruthenians rather than insistent (as the Rusynophiles of Transcarpathia are) that the Carpathian Rus' people constitute a fourth East Slavic nationality and they never tried (as the Transcarpathian and Lemko Rusynophiles do) to create a new literary language based on local dialect(s). But they did reject both the Russophile and Ukrainophile constructions, the latter more decisively than the former. As a distinct tendency, they lasted into the 1870s, but were eventually absorbed into the Russophile and Ukrainophile camps. The left-wing Dnieper Ukrainophile Mykhailo Drahomanov discerned a strong undercurrent of what I am calling Rusynism and he called *rutenshchina* in Galician Ruthenian society of the mid-1870s, that is, the proliferation among the intelligentsia of what he termed "individuals of the Austro-Seminarian-Ruthenian nationality" (*individuumy avstro-bursako-russkoi narodnosti*).[91] It is a current little in evidence thereafter, having evaporated in the heat of the polemics between proponents of the all-Russian and Ukrainian ideas.

Why did Rusynism fail to crystallize in Galicia, or at least in Eastern Galicia? The most effective way to answer that question is to look less at Eastern Galicia than at the territories where it did in fact crystallize. But *caveat lector*. The subject of Rusynism among the Transcarpathians and Lemkos is a highly controversial one at the moment.[92] Certainly scholars have reached no consensus; so far what has been achieved is that two camps have been clearly delineated (pro-Rusyn and pro-Ukrainian). Normally one would steer clear of mined terrain like this in a scholarly investigation not directly concerned with the specific topos of the current polemics, but I think there is no choice if we want to explore the intellectual territory we have set out to explore. I recognize that the interpretation I will offer of Transcarpathian and Lemkian Rusynism will dissatisfy many who are engaged in the current debate. It is not intended to be a full explanation of the phenomenon in those places where it took root; the point here is only to identify factors that might explain its absence in Galicia.

The major reason I see for the emergence of Rusynism where it did emerge is political. Ukrainophilism was weak, almost nonexistent in these territories until after World War I. Instead, the dominant national orientations among the intelligentsia here were the Magyarone orientation (*natione Hungarus, gente Ruthenus;* that is, Hungarian as far as political consciousness and high culture was concerned, with some room for an oral Ruthenian vernacular, colorful ethnographic peculiarities, and *Lokalpatriotismus*) in Transcarpathia and the Russophile orientation in both Transcarpathia and the Lemko region. Both of these orientations were anti-Ukrainian. Russophilism was, so to speak, structurally anti-Ukrainian, while the anti-Ukrainian edge of Magyaronism developed by the turn of the century as a result of the Hungarian concern over the danger of Galician Ukrainophile influences spreading to Transcarpathia, especially via Transcarpathian immigrants in the United States. Both Magyaronism and Russophilism, however, suffered a major political defeat at the end of World War I when both Greater Hungary and the Russian empire collapsed. The new political situation allowed the Ukrainian idea to make some inroads into these territories, particularly into Transcarpathia. However, an anti-Ukrainian sense of Ruthenian identity, with both Magyarone and Russophile roots, continued to exist and now took the form of Rusynophilism, that is, a localism produced by the exclusion of preferred wider alternatives and by the rejection of the one wider alternative left.

Although I consider what has been sketched in the preceding paragraph to be the crucial factor in the crystallization of Rusynism, I will also mention two subsidiary political factors. First, in the interwar era, the governments ruling these territories found it in their interests to promote local national identities. The Lemko region passed under Polish rule after the collapse of Austria-Hungary. The Polish government deliberately fostered national division among its large Ruthenian-Ukrainian minority, establishing the so-called Sokal border to prevent

Galician Ukrainian influences from penetrating into Volhynia and Polissia, cultivating the local consciousness of the Ukrainians and Belarusians of Polissia *(tutejsi)*, and funding the lingering Russophile/revived-Old-Ruthenian institutions in Galicia. It also nurtured a consciousness of separate Lemko identity, pressuring the Vatican to establish a separate Lemko Apostolic Administration in 1934 and introducing the Lemko dialect into primary schools. The government of Czechoslovakia, which inherited Transcarpathia (both Transcarpathia proper and the Prešov region) from Hungary, did not meddle so obtrusively in the debate over national identity, but by the mid-1930s it too was favoring Rusynophilism as the orientation more consistent with the interests of the Czechoslovak state, especially in the context of increasingly pro-German attitudes in the Ukrainian nationalist camp.

The second subsidiary political factor working in favor of Rusynophilism was that the Ukrainian orientation was imported into Transcarpathia by some strange bedfellows who came to be viewed with distaste by large sections of the population: Communists and Galician Ukrainian nationalists. The role of Communists in promoting the Ukrainian idea in Transcarpathia was twofold: first, beginning in the era of Ukrainization and *korenizatsiia* (the 1920s) Soviet Communists insisted that Communists in Transcarpathia, where the party was quite influential, promote a Ukrainian national identity; second, when Stalin annexed Transcarpathia (excluding the Prešov region) in 1945, he placed it in the Ukrainian Soviet Socialist Republic and imposed upon it an official socialist-in-content, but Ukrainian-in-form culture. The association of the Ukrainian national identity with Communism and with Communist methods of promoting it discredited it in the eyes of some, particularly after 1989. As for the Galician nationalists, they swooped down into Transcarpathia during the Munich era and tried to move too much too fast. Moreover, as the experience of the Galician and Transcarpathian communities in the United States of America has shown, each of these communities has its own particular cultural style, and they do not take to each other very well.

To rephrase the main political point with reference to Galicia: Rusynism did not crystallize there because the Ukrainophile current had already become hegemonic before the interwar era, when the circumstances of international politics became favorable to Rusynism.

As for the cultural sphere, we must again underscore the fact that Ukrainophilism was very weak or absent in these territories before

World War I. Transcarpathia, moreover, which had known Hungarian rule for close to a millennium, even lay outside the Polish-Russian environment, in the confrontation with which Ukrainophilism worked out its self-definition. As a result, Transcarpathia (and Russophile Lemkovina as well) did not participate in the cultural construction of the Ukrainian nationality. This was work begun at the initiative of Left Bank and Sloboda Ukraine (Kharkiv), with their recent Cossack heritage, and continued with the participation of the Right Bank and (Ukrainophile) Galicia. Transcarpathia and the Lemko regions were objects, but not subjects of the construction process.[93] Unlike Galicia, they had no input into the formation of the standard literary Ukrainian language.[94] No Transcarpathian or Lemko entered the Ukrainian national pantheon anywhere near at the levels attained by Galicians such as Ivan Franko or Metropolitan Andrei Sheptytsky. The most famous awakeners of Transcarpathia, Father Aleksandr Dukhnovych and Adolf Dobriansky, were too closely associated with Russophilism to even gain entrance to the courtyard of the national temple. In short, Eastern Galicia did, but Transcarpathia and the Lemko region did not, take part in the construction of the Ukrainian identity during the main period of its construction. The apparition of Carpatho-Ukraine in 1938–39 and the activities of the Ukrainian Insurgent Army in the Lemko region at the end of and after World War II do figure rather prominently in Ukrainian nationalist mythology, but they came, as is said in Eastern Europe, like mustard after dinner. In essence, the Galicians were stakeholders in the Ukrainian construction, the Transcarpathians and Lemkos were not.

Mention should also be made of a "technical," objective cultural difficulty with Rusynism that seems to have inhibited its development: apparently, it is very difficult to work up a Rusyn literary language. As has been noted, the Galician Old Ruthenians did not even attempt to write in dialect.[95] The Rusynophiles of Transcarpathia are struggling with the formation of a literary language to this very day. Undoubtedly, this is a technical problem on the road to solution, but the time and the form the solution is taking suggests that the Rusynophile activists are running up against a particularly tricky version of the problem of developing a standard language out of variegated vernacular dialects.[96] A glance at a dialectological map suggests why.[97] Over most of Ukraine there are a few dialects spread over fairly large expanses of territory. For example, in the area covered by the Steppe dialect one could fit several Galicias. But in the Carpathian region alone there are more dialects than in the rest of Ukraine combined. Perhaps here is a technical cultural reason for the attraction of Ukrainophilism: it presents a simplified, but intelligible linguistic system.

I do not see any particular religious factor contributing to the development or lack of development of Rusynism. It is interesting to note, however, that the common Uniatism of the Carpathian region (excluding Bukovina) was rarely invoked as a rallying point for a common Rusyn identity. Responsible for this absence, I suspect, are the Russophile roots of Rusynism and also the (related) circumstance that Rusynophilism emerged and consolidated during and immediately after a period when many Ruthenians in emigration in North America and at home in Polish Lemkovina and Czechoslovakian Transcarpathia were abandoning the Greek Catholic church for Orthodoxy.

Of social factors I have even less to say, except that Galicia and Transcarpathia developed at different rates. There was a proportionately much larger Galician than Transcarpathian Ruthenian intelligentsia, and the Galician peasantry underwent a much more fundamental political and cultural transformation before World War I than did the Transcarpathian peasantry.

Our last case, that of "Ruthenianism," is completely hypothetical, and we cannot compare it to any existing "Ruthenianism" outside Galicia. The name I have chosen to represent this hypothetical Ukrainian-Belarusian construction may be a bit confusing, considering that I have been using the term *Ruthenian* in a somewhat different sense, as a neutral term to designate the East Slavic population of Galicia. But *Ruthenian* in the Ukrainian-Belarusian sense has also entered English-language scholarship to designate the peoples of the Eastern Christian churches and the churches themselves within the Polish-Lithuanian Commonwealth. It therefore seems like the least artificial, and hence most appropriate, name to use in reference to a conception that would have re-created "Ruthenians" in that second sense. In order to avoid confusion, I will, for the remainder of this section, replace *Ruthenian* in the first sense with *Galician-Ruthenian;* when using the term in the second sense I will place it within quotation marks.

In order to propose a hypothetical construction of nationality, it is first necessary to demonstrate that there is a certain reasonableness about it. The fundamental elements of both Belarusian and Ukrainian culture developed in the course of their shared history within the

Kyivan Rus' polity. The same can be said of Russian culture, but in the mid–fourteenth century the Belarusians and Ukrainians went along one historical path, the Russians along another. Belarus and most of Ukraine passed under Lithuanian rule, Galicia under Polish rule, at a time when the Polish and Lithuanian states were entering into a close partnership (Union of Krevo [Krewo], 1385). The ancestors of the Ukrainians and Belarusians under Lithuanian rule shared a common literary-administrative language, the Belarusian-based Chancery Ruthenian. Even after all Ukrainian lands were transferred to the Polish part of the Polish-Lithuanian Commonwealth, as a result of the Union of Lublin in 1569, the Ukrainians and Belarusians, or "Ruthenians," "were viewed as one cultural-linguistic-religious community."[98] The "Ruthenians" of both branches accepted the Union of Brest, 1595–96, that is, the church union with Roman Catholicism, although the Belarusian branch did so more fully than the Ukrainian branch. Both branches participated in the "Ruthenian" cultural revival of the sixteenth century. Many prominent figures in East Slavic religion and culture of the early modern era worked in so "Ruthenian" a context that it is difficult to establish to which of the later much more clearly differentiated Ukrainian and Belorussian cultural spheres they belonged: St. Iosafat Kuntsevych was born in Volhynia but made his ecclesiastical career in Vilnius and Polatsk; his close collaborator Metropolitan Iosyf Rutsky was born in Belarus, became metropolitan of Kyiv, died in a monastery in Volhynia, and was buried in Vilnius; Simeon Polotsky was born in Belarus, studied in both Kyiv and Vilnius, worked mainly in Moscow, and felt most at home intellectually in the company of Ukrainian churchmen. By the end of the eighteenth century, both Belarus and most of Ukraine again found themselves in one polity, the Russian empire. Here the Belarusians and Ukrainians shared the same problem of national differentiation vis-à-vis the Poles to the west and the Russians to the east. The Belarusians and Ukrainians are closely related linguistically. Both are East Slavic languages that, unlike Russian, were heavily influenced by Polish. There is a dialectical region transitional between Ukrainian and Belarusian.[99] Both of their standard literary languages followed the same pattern of development, that is, the transformation of an oral vernacular into a literary vehicle (unlike Russian, which developed from a foreign literary language, Church Slavonic, that gradually incorporated more and more elements of the vernacular).[100] I think, then, that it would have been logical to construct a national identity that fell between the all-Russian and Ukrainian construction, a "Ruthenian" identity that embraced both the Belarusians and Ukrainians (including the Galician-Ruthenians). Yet I have never encountered so much as a trace of such a "Ruthenian" conception in the writings of Galician-Ruthenians.

Why not? A number of things that happened in the early modern era, and particularly the Khmelnytsky uprising, seem to have determined the ultimate differentiation of the Ukrainian and Belarusian nations.[101] But for our purposes, the question has to be looked at from the perspective of the Galician-Ruthenians in the era of national construction.

In the political category, the predominant fact is that the Belarusians were a political nullity. Their national movement began decades after that of the Galician-Ruthenians and was always weak, politically and in other respects. One of the important consequences of the Cossack uprising led by Khmelnytsky was the emergence of a Cossack polity, the hetmanate, which generated a Little Russian gentry, which was able to inaugurate a relatively dynamic national movement a generation earlier than even the Galician-Ruthenians were.[102] The Dnieper Ukrainophiles, as has been argued earlier, represented a political force, not a political force of the Russian or even Polish magnitude, but a force nonetheless; the Belarusians constituted no political force at all.

There were some cultural obstacles to the elaboration of a common "Ruthenian" nationality, although not as great as those which adherents of the Russophile nationality had to overcome. None of the potential foci of unity were free of problems. Let us take language as an example. It is conceivable that just as a Czechoslovak literary language might have come into existence on the basis of a Moravian dialect so too a "Ruthenian" literary language could have emerged on the basis of a transitional dialect spoken in Polissia. In actual fact, the central dialects of Belarusian and the southeastern dialects of Ukrainian formed the basis of the respective literary languages.[103] Central dialects in Belarusian bridged the divergences between the northeastern and southwestern dialects; the southeastern dialects of Ukrainian were spoken in the former hetmanate (Left Bank Ukraine) and Sloboda Ukraine where the Ukrainian national revival started. Hypothetically again, had the Cossacks somehow been based in Polissia instead of in the steppe, the chances of forming a common "Ruthenian" language (and nation) would have been improved. However, the phonetic evolutions of Belarusian and Ukrainian are really quite diverse—where the Belarusians soften, the Ukrainians harden, while the Belarusians change many Common Slavic *o*-sounds to *a*, Ukrainians change many to *i*. Even without the formation of separate literary languages, in other words, the two groups of dialects have followed very different paths of linguistic evolution. One can imagine overcoming the differences by devising special characters that could be pronounced both ways and one can also imagine that on the level of the new high culture the new "Ruthenians" could have overcome their folk prejudices against the way the others spoke, but the solutions would have been cumbersome and taken time.

The common history of Uniatism could have served as an important religious bond between Galician-Ruthenians and Belarusians if attachment to the church union had been less ambivalent in Galicia and, I think more importantly, if the timing of certain events had been more propitiously synchronized. The Belarusians accepted the union in 1595–96, the Galician-Ruthenians about a century later (depending on the particular locality and institution); more decisively, the union was abolished in Belarus in 1839, that is, very early in the development of the Galician-Ruthenian national movement.

Finally, as to social factors, one must note an even greater disparity in the transformation of the two societies, Galician-Ruthenian and Belarusian, than was the case for the Galician-Ruthenians and Transcarpathian Ruthenians. The Belarusians had even a smaller educated class and a peasantry even less affected by modern cultural and economic change than the Transcarpathians.[104]

Conclusions

There were in Galician Rus', as the subtitle of this article states, Icarian flights in almost all directions. The highest Icarian flight was that of the Russophiles; flights in the direction of Rusynism and "Ruthenianism" were not undertaken; the flight of the Ukrainophiles proved not to be Icarian at all. As this exploration of the alternative constructions of nationality in Galician Rus' indicates, the reasons for the choice of one construction over another were manifold and the interrelationships among them complex. Do any factors seem to emerge as primary?

The Galician Ruthenians were not, of course, the only people of

East Central Europe to confront the problem of alternative national constructions. One has only to recall Illyrism and Yugoslavism among the South Slavs, Czechoslovakism, and the contest between the all-German and Austrian ideas to realize that the phenomenon was relatively widespread. A moment's reflection on these same examples would also seem to confirm a point that I think suggests itself as well from the detailed investigation of the Galician Ruthenian situation: that, in spite of the complexity and variety of factors entering into the process, the primary determinant of the construction of a national culture was political.

NOTES

1. E. J. Hobsbawm, *Nations and Nationalism since 1780: Programme, Myth, Reality* (Cambridge: Cambridge University Press, 1990), 1–5.

2. Emil Niederhauser, *The Rise of Nationality in Eastern Europe* (Gyoma: Corvina Kiadó, 1981).

3. Ernest Gellner, *Nations and Nationalism* (Ithaca, N.Y.: Cornell University Press, 1983).

4. A locus classicus of the old literature: "A nation is a historically evolved, stable community of people, formed on the basis of a common language, territory, economic life and psychological make-up manifested in a common culture." J. Stalin, *Marxism and the National Question* (Calcutta: New Book Centre, 1975), 11.

5. From the foreword to the landmark publication of the Ruthenian cultural revival of the early nineteenth century: "We too had our bards and our teachers, but tempests and storms came upon us; our bards and teachers went dumb, and our people and our literature nodded off for a long time." *Rusalka Dnistrovaia: Ruthenische Volks-Lieder* (Buda: Pys'mom Korol. Vseuchylyshcha Peshtanskoho, 1837), iv.

6. "Awakeners? Yes. Because they set out in the firm belief, which can be verified in hundreds of manifestos, that the 'nation'—which always existed, or at least for centuries—still existed, but was asleep, people who made up this as yet subject nationality as a whole had not yet become conscious of its existence. They had to be awakened, everyone had to be made aware that they were part of a distinct nationality. Once awake, they could not fail to discover the truth about themselves, that they were indeed everything that the 'awakeners' had already known and proclaimed."

"Today, of course, we fully realize that things were very different. The sense of nationality, as they imagined it, or as they saw it elsewhere, was only just emerging. It had not slumbered in Eastern Europe; it had not existed!" Niederhauser, *Rise of Nationality*, 43–44.

7. "The basic deception and self-deception practised by nationalism is

this: nationalism is, essentially, the general imposition of a high culture on society, where previously low cultures had taken up the lives of the majority, and in some cases of the totality, of the population. . . . That is what really happens.

"But this is the very opposite of what nationalism affirms and what nationalists fervently believe. Nationalism usually conquers in the name of a putative folk culture. . . . If the nationalism prospers it eliminates the alien high culture, but it does not then replace it by the old local low culture; it revives, or invents, a local high (literate, specialist-transmitted) culture of its own, though admittedly one which will have some links with the earlier local folk styles and dialects." Gellner, *Nations and Nationalism,* 57.

8. Benedict Anderson, *Imagined Communities: Reflections on the Origin and Spread of Nationalism* (London: Verso, 1983).

9. "Admittedly, nationalism uses the pre-existing, historically inherited proliferation of cultures or cultural wealth, though it uses them very selectively, and it most often transforms them radically." Gellner, *Nations and Nationalism,* 55.

10. Descriptions of the tradition can be found in Robert T. Anderson and Gallatin Anderson, "Ukrainian Night Courting," *Anthropological Quarterly* 35, no. 1 (1962): 29–32. Owing to methodological weaknesses, the article underestimates the prevalence of night courting in the Ukrainian village. For a corrective, see Z. A. Hurevych and A. I. Vorozhbyt, *Stateve zhyttia selianky* (n.p.: DVOU, Medvydav, 1931), 41–52.

11. "Indeed, more often than not the discovery of popular tradition and its transformation into the 'national tradition' of some peasant people forgotten by history, was the work of enthusiasts from the (foreign) ruling class or elite, such as the Baltic Germans or the Finnish Swedes." Hobsbawm, *Nations and Nationalism,* 104.

12. In *Nations and Nationalism,* 58–62, Gellner works on the theoretical side of this question by developing the model of the Ruritanians and the Megalomanians. Although based on the concrete case of the Romanians and Hungarians of Transylvania, the model applies in essentials also to the case of the Ruthenians and Poles of Galicia.

13. See Frank Sysyn, "The Problem of Nobilities in the Ukrainian Past: The Polish Period, 1569–1648," in *Rethinking Ukrainian History,* ed. Ivan L. Rudnytsky (Edmonton: Canadian Institute of Ukrainian Studies, 1981), esp. 29–30, 55, 65.

14. John-Paul Himka, "The Conflict between the Secular and the Religious Clergy in Eighteenth-Century Western Ukraine," *Harvard Ukrainian Studies* 15, nos. 1–2 (1991): 35–47.

15. In 1900, 29,327 inhabitants of Lviv were Catholics of the Greek rite, but only 15,159 were Ukrainian-speaking. The Greek rite was a marker of Ruthenian ethnicity that could only be altered with some difficulty, since change of rite was regulated by the ecclesiastical authorities. Language, however, could be changed at will. The statistics thus indicate the tremendous assimilative power of the Polish urban environment. *Gemeindelexikon der im Reichsrate vertretenen Königreiche und Länder. Bearbeitet auf Grund der Ergebnisse der Volkszählung vom*

31. Dezember 1900, herausgegeben von der k.k. statistischen Zentralkommission, vol. 12: *Galizien* (Vienna, 1907), 2.

16. E. Kossak [Prawdolub], *Odpowiedź na historyę "o unii kościoła grec. kat. ruskiego" przez Michała Malinowskiego, kanonika świętojurskiego we Lwowie, w 1862 r. wydana* (Lviv: Z drukarni M.F. Poremby, 1863), 29–30.

17. In 1827 a Greek Catholic pastor donated sixty-three books to his parish library. Rather typically, thirty-one of the books were in Latin, twenty-six in Polish, and only four in Ruthenian or Old Church Slavonic (one was in Czech, one in German). Tsentral'nyi derzhavnyi istorychnyi arkhiv Ukrainy v m. L'vovi, f. 201, op. 1a, od. zh. 182, 68–69.

18. Jan Kozik, *The Ukrainian National Movement in Galicia: 1815–1849*, ed. Lawrence D. Orton (Edmonton: Canadian Institute of Ukrainian Studies, 1986), 344.

19. Peter Brock, "Ivan Vahylevych (1811–1866) and the Ukrainian National Identity," in *Nationbuilding and the Politics of Nationalism: Essays on Austrian Galicia*, ed. Andrei S. Markovits and Frank E. Sysyn (Cambridge, Mass.: Harvard Ukrainian Research Institute, 1982), 143.

20. The address goes on to make the point that in the cities "the Ruthenian language is never used. . . . the [urban] population, without regard to descent and religion, exclusively uses the Polish language." *Die Revolutionsjahre 1848/49 im Königreich Galizien-Lodomerien (einschliesslich Bukowina)*, ed. Rudolf Wagner (Munich: Verlag "Der Südostdeutscher," 1983), 59.

21. John-Paul Himka, "German Culture and the National Awakening in Western Ukraine before the Revolution of 1848," in *German-Ukrainian Relations in Historical Perspective*, ed. Hans-Joachim Torke and John-Paul Himka (Edmonton: Canadian Institute of Ukrainian Studies, 1994), 29–44.

22. Only three were to be found among the 275 individuals who belonged to the fairly representative Ruthenian voluntary association Prosvita in 1868–74: Władysław Walenty Fedorowicz, Teofil Merunowicz, and Paulin Święcicki. "Chleny tovarystva 'Prosvita,'" *Spravozdanie z dilanii "Prosvity" vid chasu zaviazania tovarystva—26. Lystopada 1868 roku, do nainoviishoho chasu* (Lviv, 1874), 26–32.

23. Kasper Cięglewicz, *Rzecz czerwono-ruska 1848 roku* ([Lviv:] W drukarni nar. Im. Ossolinskich, [1848]), 5.

24. Wagner, *Die Revolutionsjahre 1848/49*, 59.

25. An authentic exception is the case of the Albanians, who include both Roman Catholics and Orthodox. However, this is a group so linguistically distinct from all surrounding peoples that it includes not only Christians of both heritages, but even Muslims, who in fact constitute the majority of the nationality. There are also Hungarians and Poles of the Greek rite, although in both cases the vast majority is linked to the Western Christian tradition. Unlike the Albanian case, these cases represent the assimilation into the traditionally dominant national culture of elements from the traditionally subjugated national groups (Romanians and Ruthenians); the erection of a Hungarian Greek Catholic eparchy in the early twentieth century was inspired by Hungarian nationalism. On the latter, see James Niessen, "Hungarians and Romanians in

Habsburg and Vatican Diplomacy: The Creation of the Diocese of Hajdúdorog in 1912," *Catholic Historical Review* 80, no. 2 (1994): 238–57.

26. I have dealt with the impact of centralized education (in its Gellnerian conceptualization) on the Ruthenian clergy and on Ruthenian society in general and also have estimated the size of the Ruthenian secular intelligentsia over the course of the nineteenth century in "Stratificazione sociale e movimento nazionale ucraino nella Galizia dell'Ottocento," *Quaderni storici* 28, no. 3 (84) (1993): 657–78.

27. Moreover: "The marginal position of priests' sons in a semi-feudal society which provided no special niche for *Catholic* clerical *families* constituted an obvious social-psychological incentive for asserting separate ethnic identity." John A. Armstrong, "Myth and History in the Evolution of Ukrainian Consciousness," in *Ukraine and Russia in Their Historical Encounter*, ed. Peter J. Potichnyj et al. (Edmonton: Canadian Institute of Ukrainian Studies Press, University of Alberta, 1992), 133.

28. There is a vast, largely antiquated and polemical, literature on the liquidation of the Chełm Uniate eparchy. A relatively recent, scholarly treatment is Luigi Glinka, *Diocesi ucraino-cattolica di Cholm (Liquidazione ed incorporazione alla Chiesa russo-ortodossa (Sec. XIX)*, Analecta OSBM, series 2, sectio 1: Opera, 34 (Rome: PP. Basiliani, 1975). New work is being done: Theodore R. Weeks, "The 'End' of the Uniate Church in Russia: The *Vozsoedinenie* of 1875," *Jahrbücher für Geschichte Osteuropas* 44, no. 1 (1996): 28–40.

29. Volodymyr Okhrymovych, "Z polia natsional'noi statystyky Halychyny," *Studii z polia suspil'nykh nauk i statystyky* (Lviv), 1 (1909): 67.

30. *Encyclopedia of Ukraine*, ed. Volodymyr Kubijovyč and Danylo Husar Struk, 5 vols. (Toronto: University of Toronto Press, 1984–93), s.v. "Armenians" by B. Struminsky.

31. Atanasii V. Pekar, *Narysy istorii tserkvy Zakarpattia*, vol. 1: *Ierarkhichne oformlennia*, Analecta OSBM, series 2, sectio 1: Opera, 22 (Rome: PP. Basiliani, 1967).

32. This is from a list of books that the three of them borrowed from the Ossolineum Library in Lviv from December 1, 1832 to October 8, 1836: "*Rusalka Dnistrova*": Dokumenty i materialy, ed. F. I. Steblii et al. (Kyiv: Naukova dumka, 1989), 18–51.

33. John Breuilly, *Nationalism and the State* (Chicago: University of Chicago Press, 1985), 90.

34. Well summarized in Kozik, *Ukrainian National Movement*, 29–50.

35. Brock, "Ivan Vahylevych," 119.

36. Brock, "Ivan Vahylevych," 143.

37. Roman Szporluk, "Ukraine: From an Imperial Periphery to a Sover- X ६£7 · eign State," *Daedalus* 126, no. 3 (1997): 85–119.

38. A comprehensive exposition of the Russophile viewpoint on language is [Ioann Naumovych], "Iz Stril'cha. (O vnesenii O. Iakymovycha na poslidnem zasidanii Matytsy russkoi chto-do vybora odnoho diialekta russkogo dlia vysshoi lyteratury)," *Slovo* 10, nos. 82–85, 87 (1870).

39. The most representative "all-Russian" historical surveys produced

from the Russophile perspective are [Bohdan Didytskii,] "Narodnaia istoriia Rusy," serialized in *Halychanyn: Naukovo-beletrystychnaia pryloha do "Slova"* in 1867–70 (and also published separately), and Roman Surmach [Iieronym A. Lutsyk], *Narodnaia istoriia Rusy ot naidavniishykh vremen do nynishnykh dnei . . .* (New York: Ivan Hr. Borukh, 1911). The major Russophile interpretation of Galicia and Bukovina during the Austrian period is Filipp Ivanovich Svistun, *Prikarpatskaia Rus' pod vladeniem Avstrii*, 2d ed. (reprint, Trumbull, Conn.: Peter S. Hardy, 1970).

40. *Rusalka Dnistrovaia*, iv–vi.

41. Levytsky's grammar, published in 1834, was entitled *Grammatik der Ruthenischen oder Klein Russischen Sprache in Galizien*; Lozynsky's, published in 1846, was entitled *Gramatyka języka ruskiego (małoruskiego)*.

42. Proclamation of August 25, 1848, reprinted in Wagner, *Die Revolutionsjahre 1848/49*, 51.

43. Ivan Hushalevych published a bit of Mykola Kostomarov and Kotliarevsky in his periodicals *Novyny* and *Pchola* respectively. Ivan Borysikevych published Kvitka-Osnovianenko's *Marusia* separately. Kyrylo Blonsky planned to publish Kotliarevsky's *Eneida*, but did not. That was the sum total of such activity in 1848–49. Several plays by Ukrainian authors were, however, staged in Galicia in the revolutionary years. Ivan Em. Levyts'kyi, *Halytsko-ruskaia bybliohrafiia XIX-ho stolitiia s uvzhliadneniiem ruskykh izdanii poiavyvshykhsia v Uhorshchyni i Bukovyni (1801–1886)*, 2 vols. (Lviv: Stavropyhiiskii instytut, 1888–95), 1:30–50; Kozik, *Ukrainian National Movement*, 320–21.

44. The most amusing instance was the confusion of Markiian Shashkevych's pseudonym "Ruslan" with the German word for Russia, *Russland*. [Kyrylo Studyns'kyi,] *Prychynky do istorii kul'turnoho zhytia Halyts'koi Rusy v litakh 1833–47*, Vidbytka z XI i XII tomu Zbirnyka fil'ol'ogichnoi sektsii Naukovoho tovarystva im. Shevchenka (Lviv, 1909), xv–xvii, cxxvi.

45. There is a very recent exception, confirming, on the basis of newly discovered archival materials and a closer examination of publications, that the popularity of Russophilism during the revolutionary period was much greater than has been hitherto thought: Oleh Turii, "Halyts'ki rusyny: mizh moskvofil'stvom i ukrainstvom (50-i—poch. 60-kh rr.)," typescript. (Turii intends to publish a series of articles on this theme under a similar title in the yearbook of the Institute for Historical Research in Lviv; letter from Turii to the author, January 13, 1995.)

46. The leaflet was entitled "Deutsche Brüder!" dated August 23, 1848, and signed "Allgemeine Stimme der Ruthenen in Galizien." It is reprinted in Wagner, *Die Revolutionsjahre 1848/49*, 44–47.

47. See *Korespondentsyia Iakova Holovats'koho v litakh 1850–1862*, ed. Kyrylo Studyns'kyi; Zbirnyk fil'ol'ogichnoi sektsyi Naukovoho tovarystva imeny Shevchenka 8–9 (Lviv, 1905), iii–x.

48. Paul Robert Magocsi, "The Kachkovs'kyi Society and the National Revival in Nineteenth-Century East Galicia," *Harvard Ukrainian Studies* 15, nos. 1–2 (1991): 48–87.

49. Oksana Rybak, "Pershi zhinochi orhanizatsii u Skhidnii Halychyni i

Pivnichnii Bukovyni," *Ukraina v mynulomu* 1 (Kyiv-Lviv: Akademiia nauk Ukrainy, Instytut ukrains'koi arkheohrafii, 1992), 102–3.

50. Often cited, less frequently read, the most important Russophile statement on the political implications of Austria's constitutional rearrangement was Ioann Naumovych [Odyn imenem mnohykh], "Pohliad v buduchnost'," *Slovo* 6, no. 59, July 27 (August 8) 1866, 1–2.

51. John-Paul Himka, *Galician Villagers and the Ukrainian National Movement in the Nineteenth Century* (Edmonton: Canadian Institute of Ukrainian Studies; London: Macmillan; New York: St. Martin's, 1988).

52. John-Paul Himka, "Young Radicals and Independent Statehood: The Idea of a Ukrainian Nation-State, 1890–1895," *Slavic Review* 41 (1982): 219–35; Iaroslav Hrytsak, "'Molodi' radykaly v suspil'no-politychnomu zhytti Halychyny." *Zapysky NTSh* 222 (1991): 71–110.

53. See David Saunders, "Britain and the Ukrainian Question (1912–1920)," *English Historical Review* 103 (January 1988): 45–48.

54. See *Voennye prestupleniia Gabsburgskoi Monarkhii 1914–1917 gg.* (Trumbull, Conn.: Peter S. Hardy, 1964). This includes a reprint of *Talergofskii al'manakh. Propamiatnaia kniga avstriiskikh zhestokostei, izuverstv i nasilii nad karpato-russkim narodom vo vremia vsemirnoi voiny 1914–1917 gg.* (Lviv, 1924–32).

55. S. Petliura, "Z zhyttia Avstriis'koi Ukrainy. Ukrains'ki posly v Videns'komu parlamenti," *Ukraina. Naukovyi ta literaturno-publitsystychnyi shchomisiachnyi zhurnal* 1, vol. 4 (October 1907), pt. 2, 6.

56. Roman Szporluk, "West Ukraine and West Belorussia: Historical Tradition, Social Communication, and Linguistic Assimilation," *Soviet Studies* 31, no. 1 (1979): 76–98.

57. Janusz Radziejowski, *The Communist Party of Western Ukraine, 1919–1929* (Edmonton: Canadian Institute of Ukrainian Studies, University of Alberta, 1983), esp. 83–88, 140–44.

58. V. Malkin, *Russkaia literatura v Galitsii* (Lviv: Izdatel'stvo L'vovskogo universiteta, 1957). See also the response: Andrii Brahinets' et al., "Domysly i perekruchennia pid vyhliadom nauky," *Zhovten'* 2 (1959): 132–45.

59. John-Paul Himka, "Hope in the Tsar: Displaced Naive Monarchism among the Ukrainian Peasants of the Habsburg Empire," *Russian History* 7 (1980): 125–38.

60. Excellent material on pro-Russian pan-Slavism among the Czechs and other Slavic nations can be found in *Die slavische Idee: Beiträge am Matija Majar-Ziljski-Symposium vom 6. bis 10. Juli 1992 in Tratten/Posisce, Kärnten,* ed. Andreas Moritsch; *Slovanské stúdie,* special issue 1 (Bratislava: Slovak Academic Press, 1993).

61. The Russian nationalist intellectual Oleg Platonov referred to "certain linguistic or ethnographic distinctions of Ukraine and Belorussia" that "are explainable by the special features of their historical development under the many-centuries-long Polish-Lithuanian occupation." In Platonov's view, though, these distinctions are not enough to amount to "a distinct nation," and "the creation of the 'states' of Ukraine and Belorussia has an artificial and temporary character." Cited in Roman Szporluk, "Reflec-

tions on Ukraine after 1994: The Dilemmas of Nationhood," *Harriman Review* 7, nos. 7–9 (1994): 4.

62. *Korespondentsyia Iakova Holovats'koho,* cliv.

63. As a Russian official put it in 1881: "In connection with the political conditions that have arisen since the Treaty of Berlin, it is an urgent necessity that we follow vigilantly all that happens in the border regions of neighboring states, and one of the most important means of receiving useful information is the local Slavic press, especially organs devoted to us, which follow every hostile step of our opponents. Of such organs, . . . the most patriotic, influential and best organized are the Lviv paper *Slovo* and the Turčiansky Sväty-Martin paper *Národnie Noviny.*" The Russian government gave *Slovo* 2,000 Austrian gulden a year beginning in 1876; in 1881 the sum was tripled; in 1882 *Slovo* received 4,000 gulden, and a new Russophile organ, *Novyi prolom,* received 2,000; in 1884 and 1885 *Slovo* received 3,500 and *Novyi prolom* 2,500; in 1886 the total subsidy was raised to 12,000. Tsentral'nyi gosudarstvennyi istoricheskii arkhiv SSSR, Leningrad, f. 776, op. 1, d. 17, 13–16; d. 18, 9–10; d. 20, 9; d. 21, 3; d. 22, 1–4. I am citing from notes originally made by Iaroslav Dashkevych, to whom I am grateful for putting them at my disposal.

64. K. P. Pobedonostsev, *K. P. Pobedonostsev i ego korrespondenty. Pis'ma i zapiski,* 2 parts (Moscow: Gosudarsvennoe izdatel'stvo, 1923), 309, 331.

65. See John-Paul Himka, *Socialism in Galicia: The Emergence of Polish Social Democracy and Ukrainian Radicalism (1860–1890)* (Cambridge, Mass.: Harvard Ukrainian Research Institute, 1983), 48.

66. A contributor to *Slovo* in 1868 expressed concern over the mass emigration to the Chełm region, fearing that it would drain talent from the Russophiles and leave Galicia at the mercy of the Poles and Ukrainophiles. Iaroslav Hordyns'kyi, *Do istorii kul'turnoho i politychnoho zhytia v Halychyni u 60-tykh rr. XIX v.,* Zbirnyk Fil'ol'ogichnoi sektsii NTSh, 16 (Lviv: NTSh, 1917), 120.

67. Kost' Levyts'kyi, *Istoriia politychnoi dumky halyts'kykh ukraintsiv 1848–1914 na pidstavi spomyniv* (Lviv: Nakladom vlasnym, Z drukarni oo. Vasyliian u Zhovkvi, 1926), 634–35; Mykhailo Vozniak, *Ukrains'ka derzhavnist'* (Vienna: Z drukarni Adol'fa Hol'tshavzena, 1918), 123–24; Dmytro Dontsov, *Suchasne politychne polozhenie natsii i nashi zavdania. Referat vyholoshenyi na II. vseukrains'kim students'kim z'izdi v lypni 1913. roku u L'vovi* (Lviv: "Moloda Ukraina," Vydavnytstvo Ukrains'koho students'koho soiuza, 1913).

68. See John-Paul Himka, "Ukrainians, Russians, and Alexander Solzhenitsyn," *Cross Currents: A Yearbook of Central European Culture* 11 (1992): 193–204.

69. Ivan L. Rudnytsky, "The Ukrainians in Galicia under Austrian Rule," in Ivan L. Rudnytsky, *Essays in Modern Ukrainian History,* ed. Peter L. Rudnytsky (Edmonton: Canadian Institute of Ukrainian Studies, University of Alberta, 1987), 330.

70. *Korespondentsyia Iakova Holovats'koho,* l.

71. Alexey Miller, "Galicia after the Ausgleich: Polish-Ruthenian Conflict and the Attempts of Reconciliation," *Central European University History Department Yearbook* (1993): 135–43.

72. *Korespondentsyia Iakova Holovats'koho,* lvii.

73. *Korespondentsyia Iakova Holovats'koho*, l.

74. George Y. Shevelov [Iurii Sherekh], *Halychyna v formuvanni novoi ukrains'koi literaturnoi movy* (Edmonton: Department of Slavic Languages, University of Alberta, 1971).

75. "If one disregards the very few early records which had a Ukrainian tinge, the language was Belorussian based on the spoken language of the Vilna region." George Y. Shevelov, "Evolution of the Ukrainian Literary Language," in Rudnytsky, *Rethinking Ukrainian History*, 219.

76. From the point of view of nationalism, this tradition is understood as a flaw or, more defensively, as the unfortunate result of national oppression. There are, however, more positive ways to understand this tradition, just as there are more positive ways to understand Ukrainian "nonhistoricity." These and other related problems in Ukrainian cultural history require rethinking; the work of Mircea Eliade on religious culture might suggest fruitful points of departure for such a reconsideration.

77. Cited in Kozik, *Ukrainian National Movement*, 158.

78. "In Ukraine, with the exception of a few individuals, no one is thinking about creating a new literary language and new nationality." Svistun, *Prikarpatskaia Rus'*, 364.

79. The Ukrainophile national populist leader Ievhen Olesnytsky left this account of his visit to Kyiv in 1894: "I can't describe Kyiv. . . . It would captivate anyone, let alone a Ukrainian, who connects so many historical memories with it, who searches here for them, who would like to take delight in them. . . . In only one respect was I disappointed. The external character of Kyiv was not then Ukrainian, but Muscovite. Everywhere there were Muscovite signs, the Muscovite language on the street, in stores, in restaurants and cafes, and when we said that we cannot speak or understand Muscovite, they immediately tried to speak Polish. Perhaps some peasant from the village or some poor worker spoke Ukrainian here and there. This made a very painful impression. . . . My faith in the power and future of Ukraine was undermined by this. Where is that Ukraine, where is that people, to whom we fly with our hopes and upon whom we base our national ideal?" Evhen Olesnyts'kyi, *Storinky z moho zhyttia*, 2 parts (Lviv: Nakladom vydavnychoi spilky "Dilo," 1935), 2:68–70.

80. Of course, the Russophiles did not formulate the argument exactly in these terms, but they came close. Severyn Shekhovych in 1853: "The subjects not treated in our periodical [*Lada*] so far require many technical words, new for Galicia . . . and we should not and cannot make up new words" (cited in *Korespondentsyia Iakova Holovats'koho*, lxxv). Bohdan Didytsky in the same year (as paraphrased by Kyrylo Studynsky): "We, . . . and with us the other Slavs, had been enthusiastic about the language of our people, and we wrote stories and tales and composed songs, and at that time our vernacular language provided us with sufficient expressions. . . . But when we undertook to translate scholarly works, then we came to realize that we do not have enough words for more elevated concepts, that our language lacks scientific terms" (*Korespondentsyia Iakova Holovats'koho*, xciii). "Galician Rus' became convinced in 1848 that the establishment of a separate Galician Russian or Little Russian literary

language is a futile waste of time and retards the cultural progress of Austrian Rus'" (Svistun, *Prikarpatskaia Rus'*, 364).

81. Kornylo N. Ustiianovych', M. T. *Raievskii i rossiiskii panslavyzm. Spomynky z perezhytoho i peredumanoho* (Lviv: Nakladom K. Bednarskoho, 1884); *Zarubezhnye slaviane i Rossiia. Dokumenty arkhiva M.F. Raevskogo 40–80 gody XIX veka* (Moscow: Nauka, 1975).

82. Austrian State Archives, Allgemeines Verwaltungsarchiv, Ministerium des Innern, Präsidiale, 22 Russophile Propaganda, K. 2085–86.

83. Characteristically, a group of Galician Ukrainophiles (national populists) in 1867 called for the creation of a patriarchate for the Ruthenian Greek Catholic Church with the right to convoke a "people's council" *(narodnyi sobor)* to elect the patriarch and bishops. M. P. Dragomanov, "Literaturnoe dvizhenie v Galitsii," in Dragomanov, *Politicheskiia sochineniia*, ed. I. M. Grevs and B. A. Kistiakovskii, vol. 1: *Tsentry i okrainy* (Moscow: Tipografiia T-va I.D. Sytina, 1908), 368n.

84. John-Paul Himka, "The Greek Catholic Church and Nation-Building in Galicia, 1772–1918," *Harvard Ukrainian Studies* 8, nos. 3–4 (1984): 426–52, "The Greek Catholic Church and the Ukrainian Nation in Galicia," in *Religious Compromise, Political Salvation: The Greek Catholic Church and Nation-Building in Eastern Europe,* ed. James Niessen, Carl Beck Papers in Russian and East European Studies, no. 1003 (Pittsburgh: Center for Russian and East European Studies, University of Pittsburgh, 1993), 7–26, "Sheptyts'kyi and the Ukrainian National Movement before 1914," in *Morality and Reality: The Life and Times of Andrei Sheptyts'kyi,* ed. Paul Robert Magocsi (Edmonton: Canadian Institute of Ukrainian Studies, 1989), 29–46, and *Religion and Nationality in Western Ukraine: The Greek Catholic Church and the Ruthenian National Movement in Galicia, 1867–1900* (Kingston, Ontario: McGill-Queen's University Press, 1999).

85. As a model for this type of research I have in mind Miroslav Hroch, *Social Preconditions of National Revival in Europe: A Comparative Analysis of the Social Composition of Patriotic Groups among the Smaller European Nations* (Cambridge: Cambridge University Press, 1985). For a very preliminary study in this direction, see the section "The Membership of the Popular Education Society Prosvita, 1868–74," in John-Paul Himka, "Polish and Ukrainian Socialism: Austria, 1867–1890," Ph.D. diss., University of Michigan, 1977, 126–42.

86. Gale Stokes, "Cognition, Consciousness, and Nationalism," *Ethnic Groups* 10, nos. 1–3 (1993): 27–42. See also Himka, "Stratificazione sociale," 672–75.

87. Himka, "Ukrainians, Russians," 201–2.

88. The name derives from the word *rusyn*, which I and most scholars of the region translate (via the Latin *ruthenus* and more immediately via the German *Ruthene*) as "Ruthenian." However, Paul R. Magocsi has popularized the use of the term "Rusyn" in English to refer to the Ruthenians of Transcarpathia and western, Lemko Galicia and specifically to distinguish them from Ukrainians. Magocsi also coined the word "Rusynophilism," analogous to Russophilism and Ukrainophilism, to refer to the national orientation that saw the Ruthenians of the Carpathian region as a separate nationality.

89. There is a vast literature on Rusynism. For the historical background, see Paul Robert Magocsi, *The Shaping of a National Identity: Subcarpathian Rus'*, *1848–1948* (Cambridge, Mass.: Harvard University Press, 1978); Ivan L. Rudnytsky, "Carpatho-Ukraine: A People in Search of Their Identity," in Rudnytsky, *Modern Ukrainian History*, 353–73. On the current situation, see Paul Robert Magocsi, "The Birth of a New Nation, or the Return of an Old Problem? The Rusyns of East Central Europe," *Canadian Slavonic Papers* 34, no. 3 (1992): 200–223; Paul Robert Magocsi, "Carpatho-Rusyns: Their Current Status and Future Perspectives," *Carpatho-Rusyn American* 16, no. 2 (1993): 4–9, with commentaries by L'udovít Haraksim, Mykola Mušynka (*Carpatho-Rusyn American* 16, no. 3 [1993]: 4–8), Andrzej Zięba, and response by Magocsi (*Carpatho-Rusyn American* 16, no. 4 [1993]: 4–9).

90. Kubijovyč and Struk, *Encyclopedia of Ukraine*, s.v. "Old Ruthenians" by J. P. Himka and O. Sereda. Ivan Khymka, "'Apolohiia' Mykhaila Malynovs'koho: do istorii kryzy u hreko-katolyts'kii tserkvi 1882 roku i kharakterystyky pohliadiv 'sviatoiurtsiv,'" *Zapysky Naukovoho tovarystva imeni T. Shevchenka*, vol. 225: *Pratsi istorychno-filosofs'koi sektsii* (1993), 365–92. Radically different views are expressed in Paul R. Magocsi, "Old Ruthenianism and Russophilism: A New Conceptual Framework for Analyzing National Ideologies in Late 19th Century Eastern Galicia," in *American Contributions to the Ninth International Congress of Slavists: Kiev, September 1983*, vol. 2: *Literature, Poetics, History*, ed. Paul Debreczeny (Columbus, Ohio: Slavica, 1983), 305–24. Magocsi summarizes his "new conceptual framework" thus: "Before the 1870s, there were only Old Ruthenians among the Galician Ukrainian intelligentsia. Beginning in the late 1860s and early 1870s, one group, known as populists, split off. They eventually accepted the idea of identification with a distinct Ukrainian nationality. The Old Ruthenians, however, continued to exist. In the late 1890s, another group split off, known as Russophiles, who from the very beginning identified unequivocally with the Great Russian nationality. It should be remembered that despite this second split, the Old Ruthenians continued to survive, albeit in ever decreasing numbers" (309). From the previous section of the present essay ("The Ukrainian and All-Russian Ideas") some of the reasons for my rejection of these views should be clear.

91. Mykhailo Petrovych Drahomanov, "Try lysty do redaktsii 'Druha,'" *Literaturno-publitsystychni pratsi u dvokh tomakh*, 2 vols. (Kyiv: Naukova dumka, 1970), 1:413.

92. See, for example, Iaroslav Dashkevych, "Fal'shyvi etnichni menshyny v Ukraini: Pidkarpats'ki rusyny," *Ratusha* (Lviv), July 13, 1993, 2.

93. Drahomanov at the very end of his life in 1895 rued that he had always wanted to do something about Transcarpathian Ukraine, to integrate it "into our national democratic and progressive movement," but had not. He begged his followers to succeed where he had failed (Rudnytsky, "Carpatho-Ukraine," 363). They did not.

94. "The Transcarpathian variant of the literary language with a local dialectical base did not take a noteworthy place in the process of establishing

the all-national Ukrainian literary language." I. H. Matviias, *Ukrains'ka mova i ii hovory* (Kyiv: Naukova dumka, 1990), 155.

95. To my, admittedly, limited knowledge, the only serious attempts to write in dialect emanated from the Ukrainophiles, from radicals such as the Pavlyk sisters, Anna and Paraska, as well as from the Metropolitan of Halych, Andrei Sheptytsky. In both cases the very distinctive Hutsul dialect was employed.

96. In November 1992 the First Congress of the Rusyn Language was held in Slovakia. "The participants accepted the 'Romansch model,' that is to allow the development of four standards based on dialects in the countries where Rusyns live: Ukraine, Poland, Slovakia, and Yugoslavia. One standard, Vojvodinian Rusyn in Yugoslavia, already exists; the three others . . . need to be codified. The participants also agreed to meet periodically to exchange views on their own codifying work as well as to agree on as many principles as possible that will form the basis of an eventual 'fifth' Rusyn literary standard, or *koiné* that would be common to all regions." Paul Robert Magocsi, "The Rusyn Language Question Revisited," in *A New Slavic Language Is Born: The Rusyn Literary Language of Slovakia* (Boulder, Colo.: East European Monographs distributed by Columbia University Press, 1996), 37–38.

97. There is one in Matviias, *Ukrains'ka mova i ii hovory*, 124. Another is in *Encyclopedia of Ukraine*, s.v. "Dialects" by G. Y. Shevelov.

98. Frank E. Sysyn, "The Khmelnytsky Uprising and Ukrainian Nation-Building," *Journal of Ukrainian Studies* 17, nos. 1–2 (1992): 146.

99. For a clear, useful discussion of dialectical overlap and differences, see Ivan Sydoruk, *Problema ukrains'ko-bilorus'koi movnoi mezhi*, Slavistica, Pratsi Instytutu slov"ianovoznavstva Ukrains'koi vil'noi akademii nauk, 3 (Augsburg: Nakladom Tovarystva prykhyl'nykiv Ukrains'koi vil'noi akademii nauk, 1948).

100. A. Šachmatov and G. Y. Shevelov, *Die kirchenslavischen Elemente in der modernen russischen Literatursprache*, Slavistische Studienbücher, 1 (Wiesbaden: Otto Harrassowitz, 1960).

101. Sysyn, "Khmelnytsky Uprising," 146–47, 152–53.

102. See the reflections on this in Andreas Kappeler, "A 'Small People' of 25 Million: The Ukrainians circa 1900," *Journal of Ukrainian Studies* 18, nos. 1–2 (1993): 85–92.

103. N. T. Vaitovich, *Da pytannia ab farmiravanni natsyianal'nai literaturnai belaruskai movy (ab suadnosinakh litaraturnai movy i dyialektau)* (Minsk: Vydavetstva Akademii navuk BSSR, 1958); Matviias, *Ukrains'ka mova i ii hovory*, 141–60.

104. Ryshard Radzik, "Prychyny slabas'tsi natsyiatvorchaha pratsesu belarusau u XIX–XX st.," *Belaruski histarychny ahliad* 2, no. 2 (1995): 195–227.

My Past and Identities

Detroit was booming when I was born there in 1949, and it attracted immigrants from all over the eastern half of America: from the Delta, the Appalachians, and the moribund little coaltowns of Pennsylvania. My father was part of the anthracite emigration, as was my mother. I grew up in an extended family in which Polish, Ukrainian, Slovak, and Italian were tossed about by the older generation, above the heads of the monkey-in-the middle younger generation to which I belonged. It was after the war, most of the men had seen service, everyone was too busy being American to imagine that there was any point to teaching us young 'uns the old languages, which hardly any of them could read or write in any case. The food was a mixture of city chicken, hot dogs, ravioli, and gołąbki *(or* holubtsi, *depending on who was doing the talking). The older they were, the more old-country they were. My father and mother were the babies of their families and among the most assimilated. Still, there was a constant buzz of ethnicity in the air, even if none of the family had heard the word back then.*

There was also my grandmother. My birth mother had passed away when I was a baby, and some years were to go by before my father remarried. In the meantime, I was raised by my grandmother, who came to live with us. She had left the old country in 1909 but had never really gotten a handle on English. When she came to raise me, though, she made a choice that both of us later regretted: she would improve her English by raising me in that language. I later had to learn her native language, and we switched to that as our medium of communication. It would be an understatement to say that I loved my grandmother very, very much, and I spent much of my childhood trying to figure her out. Where did she come from? She said Lemberg, Austria, but it wasn't on the map. Eventually I found it in a historical atlas in my father's library and matched the location on a modern map: it was now Lvov, Russia. By about age twelve I had many things figured out, including that Grandma was Ukrainian, but Grandma was going to be constantly setting puzzles for me to solve, even long after she passed away. Many of the things she told me just didn't make sense in terms of the Ukrainian history I subsequently read and was taught. Long before I could express it, I understood that there was an important distinction to be made between the national codification of Ukrainian history and the actual past that was experienced by people who are counted as part of the Ukrainian nation.

The big jump in my consciousness came when I was fourteen. I wanted to become a priest and left home for a minor seminary, St. Basil's, in Stamford, Connecticut. I had been baptized in the Roman Catholic Church, attended a Roman Catholic school, sang in Latin in Our Lady of Sorrows' boys' choir, served as an altar boy at a Roman Catholic summer camp, and heard Sunday mass at the local Roman Catholic parish. But the discoveries of the previous few years had revealed to me that, in spite of this Roman Catholic upbringing, I was nonetheless canonically a member of an Eastern rite and that if I wanted to be a priest, I needed a special dispensation to enter the Roman priesthood. But by then I was all keen to enter Grandma's exotic church, as I thought of it, and off I went to the Ukrainian-rite seminary.

I received an incredible education at that institution over the next five years, taught by remarkable men. My teacher of Latin had done his doctorate with Moses Hadas at Columbia and had written his thesis in Latin; my music teacher was probably the most prominent conductor of the Ukrainian diaspora; my Ukrainian teacher has recently been named to succeed to the metropolitan throne of Lviv, that is, to assume leadership of the Ukrainian Greek Catholic church worldwide. Most of the teachers had doctorates and great erudition in complicated fields like patristic anthropology. Quite a few had serious academic publications to their credit. Devoted to their church and nation, they lavished their knowledge on us ingrate boys instead of making proper careers. We made fun of them all the time, but they inspired us to learn. We played sports, but we also followed the example of our preceptors, each according to his talents: arranging the sacred choral music of our church, painting icons, writing the lives of the saints, studying the traditions of the other Eastern churches.

Aside from this formal education, I learned a great deal about Ukrainians, particularly two kinds of Ukrainians: those whose parents had come after World War II and who were themselves born abroad (in other words: DPs) and those whose grandparents had immigrated before World War I, as mine had. These two groups accounted for the overwhelming majority of the seminarians, and there was always tension between them. Most of the first-immigration kids came from Pennsylvania and from an environment that retained much more of its Ukrainian character than mine had. I fit in well with these guys, from whose number my closest friends were drawn. But I was also impressed by the postwar immigrants: completely fluent in Ukrainian, possessing a worked-out nationalist worldview, tough-minded. With time, I was to gravitate more strongly toward them and to assimilate more of their culture. After I left the seminary, I always sought the company of this postwar immigration and eventually married into it.

My vocation was no match for the spirit of the times. At the end of the 1960s I left the seminary and plunged into the radical culture and radical politics of the outside world. At the University of Michigan, where I continued my education, my life consisted of militant demonstrations against the war, against racism, and against capitalist exploitation, as well as of lectures and seminars.

Michigan was an excellent place to continue my interest in things Ukrainian and develop a deeper interest in all things East European. Once again I had remarkable teachers, and peers. I came under the tutelage of Roman Szporluk, now Mykhailo Hrushevsky Professor of Ukrainian History at Harvard University. I also studied Balkan history with John Fine and Russian history with Horace Dewey. Close friends of my Michigan years included Roman Solchanyk and Patrick Moore, now prominent analysts of Ukrainian and Balkan affairs respectively, as well as Robert Donia, the Bosnian specialist, and Marian Krzyzowski, longtime editor of Studium Papers. *In these years I also met the scholars connected with the Harvard Ukrainian Research Institute; later I was to spend time with them at their home institution, and some of them were to end up with me in Edmonton.*

During this period I had to reconstruct my own Ukrainian identity. The religious underpinnings had been shattered. Moreover, I needed a Ukrainian identity that could accommodate the extreme leftism that I now espoused. My grandmother and one of the teachers at the seminary had already left me with some clues that I followed until I came upon the rich traditions of the Ukrainian socialist movements of the nineteenth and twentieth centuries. And Professor Szporluk guided me to the Ukrainian socialist thinkers that exercised the largest influence on me for many years thereafter: the father of Ukrainian radicalism, Mykhailo Drahomanov, and the Marxist historian and interpreter of Capital *and the* Grundrisse, *Roman Rosdolsky. I eventually was to write my doctoral dissertation (and first book) on the history of the socialist movement in Galicia and translate one of Rosdolsky's books into English.*

I was not the only one trying to reconcile a Ukrainian identity with the radical North American zeitgeist. I came across the journal New Directions *from New York and, really much more exciting for me at the time, the journals coming out from the Ukrainian New Left in Toronto:* Meta *and* Diialoh. *Later I was to move to Canada and marry* Meta's *coeditor.*

Before that, however, in 1974–76 I embarked on my first trip to Eastern Europe, spending a year in Cracow, six months in Leningrad, and a month each in Lviv and Kyiv. It was my first encounter with the other Ukrainians, the ones who had not left for the West. In Cracow the Ukrainians were similar to the postwar Ukrainians I knew back home: well versed in Ukrainian lore, nationalist, religious, antisocialist. We got along well in spite of many differences of opinion. In Leningrad I encountered greater variety: displaced Galicians with the nationalist worldview; other displaced Ukrainians who, like the national poet Taras Shevchenko over a century earlier, found that the alienation they experienced in the northern Russian metropolis only led them to a deeper appreciation of their roots, although, unlike Shevchenko, they did not know as much about these roots; others yet who could still remember some words of the Ukrainian language but had basically melted into "the Soviet people."

Ukraine itself offered me even more variety. On that first trip and on many other trips over the next twenty-some years, I engaged in close encounters with mighty and fledgling scholars, illiterate peasant women, enraged dissidents, sympatico and obnoxious Russians (whether one or the other, their days in authority were numbered), writers, artists, stamp collectors, crooks, saints, and biznesmeny on the make. Over the years I watched my friends rewrite their autobiographies, redefine their present and past selves, and reconstruct their identities (I should add: as I myself am perforce doing in this essay).

In 1977 I left the United States for Canada, where I was offered a contract position at the University of Alberta. Again, I was fortunate in the company I encountered. The professor of Ukrainian history was one of the great luminaries of the diaspora, Ivan Lysiak-Rudnytsky. We became close friends, even though he was a conservative and by this time I was an orthodox Marxist. Until his death in 1984, he continually gave me things to read and engaged me in discussion and debate, turning our friendship and working relationship also into a seminar. In Edmonton I was able to join the editorial board of Diialoh, which had moved there from Toronto. We had a slogan that captured our politics perfectly: "For socialism and democracy in an independent Ukraine." (Most of us later settled for the partial fulfillment of our program that history offered.) We published a journal in Ukrainian and, spicier yet, set up a modest smuggling and intelligence network in Eastern Europe and Ukraine. In addition to the deeply conspiratorial Diialoh, we also established a left-wing

Ukrainian cultural society, Hromada, which in turn gave birth to the Hromada Housing Co-operative, where some of the old stalwarts (myself included) still live. In the late seventies/early eighties life was intense, all cigarettes and public forums and layouts and debates. Key figures in the milieu included Bohdan Krawchenko, whom we nicknamed "Captain Ukraine" and who later became director of the Canadian Institute of Ukrainian Studies and still later an adviser to the independent Ukrainian government; Myrna Kostash, author of All of Baba's Children *and later head of Canada's writers' union; Halyna Freeland, founder of "Common Woman Books" and presently executive director of the Ukrainian Legal Foundation in Kyiv; and many, many others, not least of whom was my wife Chrystia Chomiak, an indefatigable activist in many progressive Ukrainian causes.*

In the later 1980s things began to change, most dramatically on the international scene, but also in my personal life. Chrystia and I had children, and I also ended up in the position formerly occupied by Professor Rudnytsky, with all the responsibilities that entailed. I managed to finish my second book, on the impact of the Ukrainian national movement on the Galician countryside, the most consistently Marxist work in my oeuvre. I decided that for my third monograph, I would write a study of the Greek Catholic church, in its relationship to the nationality question. It took me about ten years to write that book, during which time I reexamined and reevaluated many of the premises I had been working with hitherto. It has been a time extremely fertile in ideas and, especially, doubts, one fruit of which is the study of national identity published in this volume.

John-Paul Himka

Janet Hart

Reading the Radical Subject: Gramsci, Glinos, and Paralanguages of the Modern Nation

The national concept as rooted in Enlightenment political culture has received considerable attention in recent years.[1] In contrast to earlier parochialisms and more recent hybrids, *that* nation generated specific loyalty to the state and is not easily separated from the foundational agendas of modernity. Through bold insurgencies and often heated conversations about state building, citizenship, and mass mobilization, new lineages were launched in opposition to the bounded politics of ancien régimes and to fascism in Europe after 1920. The visionary potential of the modern nation has enabled the idea to cross cultural borders to become grounds for collective action, a category to be shaped by local contingencies and a significant object of study.

The final round of discussions about how to fill in the contours of the modern nation is, of course, neither imminent nor possible. What I aim to do is to contribute to the polyvalent debate about what we think we can know about how national identity was articulated by socialist intellectuals of the modern period, and to contemplate the sorts of clues that might generate new evidence about how these processes transpired. My goal, then, is to think through tendencies, in a spirit of epistemological free play, rather than to insist on naturally occurring political traits; in other words, I want to draw on what Foucault calls "experiential" possibility.[2]

To structure this discussion, I will dust off and borrow a term from ethnolinguistics and psychotherapy: *paralanguage.* The literature on this subject cites a range of nonverbal cues, from tones of voice, regional accents, registers and pitches to involuntary sounds, clicks and clucks, and head scratching; that is to say, modes and gestures, removed from the actual act of speech, that serve to encode information for listeners.[3] By the same token, paralanguage for our purposes must include the wealth of *speech acts* significant beyond mere talk.[4]

Theorists have focused on particular facets of the social construction of speech. Bourdieu, for example, attempts to trace the sociolegal conditions that give individuals the authority to speak and be heard. Talk in the public domain demands what he calls "symbolic capital," and he asserts that permission to articulate an opinion in the first place depends on some prior negotiation of power, patronage, and privilege.[5] Students of racism, colonialism, and cultural imperialism have contributed variously to our understandings of how language and the exercise and acquisition of power are intimately, but not always conspicuously, connected.[6] Habermas, also committed to placing speech in some meaningful sociological context, notes its role in reproducing social life and analyzes operative relations through what he calls "universal pragmatics" and the discourses of the "life world."[7]

Following this broader, more socially situated view of speech, how can paralanguage help clarify the dilemmas of radical selfhood and nation building in the modern era? Here, I use the concept metaphorically as a way to reflect on crucial acts of social interpretation and developmental/ontological patterns that I believe shaped the political advocacy of two intellectuals qua nation builders of the modern era, the Italian political philosopher Antonio Gramsci, and his lesser-known Greek counterpart, educationalist and resistance leader Dimitris Glinos. Political paralanguages are Geertz's "webs of significance," woven by design. They evince broad belief systems that "predict" the narratives used to galvanize, educate, preach.[8] For "modernizers" they mark distinctive vernaculars that had far-reaching consequences in terms of policy and concerted action. These moral frames, which I will explore in greater depth later, were not necessarily unique to one or two individuals, and it is possible to identify coherent directions, although we must be cautious in claiming that any given cohort marched entirely in lockstep.

Antonio Gramsci and Dimitris Glinos were among a generation of intellectuals grown in the European periphery who took the movement of antifascist unity to heart, seeing their nations' indigenous fascisms (the Italian regime was inaugurated in 1933; the dictatorship of the

Greek general Metaxas came to power three years later after a coup in 1936) as products of past distortions and incomplete democratic transitions. Both consequently devoted considerable energy to tracing and analyzing national trajectories in the wake of ostensible democratic revolutions: the Greek-minded Glinos focused on meaning-making (or lack thereof for the masses) during the revolution of 1821, the struggle to end Ottoman dominance that became a condensed symbol of freedom fighting from Bristol to Prague; the Italian-minded Gramsci saw the Renaissance as a particularly significant watershed. Gramsci's legacy has continued and even brightened throughout the postwar period, and his work has served as a touchstone for generations of Italian and non-Italian scholars, cultural critics, and activists. His posthumous role in steering the debate in postwar Italy about the future role of the Communist Party as loyal opposition was a key one. Glinos, on the other hand, was not allowed to flourish as an historically significant and binding memory in the repressive atmosphere of postwar Greece, even among those who did remember. The crucial significance of both men, however, is as participants in the antifascist movement that sought to repattern public thinking in a way that would inoculate future generations against fascism's pull.

Many scholars have noted that consciousness—insight into one's situation and potential—is not a compact and immutable thing, but rather develops over time, intensifying during critical conjunctures. Interiority, what Carolyn Steedman calls "a sense of the self within,"[9] can be centered or greatly amplified by unfolding events, resulting in shared perceptions among those touched by synchronous crises and negotiations. If we then allow some notion of collective consciousness wrought by common personal experience, for Gramsci, Glinos, and many others nation building was the articulation of a perceived social contract and certainly also a way to establish a meaningful relationship with the self.

In addition to this quest for an authentic self, one that was somehow coherent and justifiable, in its zeal to create a social force-field modern nation-building consciousness was intersubjective and outward-leaning. Imbued with the desire to connect with like-minded others and to insure the reproduction of modern values, political modernizers were driven by the imperative to model a citizenry of the future. Here they were guided by the impulse that psychologists have termed "generativity." Erik Erikson defines generativity as "the concern in establishing and guiding the next generation."[10] M. J. Maynes, among others, makes the point that the authors of working-class, socialist autobiographies in nineteenth-century Europe wrote to convey deliberate and not especially subtle messages to potential recruits. "Many of the autobiographies . . . following the suggestion of the scientific socialism then current," notes Maynes, "are consciously intended to be accounts of the transition from helpless object of history to active subject, through socialist activism. While not centered on the evolution and exaltation of individual personality and intellect, they nevertheless underscore the role of self-improvement or education in the broadest sense for a decisive transformation in their lives."[11] Within the confines of a different geopolitical reality, the conversion narratives by or about black women spiritualists served a similar purpose, namely to "connect the writer to her or his individual self as well as to collective human existence."[12] These narratives were almost certainly designed to bear witness to historic pain. Significantly, they were also assembled to provide descendants needed counsel from preeminent survivors.[13]

Narrators, then, sought to foster in fledgling citizenry a sensibility that if not always fully critical, reflected the narrator's own self-image as a political realist. As the twentieth century progressed, for many the nation (as icon), and national-*ism* (as ideology)—jelled as a *form* for communicating paradigmatic *content*,[14] that is, cautionary tales emplotted with scenes of social justice, triumph, cunning, and "right livelihood" in the Buddhist sense, realized by traveling a sapient path.[15] The storylines of these narratives were structured by contingencies of class background, regional and ethnic identity, gender consciousness, and personal ordeal. Proficiency gained from "field" experience and erudition (for a certain stratum of "organic intellectuals" often self-taught)[16] laid the foundations for communication, initiating an ongoing process. Parables were frequently given voice in formal autobiographies. But as I argue here, equally insistent generative messages can also be found in other types of writing. Thus, after 1789 the nation provided a new structure for negotiating institutional power, an arena for self-exploration and personal growth, and a grammar for the future. Consequently, all sorts of emotions and artifacts dot the semiotic plain: psychological transferences, grand passions, anxieties of status and ego, plus a full range of analogies, object lessons, mobilizing narratives,[17] and other conceptual means to strategic ends. The goals of the *transmittable* nation were also profoundly tied to historical memory, how the content of national pasts was actually remembered by "elite" narrators and their convictions about the special *role* of history—according to Karen Fields "what one cannot remember mistakenly"[18]—in configuring events.

Students of social movements have argued persuasively that the main objective of the mobilization phase of insurgencies of the modern era was invariably not to subvert authority for its own sake through random acts of violence.[19] Rather, in many cases the goal was to articulate and instill in the hopeful mass a quasi-religious course of enlightenment (in Greek, *diaphotisi*), historical analysis, and ethical practice; and in future leaders a political "super-ego" as part of the "civilizing process" that Norbert Elias considers so extensively in another context.[20] "But however these differences may arise in particular cases," Elias writes suggestively, "the general direction in the change of conduct, the 'trend' of the movement of civilization, is everywhere the same. It always veers towards a more or less automatic self-control, to the subordination of short-term impulses to the commands of an ingrained long-term view, and to the formation of a more complex and secure 'super-ego' agency" (458). On this general "transition from *warriors to courtiers*" (467), Elias goes on to say that "[c]ontinuous reflection, foresight, and calculation, self-control, precise and articulate regulation of one's own effects, knowledge of the whole terrain, human and non-human, in which one acts, become more and more indispensable preconditions of social success" (476). In these senses, the nation *as opportunity* had everything to do with the development not just of political structures, but also of revolutionary subjectivity; and the study of the nation is not easily separated from the problem of *how* we approach its construction and transmission.

Intellectuals in Politics

All my time and energy is devoted to realizing what I imagine.
Lincoln Kirstein

The various articulation processes that the modern age set in motion repeatedly tested easy assumptions about how theory and practice could be combined. Resolving the tension between the social imaginary and the concrete, between visionary possibility and material constraint, was a major challenge for radical intellectuals. Marxist pragmatists like Gramsci remained unconvinced that reforms would result naturally once key social mechanisms were triggered by the forces of history and nature. How to restructure systems of distribution and redistribution fairly, without engendering undue alarm among conservative popular elements and, equally tricky, among the uninitiated? How to deal with serious economic, political, and social legacies and problems, while not representing challenges so somberly as to discourage fresh new recruits' youthful enjoyment? How to confront both naked power and the steady drip of covert domination—hegemony, essentially—in public institutional life? How to guarantee the soundness of coalitions needed for sustained radical action? How to educate responsible, effective insurgency? As Jamaica Kincaid points out and as the unfolding contests of twentieth-century modernity confirm: "The space between the idea of something and its reality is always wide and deep and dark. . . . The space starts out empty, there is nothing in it, but it rapidly becomes filled up with obsession or desire or hatred or love—sometimes all of these things, sometimes some of these things, sometimes only one of these things."[21]

Such possible complexities of outcome did not, however, necessarily breed pessimism about the generative projects, even when frustration toward particular colleagues surfaced and despite a strong sense of urgency and occasional bouts of overbearingness, especially on Gramsci's part. Some years later, Foucault remarked that

> the job of an intellectual does not consist in molding the political will of others. It is a matter of performing analyses in his or her own fields, of interrogating anew the evidence and the postulates, of shaking up habits, ways of acting and thinking, of dispelling commonplace beliefs, of taking a new measure of rules and institutions. . . . it is a matter of participating in the formation of a political will, where [the intellectual] is called to perform a role as citizen.[22]

On the one hand, Gramsci and Glinos understood their function in terms comparable to Foucault's. As educators, theorists, and cultural critics both were committed to the informed disruption of cultures left stagnant by older hegemonies. On the other hand, their writings evince a common hope that the "political will of others," as Foucault puts it, could be educated through concerted and strategic action, an area where Foucault is agnostic and *his* intellectual less passionate. This leads us to a separate category of modern intellectuals who took part in academic conversations but who were, conjointly, civil servants and nation-builders. These *civil intellectuals* served the nation by challenging the tenets of received wisdom (citizens in Foucault's usage above), by reading voraciously[23] and thinking critically; *and* in their capacity as political leaders and "organisers of mass confidence," in Gramsci's terms.[24] They were of a different order than, for example, Zygmunt Bauman's "legislators," who did not see themselves as trading in a "value-free" zone and felt morally obligated to attempt to influence national policy and policymakers, but who for the most part inhabited a separate sphere as consultants and tended to avoid direct conversation with mass publics.[25] Civil intellectuals like Gramsci and Glinos were closer to what Jane Burbank describes as the Russian *intelligenty*.[26] They were actively and urgently involved in the business of reconstituting national civil societies to rescue them from the jaws of perceived disaster, which in their specific cases increasingly meant fascism. To be sure, it is difficult to decisively sift elements of self-interest out of the narratives produced by such "politicized" intellectuals, or to confidently isolate sincerity from the desire for star billing.[27] One fairly reliable measure, however, is the demonstrated willingness to serve time as prisoners of conscience—despite brutal circumstances—rather than renounce prior commitments, a "choice" that certainly characterizes both Gramsci and Glinos. Both, in fact, eventually died from health problems suffered during jail terms that would have been forgiven or at least substantially reduced had they been willing to cooperate with authorities.

Admitting the category of civil intellectual leads us to push against or attempt to further clarify (but not discard) Gramsci's distinction between "organic" and "traditional" intellectuals. After all, Gramsci would no doubt be the first to say that the formulation was not meant to foreclose further discussion. For Gramsci, *organic intellectuals* posed a new epistemology of social change, one that acknowledges the possibility of influential figures emerging out of local circumstances to shape public thought and mobilize various forms of collective action—professional, technical, religious, or political. Organic intellectuals represent specific social groups. They originate, if not in the societal "margins," then at some distance from the center and they help to solidify

collective identity, rising to prominence by promoting common interests, technical and sacred. Organic intellectuals can be labor leaders,
priests, school administrators, musicians, exhibition curators, club
chapter heads, police chiefs, neighborhood organizers, merchants,
financial directors—as long as they don't conform to a complacent standard and sit idly by. What distinguishes them as organic is their origin
at the heart of their social group and their "active participation in practical life, as constructor, organiser, 'permanent persuader' and not just
simple orator . . . (basing their actions on) the humanistic conception of
history, without which one remains 'specialised' and does not become
'directive' (specialised and political)."[28]

By contrast, *traditional intellectuals* are more invested in the status
quo and derive their power from earlier political constellations. They
may perform some of the same functions listed above, be members of
the clergy and even artists, but they lack a radical edge and the crucial
inclination to "participate in a particular conception of the world, have
a conscious line of moral conduct, and therefore contribute to sustain a
conception of the world or to modify it, that is to bring into being new
modes of thought."[29] In other words, traditional intellectuals are a
favored aristocracy who routinely benefit from competent but safe and
unimaginative behaviors that reify existing structures. Here, a key protagonist and shadow figure fueling Gramsci's theoretical imagination
is undoubtedly the philosopher and cultural authority Benedetto
Croce, whom he critiques at length throughout the prison notebooks
and in prior works.[30] Gramsci was also acutely conscious that, faced
with an increasingly well entrenched Fascist regime after 1922, many of
the professors and intellectual figures who had had a major impact on
his thinking during his formative student days in prewar Turin had
either succumbed quietly or defected outright.

As Nowell Smith points out, the organic/traditional couplet is not
so much based on profession as on moral and political consciousness,
in other words, on one kind of *praxis* but not another. Gramsci's interpretation does, however, lead to some confusion, since it becomes difficult to locate civil intellectuals such as Dimitris Glinos, or Gramsci himself, for that matter, especially during those conjunctures when they
were particularly influential and well placed. It is also why present-day
insurgent intellectuals and members of the academy, often deriving full
"traditional" benefits from "the system" yet conscious of the need for
innovation and structural, cultural, and institutional changes within

their milieus, who regularly use their positions to facilitate such transformations, are never really sure how to classify themselves. "Dominant" seems inflated. Furthermore, whether their alterity is based on ethnic, class, gender or multiple jeopardies, the concept does not allow for subaltern intellectuals who disrupt while at the same time drawing on past and current privileges. Gramsci notes that as a group begins to close in on success, indicating among other things that it has been able to produce its own organic intellectuals, it will seek to capture the good will of the traditional stratum in order to profit from its hegemony. This point, however well taken when applied to specific cases, only serves to lock in the duality.[31] Is the corporate lawyer of working-class origin who accepts pro bono cases to help mediate the struggle among forces in society and who manages regularly to make a difference, organic or traditional? How to classify intellectuals of "mixed heritage" who accrue cultural capital and voice in some domains but not others? Of what sort was Dimitris Glinos? Glinos was a leading figure in the demotic movement, whose principal aim was to establish a conception of "organic Greekness" within the culture by promoting modern Greek language. Born into the lower-ranking bourgeois stratum of Asia Minor Greeks, Glinos was educated at the University of Jena in Germany and was a major league player in Greek public service when his party (Venizelos's Liberal Party) was not dramatically out of favor and he was not being hounded by authorities. However, despite some early travails Glinos lived a relatively bourgeois existence during his formative years, enjoying certain basic entitlements within an essentially traditional, middle-class habitus. At the same time, he inhabited a poor nation, located low on the global hierarchy, and he was obsessed, at great personal cost, with a radical agenda that sought to clear new political space for the kind of rooted creativity that Gramsci foregrounds. Moving back to a contemporary context for a moment, are Angela Davis, Raymond Williams, Hanan Ashwari, Stuart Hall, Bill Clinton, Mary Childers, bell hooks, and Nelson Mandela no less organic for their advantages and no less traditional for their struggles? Is it possible to practice the organic faith, and simultaneously to wield the power necessary to *be* powerful? Is it possible to live traditional and think organic?

These dilemmas, in the absence of further clarifications from Gramsci, may not be entirely resolvable. Yet the distinctions he makes are crucial to political genealogies of activism. The openness of the couplet—which may or may not be a consequence of the conditions under which Gramsci wrote[32]—may be its greatest asset because it enables us to construct a more complex and situational portrait of *prominenci* and to speculate along the way about the relative effects of critical inequalities. But several further points must be made in rearticulating what are among Gramsci's most useful, if sketchy, conceptualizations.

First, it is tempting, because he poses just two categories, to cite Gramsci with the poststructural infractions of binary opposition and essentialism. But not only is such criticism coming to represent the stalest and most facile kind of point scoring, it also misconstrues Gramsci's innovation, which is meant to contribute to the debate about plural selves, not inhibit it. Thus, Stuart Hall notes, Gramsci "argues that [the] multi-faceted nature of consciousness is not an individual but a collective phenomenon, a consequence of the relationship between 'the self' and the ideological discourses which compose the cultural terrain of a society."[33] Moreover, Gramsci's characteristic emphasis on the importance of constant communication between the "leaders and the led" is in large part meant to ensure that elites avoid making policy by projecting their own potentially inappropriate subjectivities on others, and to emphasize the point that there are myriad routes to identification.[34] In "The Study of Philosophy," Gramsci refers specifically to the broad category of intellectuals when he posits "the 'historical' realisation of a new type of philosopher, whom we could call a 'democratic philosopher' in the sense that he is a philosopher convinced that his personality is not limited to himself as a physical individual but is an active social relationship of modification of the cultural environment."[35]

Second, Gramsci gives perhaps excessive weight to origins, thereby discounting the diasporic possibilities for any intellectual; in Paul Gilroy's compelling turn of phrase, "It ain't where you're from, it's where you're at."[36] Similarly, despite Gramsci's use of the broad term *social group,* structural disadvantages, especially those associated with socioeconomic class, most often come to mind as the critical building blocks of organicity. Of course class carries a less totalizing explanatory burden in Gramsci than in the work of any other Marxist philosopher of the day; and to some extent the desire to "open up" definitions of class is an anachronistic expectation, less conceivable during the modern era when Gramsci was engaged in identifying operative social forces. The theoretical role that Gramsci assigns to both origins and by implication socioeconomic class is, I would argue, the result of his historicist creed: namely that historical contexts leave distinctive marks on individual and collective consciousness and on the social texts that people produce and find persuasive.[37] However, we should not forget that Gramsci's crucial contribution to the debate was, after all, to expand the definition of "intellectual" beyond its usual scope and into more complex territory.

Finally, at a theoretical and possibly comparative level of abstraction, how should we read hybrid intellectuals who blended the traditional advantages of rank and the organic disposition to deploy subalternity and other environmental social facts to create change? This synthesis, which can never justify exact measurement or universal standards, is central to understanding Glinos, Gramsci, and other civil intellectuals of the modern period in relation to the nation and the various phases of its articulation. That it was Gramsci who distinguished between traditional and organic intellectuals is no accident. Plainly these ideal types are based on personal experience, as were many of his prescriptions for socialization and survival.[38] For Gramsci, a key feature that tied organic intellectuals to their pasts and decisively set them apart from the more established breed was—again, ideally—their penchant for nonstatic, contingent, proactive theorizing resulting in the practical resolution of communal problems. Gramsci's elaboration of a theory of praxis is substantially based on the role he envisions for organic intellectuals. However, nowhere is it chiseled either in practical terms or in Gramsci's writing that organic intellectuals retain exclusive rights to political realism or context-sensitive intellectual production. A strict dichotomy becomes particularly untenable when we consider Gramsci's own contentions that, formal vocations aside, "all men are intellectuals" and that "although one can speak of intellectuals, one cannot speak of non-intellectuals, because non-intellectuals do not exist. . . . Each man, finally, outside his professional activity, carries on some form of intellectual activity, that is, he is a 'philosopher,' an artist, a man of taste, he participates in a particular conception of the world, has a conscious line of moral conduct, and therefore contributes to sustain a conception of the world or to modify it, that is, to bring into being new modes of thought."[39] These well-known passages accent the flexibility and acceptance of compound possibilities that Gramsci is noted for, as does his assertion that "an intellectual who joins the political party of a particular social group is merged with the organic intellectuals of the group itself, and is linked tightly with the group."[40]

This brings us back to Foucault's notion of the experiential and the developmental aspects of the power/knowledge nexus. As I mentioned earlier, civil intellectuals were distinguished not only by their habitus as politicized intellectuals but also by their praxis. By this I mean that they took energetic and fairly single-minded part (the contemporary expression that comes closest to describing these men is "intense"; neither devoted much time to leisure activities or was inclined to stray very far from the business at hand) in shaping the entity called the nation to fit the foundational agendas of the modern political era as they envisioned them. These designs took more concrete form through specific associational involvements that tested their developing convictions about popular democracy, political incorporation/participation, distributive justice, and social mobilization, and all such experiences were deeply and notionally implicated in the challenge of articulating the modern nation. Gramsci's relevant vitae included stints as a journalist and editor for the socialist weeklies, *Avanti!* (Forward!) and *Il Grido del Popolo* (The people's cry) between 1915 and 1919; helping to organize the Factory Council Movement and its weekly organ, *L'Ordine Nuovo* (The new order) during the "Two Red Years" of 1919 and 1920; a leading role in inaugurating the Italian Communist Party at the Congress of Livorno in 1921; service as party representative to the Comintern from March 1922; and of course his tortured but not unproductive existence as a political prisoner under Mussolini from 1926 to his death in 1937. The highlight of Glinos's political biography was his aforementioned participation in the movement to universalize the demotic Greek language that was already in common usage and to phase out the formal, exclusionary, elite-based *katharevousa*, a passion that began early in his career and lasted until his death in 1943. Other peak experiences include service in various government ministries (notably as minister of education, charged among other things with helping to revise school textbooks) under Liberal premier Eleftherios Venizelos; launching, between 1920 and 1922, a short-lived Women's University (Anotera Yinekeia Skoli) in Athens aimed at redressing gender imbalances in Greek higher education; founding editor of the journal *Anayennisi* (Renaissance) from 1926–28 (of which Anna Frangoudaki writes that "perhaps the most important thing of all is that in the space of its two-year life *Anayennisi* tackled all the new currents of opinion, the new social scientific theories and intellectual tendencies of the times. Its pieces were all directed toward the common reader, indirectly propounding Glinos's pet theme: Greek intellectuals, help to enlighten and guide your people");[41] joining the Greek Communist Party in 1933 after contributing articles to its party organ, *Rizospastis* (The radical) and its youth paper, *Neoi Protoporoi* (Young pioneers); a trip to the Soviet Union for a conference on Soviet journalism with well-known poet Kostas Varnalis in 1934; political incarceration by the Metaxas regime from 1935 to 1940, when he took active initiative in organizing inmate education; and ultimately, his position between 1941 and 1943 as intellectual architect of the largest Greek resistance organization, the National Liberation Front (Ethniko Apeleftherotiko Metopo, or EAM),[42] which in addition to coordinating the mass uprising against the Nazi occupation of Greece also endeavored to introduce such novel social and political reforms as female suffrage and a more inclusive justice system.

Close examination of these trajectories does tend to muddy the distinctions between traditional and organic intellectuals. Like organic intellectuals, these protagonists were able to transcend major positional weaknesses and came to exercise critical influence, at certain conjunctures on a par with many so-called traditionals. But however we choose to label Gramsci, Glinos, and other civil intellectuals of the modern period, their lives were structured by their awareness of local environmental constraints and hegemonic possibilities, developed through fervent intellectual labor and direct action. They were also "emergent" in their alignment with *nouvel regime* popular forces and in that their political superegos, their stores of power and knowledge, and their places in the prevailing hegemonies were by no means fixed by prior standards of authenticity.

Paralanguages of Modern Radical Leadership

To treat the interventions of Gramsci, Glinos, or any other two thinkers as comparable is in every instance to gloss over significant complexity. Undoubtedly the speeches and writings I reflect on below derived from singular imaginations, responding to dilemmas that were situational and ought not to be read too casually. And yet taken as a whole these works show remarkable similarities. Ignoring such patterns of intellectual production we bypass an opportunity to figure, from a broader perspective, how modern nationhood was constituted and understood.

The essays written by the two men during primarily the interwar period are rife with examples of what I have termed *paralanguages of the modern nation*. To recapitulate, this is the combination of stances and recommendations that defined the modern political formation for these intellectuals and for the sake of which they consistently showed themselves willing to mortgage their personal security. Predictably, many of the premises can be directly traced to the tenets of the Enlightenment. Although the French Revolution was not the sole source of ideological raw material,[43] its focus on a civil rights agenda as a cure for absolutism and subsequently, fascism, formed the nucleus of belief. I begin, therefore, by demonstrating the ways in which Gramsci and Glinos exemplify the most salient paralanguages of modern nation building, before considering such further convergences as a burgeoning Marxist sensibility (particularly in relation to potential redistributions of power and debates in the transnational arena) and the role of local debates and alignments.

Generativity, which we have defined as a conscious bid to shape the behavior of future generations, is tied to the quintessentially modern notion of the cardinality of youth. As Philippe Aries and others have argued, the very idea of childhood and children as a class of nascent adults with special needs and rights is a modern invention.[44] That change in repertoire announced a political vision of youth and contributed significantly to the emphasis in twentieth-century political discourse on newness, freshness, innovation, and change that proved so appealing to mass audiences.[45] Morally, the young were beings to be guided in optimal directions. Instrumentally, the young became a source of support for contemporary agendas and a vital constituency.

The focus on the projected requirements of youth was therefore key to the self-conscious development of radical subjectivity and a major rationale behind programs for social transformation. The Italian nationalist Giuseppe Mazzini (1805–1872), for example, inaugurated the movement Giovine Italia (Young Italy) in 1831. This inspired a broader construct called Young Europe, spiritually linked to Young Turkey and Young China, and part of the trend to unite youthful nationalists regionally.[46] In the space of a more recent modern moment, John F. Kennedy launched the New Frontier, a metaphoric expression of his administration's policies that proved vastly persuasive in the American social imaginary of the 1960s. In that decade alone, movements from Nairobi to Paris to Albany, Georgia, underscored the magnitude of the trend.

The list of candidate examples is sweeping, and the political efficacy of the renewal narrative was amply demonstrated in the years that followed the long eighteenth century. My point, though, is that like many others Gramsci and Glinos absorbed lessons about the primacy of newness and youth into their paralinguistic framework of assumptions. As I mentioned earlier, memories of survival in the face of economic and personal hardship and severe shortages of cultural capital were never far from Gramsci's mind as he formulated his theoretical positions. Other kinds of dialogue reveal just how important the generative orientation was for him. In no mood to be indulgent, in his writings on the southern question Gramsci reproves socialist youth, specifically the hotheaded young editors of the journal *Quarto Stato* (Fourth estate), for their careless assessment of the Factory Councils.[47] Gramsci is particularly incensed at their, in his view, fatuous reading of the goals and tactics of the movement both because of what it says about their political maturity and judgment and because erroneous narratives disseminated in print have the capacity to decenter valuable collective memories. Gramsci scolds,

> In their presentation, the editors of *Quarto Stato*—who proclaim themselves to be "young people who know the Southern problem *thoroughly in its general lines*" (sic)—protest collectively at the idea that the Communist Party can be accorded any "merits." Nothing wrong so far: young people of the *Quarto Stato* type have always and everywhere expressed extreme opinions and violent protests on paper, without the paper rebelling. But then these "young people" add the following words: "We have not forgotten that the magical formula of the Turin Communists used to be: divide the big estates among the rural proletariat. This formula is at the antipodes from any sound, realistic vision of the Southern problem." And here it becomes necessary to set the record straight, since the only thing that is "magical" is the impudence and superficial dilettantism of the "young" writers of *Quarto Stato*. The "magical formula" is a complete invention. And the "young people" of *Quarto Stato* must have a low opinion indeed of their extremely intellectual readers if they dare to distort the truth in this way.[48]

On a more tender note, Gramsci's prison letters to his sons Delio and Giuliano contain not just the predictable paternal advice but also suggested sources for moral-cum-political guidance such as the writings of Rudyard Kipling[49] or Pushkin. In a letter to his sister-in-law Tatiana Schucht, Gramsci writes about *Uncle Tom's Cabin* that "in the midst of so much conventionality and propagandistic artifice, I have nevertheless found some rather forceful passages,"[50] and a week later suggests that she make a point of sending editions of that and the *Jungle Stories* to Delio. In family correspondence Gramsci recalls his childhood fascination with tall sailing ships, seafaring terms and naval battles, or encounters with local wildlife—foxes, snakes, eels, birds—on the one hand, to convey whimsy and enjoyment and on the other, to create usable allegories relevant to human negotiations, as a kind of personal stock-taking. "When I was a boy," he writes to Giuliano, "I used to draw a lot, but my drawings were labors of patience; no one had taught me. I would reproduce, enlarging them, the figures and little pictures in a comic book. I would also try to reproduce the basic colors with a system that wasn't difficult but demanded a great deal of patience. I still remember a small picture that cost me at least three months of work . . . My sisters and brothers would look on and laugh but they preferred to run and shout and left me to my endeavors."[51] But combined with benevolent appreciation, during less guarded moments Gramsci would also bluntly critique the pictures and letters his sons sent, a move that ran the risk of wounding the young spirits he sought to mentor.

Similarly, Glinos devoted considerable time and energy to youthful elements as metonymic stand-ins for whole societies at a foundational threshold. In both cases, the forceful tone of certain passages reflects the depth of commitment to the generative project. An apt example is the text of an interview (Glinos's written response) conducted in 1932 by the student periodical *Meleti—Kritiki* (Research—critique) entitled "Poioi Dhromi Anoigondai Brosta Stous Neous" (Which roads stretch before the young).[52] "Dear young people," Glinos writes somewhat grandiosely, "You ask me to tell you which roads open before you and of course, which ones I would advise you to take . . . The roads that today stretch before you are not many, they are only two. Whether or not you choose to acknowledge them, whether they try to hide them from you under a cloud of idealistic sophistry, only two roads remain before you: either you join the side of conservatism and reaction, or you join the side of revolution. *Tertium non datur* (There is no third option)."[53]

Another theme frequently associated with modernity and its Enlightenment heritage was mass education, one of the boldest and most radical challenges to ancien régimes of exclusion. The standard metanarrative posits that the state was moved to consolidate resources in public education because it needed to train future citizens for participation in the modern polity. But since industrial capitalism and entrenched interests ensured as large a pool of miscellaneously disenfranchised as officially franchised, education never lost its edge as a tool of revolutionary analysis and praxis. Both perspectives on education—as reinforcing important, albeit conservative, political structures and as key to the necessary process of rupture that would ultimately benefit the subaltern—were prominent in Gramsci's and Glinos's defining texts and should therefore be placed at the core of any composite sketch of relevant paralanguages. Glinos devoted his life to the cause of mass education through his involvement in the demotic movement. The vast majority of his essays, too, raise the banner, among them "Creative Historicism" (1920), "Women's Humanism" (1921), "The Basic Problem of Education" (1923–24), "The Greek Illness" (1926). "Toward an Understanding of Our Age—Press, Education, Clergy" (1927), "'Educational Ideals' and Mr. Papandreou" (1931), "Intellectual Forms of Reaction" (1932–33), and "National Liberation Struggle" (1942). "Creative Historicism," for example, advocates an approach to ancient texts that allows young readers to assess the lessons of the past and creatively employ them in the present.[54] "Women's Humanism" is the speech with which Glinos inaugurated his brainchild, the Women's University, designed to rectify inequities in Greek higher education. Other essays diagnose gaps and distortions in modern political reproduction in Greece, identify human and institutional obstacles, and offer ways of removing various rocks—backwardness, parochialism, crumbling to nonexistent educational infrastructure, elitism—from the road.

Comparatively, Gramsci's observations about modern education are better known,[55] although the range of writings where he addresses this theme is less appreciated. He weaves insights about education, for instance, into explorations of religion and popular culture, raising questions about how mass consent is taught and organized. Unlike many of his contemporaries on the Italian left, he refuses to dismiss the possible concurrence of spiritual belief and revolutionary commitment among workers, the role played by local Catholic clergy and believers in mobilizing social change, and the vitality of collective emotional attachment to popular literature and the potential of the latter as a site for mass education.[56] This ties into Gramsci's accent on what he terms the "national popular" (mass collective will) and on intellectuals in shaping consciousness at ground level. On the state of Italian literature, Gramsci comments that "the feelings of the people are not lived by the writers as their own, nor do the writers have a 'national educative' function: they have not and do not set themselves the problem of elaborating popular feelings after having relived them and made them their own."[57] In countries "where nationalism exists, but the situation cannot be considered a 'national-popular' one," he remarks, "the great popular masses are . . . put on a par with cattle."[58] That this perspective is shared by Glinos is evident in, among other things, his efforts to achieve wide circulation and accessibility for his journal *Anayennisi* and his editorial admonition to Greek scholars to "live with your people and unite with them, in order to guide them!"[59] Fully fifteen years later, Glinos devotes an entire section of the resistance organizing pamphlet to this idea, declaring that

> the national liberation struggle represents the highest duty of all Greeks, of all the popular strata shaped by their objective material conditions and by the collective will of the people. . . . It is a mass struggle. However such a struggle needs intellectual and political and military leadership. The people cannot fight unless organized. . . . This work of organizing the people will be realized only through intellectual supervision. And this duty falls to all those who, as a result of their position, their profession, their mission and their internal inclination, consider themselves or are the spiritual guides of the people, their intellectuals, the journalists, artists, poets, teachers, priests, judges, doctors, lawyers.[60]

The radical combination of intellectuals and masses was, in fact, the cornerstone of Gramsci's notion of the "historic bloc," a dialectical unity of elite and popular forces that would engender change based on dynamic communication between the "leaders and the led." Here, the influence of Marxist neohumanism is most apparent. For Gramsci, this orientation dated back to his earliest socialist consciousness-raising in Cagliari, Sardinia, and in Turin. For Glinos, this was the result of a more incremental but no less passionate process that culminated in his joining the Greek Communist Party in 1933, by then a mere formality. Both men often elide the distinction between education as a matter for children and young adults and education as a problem of collective consciousness at the mass level. The chief danger was fascism, which throughout much of the Mediterranean littoral loomed menacingly in view by the mid-1920s. The common motivation was the urgent need to pose credible alternatives that would appeal not just to politically green national segments, but also more extensively to mass publics whose political development had been perverted by previous "passive revolutions" (the Risorgimento and the Greek revolution of 1821, the work of a detached bourgeoisie and devoid of meaningful mass participation) and continuities of self-serving moral and cultural leadership.[61]

For Gramsci and Glinos, solutions to the truncated development of the Italian and Greek polities stem from their ideas about what it will take to overcome actually existing hierarchies and silences, which in essence involves the strategic use of education as a counterhegemonic resource. Adult education, self-education, resocialization of values and belief systems, and what Paulo Freire calls "conscientization"—the expanding capacity to analyze and act upon situatedness—are vital mechanisms, logically prior to success. Gramsci's articulation of the factory councils and the new order they were designed to embody and Glinos's efforts to establish various academies, his educational initiatives among prisoners following his arrest for "antinational" activities in 1934, and his conceptualization of EAM were all framed in pedagogical terms. Both believed that students, not just the chronologically young, should acquire a strong grounding in basic skills and principles before tackling more complex approaches to a subject. In a related vein, both saw "the education question" as substantive as well as methodological. Informed resistance and, to use an anachronism, self-actualization would come as much from knowing *how* to think one's way flexibly through a variety of contemporary problems, surrounded as they were bound to be by hidden ensnarements, as from knowing exactly *what* to think formulaically about any given challenge.

Motivated in part by the generative project, which involved ordering both the *consumption* of cultural goods and the *reproduction* of radical subjectivities and collective consciousness, the paralanguages of

modern nationhood fused watchful romanticism and unswerving cultural criticism, at least where Glinos and Gramsci were concerned. This
mixed orientation is well summarized in Gramsci's favorite phrase,
"Pessimism of the intellect, optimism of the will." Not coincidentally
given the Marxist influence, both wove suspicions about how what
Althusser would later call "ideological state apparatuses" functioned
to allow the "reproduction of the conditions of production" and to steer
the course of politics on various levels.[62] The focus was, however, such
apparatuses not in rigidly schematic but in narrative terms, which
assume neither a ready conflation with state power nor completely separate spheres of activity: that is, what kinds of stories issued from the
domain of sociological institutions and how could these be unpacked,
countered, reappropriated, and used to facilitate national-popular participation? On this front, Gramsci attacked a variety of targets too
numerous to mention that in his view symbolized dangerously wrong-
headed thinking, from Croce and Gentile to Bordiga, Tasca, and
Bukharin. He worried deeply and loudly about economism and determinism in Marxist thought and the implications for the philosophy of
praxis, and about liberal masquerades and conservative charades. Pessimism of the will was never a plausible inversion, and he wrote caus-
tically about "all those Nietzschean charlatans in verbal revolt against
all that exists, against conventionality, etc . . . and have thus made certain attitudes seem quite unserious. . . . but it is not necessary to let oneself be guided in one's own judgements by charlatans."[63] For his part,
Glinos held off joining the Greek Communist Party formally despite his
growing ideological loyalties because of profound reservations about
the mechanistic biases of influential factions within the party. He was
also in 1931 quite vigorous in critiquing the minister of education,
George Papandreou, who, like Croce and Gentile in Gramsci's analysis,
threatened to mutate the already seriously flawed face of Greek education through a disastrously idealist strategy.[64] Gramsci's absorption
with the problem of "who will educate the educators," taken from
Marx's *Theses on Feuerbach,* comes to mind.[65] Undoubtedly, trepidation
about the potential allure of hazardous alternatives also helped to
shape the contours of a host of modern political paralanguages. In this
regard, for Glinos, Gramsci, and other Marxist intellectuals, fears about
anarchism as a possible enticement shared some space with worries
about fascism and the slide into cynical realpolitik as options for the
young and politically prone.

Finally, the often poetic tone of modern political paralanguages deserves mention. This bears scant relation to the kind of idealism Gramsci laments in Croce or even at times in his old comrade Angelo Tasca, or Glinos finds so offensive in the Greek bourgeois aristocracy. It is discernible when Gramsci recalls the transformative effects of the factory councils on emblematic social actors or when Glinos expounds on the topic of revolutionary education and its capacity to empower. It can also be seen in less hopeful moments, as when Gramsci writes early on in his prison life: "If I have the assurance that Giulia and the children will not suffer any deprivation, I will really be untroubled: dear Tatiana, this is the single worry that has tormented me during this last period and not only after my arrest: I felt this storm coming, in an indistinct and instinctive way, which was therefore more tormenting."[66] On May 10, 1928, he attempts to comfort his mother:

> I don't want to repeat what I have always written to reassure you about my physical and moral states. In order to be completely tranquil, I would like you not to be too frightened or too perturbed by whatever sentence they are about to give me. I would like you to understand completely, also emotionally, that I'm a political detainee and will be a political prisoner, that I have nothing now or in the future to be ashamed of in this situation. That, at bottom, I myself have in a certain sense asked for this detention and this sentence, because I've always refused to change my opinion, for which I would be willing to give my life and not just remain in prison. That therefore I can only be calm and content with myself. Dear mother, I would really like to embrace you and hold you tight to make you feel how much I love you and how I would like to console you for this sorrow that I have caused you: but I could not have acted otherwise.[67]

Glimpses of the poetic style do not diminish the oppositional charge of these or other discursive moments. They do shed light, not only on expressive and performative aspects of what these leaders were trying to accomplish, but also on the role of *lived emotion,* to adapt E. P. Thompson's concept of lived experience; in other words, how people, especially those imbued with political qua spiritual belief, roil their way intensively and aesthetically (in the interested, not the Kantian sense) through life. A prime example is an essay by Glinos entitled

"Tria Tragoudhia" (Three songs). The piece was published in 1936 in the Communist youth newspaper *Neoi Protoporoi* (New pioneers). It begins in 1935 on the ship *Maria L.* as he and other political prisoners of the current right-wing regime are being transferred, chained to one another, from Piraeus, the port of Athens, to Ai Strati, the well-known interwar penal colony. Glinos details events on the passage between islands and the early hours of the prisoners' arrival at their destination. He draws the reader into his story with vivid, if melodramatic, descriptions of the natural environment of the so-called dry islands, fit for exiles, and the charged atmosphere of the journey as a prelude to open-ended captivity. A vignette about an episode that occurs while he is still on board the ship sets the stage:

> The captain of the "Maria L" . . . motioned me over to the helmsman. "In a moment we'll make contact with Athens on the wireless," he said to me, "so we can hear Kondili's speech . . ." And sure enough, soon scratchy, incoherent voices began to issue from the megaphone. The military dictator and regent adventurer, who had seized power and to prepare for the "honorable and free" plebiscite, sent boatloads and boatloads of democrats and antifascists to the dry islands of the Aegean, with his gasping voice was trying to spread his lies to all corners of the Greek earth. The sailor at the helm, the first captain, the third captain who was also the wireless operator, each listened to the raspy harsh tones . . . with a serene, inscrutable smile on his lips. But none said a word. They increased the weight of their own slavery. And at that moment, I felt inside myself a strange, all-encompassing feeling of freedom, the most intense since I had been arrested. And when I passed, bound in chains, between two thick lines of silent faces in Piraeus and Mitilini and when later I circulated among the passengers and the crew, I felt a deep happiness, which like a drunken harmony filled my soul, and it struck me that only we the prisoners and the exiles were truly free at that moment and all the others were living a nightmare, their chests crushed by slavery.[68]

The three songs Glinos hears and refers to in the title for him symbolize three significant, visceral, organic moments in the life of the nation. The imagery is heartfelt and at the same time calculated to appeal to audience emotion. The first song is the drone of termites, eating their way through the wood in the cabin room where Glinos has gone, exhausted and fever-stricken after the journey, to recover. Every time he closes his eyes he is haunted by this sound. By analogy, he writes that "years ago, I began to hear the monotonous, harsh, irritating concert of termites eating, to the very foundations, the enormous edifice of bourgeois society. It is decaying from roots to rafters."[69] The second song is the church bells calling the faithful to Saturday vespers. He compares this to another time, during the Turkish occupation and before the revolution of 1821, when churches were forced to operate underground and no bells could be heard. The third is the sound of the local prison collective choir singing "The Internationale." The strains fill his room with light; he speculates expansively on the possibility of rousing the entire island to action. The joy alone of hearing *that* song, rendered by *those* voices raised in harmony and solidarity, enthuses Glinos, would inspire anyone to choose exile on that barren island, "to feel the birth of a new soul within" (125).

Radical Readings

> "It will disappear whether we believe in the past or not."
>   Emma nodded her head . . ." I have always felt that the past is a mirror that persuades us, that compels us, to behave well. That is why I studied it and why I taught you, so that we would know how to live." Suddenly she looked tired. She rose from the bed with a sigh.
>   "I distrust history," Clio said. "I always have."[70]

In this essay, I tell a story about the *modern* nation as revolutionary project and—through my ineluctable *postmodern* lens—about the process of its articulation and the methodological challenge of reading the past as a citizen of the present. Often, the reading material available amounts to what Raymond Williams terms "structures of feeling," social texts that are by definition partially submerged below the archival surface. I have argued that with regard to both the evidence social historians deploy *and* historiographic practices this poses a dilemma, which can to an imperfect extent and with lowered expectations be reconciled by the semiotic device of paralanguage. Paralanguages are, fundamentally, creatures of interpretation and speculation; nevertheless they offer a means of gaining insight into cultural contexts and of opening up new worlds of conversation about the shape of the past.

Finally, I have sought to show that the political paralanguages of
Antonio Gramsci and Dimitris Glinos derive, ontologically speaking,
from their passionate aspirations to a generative politics. Such an orientation, it seems to me, only constitutes a usable past from the viewpoint of historians if we can suspend some of the cynicism wrought by
our postmodern detachment and imagine what it was like for the politically conscious to *experience* fascism as it recklessly gained speed in
Europe during the 1920s and 1930s. The urgency of the moment, coupled with mixed opportunities for consciousness raising, left gaps and
contradictions in the articulation of both the radical subject and the radical nation.[71] In a more global sense, perhaps the central lesson of the
political paralanguages of Dimitris Glinos and Antonio Gramsci is one
about history itself in relation to the modern nation. A core message
was about history and historical analysis as a resource (hence Glinos's
innovative "Creative Historicism"), but not with the chaste and dialectical approach of Hegel and Croce. "The 'theoretical' significance of this
debate," Gramsci submits, "seems to me to consist in this: that it marks
the 'logical' point at which every conception of the world makes the
passage to the morality appropriate to it, when contemplation becomes
action and every philosophy becomes the political action dependent on
it. . . . One could say . . . that this is . . . the point at which it becomes
actual and lives historically (that is socially and no longer just in the
brains of individuals), when it ceases to be arbitrary and becomes necessary—rational—real. The problem is precisely that of seeing things
historically."[72] This meant scouring the historical record for analogous
moments, comparable in terms of scene, emplotment, and protagonists;
and maintaining a critical consciousness in reading and receiving transmitted wisdoms about past events before attempting to craft future
praxis.

NOTES

1. Prominent works are Geoff Eley and Ronald Grigor Suny, eds., *Becoming National: A Reader* (New York: Oxford University Press, 1996); Partha Chatterjee, *The Nation and Its Fragments: Colonial and Postcolonial Histories* (Princeton,
N.J.: Princeton University Press, 1993), and *Nationalist Thought and the Colonial
World: A Derivative Discourse* (Minneapolis: University of Minnesota Press,
1993); George L. Mosse, *The Nationalization of the Masses: Political Symbolism and
Mass Movements in Germany from the Napoleonic Wars through the Third Reich*

(Ithaca, N.Y.: Cornell University Press, 1991), and *Nationalism and Sexuality: Middle-Class Morality and Sexual Norms in Modern Europe* (Madison: University of Wisconsin Press, 1985); Andrew Parker et al., *Nationalisms and Sexualities* (New York: Routledge, 1992); Homi Bhabha, ed., *Nation and Narration* (New York: Routledge, 1990); E. J. Hobsbawm, *Nations and Nationalism since 1780: Programme, Myth, Reality* (New York: Cambridge University Press, 1990); Benedict Anderson, *Imagined Communities: Reflections on the Origin and Spread of Nationalism* (New York: Verso, 1983); Nira Yuval-Davis and Floya Anthias, eds., *Woman-Nation-State* (New York: St. Martin's, 1989); Anthony D. Smith, *The Ethnic Origins of Nations* (New York: Basil Blackwell, 1988); Eric Hobsbawm and Terence Ranger, eds., *The Invention of Tradition* (Cambridge: Cambridge University Press, 1983); Kumari Jayawardena, *Feminism and Nationalism in the Third World* (London: Zed Books, 1989); and Miroslav Hroch, *Social Preconditions of National Revival in Europe: A Comparative Analysis of the Social Composition of Patriotic Groups among the Smaller European Nations* (New York: Cambridge University Press, 1985). For historic essays by key public intellectuals on the nationalism question, see Omar Dahbour and Micheline R. Ishay, eds., *The Nationalism Reader* (Atlantic Highlands, N.J.: Humanities Press, 1995). Also see my *New Voices in the Nation* (Ithaca, N.Y.: Cornell University Press, 1996).

Throughout this chapter I use the term *political* not so much in the Foucauldian sense of ubiquitous conflict indifferent to boundaries as in its more commonsensical institutional meaning; in other words, to denote the so-called public face of power. But this is not to deny that power struggles occur on multiple fronts or to rule out a more fine-grained approach where appropriate.

2. See Foucault, *Remarx on Marx: Conversations with Duccio Trombadori,* trans. R. James Goldstein and James Cascaito (New York: Semiotext(e), 1991) especially "How an 'Experience-Book' Is Born" (25–42) and "The Subject, Knowledge, and the 'History of Truth'" (43–82). Here I use *experience* in the sense that Foucault means when he claims that "what is essential is not found in a series of historically verifiable proofs; it lies rather in the experience which the (work) permits us to have. And an experience is neither true nor false: it is always fiction, something constructed, which exists only after it has been made, not before; it isn't something that is 'true,' but it has been a reality" (36).

On evidence as a problem that is both methodological (explicitly used to guide research and to interpret its findings) and social (inspiring behavior), see *Questions of Evidence: Proof, Practice, and Persuasion across the Disciplines,* ed. James Chandler, Arnold Davidson, and Harry Harootunian (Chicago: University of Chicago Press, 1994), especially the exchange between Joan W. Scott and Thomas C. Holt; and Carlo Ginzburg, *Clues, Myths, and the Historical Method* (Baltimore: Johns Hopkins University Press, 1992), especially "Germanic Mythology and Nazism: Thoughts on an Old Book by George Dumezil" (126–45) and "The Inquisitor as Anthropologist" (156–64).

3. Two examples are Mary Ritchie Key, *Paralanguage and Kinesics (Nonverbal Communication)* (Metuchen, N.J.: Scarecrow Press, 1975); and David Crystal,

The English Tone of Voice: Essays in Intonation, Prosody, and Paralanguage (London: Edward Arnold, 1975).

4. On this point, see Dennis Tedlock and Bruce Mannheim, eds., *The Dialogic Emergence of Culture* (Urbana: University of Illinois Press, 1995), especially R. P. McDermott and Henry Tylbor, "On the Necessity of Collusion in Conversation" (218–36) and Alton L. Becker and Bruce Mannheim, "Culture Troping: Languages, Codes, and Texts" (237–52). See also classics by Erving Goffman, *Frame Analysis: An Essay on the Organization of Experience* (Boston: Northeastern University Press, 1986), *Stigma: Notes on the Management of Spoiled Identity* (New York: Touchstone, 1986), and *The Presentation of Self in Everyday Life* (Garden City, N.Y.: Doubleday, 1959); and Peter L. Berger and Thomas Luckmann, *The Social Construction of Reality: A Treatise in the Sociology of Knowledge* (New York: Doubleday, 1967).

5. For example, Pierre Bourdieu, *Outline of a Theory of Practice* (New York: Cambridge University Press, 1987), and *Language and Symbolic Power* (Cambridge, Mass.: Harvard University Press, 1994). See also John B. Thompson, *Studies in the Theory of Ideology* (Berkeley and Los Angeles: University of California Press, 1985). In a related vein, Gramsci wrote about the "prestige theory of language." See "Language, Linguistics, and Folklore," in *Selections from the Cultural Writings,* edited by David Forgacs and Geoffrey Nowell Smith (Cambridge, Mass.: Harvard University Press, 1985), 164–95; and essay by Jonathan Steinberg, "The Historian and the *Questione della Lingua*" (198–209) in *The Social History of Language,* ed. Peter Burke and Roy Porter (New York: Cambridge University Press, 1987).

6. From this literature, see Frantz Fanon, *A Dying Colonialism,* trans. Haakon Chevalier (New York: Grove Press, 1967), *The Wretched of the Earth,* trans. Constance Farrington (New York: Grove Press, 1977), and *Toward the African Revolution: Political Essays,* trans. Haakon Chevalier (New York: Grove Press, 1988); C. L. R. James, *American Civilization* (Cambridge, Mass.: Blackwell, 1993), and *A History of Pan-African Revolt* (Chicago: Charles H. Kerr, 1995); Michele Wallace, *Invisibility Blues: From Pop to Theory* (New York: Verso, 1990); Patricia Hill Collins, *Black Feminist Thoughts: Knowledge, Consciousness, and the Politics of Empowerment* (New York: Routledge, 1991); Angela Y. Davis, *Women, Race, and Class* (New York: Vintage, 1983); bell hooks, *Feminist Theory: From Margin to Center* (Boston: South End Press, 1984), and *Black Looks: Race and Representation* (Boston: South End Press, 1992); Kwame Anthony Appiah, *In My Father's House: Africa in the Philosophy of Culture* (New York: Oxford University Press, 1992); Henry Louis Gates Jr., *Loose Canons: Notes on the Culture Wars* (New York: Oxford University Press, 1992); Cornel West, *Race Matters* (Boston: Beacon Press, 1993); Patricia Williams, *The Alchemy of Race and Rights* (Cambridge, Mass.: Harvard University Press, 1991); Manning Marable, *Race, Reform, and Rebellion: The Second Reconstruction in Black America, 1945–1990* (Jackson: University Press of Mississippi, 1991); Etienne Balibar and Immanuel Wallerstein, *Race, Nation, Class: Ambiguous Identities* (New York: Verso, 1991); Ann Laura Stoler, *Race and the Education of Desire: Foucault's History of Sexuality*

and the Colonial Order of Things (Durham, N.C.: Duke University Press, 1995; Charles Taylor, *Multiculturalism: Examining the Politics of Recognition* (Princeton, N.J.: Princeton University Press, 1994). Also see volumes edited by Richard Delgado, *Critical Race Theory: The Cutting Edge* (Philadelphia: Temple University Press, 1995) and by Bill Ashcroft, Gareth Griffiths, and Helen Tiffin, *The Post-Colonial Studies Reader* (New York: Routledge, 1995).

7. Jürgen Habermas, *The Structural Transformation of the Public Sphere: An Inquiry into a Category of Bourgeois Society,* trans. Thomas Burger, with the assistance of Frederick Lawrence (Cambridge, Mass.: MIT Press, 1987), and *Communication and the Evolution of Society,* trans. Thomas McCarthy (Boston: Beacon Press, 1979); Johanna Meehan, ed., *Feminists Read Habermas: Gendering the Subject of Discourse* (New York: Routledge, 1995); Michael Kelly, ed., *Critique and Power: Recasting the Foucault/Habermas Debate* (Cambridge, Mass.: MIT Press, 1994); Craig Calhoun, ed., *Habermas and the Public Sphere* (Cambridge, Mass.: MIT Press, 1994); Thompson, *Studies in Ideology.*

8. Paralanguage is different from a *subtext,* which involves unexpressed intention, and from *narrative,* or social explanation arranged in the form of an emplotted story. A distinction should also be made between *discourse,* a more far-flung conversation and medium of exchange among social actors, and paralanguage.

9. Carolyn Steedman, *Strange Dislocations: Childhood and the Idea of Human Interiority, 1780–1930* (Cambridge, Mass.: Harvard University Press, 1995), 4. Also see Agnes Hankiss, "Ontologies of the Self: On the Mythological Rearranging of One's Life History," in *Biography and Society: The Life History Approach in the Social Sciences,* ed. Daniel Bertaux (Beverly Hills, Calif.: Sage, 1981), 203–9; and Dan P. McAdams, *The Stories We Live By: Personal Myths and the Making of the Self* (New York: William Morrow, 1993).

10. Quoted in Bill E. Peterson and Abigail J. Stewart, "Antecedents and Contexts of Generativity Motivation at Midlife," *Psychology and Aging* 11, no. 1 (1996): 21. Important theorists in this area are John Kotre, *Outliving the Self: Generativity and the Interpretation of Lives* (Baltimore: Johns Hopkins University Press, 1989); McAdams, *Stories We Live By;* Abigail J. Stewart, "The Role of Personality Development in Shaping Vera Brittain's Feminism and Pacifism," paper presented at Centenary Conference, "A Testament to Vera Brittain," McMaster University, Hamilton, Ontario, October 16, 1993. For other helpful discussions see Peterson and Stewart, "Antecedents and Contexts," Bill E. Peterson and Eva C. Klohnen, "Realization of Generativity in Two Samples of Women at Midlife," *Psychology and Aging* 10, no. 1 (1995): 20–29; Bill E. Peterson and Abigail J. Stewart, "Using Personal and Fictional Documents to Assess Psychosocial Development: A Case Study of Vera Brittain's Generativity," *Psychology and Aging* 5, no. 3 (1990): 400–411.

11. Mary Jo Maynes, "Gender and Narrative form in French and German Working-Class Autobiographies," in *Integrating Women's Lives: Feminist Theory and Personal Narratives,* edited by the Personal Narratives Group (Bloomington and Indianapolis: Indiana University Press, 1989), 110. For more extensive

treatment of popular pedagogy through autobiography, see Mary Jo Maynes, *Taking the Hard Road: Life Course in French and German Workers' Autobiographies in the Era of Industrialization* (Chapel Hill: University of North Carolina Press, 1995).

12. Nellie Y. McKay, "Nineteenth-Century Black Women's Spiritual Autobiographies: Religious Faith and Self-Empowerment," in *Interpreting Women's Lives: Feminist Theory and Personal Narratives,* ed. Personal Narratives Group (Bloomington: Indiana University Press, 1989), 140.

13. The practice of imparting ethical *cum* political lessons to reading publics is salient in the work of a number of modern scholar/activists, including C. L. R. James, E. P. Thompson, W. E. B. Du Bois, C. Wright Mills, Hannah Arendt, E. J. Hobsbawm. Attempts to engender specific behaviors among the common folk are evident in Sojourner Truth's narrative as told to amanuensis Olive Stewart. In this vein also see Thomas C. Holt, "The Political Uses of Alienation: W. E. B. Du Bois on Politics, Race, and Culture, 1903–1940," in *Intellectuals and Public Life: Between Radicalism and Reform,* ed. Leon Fink, Stephen T. Leonard, and Donald M. Reid (Ithaca, N.Y.: Cornell University Press, 1996), 236–56; George M. Fredrickson, *Black Liberation: A Comparative History of Black Ideologies in the United States and South Africa* (New York: Oxford University Press, 1995); and Jervis Anderson, "Two Giants of Literary Cricketism," *New York Times Book Review,* August 31, 1997, 23.

14. See Hayden White's classic argument about the possible functions of the narrative form, *The Content of the Form: Narrative Discourse and Historical Representation* (Baltimore: Johns Hopkins University Press, 1989); and Roman Szporluk, *Communism and Nationalism: Karl Marx versus Friedrich List* (New York: Oxford University Press, 1988) on List's nationalist challenge. Also see C. L. R. James's *American Civilization* (Cambridge: Blackwell, 1993). As I want to claim with the nation, James sees the "American civilization" concept as expressing rich (and loaded) content.

15. See Mark Epstein, *Thoughts Without a Thinker: Psychotherapy from a Buddhist Perspective* (New York: Basic Books, 1995).

16. For a discussion of autodidacticism among German "organic" intellectuals, see Geoff Eley, "Intellectuals and the German Labor Movement," in Fink, Leonard, and Reid, *Intellectuals and Public Life,* 74–96.

17. Hart, *New Voices.*

18. Karen E. Fields, "What One Cannot Remember Mistakenly," in *Memory and History: Essays on Recalling and Interpreting Experience,* ed. Jaclyn Jeffrey and Glenace Edwall (Lanham, MD: University Press of America, 1994), 89–104. I am grateful to DoVeanna Fulton for drawing this source to my attention.

Commenting on a recent translation of Norberto Bobbio's *Profilo ideologico del Novecento* (Ideological profile of twentieth-century Italy), Massimo Salvadori assesses the epistemological roots of such approaches: "As for its literary genre, the *Profilo ideologico* belongs within a solid tradition in Italian cultural history of *saggi-bilanci* summing up the current situation and attempting to answer such questions as, At what point are we? Why? How did we get to this point? Such works, the expression par excellence of historical and political debate and of shifts in ideology and political culture, are generally written by scholars, and their intellectual materials and techniques often reflect the highest standards even when they aim at providing a direct response to the ideological interrogations that prompted them. They usually arise out of moments of acute crisis in the nation, and they often express concerned reflections that aim at holding high old hopes or generating new ones." Massimo Salvadori, foreword to Norberto Bobbio, *Ideological Profile of Twentieth-Century Italy*, trans. Lydia G. Cochrane (Princeton, N.J.: Princeton University Press, 1995), xv–xxxvi.

19. This certainly held true for movements not explicitly anarchic. Even anarcho-syndicalists of the late nineteenth and early twentieth centuries, many eccentric and stubbornly antipositivist, attempted to steer potential followers away from entirely haphazard acts whose point might be lost on broader publics and authorities, and toward a definitive (and definable) worldview. See, for example, discussion of Walter Benjamin on Georges Sorel and the concrete effects of the myth of the "proletarian strike" (Ernesto Laclau and Lilian Zac, "Minding the Gap: The Subject of Politics," in *The Making of Political Identities*, ed. Ernesto Laclau [London: Verso, 1994], 24–26). On anarcho-syndicalism also see Albert S. Lindemann, *A History of European Socialism* (New Haven, Conn.: Yale University Press, 1983). For an emblematic consideration of the role of violence in Indian nationalist reconstruction see Jawaharlal Nehru, "Socialism and Nationalism," in *Nationalism: Its Meaning and History*, ed. Hans Kohn (Malabar, Fla.: Robert S. Krieger, 1965), 175–79.

20. Norbert Elias, *The Civilizing Process: The History of Manners and State Formation and Civilization* (1939; Oxford: Blackwell, 1994), 458, 477.

21. Jamaica Kincaid, "On Seeing England for the First Time," *Transition* 51 (n.d.): 37.

22. Foucault, *Remarx on Marx*, 11–12.

23. For example, even when gravely ill in prison Gramsci displayed an astounding recall in citing sources not immediately at hand, thanks in part to vigilant censors. The depth and breadth of his earlier reading is patent.

24. Gramsci likens the function of certain intellectuals to that of capitalist entrepreneurs: "he must be an organiser of masses of men; he must be an organiser of the 'confidence' of investors in his business, of the customers for his product, etc." "The Intellectuals," in *Selections from the Prison Notebooks*, ed. and trans. Quintin Hoare and Geoffrey Nowell Smith (New York: International Publishers, 1971), 5. The consistent use of male-gendered discourse, whether to connote universal human experience or as an empirical referent, is worth acknowledging, even though a fuller treatment of Gramsci's masculinist tendencies is not possible here. However, see Teresa de Lauretis, "Gramsci Notwithstanding; or, The Left Hand of History," in *Technologies of Gender: Essays on Theory, Film, and Fiction* (Bloomington: Indiana University Press, 1987), 84–94.

25. See Stephen T. Leonard, introduction to Fink, Leonard, and Reid, *Intel-*

lectuals and Public Life, 17–18; and Zygmunt Bauman, *Legislators and Interpreters: On Modernity, Post-Modernity, and Intellectuals* (Ithaca, N.Y.: Cornell University Press, 1987).

26. Jane Burbank, "Were the Russian *Intelligenty* Organic Intellectuals?" in Fink, Leonard, and Reid, *Intellectuals and Public Life,* 97–120.

27. "Politicized intellectuals" is Leonard's term, 3. Joan W. Scott, "The Evidence of Experience," *Critical Inquiry* 17, no. 4 (1991): 773–97, has raised critical questions about self-representations and how historians interpret them.

On the left, the reflexivity of recent times, poststructuralist influences, and a fresh round of soul-searching, post-1989, have led many to reexamine radical intelligentsias with a critical new eye. See, for example, Eugene Genovese's strongly worded "open letter to the left" and concluding "riposte," with commentary by Mitchell Cohen, Eric Foner, Alice Kessler-Harris, Robin D. G. Kelley, Christine Stansell, and Sean Wilentz in *Dissent* (summer 1994): 371–88.

28. Gramsci, "The Intellectuals," 10.

29. Gramsci, "The Intellectuals," 9.

30. For extensive discussions of Croce's shortcomings, see the selections newly translated by Derek Boothman, *Further Selections from the Prison Notebooks,* ed. Derek Boothman (Minneapolis: University of Minnesota Press, 1995).

31. Gramsci, *Selections from Prison Notebooks,* 10.

32. Referring specifically to the question of levels of abstraction, Stuart Hall rightly warns against second-guessing Gramsci or somehow "helping" him to complete his thoughts ("Gramsci's Relevance for the Study of Race and Ethnicity," in *Stuart Hall: Critical Dialogues in Cultural Studies,* ed. David Morley and Kuan-Hsing Chen [New York: Routledge, 1996], 413).

33. Hall, in Morley and Chen, *Stuart Hall,* 433.

34. Gramsci, *Selections from Prison Notebooks,* 144–46.

35. Gramsci, *Selections from Prison Notebooks,* 350.

36. Paul Gilroy, "It Ain't Where You're From, It's Where You're At. . . : The Dialectics of Diasporic Identification," *Third Text* 13 (winter 1990–91): 3–16, cited in Jon Stratton and Ien Ang, "On the Impossibility of a Global Cultural Studies," in Morley and Chen, *Stuart Hall,* 383.

37. Paul Hamilton, *Historicism* (London: Routledge, 1996), esp. 110.

38. For example, in his introduction to the notes on education in the *Selections from Prison Notebooks* Quintin Hoare underscores the point that "Gramsci's success in school and university despite constant ill-health, under-nourishment and over-work was a triumph of intellectual purpose. Something of his individual experience is thus carried over into his repeated emphasis on learning as work. . . . In the last resort, the work involved in education which Gramsci emphasises so much is at one and the same the work by means of which he personally transcended his environment and the work required in the forging of a revolutionary party of the working class—the latter's 'organic intellectuals'" (25).

39. Gramsci, *Selections from Prison Notebooks,* 9.

40. Gramsci, *Selections from Prison Notebooks,* 16.

41. Anna Frangoudaki, "Glinos kai i paidheia" (Glinos and education), in Philosophical Section, Philosophy Department of the University of Ioannina, *Dimitris Glinos: Paidagogos kai philosophos* (Dimitris Glinos: Educator and philosopher) (Athens: Ekdhoseis Gutenberg, 1983), 80.

42. The EAM was initiated in September 1941 by members of the Greek Communist party, the KKE (Kommounistiko Komma tis Ellados). Prior experience with cell structure methods allowed them to give scattered, individual resistance efforts a more coherent form. Several specialized groups fell under the EAM rubric, such as EPON (Enaia Panelladhiki Organosi Neolaias, or United Panhellenic Youth Organization), the youth branch; EA (Ethniki Allilengii, or National Solidarity), the relief organization; and ELAS (Ethnikos Laikos Apeleftherotikos Stratos, or National People's Liberation Army), the military wing. Its major domestic challenger was the significantly smaller "republican" organization EDES (Ethnikos Dimokratikos Ellinikos Syndhesmos, or National Democratic Greek Union), led by General Napoleon Zervas. Zervas was frequently accused of collaboration with both the British and the Germans. After the Italian retreat in 1943, the EAM christened a large mountainous area in the central region of the country "Free Greece" (Eleftheri Ellada), installing a "government of the mountains" under the aegis of PEEA (Politiki Epitropi Ethnikis Apeleftherosis, or Political Committee of National Liberation) and ruled by an elected parliament. Its constitution included a network of participatory rights for newly mobilized citizens. Glinos was nominated for president but declined for health reasons. Following the German evacuation in October 1944, the struggle between EAM and EDES helped fuel the Greek Civil War (1946–49), which culminated in the massive defeat of forces associated with the EAM and rampant arrests, bloodshed, exilings, and movement of refugees. This phase of the conflict stretched into the 1960s and beyond creating a network of social/legal sanctions and a growing sector of political prisoners.

43. I agree with Simon During ("Literature—Nationalism's Other? The Case for Revision," in Bhabha, *Nation and Narration*, 140) that we should be cautious in presuming too facile a connection between the French Revolution and nationally conditioned political identity. Chatterjee *(Nation and Its Fragments)* has led the way in critically examining the reappropriation of modernist culture on indigenous ground.

44. Philippe Aries, *Centuries of Childhood: A Social History of Family Life* (New York: Vintage Books, 1962); Steedman, *Strange Dislocations.* John Boswell, *The Kindness of Strangers: The Abandonment of Children in Western Europe from Late Antiquity to the Renaissance* (New York: Vintage Books, 1990), takes issue with the theory that the social category of childhood is exclusive to modern vernacular, arguing that affective bonds between parents and children were also evident in premodern Europe. Moreover, despite Aries's pretensions to a nonuniversalistic problematization of childhood, his argument nevertheless reflects the blithely Eurocentric bias common to the discussion at that point.

45. For example, see Anderson, *Imagined Communities,* 108–9.

46. Kohn, *Nationalism*. Kohn has been taken to task for his organic view of nationalism—in misguidedly spatial (a thing that moves from "Enlightened" West to East), temporal (a thing that develops linearly and ultimately deteriorates into reactionary forms such as National Socialism), and cultural/psychological (tending toward the irrational and uncritically ideal) terms. See Eley and Suny, *Becoming National,* 4–5. Kohn's now clearly archaic view does not, it seems to me, seriously damage his credibility on this point.

47. "Some Aspects of the Southern Question" never actually appeared in Italy during the 1920s. Gramsci had planned to reinstate *L'Ordine Nuovo* (after the 1919–20 and 1924 conjunctures), this time as a theoretical journal with this essay as the opening editorial, but his arrest intervened. The piece was found among his papers and subsequently published in Paris in 1930. *Selections from Political Writings: 1921–1926,* ed. and trans. Quintin Hoare (Minneapolis: University of Minnesota Press, 1990), 504–5 nn. 240, 245.

48. *Political Writings, 1921–1926,* 441. Gramsci further asserts that "the fundamental concept of the Turin Communists was not the 'magical formula' of dividing the big estates, but rather the political alliance between Northern workers and Southern peasants. . . . The writers of *Quarto Stato* have invented entirely the 'magical formula' they attribute to the Turin Communists; they have thus revealed their journalistic unseriousness and a lack of scruple proper to village pharmacy intellectuals (and these too are significant political factors, which bring their own consequences)" (442–43).

49. In hindsight, an ironic choice given the broader ethical heritage of colonialism, which was at best mixed. It is of course important to bear in mind that nuanced, postcolonial-style readings of many of the texts that fired modern imaginations only became possible after subsequent changes in critical discourses.

50. Gramsci, *Letters from Prison,* ed. Frank Rosengarten (New York: Columbia University Press, 1994), August 1, 1933, 2:316.

51. Gramsci, *Letters from Prison,* 2:386.

52. The piece was republished in *Sti Mnimi Dimitri A. Glinou* (In memory of Dimitris A. Glinos), Ta Nea Biblia (New Books), Athens, in 1946 at another critical conjuncture following the German evacuation of Greece and on the eve of the civil war that led, among other things, to the massive repression of the resistance movement that Glinos helped to create. Poignantly, by then many of the recipients of Glinos's advice had either been killed in the war or would soon find themselves the targets of the repressive apparatus of the state as jailings, executions, and blacklistings of former partisans and youthful members of EAM organizations rose dramatically.

53. Glinos, "Poioi Dhromi Anoigondai Brosta Stous Neous" (Which roads stretch before the young) (1932), in *Eklektes Selidhes* (Selected writings), 4 vols. (Athens: Stohastis, 1975), 4:27–28. All of the works by Glinos cited subsequently are from this edition.

54. This is different from what Gramsci critiques as "Croce's historicism," which he sees as flawed by its Hegelian-style idealism and "an ably disguised

form of preconceptualized history, like all liberal reformist conceptions" (*Further Selections*, 376). Glinos stresses active, creative engagement with history and like Gramsci opposes this to complacent readings that fail to recognize the role of political antagonisms and power struggles in the historical process.

55. For example, "The Intellectuals," "On Education," and "State and Civil Society," in *Prison Notebooks*.

56. See Gramsci, *Further Selections*, for discussions of religion and further selections on education and *Cultural Writings* on fine arts and mass culture. Glinos acknowledges religion as hypothetically positive in form and in principle, and takes a practical view of its capacity to influence popular behavior, but like Gramsci is scathingly critical of the ways in which organized religion has represented "the main spiritual/intellectual weapon of social tyranny" ("Yia Na Katanooume Tin Epohi Mas—Typos, Paidheia, Kliros" (Toward an understanding of our age—press, education, clergy) (1927), 3:82.

57. *An Antonio Gramsci Reader: Selected Writings, 1916–1935*, ed. David Forgacs, trans. Quintin Hoare and Geoffrey Nowell-Smith (New York: Schocken Books, 1988), 365.

58. Gramsci, *Further Selections*, 256.

59. Frangoudaki, "Glinos kai i paidheia," 77.

60. Glinos, "O Laos Anazitei Tous Arhigous Tou" (The people search for their leaders), "Ti Einai kai Ti Thelei To Ethniko Apeleftherotiko Metopo" (What the EAM is and what it wants), 160–61.

61. See Gramsci's "Notes on Italian History," *Selections from Prison Notebooks*, 52–120; and Glinos, "I Elliniki Arrosteia" (The Greek illness), 2:109–23. In "Dimiourgikos Istorismos" (Creative historicism), 1:13–34, Glinos sees the Renaissance as a positive development that unleashed a variety of creative forces and from which Greece, unlike France, Italy, and other "western European" countries, failed to profit fully. In contrast, Gramsci views the Renaissance as a missed opportunity in which the Italian bourgeoisie and intellectuals linked to the papacy did not succeed in establishing a truly viable national state. But he also recognizes it as a mixed blessing, citing "the double face of Humanism and the Renaissance, which were essentially reactionary from the national-popular point of view and progressive as an expression of the cultural development of the Italian and European intellectual groups" (*Cultural Writings*, 188).

62. Louis Althusser, "Ideology and Ideological State Apparatuses (Notes toward an Investigation)," in *Lenin and Philosophy and Other Essays by Louis Althusser*, trans. Ben Brewster (New York: Monthly Review Press, 1971), 127–86.

63. Gramsci, *Selections from Prison Notebooks*, 369.

64. Glinos, "'Ta Idhanika tis Paidheias' kai O K. Papandreou" ("Educational ideals" and Mr. Papandreou), 3:99–113.

65. For example, see references to gaps in his niece Mea's education in letters to Carlo (brother), August 25, 1930, *Letters from Prison*, 1:347–50, and to Teresina (sister), May 4, 1931, *Letters from Prison*, 2:31–32.

66. Letter to Tatania Schucht, December 19, 1926, *Letters from Prison*, 1:50.

67. *Letters from Prison*, 1:206.

68. Glinos, "Tria Tragoudhia" (Three songs) (1936), 4:117–18.

69. Glinos, "Tria Tragoudhia," 122.

70. Susanna Moore, *Sleeping Beauties* (New York: Vintage, 1993), 171–72.

71. For example, Glinos's references to the "obscure and marginal status" of "the Eastern peoples, the Chinese, the Indians, the Egyptians, the Persians, the Arabs" (*Eklektes Selidhes*, 1:18) and the "fate of the blacks of Africa, the coolies and the Chinese beggars who are dying like flies in the cities and in the villages" (*Eklektes Selidhes*, 4:153), warning that the quintessentially *Western* Greek nation must not be allowed to sink to such a level of degradation; and Gramsci's occasional sexist declarations, demonstrate a less enlightened understanding than fans—including this author—would want to see, regarding how regimes of gender and race work to undermine the social-justice agenda that they otherwise advocated so eloquently. Though vitally necessary, as a genre intellectual histories are frequently silent on this score, and unfortunately an examination of such antinomies, one that incorporates the full range of discursive moments, is not possible here.

72. Gramsci, *Selections from Prison Notebooks*, 369.

Strange Rhapsody

What probably centered me most was a lived childhood[1] in Ithaca, New York, in the shadow of Cornell University. The university permeated most forms of existence in Ithaca. It was more or less a company town. Myriad jobs and commercial ventures were connected in some way with the structures up on the hill. Various events—concerts (if and when the performers and Mohawk Airlines were able to negotiate the weather), African Liberation Day celebrations in the early 1960s, Fourth of July fireworks—took place on the campus. My father, an ophthalmologist performing surgeries and refractions on students, faculty, and staff. My mother, having concentrated on raising five children, first an administrator in the ombudsman's office, then an associate dean in the graduate school, and then a vice president for human relations. Classmates' fathers were physics professors, and pundits sought out for their opinions on a range of topics. Some acquaintances were academic secretaries or directors of institutes. Others conducted research at the muddy, pungent pigbarns or performed experiments on moon beetles. When visitors came to town, we would take them to see Cornell sights: the suspension bridge, Beebe Lake, gorges that cut through woods, and the steps of Willard Straight where Ed Whitfield and colleagues were photographed with guns and bullet belts during the student takeover. Clearly the university had colonized the town and that wasn't necessarily a bad thing. Especially when we chauvinistically compared it to Spencer or Cortland or sad, sorry Syracuse.

We were an upper-middle-class black family with a relatively thin sense of boundaries. I remember one time my grandmother, newly arrived from Louisiana, was wounded that she wasn't invited to a party my parents were

---

1. Cf. E.P. Thompson's "lived experience" and Alessandro Portelli's insight that memory is "a form of consciousness." Paul Thompson, "Believe It Or Not: Rethinking the Historical Interpretation of Memory," in *Memory and History: Essays on Recalling and Interpreting Experience,* edited by Jaclyn Jeffrey and Glenace Edwall (New York: University Press of America, 1994):8. Also see Portelli, *The Death of Luigi Trastulli and Other Stories: Form and Meaning in Oral History* (Albany: State University of New York Press, 1991).

giving. Her conditioned view was that regardless of who was on the guest list, no matter what the nature of the party or how regularly you threw these bashes, you always invited family. *This practice was common in the South that she grew up in, a part of "the order of things." Such unspoken codes made African American survival possible. I remember finding this disjuncture striking, and I identified with my grandmother's loss, though at ten I really had no means to put the experience in perspective. Now, through fortysomething eyes, I look at that incident as symbolizing the many contradictions of migration and the crosswinds that would always blow through our anomalous Ithacan existence.*

I remember that for the Greyhound bus trip down to the March on Washington in 1963, my friend Nancy's neighbor Christine brought brownies made with bacon grease. It was her first baking attempt. My father, brother, and I marched with the Ithaca contingent and found a spot reasonably close to the Lincoln Memorial. I can't say that I recall "I Have a Dream" apart from what seemed like an endless round of speeches; only subsequently did it acquire its greater public ritual significance. Later in the day, around the reflecting pool we heard the Freedom Singers, mostly students, performing songs a cappella from Albany, from Mississippi, from jail: "Ain't Gonna Let Nobody Turn Me 'Round," "We Are Soldiers in the Army," "Eyes on the Prize." We arranged a concert and fundraising event to be held in Ithaca later that year, and several of the performers bunked at our house. My parents threw a community picnic, and after the meal there was impromptu singing. The students were between six and ten years older than me and in my eyes so heroic and so righteously cool, having experienced things far beyond my social vocabulary. I adored their songs and wondered about the lyrics. Feeling cramped by my agnostic upbringing, I made a mental note to find out who Paul and Silas (bound in jail) were. Dr. King spoke at Bailey Hall on the Cornell campus during this period, and among other duties, we got to pick him up at the airport. Our family developed a friendship with the McKissick family; Floyd McKissick became director of CORE (Congress of Racial Equality) in 1966. His daughter Andre stayed with us for a time, and I worshipped her for her nail polish, her stockings, her tales about SNCC guys, and her political savvy. In the mid-1960s, we attended a number of protest events. During a rally against the Vietnam War we were jeered at as we shouted slogans and waved signs on our way up State Street hill. My father zealously tried to convince my mother to allow the two older kids, me and my brother, to accompany him on a Freedom Ride. My mother vetoed this idea as too dangerous, and in the end no one went. In 1968,

I got an Afro. In a typical intergenerational conflict of the times, my parents were furious.

In Ithaca and later at Swarthmore College, I came to value a kind of ecumenical power/knowledge. At Swarthmore, I stopped wincing at the idea of being an intellectual. Institutional culture encouraged scholarship as everyday praxis. It would be misleading, however, to characterize myself as unequivocal about the terms of this identity, and during this time my perspective on what constituted the life of the mind shifted in crucial ways. There, as they say, I came of political age, part of the interim but no less militant generation that missed the 1960s by a hair. Between 1970 and 1974, insurgency still prevailed and to some degree took on even more urgent forms. Among Black students—and both Black *and its capitalization were innovations, central to our analysis—cultural nationalism and separate spheres of activity were the order of the day. Marxist and other leftist critical shadings were also seamlessly incorporated into the conversation, as were McCoy Tyner, Sun Ra, Gil Scott-Heron's untelevised revolution, a discursive and practical orientation toward the "Community," lessons about Black histories, literatures, religions. Many of us at some point acquired African names—most of us started regularly adding items of clothing to our wardrobes to symbolize our commitment to local and global struggles. A hundred or so of us ate together, congregated at the Black Cultural Center, had crushes on and romances with one another, studied or "booked" together, fought and factioned, worked on political and community projects together. Our corporate spirit was strong and relatively unforgiving. Admittedly I now look back on all this nostalgically, as a time when a more or less steady articulation of identity padded by a certain kind of security were possible. However many conflicts and feuds bubbled to the surface, the consensus was that these could not be allowed to override our basic unity and mutual affection. Without a doubt, participation in that social movement fostered my later, somewhat vicarious membership in the Greek movement.*

(Scene from a recent Black Cultural Center twenty-fifth reunion: a brother we called "Bush" for his huge Afro, now a physician, with cropped graying hair, walking down the lane with his two adolescent daughters, his shades now used to block out the sun.)

The intervening years before graduate school involved considerable movement. After graduating from Swarthmore with a B.A. in soc-anthro, I worked as a secretary in Boston for a year or so and saved enough money to quit and head for Europe to "wander," I announced. "Blacks don't wander," my relatives countered. "Better plan your future." Of course they were right, to a very significant degree. My recently heightened consciousness told me so. But something else told me this was in some global, so to speak, way my future. These were ten-dollars-a-day, sleeping-bag-on-the-jammed-floor-of-the-convent years and Traveling Youth Nation was large and vaguely socialist and sociable and vibrant. I anchored here and there, with a shifting crew of international companions and eventually ended up on an Ethiopian Airlines flight from Valetta, Malta, to Rome to Athens. I had crossed a new threshold.

It was 1975 and the junta had just fallen. For expatriates and wanderers, Greece tugged and charmed. A breezy sense of optimism and civic fervor seemed to dominate, although at the time my impressions were wide-eyed and lacked all nuance. Still, there was an unmistakable intensity of political and artistic expression, a movida *of sorts. No doubt like the initial post-Franco era in Spain, a sense of relief permeated that I was only able to place in historical context much later. It turned out that, to varying degrees, the country's encounter with fascism had stretched over a period of some fifty years. In a tiny village square on Kerkyra (Corfu), some guys were singing resistance songs, our host explained. Who could've guessed that, ten years hence, I might have cut a counterintuitive figure, a young African American woman belting out "Embros ELAS Yia Tin Ellada!"[2] and joining in the chorus of "Epesate Thimata . . ."?[3]*

I returned home. More movement. To Eugene, Oregon, for a time and secretarial work at the university. When the homogeneity of central Oregon constrained, on to Oakland, California, and similar work at UC-Berkeley in the Career Planning and Placement Office at 111 Wheeler Hall. More crisscrossings. Salsa dancing with friends from work at Caesar's in San Francisco, attending occasional pageants and holiday services with a coworker and her son, my godson, at her A.M.E. church in East Oakland, cheering my older brother as he competed in bicycle races, inner-tubing on the Russian River and otherwise circulating around northern California. After a few years typing away on my trusty IBM Selectric, which at that time was state-of-the-art secretarial technology (imagine a world where we labored clueless as to the impending computer revolution), I moved back East to begin graduate school in the Government department at Cornell University.

I was enchanted with the idea of government or political science for what I imagined it would allow me to do, namely to make everything my business. It really sounded like the way to make syncretic sense of my unbounded fasci-

---

2. "Forward ELAS (Greek Resistance Army) for Greece!" a signal song of the EAM movement.

3. A ballad, "You fell as victims . . ."

nations. Now, in retrospect, my ingenuousness regarding the possibilities brings to mind the frescoes in Siena, Italy, called "Allegories of Good and Bad Government," which in their lacquered fixity fail to acknowledge more than two basic scenarios or the dense politics embedded in politics. The discipline's tendency toward rigid structuring and its narrow conceptions of rigor have increasingly become objects of critique in more adventurous quarters of the academy. I am neither the first nor the last to despair of the cultural resistance to difference and its frequent dismissal as disintelligence within the field. In addition to the standard afflictions of graduate school and the obstacles to pursuing topics thought to constitute "low politics," if they were considered political at all, I was one of three women out of a group of twenty in my cohort and the sole black woman anyone had seen around those parts in a long time. All of this gave me ample pretext to be consistently unnerved, enraged, misunderstood. But those moments also compelled me to try, with mixed results, to find the tools to insist. To harness my idealism and compound perspectives and attempt to make them constructive. I also acquired a great deal of core knowledge about conventional epistemologies in the discipline. I learned about the formal workings of politics from a comparative standpoint, which has since stood me in very good stead, and about social movements and more general European affairs.

In 1983, having finished my qualifying exams and written a preliminary proposal, I returned to Greece to do fieldwork on a Fulbright grant. The original nine months of the grant turned into two and a half years with a renewal and other assorted monies pieced together. These years, too meandering to explore in any depth here, eventually produced a dissertation and book on gendered aspects of the Greek resistance movement and on the movement as a site where fundamental conflicts of modern politics occurred, seen through a semipostmodern lens. The experience, intrinsic to ethnography, of being several kinds of Other while studying several kinds of Other served to trouble and enhance the view. The first kindling of interest in Greece certainly helped to set the research process in motion. I suspect that the collective postauthoritarian glee I witnessed in the mid-1970s was key to my desire to study politics and my decision to focus on Greece in particular. The experience of interviewing former partisans who spent tortured years in exile and prison for alleged "antinational" crimes, who had to find a way to transcend the trauma of watching friends and comrades taken away to be shot at dawn, was very simply lifechanging and provided vivid imagery that I often drew upon to keep me focused. I became obsessed with one puzzle in particular: what kind of resistance movement, and fighting the Nazis was not a hugely controversial cause relative to many others, would represent a specter so threatening as to prompt the executions of adolescents as enemies of the state and family?

I returned home. I began sifting through fifty-odd tapes of oral histories, reading through written accounts, considering popular cultural artifacts, and attempting to write chapters. It was the exhilarating, gut-wrenching, manic experience that others had warned me it would be. I began making presentations at professional meetings and racked up frequent-flyer miles on campus visits. Serendipitously, a chance meeting with Michael Kennedy on a return flight from the Europeanists' conference in Washington, D.C., and a chat triggered by an Anthony Giddens book which one of us was reading ultimately led me to turn down offers in political science and accept my first teaching position at the University of Michigan in Sociology and Women's Studies.

My interest in Gramsci and in nationhood as articulated by specific kinds of intellectuals intensified as I was revising my dissertation into a book. I had taped interviews with women. I had assorted bits of documentation. But I realized that certain convictions expressed about the movement seemed to depict common themes as justifications for participation in the face of considerable danger. I took to heart Anderson's idea of the nation as something for which people would "willingly die" and tried to trace the message valorizing such behavior to the leaders, interrogating their understandings of what fascism meant and their notions of what its most effective antidote might be. I linked Gramsci's counterhegemonic stratagems—emphasizing education, the revolutionary "party," informed commerce between the leaders and the led—to the analogous logic that I argue was shared by Greek intellectuals such as Dimitris Glinos.

Eight years after my arrival in Ann Arbor I sit with my laptop and try to impose some order on the chaos of twenty years of production and growth. In crafting my story inevitably I've left gaps, including past lives in Boston, D.C., and New York. Currently, I now teach in the Anthropology department. This is fitting, given how much I've noticed, worked around, and tried to problematize various identities. Such struggles are what a number of anthropologists have tried to make explicit in the conversation. The boundaries of my epistemic community have continued to widen, of choice and of necessity. I am now part of an old tradition of unusual intellectual injections into the discipline and indeed a lively, amorphous interdisciplinary community that will never be stuffed back into the box.

Janet Hart

Yuri Slezkine

N. Ia. Marr and the National Origins of Soviet Ethnogenesis

Whatever about the soundness of de Selby's theories, there is ample evidence that they were honestly held and that several attempts were made to put them into practice.

Flann O'Brien, *The Third Policeman*

The world consists of nations. Nations are communities united by a common name, state, language, territory, customs, and physical features. Nations are defined by their origins. The origins of the name, state, language, territory, customs, and physical features have nothing to do with each other. Such was the Great Ethnological Predicament, discovered and sometimes discussed by eighteenth-century scholars as they pursued D'Alembert's "art of reducing, as far as possible, a great number of phenomena to a single one which can be regarded as the principle of them."[1] "*Principle* and *beginning*" being "two words that originally signify the same thing" (as Condillac put it),[2] the pursuit of principle became mostly historical. Stubbornly and perhaps uniquely among natural phenomena, nations seemed to have several principles at the same time.

The problem was particularly painful in Russia, where a few German scholars brought in to catalog the empire's endowments had concluded that, according to the best "primary sources," the Russian land had not been "Russian" for very long; the Russian state and the Russian name had come from Scandinavia; the Russian apostle Andrew had never been to Russia; and the Russian language had been—quite recently—imported by the tribes chased out of the Danube. It was all very fine for the Academy of Sciences historiographer G.-F. Müller to

assure his readers that science implied a difference "between a historical dissertation and a panegyric" and that "the origins of peoples,
mostly quite obscure; the beginnings of states, usually humble; and the
savage ways of ancestors," among other things, had "absolutely nothing to do with either fame or infamy."[3] M. V. Lomonosov knew better.
"If the modern Russian nation is descended primarily from the ancient
people who existed before the coming of the Varangians," he argued,
"then the dishonor engendered by contempt for those ancient people
affects in very large measure the modern nation."[4] Much more to the
point, the origins of peoples, the beginnings of states, and the ways of
ancestors (all of them as "ancient" as one's scientific imagination would
allow) had to be closely related to each other and to the name and territory they all shared (preferably "for ever and ever" but possibly "from
time immemorial"). The various components of the "modern nation"
taken apart by the misguided and probably ill-intentioned academic
mercenaries had to be put back together again. In Lomonosov's own
version, the ancient Russians were called Roksolans (Russians) and had
spoken Slavic (name equals language); the ancient Slavs were Sarmatians and hence had always inhabited the Russian land (name equals
language equals territory); while the apparently alien Varangians were
Slavic-speaking Prussians and hence Russians (name equals language
equals territory equals state).[5]

In the wake of the Romantic enthronement of folk cultures, the
study of each national ingredient gave birth to a more or less
autonomous academic discipline concerned, inter alia, with the delin-
eation of national boundaries through a search for national origins. The
Great Ethnological Predicament grew more dire: "cultures" were holistic, but "nations" as defined by folklorists, ethnographers, archaeologists, linguists, and geographers were not coterminous and perhaps not
even cognate. The Russian land was not equal to Russian dialects,
which was not equal to the distribution of Russian dwellings, wed-
dings, songs, or scythes. Historical syntheses tended to begin according
to the territorial principle, then shift to the ethnolinguistic, and finally
to the state before they could proceed with a national story that claimed
the unity of all meaningful elements.

The turn toward positivism in the second half of the century transformed the study of particular ethnic traits (such as language, customs,
or myths) but had very little effect on the fuzzy organic metaphors
applied to nations as whole entities. The neogrammarians' "regular

sound laws" grew on the genealogical tree of Romantic comparativism; Veselovskii's "laws" of universal literary history and "mixings" of cosmopolitan plots were ultimately attached to "folk-poetic organisms" and "national essences"; the ethnologists' evolutionary schemes were being compromised by the ethnologists' attachment to the "naturalness" of the evolution's victims; and the archaeologists' chronologies were being complicated by the discovery that recurrent assemblages of prehistoric artifacts were "cultures" associated with well-traveled tribes and their languages.[6] Russian positivism was populist: it undermined its *völkisch* foundation without questioning it.

Few scholars were as effective in this regard as the physical anthropologists, whose efforts to compile a racial map of the Russian empire and build a truly genetic classification of its many peoples had resulted in the taxonomic dissolution of the peoples in question. Based on their height, hair, skin color, and cephalic index, some Russians had turned out to be Finns, some Finns to be Balts, some Balts to be Slavs, and some Slavs to be Turks. According to the founder of Russian craniology A. P. Bogdanov, the Great Russians were the only true descendants of the ancient Slavs. According to the most prominent Ukrainian anthropologist F. Volkov, the Great Russians (and, perhaps predictably, the Poles) happened to be the only Slavic speakers who were biologically non-Slavs. And according to D. N. Anuchin's 1892 summation of the majority opinion, half the Great Russians from the central provinces were tall, upright, fair-haired Slavs with "straight noses" and "expressive eyes," while the other half consisted of stocky, swarthy Finns with narrow eyes and flat hairless faces with prominent cheekbones.[7]

One could avoid such discrepancies by dismissing the offending discipline altogether, as did the philologist A. I. Sobolevskii, who rejected the "Finnish admixture" thesis on the basis of linguistic, historic, and folkloric evidence.[8] More commonly, one could question a given discipline's choice of taxonomic indices. Archaeologists wondered what artifact combinations constituted a "culture," linguists questioned Humboldt's morphological criteria for typological classifications, and race scientists asked which physical traits formed "true indicators of race."[9] No matter what the "first principle," however, a perfect fit remained out of reach (even for Sobolevskii). Too many Slavic-speakers with Finnic faces were walking over Germanic graves.

Perhaps this was the way it was supposed to be. "We know,"

wrote Anuchin, "that 'ethnic group' *(narodnost')*, 'tribe,' and 'race' are very different concepts: membership in a certain ethnic group (or people) is based on a common culture, history, and ethnic self-identification; membership in a certain tribe is based on a common language; and membership in a certain race is based on a common physical (anthropological) type. All across Europe we see that these categories do not coincide."[10] Many scholars accepted this proposition, and some made the point of discussing inanimate fossil cultures or speechless dolichocephalous races, but virtually everyone—at one time or another—used the same generic ethnonyms when referring to archaeological finds, skull shapes, linguistic reconstructions, political entities, and geographic units. E. M. Chepurkovskii insisted on "the fundamental finding of anthropology that language and race do not coincide" even as he divided the peasant population of European Russia into Finnish, Great Russian, Little Russian, and Teutonic racial groups.[11] Anuchin's student and later the dean of Soviet physical anthropologists V. V. Bunak populated his studies of racial types (alias "tribes" alias "peoples") with the Spanish, Dutch, and Chinese.[12] And Anuchin, as we have seen, did not always follow his own advice. Indeed, most anthropometric studies in Russia were done on populations defined by language ("the anthropology of the Finns") or by ethnic/administrative territory ("the craniometric survey of Georgia"). The archaeologists routinely attributed changes in material culture to migrations, thus associating them with particular ethnic groups (the Cherniakhovskii culture was found to be Gothic, i.e., Germanic). The linguists, meanwhile, had little choice in the matter (only a handful being prepared to discard "Russian" or "German" as useless abstractions), so that discussions of language spreads were commonly perceived—and sometimes meant—to refer to the physical movement of peoples. The terminological disarray was exacerbated by relentless nationalist efforts on behalf of a retroactive national wholeness. If Lithuanians were defined according to a particular language, homeland, and cephalic index, then the longer these traits had been related, the better for the Lithuanians.[13]

By the mid-1920s the Great Ethnological Predicament had been partially alleviated through inattention. Nations and nationalities had been officially promoted to moral subjects and political units, but origins were quickly losing ground as scholars moved from diachrony and historicism to synchrony, function, and structure. The "ethnographic present" and the fully deethnicized future prevailed over "ethnogenesis"; "indices of racial affinity" and "racial hygiene" pre-vailed over race formation; the morphology and typology of archaeo-logical artifacts prevailed over evolutionary sequencing; and Baudouin de Courtenay and Ferdinand de Saussure prevailed over Wilhelm von Humboldt and Hans Conon von der Gabelentz. Linguistics, in particu-lar, became mostly structural, and most structural linguists became "applied" as N. F. Iakovlev, E. D. Polivanov, and friends set out to cre-ate new alphabets, formulate new standards, and codify new vocabu-laries in new dictionaries (this, along with an interest in the "sociology of language," appeared to constitute Marxism in language science, although no one knew for sure). Etymologies, protolanguages, and Slavic antiquities were out; "the living word," native vernaculars, and "Eastern nationalities" were in. Polivanov had good reason to compare his work to that of Cyril and Methodius.[14]

There were plenty of philologists and archaeologists who contin-ued to labor in the historicist tradition, of course, but most of them seemed uncomfortable around the modernity-bound proletarian politi-cians and Marxism-struck academic modernists. Most—but not all. Nikolai Iakovlevich Marr was a philologist and archaeologist in the his-toricist tradition who seemed as comfortable around politicians (old and new) as he appeared to be confident about the Romantic seeds of avant-garde millenarianism. A full member of the Russian Academy of Sciences from 1912 on, Marr was the dean of the Department of Orien-tal Languages of the University of St. Petersburg from 1911 to 1918; first dean of the Department of Social Science of Petrograd University; director of the Institute of Archaeology (formerly the Archaeological Commission) from 1918 to 1919; founder and president of the State Academy for the History of Material Culture (heir to the Archaeologi-cal Institute) from 1919 until his death in 1934; founder and president of the Japhetic Institute (1921–31) and of its successor, the Institute of Lan-guage and Thought (1931–34); and head of the Section of Materialist Linguistics of the Communist Academy. Marr's main claim to scholarly distinction lay in the field of Georgian and Armenian antiquities (both "spiritual" and "material"), but his real passion was the study of com-parative linguistics in pursuit of remote origins—his own, his home-land's, and everybody else's.

N. Ia. Marr was born in Georgia in 1864, the son of a Scottish father who did not speak Georgian and a Georgian mother who spoke noth-ing but Georgian.[15] "Communication in a formally mixed language" had "some effect" on the boy's Georgian vocabulary (and possibly on the man's later theory, which, in Katerina Clark's words, enabled "mummy and daddy to speak to each other, if in some primordial past"),[16] but it was the orphan status of the Georgian language itself that became N. Ia. Marr's most public obsession. By the turn of the twentieth century, most languages of Eurasia had been assigned to "families" complete with ancestors (protolanguages), siblings (the progeny of the same *Muttersprache*), and offspring (dialects on their way to becoming languages). Among the relatively few exceptions was Marr's mother tongue, which appeared unrelated to any other language except for the neighboring Mingrelian, Laz, and Svan. Appearances could be false, however, and possibly falsified on purpose. Having determined, at the age of fifteen, to "promote the Georgian language and enhance its prestige in its social milieu," and having vowed, at the age of twenty, "not to lay down his arms" until Georgia was liberated, Marr set out in search of relatives.[17] As a graduate of the Kutaisi gymnasium, he attempted to link Georgian to Turkish and English, and as a student at St. Petersburg University, he was pleased to discover, proof pending, that "the Georgian language [was] related to the Semitic family in both flesh and spirit, i.e., according to word roots and grammatical structure."[18]

Why had no one ever noticed this before? Because Indo-Europeanist linguistics (Marr refused to notice any other kind) was willfully ignorant of the languages of the Caucasus, complacently dogmatic about its procedures, and thus guilty of complicity "in the oppression of the peoples of the East by the European peoples with their lethal colonial policies."[19] "Would you like concrete proof? Here it is: note how much attention the European nations have been paying to Sanskrit—because it is related to European languages, because it has a written form (a very ancient one), and because it is highly cultured and thus representative of the great cultural beginnings of European languages. Note how much has been done to study Sanskrit as compared, say, to the Dravidian languages of the same area."[20]

In Marr's view, the ethnolinguistic quest for "Adam's biblical paradise and Hesiod's Golden Age" was designed to benefit colonial empires at the expense of everyone else (hence the insistence on a *single* protolinguistic heaven). Indo-Europeanist scholars of Indo-European backgrounds were "still looking for Elysian rivers . . . populated by their Indo-European forefathers armed with speech and high culture and ever ready to settle Europe."[21] The deliberate confusion of language and ethnicity that this scheme implied was based on "a contrived representation of national origins that did not take into account true genealogies" but did attach culture to race in a deliberate attempt to perpetuate Western ascendance over the "oppressed tribes and peoples."[22] All Western claims to scholarly objectivity were spurious because all Western research on cultural difference was inherently racist.

Marr's own ambition was to restore genealogical justice once and for all. He was going to trace the origins of nations without causing offense to anybody except the habitual offenders from among the Indo-Europeans. He was going to prove that "progress was characteristic not only of Europeans" and that, if it came right down to it, "the European race" had "brought with it the barbarism that had destroyed a flourishing [pre-Indo-European] culture."[23] He was going to erase the distinction between *Naturvölker* and *Kulturvölker* ("there are no primitive peoples in the world").[24] He was going to be "vitally *(organicheski)* interested in the equal consideration of the languages of all peoples irrespective of whether they had an ancient writing system, a new writing system, or no writing system at all, and whether they were fully or very weakly integrated in modern culture." He was going to be "especially interested in promoting the national consciousness of small and backward peoples whose mental structure was different from the mental structure inherent in the ruling languages, or the languages of the ruling peoples, that is to say, the ruling classes."[25] He was going to overthrow the dictatorship of artificial literary standards—those "enemies of the natural life of languages" that "destroy popular linguistic creativity" and corrupt the "soul of the people."[26] Most important, he was going to resolve the Great Ethnological Predicament by prescribing a logically consistent and morally unimpeachable method of combining race, language, culture, and class within a holistic evolutionary framework.[27]

Marr was not alone in his struggle. In the early 1920s—when he became a minor celebrity and a powerful academic entrepreneur—official Party pronouncements seemed to equate national inequality with class oppression; various nationality spokesmen tended to attach comparable value to their groups' unrelieved martyrdom and unrivaled accomplishments; and even the firmest of "formalists" paid homage to the "peoples of the Orient" and "the dependence of linguistic evolution

on social and economic phenomena."[28] The degree of support for
Marr's sentiments was great enough to worry the self-styled lone cru-
sader: the Indo-Europeanist enemy, besieged by Boas and Iakovlev
alike, was almost too feeble to play its part.

It was the Vienna-based "Prague" phonologist and exiled
"Eurasian" enthusiast N. S. Trubetskoi, however, who came closest to
sharing Marr's concerns, if not his linguistic methods. Clearing the East
Slavs and other redeemable Indo-Europeans of all suspicion of colonial
complicity, he accused the aggressively acquisitive and "sinfully
proud" Romano-Germanic peoples of "ravaging the souls of Europeanized peoples" and rendering them "spiritually barren and morally
indifferent."[29] The key to the West's success was not so much its "materialist-utilitarian and rationalist foundation" as its ability to fool others
with the disingenuous talk about humanity (read "Romano-Germanic
peoples"), universal civilization (read "Romano-Germanic culture"),
and cosmopolitanism (read "Romano-Germanic chauvinism"). Recom-
mended resistance strategies included cultural self-knowledge and
self-esteem, but also scholarly struggle on behalf of *territorial* "language
unions" *(Sprachbund* or *iazykovoi soiuz,* as in "Balkan," or—much more
controversially—"Eurasian"). The gratifying, if paradoxical, result of
this war on ethnic lineages was a world divided into organic, self-contained, and morally incommensurate ethnolinguistic "cultures"
attached to particular histories and landscapes. Some cultures seemed
markedly less "materialist-utilitarian" than others. Materialism-utili-
tarianism was an absolute evil.[30]

Preaching Eurasianism in Vienna proved less profitable than pursuing ethnolinguistic equity in Petrograd. But Marr was not simply in
the right place at the right time. He was the right man for the job of
devising the ultimate ethnological synthesis because he was the ultimate personification of that synthesis. Not only was he simultaneously
a linguist, archaeologist, historian, folklorist, and ethnographer. His
whole life was a reflection of universal history as he saw it and thus an
answer to the offensive yet seemingly all-pervasive question of
whether the Caucasus "had a history."[31] All of Marr's major theoretical
statements were stories of personal/national victimization followed by
personal/national vindication. "There came from the wild Caucasus a
wild man who dared teach the teachers and who was bold enough to
propose that the uncultured Georgian language, known by few and
studied by fewer, could compete in its linguistic significance with such

rich and cultured classical languages as Sanskrit, Greek, Latin, or even Old and Middle Persian."[32]

The man had excellent reasons to propose what he proposed, and the language had an excellent chance of winning the competition. The triumph of the theory blended into the final revolution against national oppression.

In 1908 Marr published his "proof" of the Georgian-Semitic relationship. With the help of sound laws that operated beyond time, place, and dialect, the two phonetic and morphological systems turned out to be strikingly similar, and a few dozen semantically linked roots (plus about nine hundred more that the author promises to produce but does not) turned out to be cognates.[33] The conclusion was that Georgian was "the most characteristic representative" of a "Japhetic branch" of a large "Noetic family," which also included the Semitic languages. To be more precise, Semites and Japhetides "were related in the manner of cousins—that is, as the children of two brothers, the Proto-Semitic and Proto-Japhetic languages."[34] This scheme was not just genealogical (and thus, according to Marr's usage, "Indo-Europeanist")—it was remarkably similar to the standard medieval Georgian family tree first outlined by Leonti Mroveli in his eleventh-century *Chronicle of Kartlian Kings* (Kartlos was the son of Targamos, "the son of Tarshis and the grandson of Noah's son Japheth").[35] Whatever did not fit the indigenous patrilineal relationship was the result of Indo-European manipulation:

> The displacement of the organic development of the Japhetic languages from the path of their original racial psychology and the decay of their primordial morphophonational *(morfo-fonatsionnoi)* life is probably due to the immigration of the Aryan race, which was foreign to them at the time, into those parts of Southwest Asia *(Peredniaia Aziia)*, Asia Minor, and Armenia that constituted the main area of settlement of the Japhetic tribes. The fact that the autochthonous proto-Armenians were subject to particularly intense Aryanization does not mean that the Georgians and those tribes that are at present more closely related to them did not suffer a similar fate. Among other things, the Aryan invasion cut the Japhetic world off from the Semitic world, pushing the less affected representatives of the former into the basins of the Kura, Chorokh [Çoruh], and Rion.[36]

At one stroke, the Georgians regained their distinguished biblical pedigree and acquired a solid claim to uncommon ethnic purity along with a bitter grievance against the Indo-Europeans. "Japhetidology" became the heavenly double of the ethnoracial Indo-Europeanism as practiced, in particular, by the Berlin University professor Gustaf Kossinna, whose German Society for Prehistory would shortly become the Society for German Prehistory.[37] (Ironically enough, the world's first Indo-Europeanist treatise—James Parsons's 1767 *The Remains of Japhet*—referred to "European languages" as Japhetic and located their homeland in Armenia.)[38]

As for Marr's Armenians, it soon turned out that their "Aryanization" was mostly a masquerade. According to one of Marr's third-person autobiographical statements, even as a university student he "had stopped being a Georgian nationalist but had not given up the nationalist platform: as a result of dealing with the various national masses of the Caucasus and learning their languages he had gradually become an internationalist in his attitude toward Caucasian society."[39] In other words, he had become a pan-Caucasian patriot, arguing repeatedly, passionately, and against vehement Georgian and Armenian opposition that all the peoples of the Caucasus shared the same "autochthonous" roots, the same relationship to the mountainous landscape, and the same "cultural elements" that had emerged "from the treasury of the most ancient experiences of the people and found expression in original monuments." There were many such monuments—literary, architectural, and ethnographic—but it was the "indigenous languages (i.e. non-Indo-European and non-Turkic)" that bore witness to the true primordial unity of the Caucasian "national psychology."[40]

Accordingly, Marr devoted himself to the study of the various languages of the Caucasus and in due course found them all to be more or less Japhetic. To quote the eleventh-century chronicler again, "the Armenians and Kartlians, Rans and Movakans, Heris and Leks, Mingrelians and Kavkasians all had the same father, whose name was Targamos. This Targamos was the son of Tarshis and the grandson of Noah's son Japheth. And this Targamos was a hero."[41] In Marr's version, the Armenian language turned out to contain a Japhetic layer that represented a "survival of the language of the aboriginal inhabitants of Armenia" and was, therefore, linked to "the very depths of the national psychology": kinship terms and numerals may be "Aryo-European," but "words for such concepts as *sky, earth, water, soul, breath,* and a significant share of the verbs expressing *spiritual effects—fear, happiness, etc.,* belong to the corpus of Japhetic elements."[42] Indeed, the Armenian language was congenitally dualistic, or "bigenetic" *(dvuprirodnyi)*— "the result of the mixing of two races, the Japhetic and the Aryan."[43] Better yet, there were two "organically distinct" Armenian languages/races: one indigenous, demotic, oral, and mostly Japhetic, the other alien, aristocratic, literary, and mostly Aryan (languages equal race equal class).[44] This was not good enough, however. By 1916 Marr had established that "neither of the languages of Armenia . . . fully lived up to the theory of Western European scholars: neither proved to be purely Aryo-European. Both turned out to be languages of the so-called 'mixed type,' namely Aryo-European and Japhetic. Thus, ethnically and linguistically one-half of Armenian nature is closely related to the Japhetic peoples of the Caucasus."[45] This fission, too, proved to be a half measure: "Even the Japhetic languages as we know them today are far from being pure. It has been shown, for example, that the Svan language is a mixture of two Japhetic branches."[46] And so on, deeper and deeper into antiquity and "national psychology." Rejecting, in effect, the concept of borrowing, Marr continued to locate mixtures within mixtures within mixtures until it appeared impossible to identify the ingredients that were being mixed.[47] Nothing, however, appeared impossible to the "madman who opened his own Pandora's box" by continuously exploring his own origins: all languages were mixed; all languages issued from the union of opposites; all languages bore a family resemblance to their parents; and no languages—in spite of the Indo-Europeans' murderous rampages—ever became extinct, surviving within other languages and ultimately making it possible to recover the primordial state of Japhetic purity.[48]

One after another, most of the living languages of the Caucasus and the dead languages of the Mediterranean succumbed to the Japhetic epidemic. Assuming language and race to be identical, and regarding "tribal name" as the most faithful and durable indicator of origin, Marr found Caucasian sources for an ever growing list of Eurasian ethnonyms/peoples ("Etruscan," "Pelasgian," and "Lezgian," for example, were derived from a Georgian word for "stork" [*lak'-lak'-i*], which meant that the ethnic groups in question were descended from a Japhetic tribe that had had a stork as its totem).[49] By 1920, the Japhetic branch had been promoted to a family in its own right, while languages from Burushaski in the Pamir to Basque in the

Pyrenees (by way of Elamite, Sumerian, and Thracian, among others) had been promoted to the status of Japhetic. The "Japhetides" turned out to have been the earliest and largest "ethnic substratum" of the Mediterranean world, "or indeed the very foundation of the Mediterranean culture, the historic source of world civilization."[50] The great migration of peoples turned out to have been "the great spread of the Japhetic tribe" from its Caucasian homeland to the Atlantic coast and possibly to Central Asia, Far East, and Africa. "The very beginnings of culture"—the invention of fire and the taming of metals ("as well as precious stones")—turned out to have been a Japhetic gift to mankind.[51] And Mount Ararat, upon which Noah's ark came to rest, turned out to have been a true "Japhetic mountain"—the "prehistoric guard" of pre-Babel beatitude. "And the whole earth was one language, and of one speech" (Gen. 11:1). "And the Lord said, Behold, the people *is* one, and they have all one language" (Gen. 11: 6). "Go to, let us go down, and there confound their language, that they may not understand one another's speech" (Gen. 11:7).

> This fairy tale is the tale of Japhetic reality. Over the entire land known to the civilized world of that time, from the Caucasus to Asia Minor to the Iberian Peninsula, there was but one language, the language of the Japhetic family. . . . There may have been an earlier blow to the unity of the Japhetic world, but the last "crushing" blow—the coup de grâce—was delivered by the Indo-European invasion, which was followed by confusion, . . . hybridization, the emergence of new mixed linguistic types, and the end of mutual comprehension.[52]

But the Indo-Europeans were not just "bandits" bent on "silencing live speech, extinguishing national psychology, laying waste to the land, and exterminating the people."[53] They were also the smug proprietors of that "global European culture" that Marr—along with countless patriots elsewhere—was so anxious to both debunk and appropriate. Accordingly,

> The Japhetic languages of Asia Minor and the insular and peninsular Japhetic languages of Mediterranean Europe—the languages of the peoples who created the culture that preceded the invasion of the Indo-European barbarians—only seemed to be destroyed. In

fact they did not sink into oblivion, did not perish, but, through participation in the process of new ethnogony and glottogony, entered everyday life, nature/speech *(prirodu-rech')*, and, naturally, the psychology of the newborn peoples. The creators of the pre-Hellenic and pre-Roman Mediterranean culture never stopped participating in the creation of the entire global European culture.[54]

Athena was Caucasian, after all, as were "the works of Homer" and "the legends of the birth of not only Moses but also Romulus and Sargon."[55]

This was not all. In the same year (1920) that he staked the Japhetides' claim to temporal and spatial priority in "global culture-creation," he took them on a journey that seemed to transcend time, space, and therefore culture-creation. The tripartite evolutionary sequence he had established was ethnoracial (Japhetides, Semites, Indo-Europeans) and linguistic ("amorpho-synthetic," agglutinative, flectional), as well as social, psychological, artistic, and economic (not spelled out).[56] Parallelism reigned at every level: "the morphology of speech reflected the morphology of the social system"; "agglutinative psychology" corresponded to agglutinative art; and so on, very neatly—except that none of it applied to the Japhetides:

> The modern Japhetic languages carry within themselves exceptionally striking relics of all three periods. Touching the skies with their head (national psychology) like the mythical hero Atlas, the Japhetides, while capable of thinking, speaking, and creating at the level of all epochs of the cultural history of mankind, including even our own modernity, are firmly attached with their trunk (the morphological structure of speech) to the soil of prehistory. In fact, they have their feet deeply rooted in that soil, preserving, through an unbroken chain of transformations spanning a number of periods, a bond with the state of the same language on the verge of the humanization of animal speech.[57]

The conquest of space is usually more straightforward than the conquest of time. In May 1922 Marr listed the Dravidians as being "genetically related" to the Japhetides but pledged "silence, for the time being, on the ethnoglottogonic problem of the indigenous population of America."[58] Several months later he commented on the "amazing typological analogies—one could even say, total identity," between the Native American and Japhetic languages. And within the space of four years he had appropriated Chuvash, Chinese, Hottentot, and, with particular gusto, the remaining Indo-European languages.[59] The class/race of the Roman plebeians was traced to the Japhetides by way of Lesbos (*ple* from *les* plus the Georgian plural suffix *b*); the great city of Paris, "illuminated by the achievements of the highest civilization," was connected to the Caucasus by the river Seine (which means "blackbird" in Mingrelian); "German" was derived from "Megrel"; "Hun" from "Svan"; "Russian" from "Etruscan"; "Ukrainian," also from "Etruscan."[60] The Japhetides had always been everywhere. All humans were Japhetic. All the words of all the languages were echoes of the ancient Japhetic tribes and their totems.[61]

By about 1924, in other words, Marr's Georgians had progressed from an orphaned ethnic group to a well-connected ethnic group to a great ethnic group to the only ethnic group to the very essence of human evolution. One man's nationality question and the world's ethnological predicament were resolved simultaneously by a daring dialectical move: if everyone was the same ethnicity, then there was no such thing as ethnicity. The racist ("Indo-Europeanist") equation of language family, culture, and race had been defeated through a much closer identification of language family, culture, and race—until there were no more language families, cultures, or races. A search for high-status ethnic kin had led to the total disaggregation of ethnicity and kinship. No more minorities and majorities, no more privileged peoples, no more nations. "It is self-evidently absurd to identify the formation of a nation with the act of physical birth from a particular pair of known parents (sometimes with a helpful reference to noble origins)—from Mommy and Daddy living in a stable household."[62] Indeed, "the very terms *ethnos* or *tribe* in their old meaning would have to be discarded," and the whole concept of Japhetic migrations would have to be abandoned.[63]

What was the new meaning of *ethnos?* Who were the "Japhetides" if not a tribe, and what accounted for their ubiquity if not migrations? After 1924, the answer was obvious enough to appear inevitable. Marxists from various quarters were trying to fit scholarly disciplines into historical and dialectical materialism; scholars of various persuasions were seriously exploring the promise of Marxism; and linguists, in particular, were growing increasingly keen on the connections between "language and society."[64] At the same time, Marr was presiding over a rapidly expanding institutional realm that included the State Academy for the Study of Material Culture, the Caucasus Section of the Commission for the Study of the Tribal Composition of the USSR, the Japhetic Institute, the Central Bureau of the Society for Local Studies, the Communist Academy, Leningrad University, and the Oriental Institutes in both Leningrad and Moscow. Between 1923 and 1925, he provided a solid political cover for his domain by becoming the chairman of the Section of Scientists and a member of the Central Committee of the Educators' Union, director of the Leningrad Public Library, a member of the Central Trade Union Council, and a permanent member of the Leningrad Soviet "of all convocations." Marr probably noticed, in other words, that some theoretical formulations were better regarded and better funded than others; and even if he did not, A. V. Lunacharskii, M. N. Pokrovskii, and V. M. Friche were quite blunt about which formulations of the Japhetic theory they found appealing.[65] All this, in addition to the apparently irresistible inner logic of the theory itself, led Marr to the discovery that Marrism was Marxist and that " 'tribe' ('ethnos') was not a racial but a socio-economic concept. Starting from the earliest forms of human collectivity, these were groups based not on blood but on economic need. Not only was there no 'Daddy-the-progenitor'—one single father—but there was no kinship. Kinship terminology, like the family itself, was a later phenomenon. Kinship terminology has been found to refer to one's social position as determined by production."[66]

Language and thought were superstructural phenomena whose evolution mirrored the evolution of the economic base.[67] The "kinetic" or "linear" speech of prehistoric man was immanent in manual labor/thought. The four original sound elements of the primeval oral language (SAL, BER, YON, ROSh) accompanied syncretic magic performances "necessary for successful production" by a pretribal collective.[68] "Embryonic" languages expressed the "diffuse nature of prelogical primitive thought, which was necessarily concrete but did not differentiate among concepts."[69] "Monosyllabic/polysemantic" languages, of which Chinese was a remarkable relic, "did not distinguish between basic and functional meanings" and corresponded to the stage of primitive communism.[70] Agglutinative languages were more archaic than flectional languages (which represented class society); languages with pharyngeal sounds were more archaic than languages without such sounds; nouns came before verbs; the pronouns came from totems; the plural preceded the singular; grammatical gender dated back to the matriarchate; and the word *horse* was used to refer to dogs, deer, elephants, and camels, thus reflecting the history of modes of transportation.[71]

Marr obviously did not know how to fit all these correspondences into a universal evolutionary chronology. Nor did he seem to worry too much about it—what mattered the most, apparently, was that all languages of the world were related without being blood relatives, "this relationship . . . based on similarities in social development and not on racial descent from common parents."[72] "Each racial language family has turned out to be a new system representing the development of a previous system, not a genetically separate group. The isolation of not only the Georgian language, but even of the Chinese language, has disappeared."[73] *Quod erat demonstrandum.*

The reason for linguistic and cultural change was "not external mass migrations . . . but revolutionary shifts that resulted from qualitatively different conditions of material life, qualitatively new technology, and a qualitatively new social system."[74] All languages were native to their soil ("autochthonous"): the various Russian dialects, for example, were genetically unrelated remnants of the Japhetic languages that had become "Slavic" due to similar socioeconomic pressures. All languages were class languages: "same-class languages from different countries—given identical social structure—are more similar typologically than the languages of different classes within the same country, the same nation."[75] "All languages great and small" were therefore "equally mortal in the face of new proletarian thought that [was] forging a classless society."[76] To be more specific, the existing "sound languages" and "formal logical" (that is, hierarchical) thinking, created by the exploiting classes in their own interest, would be transcended by the "dialectical materialist thought of the proletariat," which would provide the whole of mankind with not only one single thought process but also with one single language—the master of all time and all space.[77] To be even more specific (and possibly more postmodern),

> Our greatest accomplishment—an accomplishment brought about
> by the proletariat—is the fusion of science and its ideological tech-

nology with art and its formal technology, as well as the unity of beauty and intellect (the intellect of the dialectical materialist thought of the proletariat). This dialectical materialist thought knows neither a successor nor closure: it possesses inexhaustible possibilities of developing in width and in depth, in space and in time. This dialectical materialist thought has outgrown linear speech, no longer fits within sound speech, and, as it outgrows sound speech, it is preparing to mold—to create—a new unified language based on the final accomplishments of both manual and sound languages—a language wherein supreme beauty will merge with the highest development of the mind. Where? Only in a classless, communist society, comrades.[78]

Marr's "new theory of language" was generally ready by 1928, when the arrival of a speechless society of supreme beauty was officially prophesied for the foreseeable future.[79] The First Five-Year Plan was to be the "last and decisive battle" against all tyranny in general and the dictates of biological descent, in particular. "Little families" were to be replaced by Stalin's big one.[80] A breathlessly wordy linguistic doctrine with almost nothing between genesis without genetics and the Apocalypse without sound seemed a perfect rhetorical match for the Great Transformation of the Soviet Union.[81]

There was much more to the New Theory of Language, however (the theory being much less New than it claimed). The grand obituary to "biologism" consisted of mostly biological metaphors that suggested an organic growth from "numerous mollusk-like embryo-languages" to full proletarian fruition by "mutations" of "hybridized" organisms (all of which ultimately consisted of the same four irreducible "elements").[82] The adamant advocacy of the base-superstructure dualism was also a spirited defense of life's organic wholeness against the positivistic "formalism" of both structuralists and historical comparativists.[83] The new science designed as a proletarian weapon in the struggle for socialism was a "paleontological" descent into the "spider's deafness" of the most distant rung of "Lamarck's sliding ladder" (as Mandelstam, himself intrigued by the "spirit of Japhetic philosophizing," put it).[84] Perhaps most obviously, the final abolition of ethnicity affected different ethnic groups in different degrees. Slavic kinship might be a myth, for example, but certain Transcaucasian peoples remained "at a high stage of enlightenment" by retaining their "ancient national culture—more ancient than Russian and Western European and characterized by an eastern-borderland bigenetic (Asian/European) humanism that was superior to the one-sided and enclosed European humanism of Western countries."[85] Some Japhetides were clearly more Japhetic than others, and so some Japhetidologists seemed especially sympathetic to the discovery that the existing ethnolinguistic order was an imperialist artifice; that all non-Japhetic scholarship was carried out by colonial administrators and missionaries in the service of the Indo-European bourgeoisie; and that the language of the future would supercede the "always class-bound, culture-bound, and inevitably imperialistic traditional international languages" by incorporating the speech of those regions that "until now have been stigmatized as places of exile and doomed as colonial or 'native.'"[86]

Marr claimed to be gratified, therefore, and not at all surprised, that the Japhetic writings shunned by the "Indo-Europeanists" in Leningrad, Moscow, Erevan, and Tbilisi were being "warmly welcomed and lovingly printed in Dagestan, in Abkhazia, in Cheboksary by the Chuvash, in the young University of Azerbaijan, in the equally young scholarly community of the Azerbaijani Republic, in the fresh milieu of the still scattered new centers of scientific self-knowledge in Vladikavkaz, among the Osetians; in Ust'-Sysol'sk, among the Komi, etc."[87] When the Cultural Revolution called for a complete fusion of scholarship and politics, it was these "promotees" from "fresh milieus" who forced "the entire army of ethnographers, archaeologists, and folklorists" (not to mention the newly prominent linguists) to abandon "biologism," racism, "psychologism," "creeping empiricism," and all the other stratagems that cast doubt on the "eventual success of the Soviet policy of fostering the cultural development of the most backward national groups."[88]

Ethnographers renounced the transcendental claims of such bourgeois concepts as culture, ethnos, and diffusion, pledging themselves to the study of "specific societies, particularly those that still find themselves at the early stages of development."[89] Within three years, the "dizzying" success of the First Five-Year Plan resulted in the official disappearance of such societies from the face of the USSR and in the (inconclusive) banning of ethnography for impersonating a Marxist science and perpetuating the colonial distinction between *Kulturvölker* and *Naturvölker*.[90] Many of the former ethnologists were reassigned as Marrist historians specializing in primitive communism and its rapidly disappearing survivals. One of their primary commissions was to engage in the study of "ethnogenesis," or the origins of entities that did not seem to have any historical-materialist substance.[91]

Archaeologists denounced formalist "objectology" (*veshchevedenie*) and racist migrationism in order to become "historians of material culture," dedicated to the reconstruction of the full range of social relations within socioeconomic formations as well as to the "study of today's survivals with the goal of their correct liquidation."[92] Having been persuaded, however, that the existence of archaeology under any name was "tantamount to the anti-Marxist and anti-Leninist attribution of a special form of [dialectical] development to mere artifacts," they disbanded themselves altogether before settling on the role of material-source experts and hence "de facto historians of distant epochs" (more recent epochs being accessible through other sources).[93] The key to the correct interpretation of excavated objects was the New Theory of Language, and the guide to the correct methodology was Marr's "genetic approach."[94] Of the two leading archaeological revolutionaries, one discovered that the East Slavs were descended from "totemic production groups with Japhetic speech and a homogeneous totemic socioeconomic system," while the other proved that the Black Sea Goths were "formed autochthonously and by stages" from preexisting local populations.[95]

Folklorists withdrew from rump ethnography and moved into literary studies, defining their niche of "ideological superstructure" as the "oral-poetic creativity of the broad popular masses, . . . ultimately conditioned, in its formation and development, by a given mode of production and the corresponding relations of production." Useful "for the reconstruction of the history of society," folklore provided a valuable key to the understanding of popular consciousness as it evolved from "primitive thought" to "socialist content." Marr's "paleontological analysis," in particular, could reveal prehistoric meanings—and hence prehistoric social realities—behind literary plots, tropes, and motifs. The reason it could do so was because literary devices did not migrate any more than did ethnic groups, surviving as semantically transfigured but physically recognizable relics of earlier cognitive-linguistic stages. Today's metaphor was yesterday's identity of meaning.[96]

Physical anthropologists rose up resolutely against "biologism" in general and "zoologism" in particular. Races existed "objectively in nature" (not just in people's minds), but their reality as "biological collectives" was "superceded" (*snimat'*, from the Hegelian *aufheben*) by social groups based on class and ethnicity. Human biodiversity was qualitatively different from animal biodiversity because the various human races had lost their species instinct (displaced for the most part by social calculations); become thoroughly mixed (except for a few isolated groups); abandoned natural selection in favor of social selection; and cut loose their association with particular geographic areas and their dependence on the natural environment. There was no causal connection between biological race on the one hand and particular "linguistic, cultural, and other social groups" on the other. "No cephalic indexes, no racial traits of any kind will prevent the most culturally backward peoples from advancing toward higher cultural and political forms provided the appropriate socioeconomic conditions are present." Meanwhile, Soviet race science (*rasovedenie*) would continue to exist because "in spite of all the above tendencies, racial distinctions will survive for a very long time as a certain biological reality that is not permanent but can still be observed with a naked eye or, in more complicated cases, through anthropological analysis." Given that this biological reality was "contained within social entities"; that social entities of real consequence were class and nationality; and that the racial study of classes was—for reasons that were never spelled out—an absurd proposition, the task of Soviet race science was "to study the biological peculiarities of ethnic groups." The definition of ethnic groups (and the degree of their "reality") was not the responsibility of race scientists.[97]

Linguistics was the only discipline where young Marrists had serious competition for the Marxist mantle. In February 1929 E. D. Polivanov—a ten-year Party veteran as well as a Petrograd University professor of Far Eastern languages, a founding member of the Society for the Study of Poetic Language, and a leading theoretician of the alphabet reform in Central Asia—publicly accused Marr of "appalling ignorance of the most basic concepts of all branches of linguistics, from speech physiology to the comparative-historical grammar of any group of languages."[98] Citing scores of absurd etymologies, odd transcriptions, logical non sequiturs, and all manner of other "horrors," Polivanov concluded that the Japhetic theory had nothing to do with either Marxism or linguistics, and urged his audience at the Communist Academy to work on a new theory based on "facts rather than faith." The problem was that the audience consisted mostly of the Marrist "faithful" (as Polivanov himself put it), and that the main article of their faith was a principled refusal to distinguish between faith and facts, and hence between Marxism and linguistics. "Quixotic" to a much greater degree than he seems to have realized ("I accept this term, it was well-chosen by comrade Il'inskii"),[99] Polivanov appealed to the authority of his Western peers; bemoaned the propensity of minority graduate students to "speak even when they do not know the subject"; grudgingly excused Stalin for "not knowing the terminology"; compared Marr to a man who showed up at a chemistry conference claiming that water consisted of four mysterious elements rather than hydrogen and oxygen; and generally made a nuisance of himself by claiming repeatedly that "facts were facts" and that scientific work by trained professionals was the only way of establishing them, whether ignorant outsiders liked it or not and whether those involved happened to be bourgeois or proletarian.[100]

> What do you want? Do you want guidelines that consist of true general statements that may be correct and acceptable from a Marxist point of view but that are not based on linguistic facts? But this is not linguistics— Marxism perhaps, or maybe the theory or history of science, but not linguistics. Only when all Marxist propositions, all propositions of dialectical materialism are based on facts—only then will I say that you have Marxist linguistics.[101]

Polivanov was banished to Samarkand, and in the fall of 1930 his pursuers turned on each other. The young members of Language Front (*Iazykfront,* a clone of RAPP's [Russian Association of Proletarian Writers] *Litfront*] were fluent in the new idiom, as well as quite sure that science was contingent on class and perhaps ethnicity, but they found Marrism's preoccupation with origins to be mechanistic, backward-looking, and hence detrimental to socialist "language construction." The Marrists, for their part, defended the cutting-edge modernity of their paleontology and castigated their opponents for reactionary idealism and covert Indo-Europeanism. After two years of uneven struggle (the Front's only institutional base was the Commissariat of Enlightenment), the latecomers to linguistic Marxism were defeated, disbanded, and posthumously humiliated by being equated with Polivanov.[102]

What all these Marrist pronunciamentos had in common was their attempt to rehabilitate low-status ethnic groups by questioning, and perhaps shattering, the concepts of ethnos, race, national history, and national culture. For the first time since the eighteenth century, the Lomonosov solution to the Great Ethnological Predicament was being rejected fully and unequivocally. The fixation on origins remained (and was justified by constant references to Engels's-dictum-turned-Soviet-reality that the only real science was history—human and natural), but the idea of the common and ancient provenance of all national ingredients was declared to be a "fiction" and a "mirage" when it was not being dismissed as "indescribably foolish and trivial nonsense."[103] Witness, for example, the various attempts by "bourgeois scholars" to identify the ancient Scythians with Slavs, Germans, Finns, or Iranians.

> All of them without exception, whatever their point of view, base their research on the modern ethnographic—in effect political—map. No one wonders if it is scientifically appropriate or if there were any Slavs, Germans, Finns, and Iranians in the Scythian period. Everyone takes for granted the unproven fact that all of these peoples existed in remote antiquity, arbitrarily projecting some piece of the modern map onto the distant past. And amid all the quarrels and recriminations, no one seems to realize that they find themselves within a vicious circle insofar as they assume precisely those things that need to be proven.[104]

At the root of this delusion was the Indo-Europeanist belief in eternal ethnos (inspired, according to Aptekar', by the desire of the nineteenth-century German Romantics to "weasel their way out of a despised European provincialism" into "a good noble genealogy").[105]

> The concept of a gradual coming together of an ethnos does not exist in bourgeois science. Ethnos is assumed to be fundamentally stable, and so are, in the final analysis, races, cultures, and languages. When the notorious *Nordische Rasse* . . . first appeared in the Mesolithic period, it already possessed all the traits that characterize it now: long-headedness, tallness, a particular facial index, etc. Along with these traits, the northern proto-Indo-Germanic race had—also from the very beginning—certain cultural proclivities that became manifest in the subsequent development of its cultural area. By the same token, all the peculiarities of a given lan-

guage family are contained within the protolanguage. Evolution becomes teleological.[106]

A curious accusation coming from a Marxist, perhaps, but it was the nature of the telos that mattered. The bourgeois scholars as described by the Marrists were high priests of the nation-state, and so they "fantasized about the great 'states' of antiquity that had never existed"; staked national claims to particular pots, bones, and therefore lands; labored assiduously to "make cephalic indexes fit culture areas"; and generally devoted themselves to self-serving myth-making.[107] The Marrists as described by themselves, on the other hand, knew that there was "no fateful link between ethnic groups and the collections of variously shaped objects known as 'cultures,'" ridiculed the "theory of the original connection between modern language groups and particular races," and never tired of quoting Marr's passionate refusal to consider "human tribes" to be "zoological types akin to horse or cow breeds, with tribal traits inherited ab ovo."[108]

Meanwhile, the political authorities were pulling their share of the weight by arresting non-Russian ethnologists as bourgeois nationalists; Russian historians, as White sympathizers; "regional studies" enthusiasts, as "creeping empiricists"; and most Slavic philologists, as sentimental Slavophiles turned saboteurs.[109] According to one scholarly indictment with penitentiary consequences, the field of Slavic studies was devoted "to the study of 'a single Slavic type with common physical and spiritual characteristics,' to the defense of its unique nature, and to the promotion of its consequent messianic role, thus always representing a science deliberately and entirely saturated with zoological nationalism." Both in the "so-called Slavic countries" and in the Soviet Union, the Herderian reification of the *Volk* based on the imagined connection between "blood descent and the physical conditions of existence as determined by territory" was tantamount to a "slide into fascism."[110] Fascism was, of course, a very real threat outside the Soviet Union—and therefore, according to the now familiar logic, a very real threat within Soviet academia.

By the end of 1934 most ethnological disciplines (but not most ethnologists) had been proclaimed to be Marrist; Marrism had been proclaimed to be a subset of Marxism; and Marr himself had been decorated with the Order of Lenin, buried beside Lomonosov, and beatified through a series of "memory immortalization" decrees.[111] Unfortunately for the victorious Marrists, however, the Great Transformation had already begun to give way to the "Great Retreat," or at any rate to a quite substantial transformation in a new direction. In 1932, ethnographers and archaeologists had been told to stop questioning "historically given ethnic and national peculiarities," and in 1934 special government decrees had denounced Marr's historiographic counterpart M. N. Pokrovskii for serving up "abstract definitions of socioeconomic formations" instead of a "coherent," "lively," and "entertaining" historical narrative centered on the "peoples of the USSR."[112] Soon after Marr's death on December 20, 1934 large portions of his New Theory (including the four irreducible "elements") disappeared from scholarly discourse; during the terror of 1937–38 some of his closest disciples (as well as opponents) disappeared into the Gulag; and in 1938–39 the whole of Marrism was apparently rendered irrelevant by the Party's demand that historians, anthropologists, archaeologists, folklorists, and linguists join forces in pursuit of Lomonosov-style national origins, with special attention to the "determination of the antiquity of Russian, Ukrainian, and Belorussian settlement on the territories that they currently occupy."[113] The 1938 drafts of Soviet and world history textbooks began with "ancient tribes" that gave birth to less ancient tribes in a clearly genealogical fashion; in that same year the Slavic origins of the Russian state and the murky origins of the Germans and the Japanese became the object of special scholarly scrutiny; and in 1941 the leading Marrist deconstructor of race took obvious pleasure in showing that Germans were more Mongoloid than Eastern Europeans (those from Hanover and Baden, for example, "turned out to be clearly 'Mongoloidized' (zamongolizirovanny) as compared to the Voronezh Russians or Vychegda Komi, and only a little less so than the North Caucasus Turkmen, who are half Mongoloid").[114] Nazi race science was no longer a demon to be exorcised—it was a rival to be defeated "on its own territory."

Marr was not formally expelled from the Marxist pantheon, however, so that Soviet ethnologists from various disciplines found themselves in a no-man's-land between two worlds that had nothing to do with each other: the official blood-and-soil nationalism and the no less official socioeconomic Marrism. Some felt perfectly at home there: the celebration of particular ethnic groups by means of an apparent denial of ethnic continuity had been at the core of the New Theory. The historian N. S. Derzhavin, for example, toiled tirelessly in the field of "Slavic ethnogenesis" while continuing to argue that there was "no point in trying to determine at what time this or that people came into existence."[115] The anthropologist G. F. Debets ridiculed the Indo-European confusion of race and language while conducting his own "racial analysis of the Veps" among "those who, in their domestic environment, use the Veps language in preference to Russian or at least on an equal footing with it."[116] Others cited Marr, mentioned "stadialism," and then pointedly ignored both in pursuit of a research objective that took for granted migrationism, tribal genealogy, and the longevity of the "ethnos."[117] Yet others appeared to reject the whole "Marrist-therefore-Marxist-therefore-valid" formula and made Polivanov-like appeals to independent scientific criteria that went unpunished and possibly not unheeded. "They have tried hard to turn us, historians who rely on real facts, into poets," protested the recently released but apparently unreformed V. I. Picheta at the March 1940 session of the History and Philosophy Section of the Academy of Sciences. "Instead of this hypothesis I can propose any other hypothesis, and then the battle of our hypotheses will become reminiscent of medieval scholasticism."[118] Beginning in 1937 Western classics of "formalism" and "Indo-Europeanism" were being translated into Russian, cited generously, and reviewed on their own terms; and at the end of the war the non-Marrist linguist V. V. Vinogradov was brought back from exile (his second after the 1934 "trial of the Slavists"), made dean of the recently resurrected Philology Department of Moscow University, awarded the Lomonosov (!) prize for *The Russian Language,* and in 1946 elected full member of the Academy of Sciences, bypassing the "corresponding member" stage.[119]

Not a moment too soon, as it turned out. In the late summer of 1946 Zhdanov launched his offensive on the culture front, and by late 1947 it had been revealed that Vinogradov's *Russian Language* was not "a Russian book on the Russian language" but a lot of "vacuous and pernicious nonsense" dressed up as "pseudoscientific objectivity."[120] "The reign of Zhdanov" (much of it posthumous) was a more or less self-conscious attempt to revive the flagging spirit of the Cultural Revolution: all knowledge was either Marxist or anti-Marxist; all claims to objectivity were vacuous and pernicious nonsense; all Soviet scholars had to be Marxists "in deed"; all practicing Marxists had to agree on what Marxism meant in practice; the true meaning of Marxism emerged from "lively discussions" refereed by Party guardians of "party-mindedness." More specifically (after August 1948), Marxism meant a rejection of genetic determinism and an interdisciplinary endorsement of Lysenko's Lamarckianism.[121]

The Soviet nationality theorists seemed to have no choice. Marr was the officially accredited prophet of Marxism among ethnologists and an obvious double of the newly accredited prophet of Marxism among biologists. The new cultural revolution had to complete the work of the old Cultural Revolution. The surviving Indo-Europeanists and all other formalists/comparativists had to "disarm" before the teaching of Marr because the teaching of Marr was "an integral part of the ideology of socialist society" and thus "the only general theory and the only scientific theory for all the particular linguistic disciplines."[122]

> It is not enough to recognize the New Theory in words alone, nor is it enough to refrain from fighting against N. Ia. Marr—it is necessary to be a consistent and uncompromising fighter for N. Ia. Marr! Either the triumph of materialist linguistics founded by N. Ia. Marr, or the misery of existence in the swamp of Indo-Europeanism. There is and there can be no "third way," no "golden mean" of any kind![123]

After more than ten years of compromise and equivocation, all ethnic genealogies were once again proscribed—this time for the additional reason that they were analogous to the "primary and immutable agents of heredity" contrived by the bourgeois geneticists.[124] Linguists promised to continue Marr's struggle against inheritable folk essences, ancestral protolanguages, and specious structuralisms (Saussure was a default geneticist because he divorced language from its social base).[125] Archaeologists forswore migrationism and "objectology," ethnographers insisted on the "historicity" of ethnicity, folklorists expelled functionalists along with "traveling plots," and physical anthropologists attacked racism by emphasizing "the influence of external conditions on man's physical type—on the transformation of his inheritable nature" (V. V. Bunak, who suggested that eating an extra kilo of sugar "does not mean that one's skull shape will change or any such thing," had to apologize and admit "the unconditional correctness of the principles of Soviet Darwinism as formulated by the academician T. D. Lysenko").[126] In late 1949 the Agitprop Department of the Party's Central Committee reviewed the battlefield and found the degree of Marrization to be woefully inadequate.[127] The Presidium of the Academy of Sciences resolved to reissue Marr's works and Marr's biography; establish a special Marr Commission on the Languages and Scripts of the Peoples of the USSR; institute a Marr Medal and a Marr Prize; celebrate Marr's death as well as his birthday; and stage a Marrist-dominated discussion "aimed at the conclusion of the evaluation of the situation in Soviet linguistics."[128] Non-Marrist professors were blackballed, demoted, and dismissed. Non-Marrist books were banned. Marr himself was proclaimed a "resolute enemy of cosmopolitanism."[129]

A cultural revolution (complete with "scholar brigades" and pugnacious graduate students) in the land of socialist realism was a rather incongruous affair. A Marrist revolution amid the postwar patriotic campaign was downright bizarre. Both the original Great Transformation and its postwar aftershock absolutized the us-against-them dichotomy (with "no third way of any kind"), but the meaning of both "us" and "them" had of course changed: "proletarian" was now "Soviet" (divided unequally by nationality), and "bourgeois" was now "foreign" (with some preference for "Anglo-Americans").[130] Foreigners masked their racism as cosmopolitanism, while Soviets openly enjoyed their patriotism because it was wholesome as well as pleasurable. "Humankind is divided into nations. Each nation has its own national culture, its own mores and customs, its own special way of life. Every nation treasures its national uniqueness, loves it, is proud of it, and does not want to trade it for a cosmopolitan gruel."[131] Scholars, like everyone else, were expected to contribute to the making of the rich national soup: "every scientific discovery belongs to a particular nation, and every new theory is put forward by a scholar belonging to a certain nation."[132] Ethnologists, in particular, had to get back to their primary responsibility of studying national cultures—"because if each nation has certain peculiarities that are uniquely its own, then these peculiarities, or rather, each nation's national culture, need to be studied."[133] No more "abstract stages" diluting the "wonderful, centuries-old epic tradition of the Uzbek people"; no more "cosmopolitan-racist" campaigns to dissolve the Tajiks, Persians, and other peoples of the Iranian language group in some faceless 'Iranian' ethnic element; no more "preposterous, reactionary attempts to destroy the national uniqueness of the *Kalevala* through pointless, ridiculous comparisons."[134] One could no longer cover one's back with a few quotes from Marr—one had to be equally passionate about deconstructing nationality and building it up. The challenge was to be Marrist and anti-Marrist at the same time; to wear one's Marr medal while bemoaning his "abstract stages"; to keep referring to Marr's work without ever reading it.

Deliverance and absolution could only come from above. In the spring of 1949 the most brazen Soviet anti-Marrist, Arnold Chikobava, was asked by the first secretary of the Georgian SSR to summarize his views in a special essay. Vilified relentlessly by the new cultural revolutionaries in Moscow and Leningrad, Chikobava was one of the most prominent academics in Tbilisi—perhaps because he approved of the "Japhetic" phase of Marrism while rejecting the theory of stages on nationalist as well logical grounds.[135] "The Japhetic (or Ibero-Caucasian) languages," he wrote in his Party-commissioned paper, "do not constitute some mythical evolutionary stage, frozen in its development just to suit the far-fetched scheme of the Japhetic Theory. The Japhetic languages are living representatives of an ancient and numerous group of languages, whose speakers are known in the history of mankind as the creators of the ancient Near Asian civilization, which gave rise to the ancient Greco-Roman civilization, and consequently, to the whole of Western European culture."[136] On the evening of April 10, 1950, Chikobava and the four highest-ranking Georgian officials arrived at Stalin's dacha for a chat about linguistic theory. The host, who had obviously read the Tbilisi essay, told Chikobava to write a larger "discussion piece" ("You go ahead and write it, and we'll see. If we like it, we'll print it"). Chikobava wrote it, Stalin liked it, and after two more editorial summits Chikobava's attack on the New Theory was printed in *Pravda* on May 9.[137] In the following "free discussion" (the most widely publicized and, for the average *Pravda* reader, probably the most obscure in recent memory), some heartened dissidents accused Marr of being un-Marxist, unscientific, anti-Russian, and possibly insane; some prudent scholars pointed out certain errors and contradictions in his theory; and a few puzzled but steadfast Marrists defended what they assumed to be the official orthodoxy (it was not quite two months, after all, since the Presidium of the Academy had ordered the cessation of all work on comparative grammars!).[138]

On June 20, 1950, Stalin broke the suspense by publishing his own—and hence everybody else's—views on linguistics (the piece was typographically indistinguishable from other discussion entries, so that the reader had to scan the standard boxed-in introduction or wait for the signature at the bottom to know that it was the Truth).[139] The truth, as usual, proved self-evident when revealed: language was neither superstructure, nor base, nor any "intermediate phenomenon" (one is reminded of Lenin's equally dialectical vision of Bolshevik sexuality: "neither monk, nor Don Juan, nor the intermediate attitude of the German philistines").[140] Languages could only belong to "whole societies"; "societies" were always equal to ethnic groups (from tribe to nation); and ethnic groups—inseparable as they were from languages and therefore thinking—existed "incomparably longer than any base or any superstructure."[141] Classes and "epochs" came and went, but nationalities remained. "History"—itself rather circular in Stalin's conception, "tells us that national languages are not class languages but nationwide languages, common to all of the nation's members and unified for the nation."[142] Some national languages were genetically related to each other, and some were more durable than others. "The linguistic kinship of the Slavic nations" was completely obvious, while "mixing" was a matter of one language prevailing over another: "such was, for example, the case with the Russian language, which over the course of its development became mixed with languages of various other peoples but has always come out victorious."[143] As for Marr, he was a hopelessly confused "simplifier and vulgarizer of Marxism of the 'RAPPist and 'proletkultist' variety," who "introduced into linguistics an immodest, arrogant, and supercilious tone that is alien to Marxism."[144] Marr's "so-called students" added insult to injury by instituting a "regime alien to science," firing "valued workers," and making appointments "based not on merit but on the unquestioning acceptance of N. Ia. Marr's teaching." The result was a profound crisis in Soviet linguistics, for "it is generally known that no science can develop and flourish without a struggle of opinions, without freedom of criticism."[145]

Thus, twenty-one years after Polivanov's last stand at the Communist Academy and twelve years after his death in the Gulag, "the leader and teacher of the Soviet peoples" publicly endorsed his views on scientific autonomy in general and Marrist linguistics in particular. In a direct allusion to a paper he surely never read, Stalin called Marr's theory of class-based linguistic revolutions "quixotic," and compared it to postrevolutionary "pseudo-Marxist" projects of replacing bourgeois railroads with new, proletarian ones (Polivanov had argued—"quixotically," in his own estimation—that Marr's theory was "tantamount to a demand that at the moment of the revolution all the pistons of a loco-motive start working differently compared to how they had worked under the czar").[146] Inconsistently and inconclusively but with obvious relish, Stalin launched a public assault on two of the most sacred cows of his "revolution from above": the absolute "party-mindedness" of all knowledge and the rhetorical primacy of class over nationality. In July 1948 the leader of the peoples had deleted the statement "all sciences are class-based" from the text of Lysenko's speech to the Agricultural Academy ("Ha-ha-ha!!!" he wrote on the margin, "But what about mathematics? What about Darwinism?").[147] In April 1950 he had told Chikobava: "Lysenko is making life impossible for everyone. We are going to be criticizing him!"[148] Now he was saying that no "closed group of infallible leaders" could substitute itself for the contentious and apparently self-contained process of the scientific quest for knowl-edge.[149] He was infallible all right, but his decision-making power, he now claimed, depended on the disciplinary "struggles" waged by pro-fessional scholars.

Professional scholars in various disciplines responded to the leader's call with varying degrees of enthusiasm (hoping as many of them did to guess the final decision before engaging in disciplinary struggles).[150] Only the formerly Marrist fields had their tasks perfectly well defined. Linguists, reassured that languages were "ancient," "resilient," and inseparable from the history of the nations that "cre-ated and spoke them," could concentrate on the genealogical connec-tions and nation-building significance of "national languages."[151] Liter-ary historians were free to rid themselves of the already marginalized plot paleontologists in order to focus on "national form" in general, and folklore as the deepest "source of national art," in particular (the "forgotten" Russian national form was of paramount concern).[152] Race scientists could proceed from the premise that their findings were "mere reflections in anthropological data of migrations and mixings of tribes, nationalities, and nations," which meant that by studying race formation, anthropologists could contribute to the history of tribes, nationalities, and nations.[153] Ethnographers, who had had their 1932 death sentence formally suspended, could fully and unabashedly devote themselves to the study of "ethnos" as a generic concept that covered the evolutionary hierarchy of tribes (ethnicity of primitive communism), nationalities (ethnicity of slave-holding and feudal societies), and nations (ethnicity of capitalism and socialism).[154] Archaeologists, who had replaced linguists and folklorists in the limelight, could build on the "resilience" thesis in order to trace ethnic genealogies as far back as possible (nothing seemed impossible in the case of the Slavs, who were found to have "firm local roots" in Moldavia and the Crimea, for example, but some of the other peoples were also doing well thanks to the efforts of their scholarly descendants in republican capitals).[155] And V. V. Vinogradov could preside over Soviet philology from his new position as the head of the Language and Literature Section of the Academy of Sciences.[156]

It was the joint search for "ethnogenesis," however, that emerged as the most important task of the scholars who had been cut loose from the New Theory of Language. The professedly Marxist Marrism of rootless cosmopolitanism and revolutionary leaps was finished; the explicitly nationalist Marrism of ethnoracial genealogies and national essences reigned supreme. The world consisted of ethnic groups; ethnic groups were communities sharing certain attributes; modern communities derived their status and identity from the time and circumstances of their origins; the origins of the various ethnic attributes were notoriously difficult to reconcile. It was the job of specially trained scholars to chart the progress of ethnic attributes and determine the time of their coming together, thereby providing a modern nation(ality) with a duly stamped birth certificate. Advertised in the eighteenth century and updated by the young Marr in the early twentieth, this job was now presented as a collective enterprise: if ethnogenesis was "a historical process of the formation of a given ethnic community, i.e., the formation of its anthropological [racial], linguistic, and ethnographic traits," then it could only be uncovered by anthropologists, linguists, and ethnographers working together.[157] Fossil skulls belonged to people who had spoken a particular language and made particular tools in particular dwellings; protolanguages were spoken by people with particular skulls who had made particular tools in particular dwellings; unearthed dwellings contained people who had spoken particular languages, and so on. All of them, if assembled and named, were someone's more or less worthy ancestors: some Tatar and Chuvash scholars argued over the Bulgars; some Georgian and Armenian scholars argued over Urartu; some Russian scholars argued with the uninvited Varangians, and one Uzbek scholar proved conclusively that the "primordial, indigenous, original inhabitants" of the present-day territory of Uzbekistan were nearly identical to the present-day Uzbeks in language, physical type, and horse-breeding excellence.[158] It seemed obvious as well as officially sanctioned that "every nationality wanted to know where it came from, and where the origins of its language, culture, and peculiar traits lay."[159] It was equally obvious that not all answers were acceptable. Marr's final solution of the Great Ethnological Predicament proved temporary.

NOTES

This essay first appeared in *Slavic Review* 55, no. 4 (1996): 826–62 and is reprinted with permission of the AAASS. I am grateful to Sergei Arutiunov, Daniel Brower, Sheila Fitzpatrick, Francine Hirsch, Alexander Kazhdan, Johanna Nichols, Ethan Pollock, Nicholas V. Riasanovsky, Alexander Vucinich, Reginald Zelnik, and *Slavic Review*'s anonymous reviewers for stimulating comments and helpful suggestions. I apologize to Reader No. 1 for not being able to follow all of his/her excellent recommendations while also keeping the essay's original focus and size.

1. Quoted in Charles Frankel, *The Faith of Reason: The Idea of Progress in the French Enlightenment* (New York: Columbia University Press, 1948), 44.

2. Hans Aarslef, *From Locke to Saussure: Essays on the Study of Language and Intellectual History* (Minneapolis: University of Minnesota Press, 1982), 158–59.

3. See the Müller-Lomonosov debate in M. V. Lomonosov, *Polnoe sobranie sochinenii*, 11 vols. (Moscow: AN SSSR, 1952), 6:67–68.

4. Lomonosov, *Polnoe sobranie sochinenii*, 6:77–78.

5. Lomonosov, *Polnoe sobranie sochinenii*, 6:25–80. The preceding discussion is based on Yuri Slezkine, "Naturalists versus Nations: Eighteenth-Century Russian Scholars Confront Ethnic Diversity," *Representations* 47 (summer 1994): 170–95.

6. A. N. Veselovskii, *Sobranie sochinenii* (St. Petersburg: Imperatorskaia Akademiia nauk, 1913–14), 1:7, 10, 44; 16:86; A. N. Veselovskii, *Izbrannye stat'i* (Leningrad: Khudozhestvennaia literatura, 1939), 501–14; Yuri Slezkine, *Arctic Mirrors: Russia and the Small Peoples of the North* (Ithaca, N.Y.: Cornell University Press, 1994), 124–26; Bruce G. Trigger, *A History of Archaeological Thought* (Cambridge: Cambridge University Press, 1989), 161–63.

7. D. N. Anuchin, "Velikorussy," in *Entsiklopedicheskii slovar'* (St. Petersburg: F. A. Brokgauz and I. A Efron, 1892), 5A:837. On A. P. Bogdanov and F. Volov, see M. G. Levin, *Ocherki po istori antropologii v Rossii* (Moscow: AN SSSR, 1960), 101, 123–25.

8. See A. Sobolevskii's review of N. Iu. Zograf, *Antropometricheskiia izsledovaniia muzhskago velikorusskago naseleniia Vladimirskoi, Iaroslavskoi i Kostromskoi gubernii* (Moscow, 1892) in *Zhivaia starina* 3, no. 1 (1893): 115–22. Anuchin's summary is based on Zograf's work.

9. Levin, *Ocherki,* 133; N. G. Zalkind, *Moskovskaia shkola antropologov v razvitii otechestvennoi nauki o cheloveke* (Moscow: Nauka, 1974), 83.

10. Quoted in Levin, *Ocherki,* 124–25.

11. E. M. Chepurkovskii, "O neobkhodimosti edinogo plana rabot po antropologicheskomu analizu naseleniia Rossii i zhelatel'nosti etnograficheskogo issledovaniia nekotorykh opredelennykh oblastei," *Russkii antropologicheskii zhurnal* 13, nos. 1–2 (1923): 99–101.

12. See, for example, V. V. Bunak, "O smeshenii chelovecheskikh ras," *Russkii evgenicheskii zhurnal* 3, no. 2 (1925): 121–38.

13. For interesting discussions of similar problems in other contexts, see Malcolm Chapman, *The Celts: The Construction of a Myth* (New York: St. Martin's, 1992); and Colin Renfrew, *Archaeology and Language: The Puzzle of Indo-European Origins* (London: Jonathan Cape, 1987).

14. E. D. Polivanov, *Stat'i po obshchemu iazykoznaniiu* (Moscow: Glavnaia redaktsiia vostochnoi literatury, 1968), 195. For very useful surveys, see Wolfgang Girke and Helmut Jachnow, *Sowjetische Soziolinguistik: Probleme und Genese* (Kronberg: Scriptor Verlag, 1974), 18–50; Thomas John Samuelian, "The Search for a Marxist Linguistics in the Soviet Union, 1917–1950," Ph.D. diss., University of Pennsylvania, 1981; and Michael G. Smith, "Soviet Language Frontiers: The Structural Method in Early Language Reforms, 1917–1937," Ph.D. diss., Georgetown University, 1991. For an interesting interpretation, see Patrick Sériot, "Changements de paradigmes dans la linguistique soviétique des années 1920–1930," *Histoire Epistémologie Langage* 17, no. 2 (1995): 236–51.

15. For biographical information on Marr, see "Avtobiografiia" (1927), in N. Ia. Marr, *Izbrannye raboty,* 5 vols. (Leningrad: GAIMK, 1933), 1:6–13 (hereafter *IR); V. A. Mikhankova, *Nikolai Iakovlevich Marr* (Moscow: AN SSSR, 1948), and "Iz vospominanii o N. Ia. Marre," *Problemy istorii dokapitalisticheskikh obshchestv* 3–4 (1935).

16. Marr, "Avtobiografiia," 1:6; Katerina Clark, *Petersburg, Crucible of Cultural Revolution* (Cambridge, Mass.: Harvard University Press, 1995), 216.

17. Mikhankova, *Nikolai Iakovlevich Marr,* 8; Marr, "Avtobiografiia," 1:9. See also V. B. Aptekar', *N. Ia. Marr i novoe uchenie o iazyke* (Moscow: Gosudarstvennoe sotsial'no-ekonomicheskoe izdatel'stvo, 1934), 11–13; V. M. Alpatov, *Istoriia odnogo mifa* (Moscow: Nauka, 1991), 14; V. M. Zhirmunskii, "Lingvisticheskaia paleontologiia N. Ia. Marra i istoriia iazyka," in *Protiv vul'garizatsii i izvrashcheniia marksizma v iazykoznanii,* ed. V. V. Vinogradov and B. A. Serebrennikov, 2 vols. (Moscow: AN SSSR, 1952), 2:172–208.

18. N. Ia. Marr, "Priroda i osobennosti gruzinskogo iazyka" (1888), *IR* 1:15.

19. N. Ia. Marr, "K voprosu o zadachakh armianovedeniia" (1899), *IR* 1:17, "Vvedenie k rabote 'Opredelenie iazyka vtoroi kategorii Akhmenidskikh klinoobraznykh nadpisei po dannym iafeticheskogo iazykoznaniia'" (1912), *IR* 1:50–51, "Ob iafeticheskoi teorii" (1924), *IR* 3:1. Political anticolonialism becomes a dominant theme in early 1920 (see "Iafeticheskii Kavkaz i tretii etnicheskii element v sozidanii sredizemnomorskoi kul'tury," *IR* 1:90–93), but a vigorous dislike of the linguistic establishment and a conviction that true

scholarship is guided by "the innate feeling of affection for one's native antiquities and folktales" animates Marr's earliest work (the quote is from Marr's speech at his dissertation defense in May 1899, *IR* 1:18).

20. Marr, "Ob iafeticheskoi teorii," 3:1.

21. Marr, "Ob iafeticheskoi teorii," 3:49. See also P. S. Kuznetsov, "Oshibki N. Ia. Marra v ego vzgliadakh na rodstvo i istoricheskoe razvitie iazykov," in Vinogradov and Serebrennikov, *Protiv vul'garizatsii*, 2:210–12.

22. N. Ia. Marr, "Chem zhivet iafeticheskoe iazykoznanie?" (1921), *IR* 1:176, and "Ob iafeticheskoi teorii," 3:1.

23. Marr, "Chem zhivet," 1:177. Cf. a recent feminist restatement of this thesis in Marija Gimbutas, *The Language of the Goddess* (San Francisco: Harper and Row, 1989). "We are still living under the sway of that aggressive male [i.e. Indo-European] invasion and only beginning to discover our long alienation from our authentic European Heritage—gylanic, nonviolent, earth-centered culture" (xxi). The coinage "gylanic" denotes sexual equality. See also David W. Anthony, "Nazi and Eco-Feminist Prehistories: Ideology and Empiricism in Indo-European Archaeology," in *Nationalism, Politics, and the Practice of Archaeology*, ed. Philip L. Kohl and Clare Fawcett (Cambridge: Cambridge University Press, 1995), 82–96.

24. N. Ia. Marr, "Znachenie i rol' izucheniia natsmen'shinstva v kraevedenii" (1927), *IR* 1:235.

25. N. Ia. Marr, "Osnovnye dostizheniia iafeticheskoi teorii" (1924), *IR* 1:215. Marr was greatly influenced by Lucien Lévy-Bruhl's *Primitive Mentality*. For an analysis, see Lawrence L. Thomas, *The Linguistic Theories of N. Ja. Marr*, University of California Publications in Linguistics 14 (Berkeley and Los Angeles: University of California Press, 1957), 78–81.

26. N. Ia. Marr, "Kavkazovedenie i abkhazskii iazyk" (1916), *IR* 1:59, 70.

27. "Great Ethnological Predicament" is my own term, of course, but the feeling that nations and their origins were in theoretical trouble was quite widespread if not always clearly defined.

28. Girke and Jachnow, *Sowjetische Soziolinguistik*, 18–50; Smith, "Soviet Language Frontiers," 101–23. The last quote is from E. D. Polivanov, "Gde lezhat prichiny iazykovoi evoliutsii," in *Stat'i po obshchemu iazykoznaniiu*, 75–89.

29. N. S. Trubetskoi, "Vavilonskaia bashnia i smeshenie iazykov" (1923), in *Evraziia: Istoricheskie vzgliady russkikh emigrantov*, ed. L. V. Ponomareva (Moscow: Institut vseobshchei istorii RAN, 1992), 143.

30. See, in particular, Trubetskoi, "Vavilonskaia bashnia"; "Ob istinnom i lozhnom natsionalizme," in *Iskhod k Vostoku* (Sofia: n.p., 1921), 71–85; and *Evropa i chelovechestvo* (Sofia: Rossiisko-bolgarskoe knigoizdatel'stvo, 1920). For Trubetskoi-Marr parallels, see Patrick Sériot, "Un conflit de métaphores: Eurasistes et marristes," in *Histoire des idées linguistiques*, ed. Sylvain Auroux, vol. 8 (Brussels: Madarga, 1995); and Smith, "Soviet Language Frontiers," 159. For implicit but highly suggestive comparisons, see Boris Gasparov, "The Ideological Principles of Prague School Phonology," in *Language, Poetry, and Poetics: The Generation of the 1890s: Jakobson, Trubetzkoy, Majakovskij*, ed. Krystyna

Pomorska (Berlin: Mouton de Gruyter, 1987), 49–78; Patrick Sériot, "Aux sources du structuralisme: Une controverse biologique en Russie," *Etudes de lettres*, January–March 1994, 89–104, and "La double vie de Trubetzkoy, ou la clôture des systèmes," *La gré des langues* 5 (1993): 88–115. For the English translations of Trubetskoi's essays, see N. S. Trubetzkoy, *The Legacy of Genghis Khan and Other Essays on Russian Identity*, ed. Anatoly Liberman (Ann Arbor: Michigan Slavic Publications, 1991).

31. N. Ia. Marr, "Predislovie k 'Iafeticheskomu sborniku, t. V" (1927), *IR* 1:251.

32. N. Ia. Marr, "Iafetidologiia v Leningradskom gosudarstvennom universitete" (1930), *IR* 1:255.

33. N. Ia. Marr, "Predvaritel'noe soobshchenie o rodstve gruzinskogo iazyka s semiticheskimi" (1908), *IR* 1:24. For a detailed critique of Marr's methodology, see Thomas, *Linguistic Theories of Marr*, 5–18 and passim. See also Girke and Jachnow, *Sowjetische Soziolinguistik*, 50–62.

34. Marr, "Predvaritel'noe soobshchenie," 1:23, 26.

35. Leonti Mroveli, *Zhizn' kartliiskikh tsarei*, trans. and ed. G. B. Tsualaia (Moscow: Nauka, 1979), 21. I am grateful to Sergei Arutiunov for pointing out the connection.

36. Marr, "Predvaritel'noe soobshchenie," 1:36–37.

37. See Trigger, *History of Archaeological Thought*, 163f.; and Ingo Wawjorra, "German Archaeology and Its Relation to Nationalism and Racism," in *Nationalism and Archaeology in Europe*, ed. Margarita Díaz-Andreu and Timothy Champion (London: University College London Press, 1996), 173–75.

38. See J. P. Malory, *In Search of the Indo-Europeans: Language, Archaeology, and Myth* (London: Thames and Hudson, 1989), 10–11, 143.

39. Marr, "Iafetidologiia v Leningradskom gosudarstvennom universitete," 1:271.

40. N. Ia. Marr, *Kavkaz i pamiatniki ego dukhovnoi kul'tury. Perepechatano iz Izvestii Akademii nauk za 1912 god* (Petrograd, 1919), 15–16. See also N. Ia. Marr, *Ob istokakh tvorchestva Rustaveli i ego poeme* (Tbilisi: Izdatel'stvo Akademii nauk Gruzinskoi SSR, 1964), esp. 17–42; Aptekar', *N. Ia. Marr*, 22–25, 32; Mikhankova, *Nikolai Iakovlevich Marr*, 134–35, 143, 239–45. Marr's pan-Caucasian patriotism became a substantial political asset after the formation of the Transcaucasian Federation in 1922.

41. Mroveli, *Zhizn' kartliiskikh tsarei*, 21.

42. Quoted in Thomas, *Linguistic Theories of Marr*, 23, 30. Cf. Trubetskoi: "In matters of the 'soul' Slavs were drawn toward Indo-Iranians; in matters of the 'body,' . . . to the Western Indo-Europeans." Proof: "Among specific coincidences of Proto-Slavic and Proto-Iranian lexicons, the terms referring, one way or another, to religious feelings, represent a very significant proportion. Specific coincidences of the Proto-Slavic and Western European [*sic*] languages are of a completely different nature. There may be more of them than between Proto-Slavic and Proto-Indo-Iranian, but . . . words to do with technology pre-

dominate decisively." N. S. Trubetskoi, "Verkhi i nizy russkoi kul'tury (Etnicheskaia osnova russkoi kul'tury)," in *Iskhod k Vostoku*, 91–92. For an analogous (one might say, "Eurarabic") construct elsewhere in Europe, see Margarita Díaz-Andreu, "Islamic Archaeology and the Origin of the Spanish Nation," in Díaz-Andreu and Champion, *Nationalism and Archaeology*, 78–79.

43. Marr, *Kavkaz i pamiatniki*, 19. Also Marr, "K voprosu o zadachakh armianovedeniia," 1:20.

44. Marr, "K voprosu o zadachakh armianovedeniia," 1:20, "O Chanskom iazyke" (1910), *IR* 1:39, "Kavkazovedenie i abkhazskii iazyk," 1:69.

45. Marr, "Kavkazovedenie i abkhazskii iazyk," 1:69.

46. Marr, "Kavkazovedenie i abkhazskii iazyk," 1:69.

47. Thomas, *Linguistic Theories of Marr*, 28–34.

48. Marr, "Iafeticheskii Kavkaz i tretii etnicheskii element," 1:90–91. The "madman" quote is from another one of Marr's ironic self-characterizations. See "Iafetidologiia v Leningradskom gosudarstvennom universitete," 1:255.

49. Thomas, *Linguistic Theories of Marr*, 48–51.

50. Marr, "Iafeticheskii Kavkaz i tretii etnicheskii element," 1:94, 116.

51. Marr, "Iafeticheskii Kavkaz i tretii etnicheskii element," 1:118–20, 110–11.

52. Marr, "Iafeticheskii Kavkaz i tretii etnicheskii element," 1:120–21.

53. Marr, "Iafeticheskii Kavkaz i tretii etnicheskii element," 1:91.

54. Marr, "Iafeticheskii Kavkaz i tretii etnicheskii element," 1:121.

55. N. Ia. Marr, "Predislovie k nemetskomu izdaniiu raboty 'Iafeticheskii Kavkaz i tretii etnicheskii element v sozidanii sredizemnomorskoi kul'tury'" (1923), *IR* 1:151.

56. Marr, "Iafeticheskii Kavkaz i tretii etnicheskii element," 1:98–101, 116–17.

57. Marr, "Iafeticheskii Kavkaz i tretii etnicheskii element," 1:98, 116, 101.

58. N. Ia. Marr, "Knizhnye legendy ob osnovanii Kuara v Armenii i Kieva na Rusi" (1922), *IR* 5:65, "Iafetidy" (1922), *IR* 1:133.

59. Marr, "Predislovie k nemetskomu izdaniiu," 1:151; Thomas, *Linguistic Theories of Marr*, 85–86.

60. N. Ia. Marr, "Sena, Liutetsiia i pervye obitateli Gallii—etruski i pelasgi' (1922), *IR* 1:138–43, 147; Thomas, *Linguistic Theories of Marr*, 55; I. K. Zborobskii, "N. Ia. Marr i ukrainskii iazyk," *Iazyk i myshlenie*, 8 (1937): 36–38; V. D. Levin, "Kritika vzgliadov N. Ia. Marra i ego posledovatelei na proiskhozhdenie russkogo iazyka," in Vinogradov and Serebrennikov, *Protiv vul'garizatsii*, 1:244–46.

61. Marr was not the only national chronicler bent on retroactive greatness—just the most well placed and successful. For similar scholarly efforts on behalf of the Tatars, Chuvash, Mari, and Belorussians, see Victor A. Shnirelman, "The Faces of Nationalist Archaeology in Russia," in Díaz-Andreu and Champion, *Nationalism and Archaeology*, 226–30. Outside the USSR, it was probably Heinrich Himmler's onetime favorite Herman Wirth who came closest to Marr in both style and spirit. In his 1928 *Der Aufgang der Menscheit*, Wirth

announced his discovery of a primeval "Atlanto-Nordic" race that had taken advantage of its "metaphysical-transcendental" gift in order to fulfill its "world-historical mission" of spawning all the known world cultures. (In 1938, Wirth was dropped by the Nazis in favor of the much less inclusive Hans Reinerth.) See Wawjorra, "German Archaeology," 180–82. The term for this condition is Goropianism (after Goropius Becanus, who traced all languages to Dutch). Another prominent victim was the founder of Indo-Europeanism, James Parsons, who derived the whole family from Irish.

62. N. Ia. Marr, "Terminy iz abkhazo-russkikh etnicheskikh sviazei 'Loshad'' i 'trizna'" (1924), *IR* 5:119.

63. N. Ia. Marr, "Znachenie i rol' izucheniia natsmen'shinstva," 1:241, and "Osnovnye dostizheniia iaeticheskoi teorii," 1:197.

64. For the relationship between Marxism and Soviet science, see, in particular, Loren R. Graham, *Science, Philosophy, and Human Behavior in the Soviet Union* (New York: Columbia University Press, 1987); David Joravsky, *Soviet Marxism and Natural Science, 1917–1932* (New York: Columbia University Press, 1961); David Joravsky, *Russian Psychology: A Critical History* (Oxford: Basil Blackwell, 1989); and Alexander Vucinich, *Empire of Knowledge: The Academy of Sciences of the USSR (1917–1970)* (Berkeley and Los Angeles: University of California Press, 1984), esp. 149–70. For the rise of the "sociological method" in Soviet linguistics, see Girke and Jachnow, *Sowjetische Soziolinguistik*, 16–50; Smith, "Soviet Language Frontiers," 87–106; and Samuelian, "Search for Marxist Linguistics," 255–63, 278–80, and passim.

65. Clark, *Petersburg*, 218; M. V. Gorbanevskii, *V nachale bylo slovo . . . Maloizvestnye stranitsy istorii sovetskoi lingvistiki* (Moscow: Universitet druzhby narodov, 1991), 42–45; Samuelian, "Search for Marxist Linguistics," 272, 309; Thomas, *Linguistic Theories of Marr*, 89.

66. Marr, "Znachenie i rol' izucheniia natsmen'shinstva," 1:241. See also 1:236; "Pochemu tak trudno stat' lingvistom-teoretikom" (1928), *IR* 2:399; and "Terminy iz abkhazo-russkikh etnicheskikh sviazei," 5:119.

67. The unity of language and thought was a crucial revolutionary—and later Stalinist—concept. By transforming language, one transformed thought, and ultimately reality. See Clark, *Petersburg*, 201–23.

68. N. Ia. Marr, "Obshchii kurs ucheniia ob iazyke" (1927), *IR* 2:85f.

69. N. Ia. Marr, "Lingvisticheski namechaemye epokhi razvitiia chelovechestva i ikh uviazka s istoriei material'noi kul'tury" (1926), *IR* 3:57.

70. N. Ia. Marr, "Aktual'nye problemy i ocherednye zadachi iaeticheskoi teorii" (1928), *IR* 3:1. See also Marr, "Pochemu tak trudno stat' lingvistom-teoretikom," 2:405.

71. Thomas, *Linguistic Theories of Marr*, 103–7.

72. N. Ia. Marr, "Postanovka ucheniia ob iazyke v mirovom masshtabe i abkhazskii iazyk" (1928), *IR* 4:58.

73. Marr, "Avtobiografiia," 1:11.

74. Marr, "Postanovka ucheniia ob iazyke," 4:61.

75. Marr, "Pochemu tak trudno stat' lingvistom-teoretikom," 2:415.

76. N. Ia. Marr, "Iazyk i myshlenie" (1931), *IR* 3:121.

77. Marr, "Iazyk i myshlenie," 3:118.

78. Marr, "Iazyk i myshlenie," 3:111–12. Cf. Thomas, *Linguistic Theories of Marr*, 108–11.

79. Marr's overview of his new doctrine was delivered as a series of lectures at the State University of Azerbaijan in Baku in 1927, and published in 1928. See *IR* 2:3–126, and Mikhankova, *Nikolai Iakovlevich Marr*, 341.

80. See Katerina Clark, *The Soviet Novel: History as Ritual* (Chicago: University of Chicago Press, 1981), 114–29 and passim.

81. Marr's prose is frequently and not always deliberately at odds with Russian grammar and "formal logical thinking"; his lectures appear to have been virtually incomprehensible (see "Iz vospominanii o N. Ia. Marre," 158).

82. Marr, "Ob iafeticheskoi teorii," 3:31; A. V. Desnitskaia, "O roli anti-marksistskoi teorii proiskhozhdeniia iazyka v obshchei sisteme vzgliadov N. Ia. Marra," in Vinogradov and Serebrennikov, *Protiv vul'garizatsii*, 1:49–51.

83. For an extremely interesting examination of Marr, Bakhtin, and Lysenko as representatives of a "neo-Romantic" strain within the late avant-garde, see Boris Gasparov, "Development or Rebuilding: Views of Academician T. D. Lysenko in the Context of the Late Avant-Garde," in *Laboratory of Dreams: The Russian Avant-Garde*, ed. John E. Bowlt and Olga Matich (Stanford: Stanford University Press, 1996). See also V. V. Ivanov, *Ocherki po istorii semiotiki v SSSR* (Moscow: Nauka, 1976), 12–65 and passim.

84. See his "Lamark," in Osip Mandel'shtam, *Sobranie sochinenii v dvukh tomakh* (Washington: Inter-Language Literary Associates, 1964), 1:168–9; and "Puteshestvie v Armeniiu," in Osip Mandel'shtam, *Sochineniia v dvukh tomakh* (Moscow: Khudozhestvennaia literatura, 1990), 2:100–132, esp. 105–6. For a discussion, see Gasparov, "Development or Rebuilding." For a suggestive explication of "Lamarck," see Gregory Freidin, *A Coat of Many Colors: Osip Mandelstam and His Mythologies of Self-Presentation* (Berkeley and Los Angeles: University of California Press, 1987), 224–28.

85. Marr, "Knizhnye legendy," 5:47; N. Ia. Marr, "Iazykovaia politika iafeticheskoi teorii i udmurtskii iazyk" (1930), *IR* 1:282.

86. Marr, "Iazykovaia politika iafeticheskoi teorii i udmurtskii iazyk," 1:286–7, and "K voprosu ob edinom iazyke" (1928), *IR* 2:394–95.

87. Marr, "Predislovie k 'Iafeticheskomu sborniku, t. V'," 1:250. On various ethnogenetic projects by the "young scholarly communities," see Shnirelman, "Faces of Nationalist Archaeology," 226–30.

88. N. M. Matorin, "Sovremennyi etap i zadachi sovetskoi etnografii," *Sovetskaia etnografiia* 1–2 (1931): 11; S. Tokarev, review of Franz Boas, *The Mind of Primitive Man*, in *Etnografiia* 1 (1928): 132; Sheila Fitzpatrick, "Cultural Revolution as Class War," in Fitzpatrick, ed., *Cultural Revolution in Russia, 1928–1931* (Bloomington: Indiana University Press, 1978), 3–38.

89. "Soveshchanie etnografov Leningrada i Moskvy 5/IV–11/IV 1929 g.," *Etnografiia* 2 (1929): 118.

90. As Marr's main spokesman in Moscow, V. B. Aptekar', put it at the

Sociology Section of the Society of Marxist Historians (May 7, 1928), "If you look into the history of ethnology, you'll see that it was created by priests, missionaries, merchants, slave-owners, and travelers who founded colonies." Arkhiv RAN, f. 377, op. 2, d. 115, l. 88. See also d. 130, ll. 2–38; d. 139, ll. 7–20; and op. 4, d. 29, l. 12.

91. Cf. Sergei Tolstov, "K probleme akkul'turatsii," *Etnografiia* 1–2 (1930); Matorin, "Sovremennyi etap," 19–23; and "Rezoliutsiia vserossiiskogo arkheologo-etnograficheskogo soveshchaniia 7–11 maia 1932 goda," *Sovetskaia etnografiia* 3 (1932): 14. See also Slezkine, *Arctic Mirrors*, 246–64.

92. Arkhiv RAN, f. 377, op. 2, d. 129, ll. 1–9; "Tselevaia ustanovka i novye zadachi GAIMK," *Soobshcheniia Gosudarstvennoi akademii istorii material'noi kul'tury* 2 (1931): 2; A. N. Bernshtam, "Zhilishche Krymskogo predgor'ia: opyt sotsiologicheskogo analiza," *Izvestiia Gosudarstvennoi akademii istorii material'noi kul'tury* 9, nos. 6–7 (1931): 2.

93. S. N. Bykovskii, "O predmete istorii material'noi kul'tury," *Soobshcheniia Gosudarstvennoi akademii istorii material'noi kul'tury* 1–2 (1932): 3–4; "Rezoliutsiia vserossiiskogo arkheologo-etnograficheskogo soveshchaniia," 4–9; V. I. Ravdonikas, "Arkheologiia na Zapade i v SSSR v nashi dni," *Soobshcheniia Gosudarstvennoi akademii istorii material'noi kul'tury* 9–10 (1932): 20.

94. I. I. Meshchaninov, "Piry Azerbaidzhana," *Izvestiia Gosudarstvennoi akademii istorii material'noi kul'tury* 9, no. 4 (1931): 2; S. N. Bykovskii, "O roli izucheniia iazykovykh iavlenii v bor'be za novuiu istoriiu material'noi kul'tury," *Soobshcheniia Gosudarstvennoi akademii istorii material'noi kul'tury* 11–12 (1931): 4–7.

95. S. N. Bykovskii, "Iafeticheskii predok vostochnykh slavian—kimmeriitsy," *Izvestiia Gosudarstvennoi akademii istorii material'noi kul'tury* 8, nos. 8–10 (1931): 94; V. I. Ravdonikas, "Peshchernye goroda Kryma i gotskaia problema v sviazi so stadial'nym razvitiem Severnogo Prichernomor'ia," *Izvestiia Gosudarstvennoi akademii istorii material'noi kul'tury* 12, nos. 1–8 (1932), quoted in Mikhail Miller, *Archaeology in the USSR* (New York: Frederick A. Praeger, 1956), 81. See also A. A. Formozov, "Arkheologiia i ideologiia (20–30-e gody)," *Voprosy filosofii* 2 (1993): 70–82; and Victor A. Shnirelman, "From Internationalism to Nationalism: Forgotten Pages of Soviet Archaeology in the 1930s and 1940s," in Kohl and Fawcett, *Nationalism, Politics*, 126–29.

96. A. N. Lozanova, "K blizhaishim zadacham sovetskoi fol'kloristiki," *Sovetskaia etnografiia* 2 (1932): 4, 6, and passim. See also "Diskussiia o sushchnosti i zadachakh fol'klora v leningradskom Institute rechevoi kul'tury," *Sovetskaia etnografiia* 3–4 (1931): 239–42; "Diskussiia o znachenii fol'klora i fol'kloristiki v rekonstruktivnyi period," *Literatura i marksizm* 5 (1931): 91–114 and 6 (1931): 105–23; and O. M. Freidenberg, "Vospominaniia o Marre," *Vostok-Zapad* 3 (1988): 181–204. For outstanding examples of Marrist literary history ("paleontology"), see I. Frank-Kamenetskii, "Pervobytnoe myshlenie v svete iafeticheskoi teorii i filosofii," *Iazyk i literatura* 3 (1929): 70–155; *Tristan i Isol'da: Ot geroini liubvi feodal'noi Evropy do bogini matriarkhal'noi Afroevrazii* (Leningrad: AN SSSR, 1932); and O. Freidenberg, *Poetika siuzheta i zhanra: Period antichnoi lit-*

eratury (Leningrad: Khudozhestvennaia literatura, 1936). On Freidenberg, see Kevin Murphy Moss, "Olga Mikhailovna Freidenberg: Soviet Mythologist in a Soviet Context," Ph.D. diss., Cornell University, 1984; Nina Perlina, ed., *Ol'ga Mikhailovna Freidenberg*, a special issue of *Soviet Studies in Literature* 27, no. 1 (1990–91); and Iu. M. Lotman, "O. M. Freidenberg as a Student of Culture," in *Semiotics and Structuralism: Readings from the Soviet Union*, ed. Henryk Baran (White Plains, N.Y.: International Arts and Sciences Press, 1976), 257–67.

97. A. I. Iarkho, "Protiv idealisticheskikh techenii v rasovedenii SSSR," *Antropologicheskii zhurnal* 1 (1932): 9–23 (all the quotations are from this article). For a very spirited discussion of whether true Marxists should preserve the concept of race ("the ultimate question being: are the Uzbeks capable of the same development as the Great Russians?"), see Arkhiv RAN, f. 377, op. 2, d. 52 (the quotation is from l. 32). See also M. A. Gremiatskii, "Problema rasy v antropologii," *Trudy chetvertogo vsesoiuznogo s"ezda zoologov, anatomov i gistologov v Kieve, 6–12 maia, 1930* (Kiev-Khar'kov: Gosmedizdat USSR, 1931), 298–300; A. I. Iarkho, "Osnovnye napravleniia rasovoi antropologii v SSSR," *Trudy chetvertogo*, 330–32; M. Plisetskii, "Na antropologicheskom fronte," *Sovetskaia etnografiia* 1 (1932): 91–101; G. I. Petrov, "N. Ia. Marr i problema rasogeneza," *Problemy istorii material'noi kul'tury* 5–6 (1933): 37–45; and T. Trofimova and N. Cheboksarov, "Znachenie ucheniia o iazyke N. Ia. Marra v bor'be za marksistko-leninskuiu antropologiiu," *Antropologicheskii zhurnal* 1–2 (1934): 28–54. For the (rather less happy) fate of the other sociobiological disciplines, see Mark B. Adams, "The Soviet Nature-Nurture Debate," in *Science and the Soviet Social Order*, ed. Loren R. Graham (Cambridge, Mass.: Harvard University Press, 1990), 94–138; and Mark B. Adams, "Eugenics in Russia 1900–1940," in *The Wellborn Science: Eugenics in Germany, France, Brazil, and Russia*, ed. Adams (Oxford: Oxford University Press, 1990), 153–216.

98. E. D. Polivanov, "Stenogramma 4 fevralia 1929 g: 'Problema marksistkogo iazykoznaniia i iafeticheskaia teoriia'," in *Trudy po vostochnomu i obshchemu iazykoznaniiu* (Moscow: Glavnaia redaktsiia vostochnoi literatury, 1991), 509.

99. Polivanov, "Stenogramma," 546. G. A. Il'inskii was the only participant in the discussion who supported Polivanov.

100. Polivanov, "Stenogramma," 509, 511, 513, 521–22, 530–33, 535, and passim. For a similar, and probably the last, public statement of this kind, see a speech by the physicist Ia. I. Frenkel' as cited in Vucinich, *Empire of Knowledge*, 156.

101. Polivanov, "Stenogramma," 512. Polivanov's own attempt to define Marxist linguistics did not go beyond general observations on the social nature of language. See "Stenogramma," 536–43, and Polivanov, *Stat'i po obshchemu iazykoznaniiu*, 176–77.

102. For Language Front manifestos, see "Obrashchenie gruppy 'Iazykovednyi front'," *Literatura i iskusstvo* 1 (1930): back cover, and *Revoliutsiia i iazyk* 1 (1930). For surveys, see Alpatov, *Istoriia odnogo mifa*, 87–111, and Smith, "Soviet Language Frontiers," 170–204.

103. V. I. Ravdonikas, "Arkheologiia na Zapade i v SSSR v nashi dni," 13, and "Akheologiia na sluzhbe imperializma," *Soobshcheniia Gosudarstvennoi akademii istorii material'noi kul'tury* 3–4 (1932): 27. For a very useful survey of "internationalism" in Soviet archaeology, see Shnirelman, "From Internationalism to Nationalism."

104. S. N. Bykovskii, "Plemia i natsiia v rabotakh burzhuaznykh arkheologov i istorikov i v osveshchenii marksizma-leninizma," *Soobshcheniia Gosudarstvennoi akademii istorii material'noi kul'tury* 3–4 (1932): 5–6.

105. V. B. Aptekar', "Iafeticheskaia teoriia N. Ia. Marra i istoricheskii materializm," Arkhiv RAN, f. 377, op. 2, d. 110, l. 5.

106. Ravdonikas, "Arkheologiia na sluzhbe," 21.

107. S. N. Bykovskii, "O klassovykh korniakh staroi arkheologii," *Soobshcheniia Gosudarstvennoi akademii istorii material'noi kul'tury* 9–10 (1931): 4–7; Ravdonikas, "Arkheologiia na sluzhbe," 27 and passim. See also A. V. Shmidt, "O rabotakh russkikh arkheologov po finnam," *Soobshcheniia Gosudarstvennoi akademii istorii material'noi kul'tury* 3–4 (1932): 35–43.

108. V. I. Ravdonikas, "O rabote D. N. Edinga 'Sarskoe gorodishche'," *Soobshcheniia Gosudarstvennoi akademii istorii material'noi kul'tury* 4–5 (1931): 64; G. Debets, "Tak nazyvaemyi 'vostochnyi velikoruss'," *Antropologicheskii zhurnal* 1–2 (1933): 54; Marr, *IR* 5:314.

109. Zh. I. Alferov et al., eds. *Akademicheskoe delo 1929–1931 gg. Dokumenty i materialy sledstvennogo dela, sfabrikovannogo OGPU* (St. Petersburg: RAN, 1993); F. D. Ashnin and V. M. Alpatov, *"Delo slavistov": 30-e gody* (Moscow: Nasledie, 1994); S. B. Bernshtein, "Tragicheskaia stranitsa iz istorii slavianskoi filologii (30-e gody XX veka)," *Sovetskoe slavianovedenie* 1 (1989): 77–82; V. S. Brachev, "'Delo' akademika S. F. Platonova," *Voprosy istorii* 5 (1989): 117–29; A. N. Goriainov, "Slavianovedy—zhertvy repressii 1920–1940kh godov. Nekotorye neizvestnye stranitsy iz istorii sovetskoi nauki," *Sovetskoe slavianovedenie* 2 (1990): 78–89; B. S. Kaganovich, *Evgenii Viktorovich Tarle i peterburgskaia shkola istorikov* (St. Petersburg: Dmitrii Bulanin, 1995), 38–54. For the fate of the "regional studies" *(kraevedenie)* movement, see Eileen Maniichuk's "Observing Homeland and Hinterland: The Construction of Local Identity in Soviet Ethnography and Kraevedenie, 1917–1937," Ph.D. diss. University of Toronto, 1996; and A. Akin'shin and O. Lasunskii, "'Delo kraevedov' Tsentral'nogo Chernozem'ia," *Otechestvo* 1 (1990): 56–66.

110. Dim. Dimitrov, "Slavianskaia filologiia na putiakh fashizatsii (k kharakteristike ee sostoianiia na Zapade)," *Iazyk i myshlenie* 5 (1935): 125–33.

111. See "Ob uvekovechenii pamiati N. Ia. Marra" and other materials in *Problemy istorii dokapitalisticheskikh obshchestv* 3–4 (1935), esp. 3–6, 255–59. See also Mikhankova, *Nikolai Iakovlevich Marr*, 427–28; Alpatov, *Istoriia odnogo mifa*, 110–11. By all accounts, Marr was buried at the Alexander Nevsky Necropolis, but Alpatov reports having been unable to find his grave there. See *Problemy istorii dokapitalisticheskikh obshchestv* 3–4 (1935): 258, and Alpatov, *Istoriia odnogo mifa*, 110n.

112. N. M. Matorin, "15 let Oktiabr'skoi revoliutsii," *Sovetskaia etnografiia*

5–6 (1932): 12–13, and "Na fronte istoricheskoi nauki. V Sovnarkome Soiuza SSR i TsK VKP(b)," *Sovetskaia etnografiia* 1 (1936): 3.

113. Alpatov, *Istoriia odnogo mifa*, 112–42; René L'Hermitte, *Marr, marrisme, marristes: Une page de l'histoire de la linguistique soviétique* (Paris: Institut d'études slaves, 1987), 47–54; E. P. Aksenova and M. A. Vasil'ev, "Problemy etnogonii slavianstva i ego vetvei v akademicheskikh diskussiiakh rubezha 1930–1940kh godov," *Slavianovedenie* 2 (1993): 91–92; and Shnirelman, "Faces of Nationalist Archaeology," 233–36, and "From Internationalism to Nationalism," 132–38. For the composition of the special "Ethnogenesis Commission" at the History and Philosophy Section of the Academy of Sciences, see "Khronika," *Vestnik Akademii nauk SSSR* 4–5 (1939): 175. For some early results of the new ethnogenetic research, see "Na sessii OON AN SSSR (oktiabr' 1938 g.)," *Vestnik drevnei istorii* 4 (1938): 259–65, and "Doklady na soveshchanii Kommissii po etnogenezu pri Otdelenii istorii i filosofii," *Kratkie soobshcheniia o dokladakh i polevykh issledovaniiakh Instituta istorii material'noi kul'tury* 9 (1941): 3–62. The terror of 1937–38 seems to have had little regard for scholarly differences: E. D. Polivanov, his lone defender G. A. Il'inskii, and his chief accuser V. B. Aptekar' were executed within weeks of each other.

114. "Skhema piatitomnika po istorii SSSR," *Istorik-marksist* 1 (1938): 174–204; "Proekt skhemy mnogotomnika vsemirnoi istorii," *Istorik-marksist* 2 (1938): 143–91; V. Parkhomenko, "K voprosu o 'Normanskom zavoevanii' i proiskhozhdenii Rusi," *Istorik-Marksist* 4 (1938): 106–11; "Soveshchanie po voprosam etnogeneza," *Istorik-Marksist* 6 (1938): 201; N. N. Cheboksarov, "Mongoloidnye elementy v naselenii Tsentral'noi Evropy," *Uchenye zapiski MGU* 63 (1941): 238. Cf. Trofimova and Cheboksarov, "Znachenie ucheniia o iazyke," 39. Also M. I. Artamonov, "Doklady na sessii Otdeleniia istorii i filosofii AN SSSR: Spornye voprosy drevneishei istorii slavian i Rusi," *Kratkie soobshcheniia o dokladakh i polevykh issledovaniiakh Instituta istorii material'noi kul'tury* 6 (1940): 3–14.

115. Aksenova and Vasil'ev, "Problemy etnogonii," 99.

116. G. F. Debets, "Vepsy," *Uchenye zapiski MGU* 63 (1941): 139. Cf. Debets, "K probleme rasovogo tipa 'protofinnov'," *Uchenye zapiski MGU* 63 (1941): 11–20, and especially "Rasy, iazyki, kul'tury," *Nauka o rasakh i rasizm*. Nauchno-issledovatel'skii institut antropologii Moskovskogo gosudarstvennogo universiteta. Trudy, vyp. IV (Moscow: AN SSSR, 1938), 105–22.

117. Alpatov, *Istoriia odnogo mifa*, 112–37; L'Hermitte, *Marr*, 47–54.

118. Aksenova and Vasil'ev, "Problemy etnogonii," 99. See also Alpatov, *Istoriia odnogo mifa*, 136–37.

119. Alpatov, *Istoriia odnogo mifa*, 138–42; Ashnin and Alpatov, *"Delo slavistov,"* 162, 168; L'Hermitte, *Marr*, 47, 54. For the general situation in Soviet science during this period, see Vucinich, *Empire of Knowledge*, 179–210.

120. B. N. Agapov and K. L. Zelinskii, "Net, eto ne russkii iazyk," *Literaturnaia gazeta*, November 29, 1947. Quoted in Alpatov, *Istoriia odnogo mifa*, 144. See also Ashnin and Alpatov, *"Delo slavistov,"* 178–80.

121. See, in particular, David Joravsky, *The Lysenko Affair* (Chicago: Uni-

versity of Chicago Press, 1970); and Valerii Soifer, *Vlast' i nauka. Istoriia raz-groma genetiki v SSSR* (Tenafly, N.J.: Hermitage, 1989).

122. F. P. Filin, "O dvukh napravleniiakh v iazykovedenii," *Izvestiia Akademii nauk SSSR. Otdelenie literatury i iazyka* 7, no. 6 (November–December 1948): 488.

123. Filin, "O dvukh napravleniiakh v iazykovedenii," 496. See also A. G. Spirkin, "Nauchnaia sessiia, posviashchennaia 85-letiiu so dnia rozhdeniia i 15-letiiu so dnia smerti N. Ia. Marra," *Voprosy filosofii* 3 (1949): 326–37.

124. I. I. Meshchaninov, "O polozhenii v lingvisticheskoi nauke," *Izvestiia Akademii nauk SSSR. Otdelenie literatury i iazyka* 7, no. 6 (November–December 1948): 473.

125. Meshchaninov, "O polozhenii," 474. For "discussions" among linguists, see Alpatov, *Istoriia odnogo mifa*, 143–67, and L'Hermitte, *Marr*, 55–67.

126. A. L. Mongait and G. B. Fedorov, "Review of A. V. Artsikhovskii, *Vvedenie v arkheologiiu*," *Kratkie soobshcheniia o dokladakh i polevykh issledovaniiakh Instituta istorii material'noi kul'tury* 28 (1949): 123–26; S. P. Tolstov, "Sovetskaia shkola v etnografii," *Sovetskaia etnografiia* 4 (1947): 14–19; "Zadachi etnografov v sviazi s polozheniem na muzykal'nom fronte," *Sovetskaia etnografiia* 2 (1948): 3–7; V. K. Sokolova, "Diskussii po voprosam fol'kloristiki na zasedaniiakh Sektora fol'klora Instituta etnografii," *Sovetskaia etnografiia* 3 (1948): 139–46; V. Kirpotin, "O nizkopoklonstve pered kapitalisticheskim Zapadom, ob Aleksandre Veselovskom, o ego posledovateliakh i o samom glavnom," *Oktiabr'* 1 (1948): 3–27; "Protiv idealizatsii ucheniia A. Veselovskogo," *Izvestiia Akademii nauk SSSR. Otdelenie literatury i iazyka* 7, no. 4 (1948): 362–64; "Protiv burzhuaznogo liberalizma v literaturovedenii (po povodu diskussii ob A. Veselovskom), *Kul'tura i zhizn'*, March 11 and March 31, 1948; M. Levin, Ia. Roginskii, N. Cheboksarov, "Anglo-amerikanskii rasizm," *Sovetskaia etnografiia* 1 (1949): 18–39; "Itogi sessii VASKhNIL i sovetskaia antropologiia," *Sovetskaia etnografiia* 1 (1949): 182–83; V. Bunak, "Pis'mo v redaktsiiu," *Sovetskaia etnografiia* 1 (1949): 2.

127. RTsKhIDNI, f. 17, op. 132, d. 164, ll. 16–39. The Agitprop sponsored (RTsKhIDNI, f. 17, op. 132, d. 132, l. 39) two special publications on the subject: N. Bernikov and I. Braginskii, "Za peredovoe sovetskoe iazykoznanie," *Kul'tura i zhizn'*, 11 May, 1949 and 10 July, 1949; and G. Serdiuchenko, "Ob odnoi vrednoi teorii v iazykovedenii," *Kul'tura i zhizn'*, 30 June, 1949.

128. RTsKhIDNI, f. 17, op. 132, d. 164, ll. 17, 27–9, 33, 42–3. The quotation is from l. 42.

129. RTsKhIDNI, f. 17, op. 132, d. 164, l. 21. For an enlightening discussion of "discussion" as a genre (and a good summary of the linguistic discussion in particular), see Alexei Kojevnikov, "Games of Soviet Democracy: Ideological Discussions in Sciences around 1948 Reconsidered, " *Max-Planck-Institut für Wissenschaftsgeschichte,* Preprint 37 (1996): 1–31.

130. Cf. K. O. Rossiianov, "Stalin kak redaktor Lysenko: K predystorii avgustovskoi (1948) sessii VASKhNIL," *Voprosy filosofii* 2 (1993): 56–69.

131. I. I. Potekhin, "Zadachi bor'by s kosmopolitizmom v etnografii," *Sovetskaia etnografiia* 2 (1949): 17.

132. Potekhin, "Zadachi bor'by s kosmopolitizmom v etnografii," 20.

133. P. I. Kushner (Knyshev), "Uchenie I. V. Stalina o natsii i natsional'noi kul'ture i ego znachenie dlia etnografii," *Sovetskaia etnografiia* 4 (1949): 17.

134. V. Sokolova, Review of V. M. Zhirmunskii and Kh. T. Zarifov, *Uzbekskii narodnyi geroicheskii epos* (Moscow: Khudozhestvennaia literatura, 1947), in *Sovetskaia etnografiia* 2 (1949): 226; S. Tolstov, "Kniga po istorii tadzhikskogo naroda," *Kul'tura i zhizn'*, 22 April, 1950; "Bessmertnyi epos karelo-finskogo naroda," *Sovetskaia etnografiia* 2 (1949): 6.

135. Chikobava was one of the first members of the new Georgian Academy of Sciences, the chair of the Department of the Languages of the Caucasus at the University of Tbilisi, the head of the Section of the Caucasus Mountain Languages at the Institute of Linguistics of the Georgian Academy, and the editor-in-chief of the eight-volume Dictionary of the Georgian Language. See Alpatov, *Istoriia odnogo mifa*, 170.

136. A. S. Chikobava, "Stadial'naia klassifikatsiia iazykov akad. N. Marra," *Ezhegodnik iberiisko-kavkazskogo iazykoznaniia* 12 (1985): 19.

137. A. S. Chikobava, "Kogda i kak eto bylo," *Ezhegodnik iberiisko-kavkazskogo iazykoznaniia* 12 (1985): 9–14; Arn. Chikobava, "O nekotorykh voprosakh sovetskogo iazykoznaniia," *Pravda*, 9 May, 1950.

138. *Pravda*, 9 May–4 July, 1950 (every Tuesday); RTsKhIDNI, f. 17, op. 132, d. 336, ll. 4–6; Alpatov, *Istoriia odnogo mifa*, 167, 169–90.

139. *Pravda* 20 June, 1950. For comments on the formatting, see L'Hermitte, *Marr*, 69, and Alpatov, *Istoriia odnogo mifa*, 181.

140. I. V. Stalin, *Sochineniia*, ed, Robert H. McNeal, 3 vols. (Stanford: Hoover Institution, 1967), 3:150 and 114–22; Klara Zetkin, *Reminiscences of Lenin* (New York, 1934), 11–12, quoted in Joravsky, *Russian Psychology*, 239.

141. Stalin, *Sochineniia* 3:122–23, 119, 134, and passim.

142. "Istoriia govorit, chto natsional'nye iazyki iavliaiutsia ne klassovymi, a obshchenarodnymi iazykami, obshchimi dlia chlenov natsii i edinymi dlia natsii." Stalin, *Sochineniia* 3: 123.

143. Stalin, *Sochineniia* 3:147, 143.

144. Stalin, *Sochineniia* 3:146–47.

145. Stalin, *Sochineniia* 3:144.

146. Stalin, *Sochineniia* 3:130; Polivanov, "Stenogramma," 538. Cf. Alpatov, *Istoriia odnogo mifa*, 197–98.

147. Rossiianov, "Stalin kak redaktor Lysenko," 65.

148. Chikobava, "Kak i kogda," 13.

149. Stalin, *Sochineniia*, 3:146. For a later restatement of these views, see "The Economic Problems of Socialism in the USSR," in *Sochineniia* 3:188–245, esp. 189–91.

150. Joravsky, *The Lysenko Affair*, 150–55; Joravsky, *Russian Psychology*, 405–6; Vucinich, *Empire of Knowledge*, 247–56. The assumption that professional standards were valid in their own right was clearly shared by most, however. A special Politburo commission on Academy elections questioned its own legitimacy by distinguishing between a "political" veto (based on the existence

of "compromising materials") and a "professional" one (based on an insufficient number of "serious publications"). Scholars who protested to the Central
Committee about the persecution of non-Marrists emphasized the fact that the
leader of the pogrom (G. P. Serdiuchenko) "did not have serious scholarly publications and was primarily engaged in administrative work and teaching." It is
remarkable how many people who responded to Stalin's article seemed to take
his injunctions seriously. "You write that no science can develop without a
struggle of opinions, without freedom of criticism," begins the letter from a
high school teacher in Tula province. "I am sure, therefore, that you will not
object to criticism of your own writings. Please allow me to expound my
views." RTsKhIDNI, f. 17, op. 125, d. 445, ll. 102, 144; op. 132, d. 336, ll. 5, 141.

151. Stalin, *Sochineniia* 3:134, 138–39, 143. For major programmatic statements, see *Izvestiia Akademii nauk SSSR. Otdelenie literatury i iazyka* 9, nos. 1 and
2 (1950); P. Ia. Chernykh, "O sviazi razvitiia iazyka s istoriei naroda v svete trudov I. V. Stalina po iazykoznaniiu," *Izvestiia Akademii nauk SSSR. Otdelenie literatury i iazyka* 10, no. 3 (1951): 240–56; V. P. Petrus', "Slavianskaia iazykovaia
obshchnost' i slavianskie iazyki," *Izvestiia Akademii nauk SSSR. Otdelenie literatury i iazyka* 10, no. 4 (1951): 354–66; and Vinogradov and Serebrennikov, *Protiv vul'garizatsii.*

152. The quotes are from "V Institute mirovoi literatury," *Izvestiia Akademii
nauk SSSR. Otdelenie literatury i iazyka* 9, no. 2 (1950): 150; and V. I. Chicherov,
"O porochnykh vzgliadakh N. Ia. Marra i ego posledovatelei v oblasti fol'k-
loristiki," *Sovetskaia etnografiia* 3 (1952): 3–4. See also A. I. Beletskii, "Znachenie
trudov I. V. Stalina po iazykoznaniiu dlia sovetskogo literaturovedeniia,"
Izvestiia Akademii nauk SSSR. Otdelenie literatury i iazyka 10, no. 1 (1951): 21; and
A. M. Astakhova, "Znachenie trudov I. V. Stalina po voprosam iazykoznaniia
dlia razvitiia nauki o narodnom poeticheskom tvorchestve," *Izvestiia Akademii
nauk SSSR. Otdelenie literatury i iazyka* 10, no. 6 (1951): 533–46.

153. G. F. Debets, M. G. Levin, and T. A. Trofimova, "Antropologicheskii
material kak istochnik izucheniia voprosov etnogeneza," *Sovetskaia etnografiia* 1
(1952): 24–25 and passim; and N. N. Cheboksarov, "K voprosu o proiskhozhdenii narodov ugrofinskoi iazykovoi gruppy," *Sovetskaia etnografiia* 1 (1952):
36–50. See also M. F. Nesturkh, *Chelovecheskie rasy* (Moscow: Uchpedgiz, 1958).

154. S. A. Tokarev and N. N. Cheboksarov, "Metodologiia etnogenetich-
eskikh issledovanii na materiale etnografii v svete rabot I. V. Stalina po
voprosam iazykoznaniia," *Sovetskaia etnografiia* 4 (1951): 76. Also S. P. Tolstov,
"Znachenie trudov I. V. Stalina po voprosam iazykoznaniia dlia razvitiia sovetskoi etnografii," *Sovetskaia etnografiia* 4 (1950): 3–23, and Tolstov, "Itogi pere-
stroiki raboty Instituta etnografii AN SSSR v svete truda I. V. Stalina 'Marksizm
i voprosy iazykoznaniia'," *Sovetskaia etnografiia* 3 (1951): 3–14. See also Slezkine,
Arctic Mirrors, 308–23.

155. The quote is from "Itogi arkheologicheskikh issledovanii v 1946–50
godakh," *Vestnik Akademii nauk SSSR* 8 (1951): 107. See also S. V. Kiselev,
"Voprosy arkheologii pervobytnogo obshchestva v svete trudov I. V. Stalina po
iazykoznaniiu," *Kratkie soobshcheniia o dokladakh i polevykh issledovaniiakh Insti-*

tuta istorii material'noi kul'tury 36 (1951): 3–13; "Obsuzhdenie trudov I. V. Stalina po voprosam iazykoznaniia," *Kratkie soobshcheniia o dokladakh i polevykh issledovaniiakh Instituta istorii material'noi kul'tury* 36 (1951): 203–9; "Sessiia otdeleniia istorii i filosofii," *Vestnik Akademii nauk SSSR* 8 (1951): 42–43; E. V. Veimarn and S. F. Strzheletskii, "K voprosu o slavianakh v Krymu," *Voprosy istorii* 4 (1952): 94–99; A. P. Smirnov, "K voprosu o slavianakh v Krymu," *Vestnik drevnei istorii* 3 (1953): 32–45; Miller, *Archaeology in the USSR*, 132–68; and *Protiv vul'garizatsii marksizma v arkheologii* (Moscow: AN SSSR, 1953), 45–47 and passim.

156. Ashnin and Alpatov, *"Delo slavistov,"* 180, RTsKhIDNI, f. 17, op. 132, d. 336, ll. 77–78, 87.

157. I. S. Gurvich, ed., *Etnogenez narodov Severa* (Moscow: Nauka, 1980), 4.

158. M. Ermatov, *Etnogenez i formirovanie predkov uzbekskogo naroda* (Tashkent: Uzbekistan, 1968), 8–9, 15–16, and passim. For a survey of the Tatar-Chuvash controversy, see Victor A. Shnirelman, *Who Gets the Past? Competition for Ancestors among Non-Russian Intellectuals in Russia* (Washington: Woodrow Wilson Center Press, 1996). See also Philip L. Kohl and Gocha R. Tsetskhladze, "Nationalism, Politics, and the Practice of Archaeology in the Caucasus," in Kohl and Fawcett, *Nationalism, Politics,* 149–74.

159. P. N. Tret'iakov, "K voprosu o vozniknovenii i drevnei istorii finno-ugorskikh plemen Povolzh'ia," in *Etnogenez mordovskogo naroda* (Saransk: Mordovskoe knizhnoe izdatel'stvo, 1965), 7. For very thoughtful early analyses of the Soviet ethnological predicament, see G. S. Knabe, "Vopros o sootnoshenii arkheologicheskoi kul'tury i etnosa v sovremennoi zarubezhnoi literature," *Sovetskaia arkheologiia* 3 (1959): 243–57; and A. L. Mongait, "Arkheologicheskie kul'tury i etnicheskie obshchnosti," *Narody Azii i Afriki* 1 (1967): 53–76.

How I Became
Multicultural

I became Soviet in 1963 when the USSR beat Czechoslovakia in the World Hockey Championship on an empty-net goal by Leonid Volkov. I became Russian at about the same time and for the same reason. I became exuberantly Soviet in 1964 when I joined the Octobrist (Lenin's Grandchildren's) League, and then again briefly in 1966 when I was admitted to the All-Union Pioneer Organization.

I became half-Jewish in 1967 when I told my father that Mishka Ryzhevskii from apartment 13 was a Jew, and my father said: "Let me tell you something."

I became mostly Jewish around 1968, when I became anti-Soviet. My father, who was already anti-Soviet, did not have the option of becoming Jewish.

I was officially classified as Russian in 1972 when I received my internal passport (on the occasion of my sixteenth birthday). I was temporarily reclassified as Soviet in 1978 when I received my external passport (on the day I was hired by the Ministry of the Merchant Marine).

I became Swedish for a day and a half in 1978 when I borrowed the identification papers of one Gunnar Gunnarsson (place of birth Göteborg, permanent residence Boda) for the purpose of surviving a visit to the rebel-held part of Sofala Province, in the People's Republic of Mozambique.

I became a published author in 1981 when Progress Publishers printed my Portuguese translation of L. M. Maksudov's Ideological Struggle at the Present Stage. *My attempt to translate a manual on mechanical engineering for Peace Publishers was aborted due to my complete unfamiliarity with the subject matter.*

I became Iouri Slezkine in 1981 when the Department of Visas and Permissions of the Ministry of Internal Affairs of the USSR received special per-

mission to transliterate my name into French. Shortly thereafter, I was dismissed from the All-Union Union of Communist-Leninist Youth and from the Soviet Army reserve.

I became Portuguese in 1982 after reassuring a Lisbon immigration official that I had been in the Soviet Army reserve because it was obligatory. Later that year, I briefly became British in order to qualify for the position of English instructor at the Portuguese National Guard.

I became an intellectual in the fall of 1982 for the purpose of graduate admissions. I had applied to graduate school for the purpose of legally entering the United States. I entered the United States after reassuring a U.S. consular official that I had belonged to the All-Union Union of Communist-Leninist Youth because it was a college requirement. I had made enough money for a one-way ticket to Houston by completing a translation of Gabe Mirkin's Sports Medicine *despite my complete unfamiliarity with the subject matter.*

I became a Texas patriot in 1985 after two trips to Johnson City and one trip to Van Horn. I became an American in 1988 after naming most of the thirteen original colonies and two U.S. senators. I renamed myself "Yuri" on the same occasion.

I stopped being Soviet for most practical purposes in 1986 when my Soviet passport expired. I stopped being Soviet altogether in 1991 when the Soviet Union ceased to exist. I reverted to being Soviet in 1993 when I saw Igor Larionov play for the San Jose Sharks. I became exuberantly Russian at about the same time and for the same reason.

Yuri Slezkine

Andrzej Walicki

Intellectual Elites and the Vicissitudes of "Imagined Nation" in Poland

There is nothing new in the thesis that nations are not "natural" and everlasting subdivisions of humanity. There is no need to constantly repeat that modern nations are of relatively recent origin. People interested in the problem should have realized that this has been made clear more than a hundred years ago, mostly by Marxists in the multinational Habsburg empire, and that the best, classical works on this subject were published at the very beginning of our century.[1]

What is new in the current discussions about nationalism and nations is the emphasis *on the subjective factor* in the nation-building processes. It is now claimed that nations are artifacts, that they owe their existence to nationalist imagination, or even deliberate invention, and, therefore, that it was nationalism that created nations, and not the other way around. In this way scholars seeing themselves as Marxists[2] rejected the standard Marxist view of nations as products of objective socioeconomic development, necessary results of bourgeois-democratic progress; they formulated instead a conception of nations as "imagined communities," as phenomena "constructed essentially from above," by untrustworthy nationalist ideologies, and, therefore, based upon a very shaky foundation.[3]

This total reversal of the earlier Marxist position involved, of course, an obvious departure from historical materialism. On the other hand, however, it only strengthened the old Marxist illusion that nations are somehow less real and less legitimate than social classes. This might have not been intended by some of the quoted authors, but the reception of their theories is, as a rule, quite unambiguous in this matter. It is methodologically legitimate to write about "awakening" a social class, about raising it from being "in itself" to conscious existence "for itself," but it is no longer legitimate to apply this terminology to nations: as products of nationalist imagination (it is argued), nations cannot exist prior to nationalism. The assumption that nations can "exist without realizing it" is contemptuously dismissed, as deriving from a naive, "preconstructionist" methodology.[4]

From my own point of view the "constructionist" trend in the studies of nationalism is a one-sided and exaggerated reaction against the resurgence of the "primordialist" view of nations, bound up with the "ethnic revival" in our world.[5] It is one-sided because too many facts contradict the definition of nations as something contingent,[6] merely invented, or imagined. It is exaggerated because emphasizing the role of objective factors in the making of the modern nation does not have to entail the acceptance of a "primordialist" position. Miroslav Hroch's book is a good illustration of this simple truth.

Having said this, I would like to stress that I see the "construction-ist" theories as containing an important element of truth: an element completely neglected by those scholars who try to explain everything in terms of economic and social history. As an intellectual historian I am pleased to acknowledge that the "constructionists" are right in pointing out the important, active role of ideas and intellectual elites in shaping national identities. If this is so, then, as Roman Szporluk has rightly observed, "it matters a lot *what* a nation imagines itself to be."[7] This, in turn, depends on self-definition, national mythologies, images of national history and concept of national mission created by intellec-tual elites, or even by individual thinkers or writers. Hence intellectual history deserves to be treated as an important and relatively autonomous factor in the explanation of national consciousness and national movements.[8]

One could say, of course, that there is little new in these observa-tions. Indeed, patriotic thinkers and writers of the Romantic epoch knew very well how great was the role of ideas and imagination in the shaping of nation. Polish philosophers of that time wanted to mold Pol-ish national identity through creating a distinctive Polish philosophy; the great Polish poet, Cyprian Norwid, defined national artists as orga-nizing national imagination in the same way in which statesmen orga-nize national forces.[9] In noncontinuous nations, which had to experi-ence a process of "national awakening,"[10] the role of individual "organizers of national imagination" was even greater: the historian

František Palacky, who defined the meaning of Czech history, deserved to be called "the father of the Czech nation."[11] In the case of Slovaks, who, in the nineteenth century, had been a completely "new" nation, deprived of any historico-political traditions of its own, the part played by individual intellectuals at the initial state of national development was decisive. The nation-creating activity of L'udovit Štúr, who consciously decided which Slovak dialect should become the basis of Slovak literary language and separate national identity, is probably the closest approximation (at least in the European conditions) to Gellner's conception of "inventing" a nation.

However, these well-known facts need an adequate theoretical explanation, and I have no doubt that such an explanation should make use of Gellner's and Anderson's contributions. The explanatory functions of their "constructionist" approach can be preserved if it ceases to be coupled with risky generalizations, if it is not treated as the only, universally applicable key to all national phenomena. The relative weight of the subjective and objective factors in the making of nations is different in different countries and in different historical periods. Hence all theoretical generalizations should be based upon careful case studies.

The present article is a very brief and, therefore, somewhat over-simplified summary of my views on the successes and failures, intended and unintended results of the multiple attempts of Polish intellectual elites, at different periods of Polish history, to create the Polish nation, or, at least, to influence its making.

From a Medieval Nationality to the Multiethnic Nation of the Gentry

The view of nations as products of the all-European breakdown of feudal structures, initiated by the French Revolution, is not a recent discovery in Poland. In fact this view was well represented in Polish historiography already at the very beginning of our century.[12] However, it was seriously questioned by the Polish medievalists of the interbellum period.[13] All of them stressed that Poland, in contrast to the Holy Roman Empire of the German nation, reached the stage of a cohesive medieval nationhood in the Middle Ages. The ties uniting the inhabitants of the medieval Polish state could not be reduced to dynastic and religious loyalties. Unlike France, Poland had not experienced a foreign conquest; it was ethnically homogeneous; its rulers from the Piast dynasty were legitimate successors of pre-Christian tribal authorities, consciously trying to unite all ethnic Poles (or rather all kindred, proto-Polish tribes) in a single state. And the state-building elite was fully aware of the need of a sort of national consciousness and national ideology.

Some Polish historians see the emergence of a well-crystallized Polish national consciousness already at the end of the eleventh century. The main argument for this thesis is the chronicle of a Benedictine monk named Gallus Anonymus (compiled 1113–16): it contains an elaborate national ideology, stressing that Poland was not the property of the monarch, glorifying its past, and using a rich patriotic phraseology ("honor patriae," "laus patriae," "pro patria mori"). During the period of the Feudal Fragmentation (1138–1320) and Tartar invasions this patriotic ideology, further developed in the chronicle of Master Wincenty Kadłubek, was the most powerful factor keeping alive the image of a single Polish nation and the idea of reuniting the dismembered parts of its body in a single kingdom.

Among the plebeian masses the national feeling was awakened as a result of ethnic conflicts created by the inundation of Poland by German colonists, often perceived as arrogant and unjustly privileged. The Polish clergy sharply reacted against attempts to establish in Poland German churches and monasteries subject to the jurisdiction of German ecclesiastical authorities. They formally demanded that the announcements and prayers for the governing princes and fatherland be rendered in Polish in all churches in Poland. All patriots agreed that all sons of Poland *(Poloniae filii)* should defend Poland against the German danger, to preserve the Polish rule in all lands belonging to the Polish nation *(natio Polonica)*, and to strive for national unification.[14]

The task of unification was completed with the coronation of Władysław the Short as king of Poland in 1320. Shortly before that date Władysław had to suppress the revolt of the German burghers headed by Mayor Albert from Cracow, and to punish the rebels for their "treason against the Polish nation."[15] He was also involved in a conflict with the Teutonic Knights who in 1308 seized Pomerania. Władysław tried to settle this conflict by appealing for the papal arbitration. It has been rightly noticed that the three attempts at arbitration by papal representatives turned out to produce a kind of "Gallup Poll" about the Polish character of Pomerania.[16] The witnesses of the Polish side, representing all segments of the Pomeranian population, testified that Pomerania had always been a part of Poland and that the language of its people was Polish. These arguments, although largely ignored by the arbiters, showed that the language of the population was for the Poles an important factor in settling political disputes. It was so, because already in the thirteenth century the Polish elite identified the nation with its language and drew from this the conclusion that the state frontiers should coincide with the territorial scope of the national language.[17]

On the basis of these facts most Polish historians, including Marxists, tend to agree that the starting point in the long process of making the Polish nation was the medieval Polish nationality that had emerged at the turn of the thirteenth century.

The next phase in the nation-building process in Poland was the Jagiellonian empire, known as the Polish-Lithuanian Commonwealth, or "Rzecz Pospolita" (Res Publica). Its emergence generated a process that led, ultimately, to the creation of a unique political system—the Noble Democracy, or democracy of the gentry. It was a democracy because it was based upon the principle of the sovereignty of the people; it saw itself as a republican state, setting against the dynastic principle the "will of the nation," hence a form of civic nationalism. On the other hand, the "nation" of the Commonwealth was composed of, and limited to, the members of the gentry; hence it was the "noble nation," the nation of the gentry. True, the gentry of the Commonwealth were a very numerous and extremely differentiated group whose members, from the great magnates to the noble proletariat, saw themselves, at least in theory, as juridically and politically equal. Their civic and political rights were impressive by any standards, and the number of "active citizens" in their state was in fact much greater than in the nineteenth-century France, or England, before the introduction of the universal suffrage. Nevertheless, participation in the collective sovereignty of the nation was formally restricted to one estate only.

It is obvious that the transformation of the Polish state from an ethnically homogeneous (or almost homogeneous) medieval monarchy into a multiethnic, multireligious, and multilingual federal republic of the gentry must have changed the content of Polish nationalism. Let us briefly characterize some of these changes.

First and foremost, it was a shifting from the ethnolinguistic national patriotism to a form of multiethnic civic nationalism, based upon a vision of common political destiny and cemented by a fierce attachment to republican libertarian values. The nation of the gentry was conceived as a political, not an ethnic, community, and precisely this made it powerfully attractive to the gentry of the entire commonwealth, irrespective of their ethnicity and language. An influential sixteenth-century writer, Stanisław Orzechowski, was not mistaken in attributing this integrating effect to the attractiveness of Polish liberties.[18] Significantly, he was not a native Pole but a polonized Ukrainian, who described himself as "gente Ruthenus, Natione Polonus"—politically a Pole, although ethnically a Ruthenian. This non-Polish ethnic background did not prevent him from seeing the Poles as a chosen nation and himself as a part of their mission.

Integrating different ethnic elements into a single cohesive nation involved a conscious creation of a national ideology. An important part of this ideology was purely political. Numerous writers promoted a new type of national pride, stemming from the image of the Jagiellonian Commonwealth as a unique land of freedom. As ardent pupils of the ancients, they defined nation as a sovereign political community, using such terms as *societas, civitas,* and *res publica.* This was common not only in the sixteenth century, the period of humanism and the "golden age" of the gentry democracy, but also in the seventeenth century—the time of Counter Reformation and of the relative decline of the Commonwealth. Thus, for instance, a seventeenth-century writer and politician, Łukasz Opaliński, put forward a modern-sounding theory about civil society *(societas civilis),* which arises from the development of human needs, and *respublica* or *civitas,* as the large, organized society of an entire people *(magna illa unius populi civitas),* whose soul is the law.[19]

However, the ideologists of the "noble nation" were not satisfied with an exclusively political basis for national unity; they wanted to facilitate the process of integration by endowing the multiethnic nation with a feeling of being united by the common ancestry. This was done by claiming that the entire gentry of the commonwealth constituted a "Sarmatian nation," descendants of the ancient, powerful, and famous Sarmatians. As a rule, this theory tended to identify the medieval history of the invented "Sarmatian nation" with exclusively Polish historical tradition; nevertheless, some writers made considerable efforts to integrate Polish history with the history of the Kievan Rus' and Lithuania. Thus, for instance, Matys Stryjkowski published (in Polish, 1582) a rich and interesting *Chronicle of Poland, Lithuania, Samogitia, and of All*

Rus'—the first integrated history of all lands of the Commonwealth.[20] In the next century Wojciech Dębołęcki tried to integrate the history of Polish and Lithuanian-Ruthenian nobility in a fantastic story of their common descent from the "Royal Sarmatians," descendants of the Scythians, whose history, in turn, derived directly from the biblical Adam. He concluded from this that "Sarmatians" were the chosen nation, destined to rule over the world.[21]

It should be stressed that the multiethnic character of the "noble nation" must not be confused with a genuine multiculturalism. The ideologists of Sarmatianism took it for granted that national culture should be homogeneous, and that the basis for cultural unification should be provided by the Polish culture, perceived as the most developed culture of the realm. At the same time, however, the expansion to the East and the Eastern-oriented politics of the Commonwealth exposed the gentry to a strong, although rather external, Muslim influence. The other side of this was the increasing self-complacency, fondness for cultural uniqueness, and conscious turning away from the monarchist and corrupting West.[22] In the seventeenth century even the German nobles from the northern provinces of the Polish-Lithuanian state learned to grow Sarmatian mustaches and to wear the orientalized dress named *Kontusz*. Membership in the gentry was open to different ethnic elements but offered little room for cultural autonomy. In the Lithuanian part of the Commonwealth baptized Jews were almost automatically ennobled, but this entailed a total cultural transformation: the new noble, *origine Judaeus,* had to dress himself as a Sarmatian, to carry a saber, to ride a horse, and so forth.[23]

Cultural unity, as conceived by the ideologists of the "noble nation," did not include the imposition of a single official language of the state. In the Grand Duchy of Lithuania six languages (Polish, Latin, Ruthenian, German, Armenian, and Hebrew) received official recognition.[24] The language of official documents was a Ruthenian dialect (close to Belorussian), and nobody cared to replace it with Latin or Polish. Nevertheless, the embracing of the Sarmatian theory by the Lithuanian and Ruthenian gentry helped to produce the unexpectedly quick voluntary polonization (including linguistic polonization) of the non-Polish gentry of the Commonwealth. This, of course, greatly strengthened the cultural cohesion of the multiethnic "nation of the gentry"; at the same time, however, it deprived the non-Polish peoples of the Polish-Lithuanian state of their "historical classes" and thereby greatly delayed their separate national developments.

From the point of view of the making of the Polish nation, the centuries of the Noble Democracy brought about paradoxical and ambiguous consequences. On the one hand, membership in the Polish nation was extended to non-Polish nobles, which resulted in a spectacular increase of the number of patriotic and culturally creative Poles. On the other hand, the notion of "being a Pole" came to be firmly associated with the noble status, which, of course, severed the ties between Polish gentry and Polish peasantry, delaying thereby the development of an ethnolinguistic Polish nation. One is tempted to say that, in comparison with the fourteenth century, it was not only a delay but an outright regress.

The republican character of the political ideology of the "noble nation," especially the widespread use of the classical republican rhetoric in Renaissance Poland, can serve as an argument that this ideology should be classified as a form of republican patriotism and that the term *nationalism* is not applicable to it at all. Additional support for this view can be found in the recently published book by Maurizio Viroli, who argues that patriotism and nationalism are typologically different and mutually exclusive concepts. In fact, however, Viroli's book provides also strong reasons for treating the republican patriotism of Polish and polonized gentry of the Commonwealth (republican patriotism of the nonpolonized Ruthenian gentry is a different question) as a component of its "political nationalism." According to Viroli, patriotism implies the ideal of the city that does not need cultural, or moral, or religious unity.[25] If so, it should be clear that political ideology of the "noble nation" was something different, closer to nationalism (in the broad sense of the term) than to the urban pattern of classical patriotism. It was from the very beginning a form of cohesive corporate consciousness, strongly committed to the unity of moral and historical traditions, and it developed in the direction of religious and cultural homogeneity, entailing a wholesale polonization of the multiethnic nobility of the Commonwealth. Hence, if we want to characterize the ideology of the Noble Democracy as a whole, without artificially separating its early period from its culmination in Sarmatianism, it is much better to describe it as a form of "political nationalism" and a stage in the development of *national* consciousness in Poland.

Imagining a Modernized Nation

The first half of the eighteenth century witnessed a total decline of the Commonwealth. Having lost their civic spirit, the middle gentry withdrew from public affairs, while the poor, landless nobles degenerated into clients of the great magnates, thus allowing the transformation of the "gentry democracy" into an oligarchic anarchy. The army, which at the end of previous century defended the Habsburg Empire against the Turkish invasion, almost disappeared, the economic backwardness of the country was rapidly increasing, and its national independence was more and more menaced by the neighboring absolute monarchies. As a somewhat delayed reaction to this, there emerged a movement for reforms, seeing the salvation of Poland in strengthening the executive power at the expense of the "golden freedom" of the gentry. Its first great achievement was the establishment in 1773 of the Commission for National Education, the first ministry of education in Europe, which took possession of the network of schools belonging to the recently dissolved Jesuit order and thoroughly modernized the entire educational system of the state, consciously promoting the goal of cultural homogeneity. The culmination of the reformist movement was the so-called great Diet, or Four Years' Diet (1788–92), which produced the new fundamental law known as the May Constitution (1791). It transformed the gentry republic into a hereditary constitutional monarchy with modern government and biennial parliaments. Political rights were made dependent on the ownership of land, which meant that many burghers were raised to the status of "active citizens," while the landless gentry—the clients of magnates—were deprived of political rights. Thus, the replacement of republican principles by monarchical ones entailed the abandonment of the most cherished idea of the gentry democracy: the idea of political equality of all members of the nobility.

The deliberations of the great Diet were preceded and accompanied by an all-national discussion that helped to crystallize two different programs of national revival: the republican program of the so-called enlightened Sarmatianism and the monarchical program of the westernizing Party of Reform.[26]

The main vulnerability of the first program was its close connection with the republican ideology of conservative gentry. Nevertheless, even the republicanism of Michał Wielhorski, the main ideologist of the conservative Confederation of Bar (1768–72), could not be reduced to a defense of the feudal liberties—it was modern and "enlightened" enough to inspire Rousseau's *Considerations on the Government of Poland*, a treatise warmly sympathizing with the gentry republic.[27] And at the time of the Four Years' Diet the modernizing element of the republican ideology was often coming to the fore, as an alternative national program.

The central element in the republican view of the nation was the idea of popular sovereignty. The ideologists of the "noble republicanism" defined the nation as a collective subject of the sovereign political will, that is, as the opposite of a population subject to a monarch. From this point of view "nation" and absolute monarchy were, of course, mutually exclusive, while a participatory republic was the only form of mature nationhood; even England did not deserve to be called a nation because its political freedom was too limited.[28] Many theorists of gentry republicanism concluded from this that Poland-Lithuania was the only true nation in Europe. Interestingly, the most enlightened among them, for instance Michał Wielhorski (mentioned above), or the castellan of Vitebsk, Adam Rzewuski, did not try to defend the view that the nation should be restricted to one estate only; on the contrary, they insisted that this was a transient phenomenon, caused by special historical circumstances, and declared their willingness to see the rights of active citizenship made universal, related to the entire population of the country. Adam Rzewuski wrote: "O, how ardently I want that no privileged class would exist and that burghers and peasants become simply humans and Poles."[29]

The national program of the mainstream reformers stemmed from their view that Poland needed above all political and cultural westernization, that is putting an end to the Sarmatian uncritical celebration of republican values and national uniqueness. It is significant that Hugo Kołłątaj, the main architect of the May Constitution, interpreted modernization in terms of a nation-building process: as a transition from the "nation of the gentry" to the "new nation"—the "nation of proprietors," in which active citizenship would depend on property qualifications. He wanted the "new nation" to be homogeneous, speaking the same language and living under the same laws. This view was the Polish equivalent of the Jacobin conception of the nation, keenly suspicious of regional and cultural differences as incompatible with national unity and modernization. In the Polish conditions it meant the unification of laws, the liquidation of the autonomous status of Lithuania, and programmatic polonization of the entire population of the state. The rights of religious minorities were to be respected, but only in strictly religious matters. Thus, for instance, Jews were to be deprived of their autonomy, subject to Polish jurisdiction, forced to attend Polish schools and dress like westernized Poles; even their beards were to be cut off, like the beards of boyars in Russia. The Commission for National Education was to serve as a powerful instrument for implementing this program.

It should be stressed that Kołłątaj's conception of a homogeneous nation had nothing in common with special interest in the irrational cultural ties, including the mystique of national language. To paraphrase Ernest Gellner, we can say that his nationalism was simply a species of patriotism favoring cultural homogeneity. His conception of nation was political, rationalist, inspired by those ideas of the French Enlightenment that paved the way for the Jacobin nationalism. It represented the Polish version of what came to be known as "the French model of the nation."

The May Constitution reflected Kołłątaj's ideas, but the second partition of Poland prevented their implementation. The constitution had no chance to become the supreme law of the country. It remained a piece of paper, greatly celebrated today as a sui generis "last will" of the independent Polish state. But it is almost forgotten that it had been revoked, in fact, by Tadeusz Kościuszko, the democratic leader of the national uprising of 1794, who declared that the form of political system in Poland would be determined by a new Diet. And it is rarely remembered that the legacy of the May Constitution was not accepted by the Polish democrats of the Romantic epoch; that all of them—from moderates, like Joachim Lelewel, to extreme radicals, like Edward Dembowski—unequivocally rejected it, as monarchical, sanctifying inequality and betraying Polish national values.

What were the reasons of these severe judgments?

They were quite plain, not difficult to understand. As a program of national revival the May Constitution was indeed a rather conspicuous failure of imagination. It did very little to improve the situation of peasants, certainly not enough to make them patriotically loyal to the existing Polish state. At the same time it disfranchised the masses of the poor gentry, who might have been the clients of reactionary magnates but, nonetheless, could not be replaced as bearers of national consciousness and its disseminators among the nonnoble population. It was not realistic to believe that the nation of the gentry could be transformed at one stroke into a nation of property owners. After partitions, the petty gentry, despite all its shortcomings, became the main social basis of Polish movements for national independence. As a very numerous stratum, having little to lose and endowed with a vivid sense of its civic and national rights, it proved to be Poland's asset rather than liability.

It seems justified to claim that the true "testament" of eighteenth-century Poland is to be found in the proclamation of the Kościuszko uprising, not in the legislative acts of the great Diet. Kościuszko's main idea, taken up by the nineteenth-century Polish radicals, was to emancipate the peasants and thus make them Polish patriots. In his émigré pamphlet *Can the Poles Win Through to Independence?* (1800) he visualized the peasant masses, with scythes in their hands, fighting bravely for Poland and making her invincible.[30] He believed this to be possible because the emancipated peasants would make Poland "the sixteen-million-strong nation," galvanized to battle by the spirit of liberty. Reference to sixteen millions makes it clear that he saw as potential Poles all inhabitants of the former commonwealth, irrespective of their language and religious affiliation.

Imagining a Reborn Nation

The two eighteenth-century programs of national revival had one important feature in common: in both of them the concept of nation had a distinctively *political* content, referring to citizenship, and not to ethnicity. Precisely because of this, after the defeat of the Kościuszko uprising and the final partition of Poland (1795) many Polish patriots identified the end of the Polish state with a dissolution of the Polish nation. This was reflected even in the song that was to become the Polish national anthem: its words "we shall *again* be Poles" assumed that the Polish nation had temporarily ceased to exist and would return into being after regaining its independent statehood.

The defeat of the Napoleonic France made it clear that an independent Polish state was not a feasible ideal for the predictable future and thus necessitated a thorough redefinition of the Polish nation. It could no longer be defined in purely political terms because an independent Polish state disappeared from the map of Europe and the only political unit bearing the name of Poland was the tiny Kingdom of Poland, an autonomous part of the Russian Empire. On the other hand, the profound sense of political legitimacy prevented Polish patriots from embracing the ethnolinguistic conception of nationality. Such a conception, by the way, was by then very unusual; even the signatories of the Treaty of Vienna used the name *Poles* to refer to the entire population of the prepartition Polish state.[31] The new concept of the Polish nation had to support the conviction that the national unity of all lands of the former commonwealth could be maintained even under partitions. Hence it had to be *historico*-political, stressing that Poland still existed in her old frontiers as a historical nation, cemented by strong traditions and endowed with "nonlapsed political rights" to regain its lost statehood.

In this way Polish patriots set against the dynastic legitimism of the Holy Alliance a new principle of political legitimacy: the "legitimism of nations," or the principle of national self-determination. It was not yet the *modern* principle of national self-determination, based upon the ethnolinguistic concept of nation. But precisely because of this it was more in tune with the prevailing political views of the epoch and more convincing in its logic, especially in its invocation of *historical* rights, even to the monarchs themselves.

Of course, in order to survive as a nation without political independence it was necessary to put more and more emphasis on the nonpolitical factors of national unity. The most important among these was literary culture. Maurycy Mochnacki, the best theorist of the early Polish romanticism, called Polish literature of his time an organ of national self-consciousness, a proof that Poles "had recognized themselves in their essence."[32] He assumed that Polish literary culture would help to unite all lands of historical Poland, including the Ukraine; the "borderlands" were expected to produce distinctive regional traditions in Polish literature, contributing thereby to the enrichment of the Polish national spirit.[33] This proved to be an extremely successful cultural program: the literature of partitioned Poland willingly accepted the task of promoting national consciousness, performed this brilliantly, and deserved to be seen as a most powerful factor of national unity. But there was also a somewhat unexpected consequence of this success: the growing importance of literary language prepared the ground for defining the nation linguistically rather than politically.

The liquidation of the remnants of the Polish statehood after the unsuccessful insurrection of 1830–31 made it even more difficult to define the Polish nation in political terms. It was necessary to make national existence completely independent of political circumstances by firmly grounding Poland's foundation in the realm of the spiritual. The Romantic generation did this by defining the nation as a community of *tradition* and *spirit*, but above all of a universal historical *mission*. Polish democrats saw this mission as fighting for freedom and brotherhood of all nations; Polish messianic poets—Adam Mickiewicz and Juliusz Słowacki—interpreted it religiously, treating Poland as a chosen instrument of a "new revelation" that was to bring about the ethicization of politics and universal regeneration. But all patriots, irrespective of political persuasion, took it for granted that Poland's historical mission was common to all the lands of the Jagiellonian Commonwealth.

Continued loyalty to the Old Commonwealth found expression in the three different conceptions of its possible restoration: the multicultural, the unitarist, and the federal.

The *multicultural* conception was a romantic idealization of the old, multiethnic and multireligious commonwealth. Linguistic, religious, and cultural differences were to be tolerated, even valued and regarded as fully compatible with national unity. Joachim Lelewel, the great romantic historian, probably went farthest in this direction. He predicted that language or religious belief might no longer enter into the concept of nation, and dreamed of a Poland where "no differences would exist among the peoples of which it is composed": Polish, Lithuanian, German, Samogitian, Ruthenian.[34] He was equally tolerant of regional differences and apprehensive of centralist leanings of the eighteenth-century reformers. The great Romantic poet, Adam Mickiewicz—whose masterpiece, *Master Thaddeus*, begins with words "Lithuania, my fatherland"—professed similar ideas and ingrained them in the national consciousness.

In spite of this, the majority of politically active Poles of the Romantic epoch, especially democrats, embraced the *unitarist* conception of the nation, the so-called French conception. They were fairly united in their support for the integration of the historic territories of the commonwealth, combating all tendencies not only toward separatism but even toward regionalism, and after the emancipation and education of serfs they expected swift results in polonization.[35] They despised the May Constitution, but, nonetheless, the unitarist tendency in their national ideology was basically in accord with the political thinking of the eighteenth-century Party of Reform. The revolutionary manifesto of the Cracow uprising of 1846—an uprising led by a romantic revolutionary and a passionate critic of the Enlightenment, Edward Dembowski—proclaimed the ideal of an integrated and unified democratic nation within the frontiers of 1772.[36] Thus it fully disregarded the autonomous status of Lithuania. The manifesto further stressed this by a significant change in the national arms, from which the Lithuanian chase (a warrior on horse) was eliminated, now leaving the entire space of the emblem to the Polish white eagle.

The third conception—that of the "federal nation"—formed the thinking of the organizers and leaders of the January insurrection of 1863. In contrast to the Cracow uprising, the beginning of the 1863 insurrection was marked by a manifesto that called to arms the *three nations* of the Old Commonwealth: Poles, Lithuanians, and Ukrainians. Its banner showed the triune emblem of the federation composed of the Polish eagle, the Lithuanian chase, and the Ruthenian archangel. In their dealings with the non-Polish nationalities of the former Commonwealth, the insurgents used their respective languages, including the Belorussian. In the negotiations between the Polish and Russian revolutionaries, which took place before the uprising, the Polish side agreed to respect the rights of democratic self-determination on the nationally mixed territories. At the same time, however, the Poles made clear that they hoped to influence events and to bring about a voluntary union of these nationalities with Poland, thus restoring the Old Commonwealth in the form of a free federation—one that would correct the fatal mistake of not recognizing the rights of the Ukrainian population. The best traditions of the Polish-Lithuanian Commonwealth were to be revived in a democratic federation composed of three basic units: Poland, Lithuania, and Ukraine.

The federal conception differs from the multicultural and unitarist by clearly recognizing that despite their close links with Poland, Lithuania and Ukraine were separate nations. This recognition, which was given somewhat grudgingly, was prompted by several causes, such as the progress of the Ukrainian national awakening, the growing influence of political theories defining nations in ethnolinguistic terms, and, last but not least, the increasing awareness among the Poles themselves that the Polish language and Catholic religion were the most reliable elements of Polish self-identity. Thus, the federal conception to the Poles who embraced it did not imply membership in a multicultural federated nation but rather in a *Polish* nation that would be part of a federation within which the distinctive national cultures of the former Commonwealth would be preserved and mutually respected. In this way the federal option combined a nostalgia for the historic, multiethnic fatherland with an increased awareness of belonging to a culturally well defined, Polish-speaking, and Catholic nation. Owing to this, the January insurrection was more ardently and ostentatiously Catholic than previous Polish uprisings, which had been either religiously neutral (as the uprising of 1830–31), or even colored by a dose of anticlericalism (as was the Kościuszko insurrection of 1794 and the Cracow uprising of 1846).[37] Recognizing the Ukrainians as a separate nation therefore had a double meaning. On the one hand it was, of course, the long-delayed recognition of Ukrainian aspirations to nationhood, but on the other hand it recognized the difference between the Polish-speaking, Catholic population (Poles in the ethnolinguistic and cultural sense) and the Eastern Slavs.

As we can see, the federal conception was in fact the first important step toward abandoning the increasingly anachronistic idea of a single political nation. But it was still very far from a consistent commitment to the ethnolinguistic criteria of nationality. For the generation of 1863 it was too difficult to imagine that Lithuanian or Ukrainian Poles might ever be treated as a national minority. It was expected that Lithuania and Ukraine would achieve separate nationhood as multicultural countries, allowing local Poles to define themselves as Lithuanians or Ukrainians of Polish culture, combining loyalty to their respective nations with continuing attachment to the Jagiellonian tradition.[38]

On the whole, the generation of 1863 wanted to make the notion of the Polish nation as inclusive as possible. The best proof of this was the universal enthusiasm about the pro-Polish feelings among the Warsaw Jews, who actively participated in the patriotic manifestations on the eve of the uprising. They became immediately recognized as "Poles of the Mosaic persuasion" and extolled in literature as heroic participants, or even organizers and leaders of the Polish struggle for independence. It is worthwhile to point out that this euphoria was not bound up with hoping that the Jews would convert to Catholicism. On the contrary: writers of that time propagated the idea of incorporating the Jews in the Polish nation without changing their religion and renouncing their ancient historic heritage. It became popular to stress the essential identity of the Jewish and Polish messianic hopes, to present Jews and Poles as "the two Israels," the two chosen nations whose mysterious alliance had now been sealed by blood and established forever.[39] The spread of the symbolic image of "the Jew with the cross," fighting together with the Poles under a common national flag, was accompanied by a conscious Old Testament stylization of Polish patriotism: Polish messianic poets were compared to biblical prophets, freedom fighters were identified with the Maccabees, Poland was referred to as Zion, and Warsaw as Jerusalem.[40]

The defeat of the January uprising marked the end of many romantic illusions. The last remnants of the autonomy of the Kingdom of Poland, as well as its very name, were now eliminated, and the Poles, deprived even of school instruction in Polish, had to concentrate on the elementary tasks of national survival. This gave birth to different programs of peaceful "organic work," both conservative, which stressed the need for rallying Poles around the Church, and liberal, which, like the influential program of the so-called Warsaw Positivists, embraced the cause of economic and social modernization.[41] In both cases "Polishness" was put on the defensive, and this, of course, favored the transition to the narrow, ethnolinguistic definition of the nation. An additional important factor in this process was the increased role and greater social visibility of German and Jewish elements in the rapidly developing capitalist industry of the kingdom. The working class of the former kingdom (now called "Vistula land") constituted itself as a multiethnic body in which the Polish speakers were in a subordinate position, subject to brutal treatment by German foremen and seeing themselves as exploited not so much by an impersonal "system" but, rather, by well-defined aliens—German and Jewish factory owners.

But there was also a positive side of this new situation. Twenty years after the uprising it became clear that it was wrong to fear that the emancipation of Polish peasants by the Russian authorities would make them loyal subjects of the Russian Empire, indifferent to national oppression. In fact the transformation of the feudal peasantry into emancipated property owners consolidated their ethnic identity and thus created solid foundations for the new, ethnolinguistic nations. The Lithuanian peasants became consciously Lithuanian, no longer willing to join the Polish insurrectionists (as they did, in contrast to Ukrainians, in 1863). But a similar process took place among the Polish peasants: their consciousness was becoming quickly "nationalized" through the increasing awareness of national oppression, the elementary national needs (such as the use of native language in schools and offices), and, also, the inevitable conflicts with the non-Polish petty bourgeoisie.

The first and most radical attempts to take these developments into account and to adequately reformulate the tasks of the nationalist Polish intellectuals appeared in 1886. One of them, published in the Warsaw populist weekly *Głos* ("Voice"), was entitled "Two Civilizations."[42] Its author, Jan Ludwik Popławski, claimed that Poles had always been divided into two nations—the historical "nation of the privileged" and the ethnic "nation of the peasantry." The former entered the last phase of its inevitable decline: the latter, representing a separate civilization qualitatively different from the culture of the gentry, was the mainstay of national existence and the only basis for Poland's national and social regeneration.

Another manifesto of the new "peasantist" nationalism was "The Programmatic Sketches" published in Bolesław Wysłouch's *Przegląd Społeczny* (Social Review).[43] The author went so far as to treat the tradition of the "political nation" of the gentry as mostly irrelevant for the modern, peasant-based nations of the former Commonwealth. In his view, the Polish-Lithuanian Union proved beneficial only for the gentry and did not lay foundation for a fusion of the two nations. Polish rule over Ukrainian and Belorussian peasants was just a foreign yoke that could not be justified by invoking the superiority of the Polish culture. The principle of national self-determination should be applied to each ethnolinguistic nationality. This meant in practice that Poles had a right only to their "ethnographic" territory, which would bring them some gains in the West (upper Silesia and Mazuria) and severe losses in the East. It was specifically insisted that Lwów, in spite of its predominantly Polish character, should be left on the Ukrainian side.

Not surprisingly the mainstream public opinion in Poland proved to be unprepared to immediately accept these conclusions. Interestingly, negative reactions to the idea of an "ethnographic Poland" were especially strong on the left. Wysłouch's theses were subject to sharp criticism by Bolesław Limanowski, a non-Marxist socialist who was to become one of the founders of the Polish Socialist Party (PPS, founded in 1892). He condemned ethnically based nationalism (which he opposed to "patriotism") as fostering chauvinistic intolerance for minorities.[44] Unlike the thinkers of the Romantic epoch, with whom he otherwise shared many ideas and illusions, he was aware of the growth of national aspirations among the non-Polish peoples of the former

Commonwealth, but hoped that memories of common history would prevail and that all problems could be solved on the basis of democratic freedom and regional autonomy. Hence he imagined the restored Polish state as a Switzerland of eastern Europe.[45]

As a rule, left-wing Polish intellectuals warmly sympathized with such views. Only few of them would go as far as Edward Abramowski, another founder of the PPS, who declared on the eve of World War I that the "Polish nation has always been composed of these three peoples: Polish, Lithuanian, and Ukrainian," and "what God himself has united, nobody can disunite."[46] But most of them wanted to believe that the legacy of the Jagiellonian Commonwealth was not entirely destroyed, that peoples from the former "eastern borderlands" still gravitated toward Poland and needed some form of Polish guidance. The other side of these beliefs was the view of ethnically based nationalism as a dangerous force, appealing to the primitive tribal instincts and destroying the complex, historically created forms of human community.

However, in the early 1890s it became evident that ethnic nationalism had its social base not only in peasantry and petty bourgeoisie, but in the working class as well. In May 1892 sixty thousand textile workers of Łódź revolted against the ethnic segregation of job categories in factories.[47] Their struggle, lasting nine days, accompanied by anti-Jewish pogroms and bloodily suppressed by the authorities, boosted the morale of both patriotic socialists and integral nationalists. The first called into being the PPS under direct influence of the Łódź revolt; the second in 1893 organized themselves in the elitist National League and soon afterward into a mass organization called the National Democratic Party. Socialist patriots, who counted among themselves Józef Piłsudski, wanted to channel the national feeling of the workers in the direction of struggle for independent democratic Poland. National Democrats ("endeks")—headed by Roman Dmowski, the politician who was to sign the Treaty of Versailles in the name of the restored Poland—wanted to fuel ethnic conflicts and subordinate them to a more broadly conceived national interest. They defined the latter as irreconcilably opposed to the interests of Jews and other national minorities, but implying a support for the Polish landowners in the predominantly non-Polish eastern lands.

The growing politicization of the masses, resulting, among other things, from the activity of the PPS and the endeks in the revolution of

1905, made it more and more clear that even the working class, believed to be the most internationally minded of all classes, was deeply divided along ethnic lines. Political awakening showed beyond doubt that ethnic divisions were present everywhere as a fact of life that could no longer be ignored. This forced Polish political parties to accept in practice (although, as a rule, with many reservations) the ethnolinguistic conception of the nation. Patriotic socialists accepted it grudgingly, trying to save as much as possible from the old concept of a nation as historico-political community; some of them followed Piłsudski in his stubborn clinging to the federal ideas of 1863. National Democrats took the ethnic conception as their starting point but, in contrast to the early views of Popławski, tried to combine ethnic nationalism with the heritage of the old Poland; they did it by laying claims to a national territory extending to all lands where, in their view, Polish civilization and the physical presence of a Polish minority were strong enough to ensure successful polonization (in Dmowski's view this applied to the entire ethnic Lithuania). In this way the old tradition of Polish "political nationalism" disintegrated on both sides of political spectrum, undermining the belief in the legitimacy and possibility of restoring Poland in her former shape. On the eve of the World War I only a few incorrigible idealists cherished the illusion that ethnically non-Polish peoples of the former Commonwealth could be treated as Poles, or potential Poles.

The first years of the newly independent Poland provided many telling arguments for the view that only ethnic Poles could be seen as a reliable basis for the Polish state. The proclamation of independence coincided with the outbreak of a cruel fratricidal struggle between Poles and Ukrainians in the Eastern Galicia. In 1920 Polish workers and peasants, in defiance of Communist internationalism, defended the "bourgeois Poland" against the invading Red Army. At the same time the capture of Wilno (Vilnius) by General Lucjan Żeligowski disrupted for good Poland's relations with Lithuania. Many leaders of the national minorities refused to recognize Polish borders and the legitimacy of the reborn state; even Jews had many doubts about it and, as a rule, saw themselves as a national minority, not as "Poles of Mosaic persuasion."[48] In 1922 the minorities' bloc in the parliament, led by a Zionist Yitsak Grünbaum, was perceived as violently anti-Polish.[49] The tensions resulting from this culminated in the assassination of Gabriel Narutowicz, the first president of the Republic, by a chauvinistic Pole.

Small wonder that the rest of the interwar period was a history of brutal ethnic conflicts, including acts of political terrorism, as well as burning of Polish manor houses, by Ukrainian nationalists and the retaliatory pacifications of Ukrainian villages by the Polish Uhlans. A part of this picture was the growth of anti-Semitism, increasingly violent and racist.[50]

During World War II citizens of the prewar Poland witnessed not only the German atrocities but also the resumption of the Polish-Ukrainian war in the Eastern Galicia, in a form much more brutal than in 1918–19. Despite the westward shifting of Poland's eastern border, this war continued in People's Poland, ending only when the Polish Communist authorities, encouraged by Stalin, decided to raze Ukrainian villages to the ground and to disperse their population. At the same time the overwhelming majority of Polish Jews, who had survived the Holocaust, left Poland for Israel, or other destinations in the world. And this was only a very small part of gigantic resettlement operations, which affected millions of people: Poles from the former "eastern borderlands" and Germans from the German provinces incorporated into the new Poland.

Some Conclusions

Let us return now to the problems of the theory of nationalism, raised in the recent literature on the subject. Many Western theorists of nationalism, especially in America, used to oppose the "political" or "civic" nationalism to the narrower, ethnolinguistic nationalism, accepting the former and criticizing the latter.[51] Some of the Western critics of nationalism, following Lord Acton, question the very principle of national self-determination as leading to dangerous, disruptive consequences in international relations.[52] In the last decade (or decades) it became fashionable to treat nations as artifacts, invented or imagined by nationalist ideologists.

The political/ethnic dichotomy is of crucial importance for the understanding of the history of nation building in Poland. It was in fact a history of two different national formations: the ethnolinguistic nationality, which acquired a rudimentary self-consciousness already at the turn of the thirteenth century, and the multiethnic (though not multicultural) political nation of the gentry. The latter, formed as a result of the union of Lublin in 1569, was the collective sovereign in a very peculiar form of empire: not a dynastic empire but an empire based upon the principle of popular sovereignty, vested in the multiethnic "noble nation." The construction of this nation, its cultural unification, cementing it by common historical tradition and a vivid sense of common destiny, was perceived as the greatest achievement of the Polish nobility. The inner bonds uniting this nation proved strong enough to secure its survival in the stateless condition, its cultural development as a single nation (despite partitions) and its inexorable will to regain its national sovereignty.

Acton was right in seeing this as giving rise to an entirely new legitimizing device—the principle of national self-determination, and thus "awakening the theory of nationality in Europe."[53] But the "legitimism of nations," which the nineteenth-century Polish patriots set against the dynastic legitimism of the Holy Alliance, was, as a rule, very different from the desire to redraw the map of Europe along the ethnic and linguistic lines. The intellectual elite of the "resurgent Poland" (Lelewel's expression) were used to think of nations in political, not ethnic terms. Its representatives wanted to restore the Polish state in its old, historical frontiers. Like all European intellectuals of the first half of the nineteenth century, they could hardly imagine Ukrainian or Lithuanian peasants constituting themselves as separate ethnic nations, in a conscious opposition to Polishness. It was much easier for them to imagine the restored Poland extending civil and political rights to all its inhabitants, educating their children in Polish schools, and thus making them politically and culturally Polish. The easiness with which the sixteenth-century Lithuanian and Ukrainian nobility embraced Polish national patriotism and Polish culture, as a result of extending to them the rights enjoyed by the Polish gentry, created the illusion that the modern, all-inclusive Polish nation could be created by the simple act of an upward equalization of the entire population of the restored state.[54]

This was, admittedly, a fatal miscalculation, stemming ultimately from an underestimation of the "objective" aspects of nationalism. The multiethnic "noble nation" of the old Poland was indeed a product of conscious political will, helped by conscious efforts of historians, mythmakers, and other "organizers of the national imagination" (to use Norwid's expression).[55] Its history is a splendid illustration of how nations are "constructed," "invented," or "imagined." At the same time, however, it showed that the will and imagination of the political and cultural elites were not omnipotent, that nations could be "constructed" to a certain extent only, that modern nations, whether we like it or not, needed a firm ethnic basis, and that ethnic conflicts could not be exorcised by "inventing" or "imagining" a nonethnic, purely political (let alone spiritual) definition of nation.

It is true that Poland greatly contributed to the general "national awakening" in East Central Europe; but it is no less true that the results of this awakening came into a sharp conflict with the political aims and territorial claims of patriotic Poles. For a long time Polish nationalists were simply unaware of this. At a later stage they tried to avoid the conflict by making several half-hearted concessions to the nationalist aspirations of the non-Polish peoples of the "eastern borderlands," hoping to save thereby as much as possible from the legacy of the former Commonwealth. To no avail! Ultimately all peoples of Central and Eastern Europe, *including the Poles,* constituted themselves as modern nations on the basis of the *ethnic* self-determination.[56]

Thus the Polish case does not confirm the view that nations are products of nationalism and that national communities are distinguished "by the style in which they are imagined."[57] It shows rather a marked contrast between nationalism as the ideology of the elite and nationalism as a historical process that formed the modern Polish nation. The elite nationalism of the "resurgent Poland," that is, Poland of the time of great national uprisings, was different in substance and in style from the popular nationalism, which reflected the spontaneous process of the "nationalization of the masses." The dominant discourse of the elite nationalism revolved around the restoration of a multiethnic state that would raise all its inhabitants to the level of conscious patriotic citizenship; hence it tended to de-emphasize the ethnic differentiation.[58] In contrast to this, the modern Polish nation developed under partitions as an ethnolinguistic entity, on the ethnic territory of the medieval Poland. It was shaped to a certain extent by the gentry nationalism but owed its existence to the objective process of socioeconomic modernization within the confines of a preexisting ethnic nationality. Its emergence called into being the new, populistic forms of nationalism, very different from the libertarian civic nationalism of the liberal-minded intellectuals.

This does not mean that the older tradition of libertarian nationalism has become extinguished in Poland. It has survived, mostly among the intelligentsia, and plays an important part in Polish political life. It

is significant, however, that it not define itself as a variety of nationalism. In the vocabulary of Polish politics the word nationalism is a pejo-
rative term, reserved for the manifestations of intolerant, xenophobic
ethnocentricity.

NOTES

© 1997 by The American Council of Learned Societies. This essay was first
published in *East European Politics and Societies*, 11, no. 3 (1997): 227–53 and is
reprinted with permission.

1. See Synopticus [Karl Renner], *Staat und Nation* (Vienna, 1899); and Otto
Bauer, *Die Nationalitätenfrage und die Sozialdemokratie* (Vienna, 1907). The main
conceptions of the Austro-Marxist theory of nation were formulated by Karl
Kautsky in his "Die Moderne Nationalität" (*Die Neue Zeit*, vol. 5, 1887) and several other articles. Among non-Marxist works on nationalism the most important was then Friedrich Meinecke's *Weltbürgertum und Nationalstaat* (Munich,
1907). It is regrettable that some authors treat nationalism as a *new* field of
research, ignoring the previous literature on the subject.

2. See Benedict Anderson, *Imagined Communities: Reflections on the Origin and
Spread of Nationalism*, 2d ed. (London: Verso, 1991); Eric J. Hobsbawm, *Nations and
Nationalism since 1780* (Cambridge: Cambridge University Press, 1990); Ernest
Gellner, *Nations and Nationalism* (Ithaca, N.Y.: Cornell University Press, 1983).

One of the earliest and most radical formulations of the view that nations
are in fact "invented," or even "fabricated," by nationalism is to be found in
Gellner's *Thought and Change* (London: Weidenfeld and Nicholson, 1964),
where we read, "Nationalism is not the awakenings of nations to self-consciousness; it invents nations where they did not exist" (169). Anderson's thesis
is in fact less radical because he sees the creation of nations not so much as a
deliberate "invention" but, rather, as "the spontaneous distillation of a complex
<crossing> of discrete historical forces" (Anderson, *Imagined Communities*, 4).

For a defense of the view that nationalisms are products of nations, and not
vice versa, see Miroslav Hroch, *Social Preconditions of National Revival in Europe*
(Cambridge: Cambridge University Press, 1985).

3. I mean, of course, Anderson and Hobsbawm. For the quoted words
about constructing nations from above see Hobsbawm, *Nations and Nationalism*,
10.

4. For an example of this disdainful attitude toward scholars who dare to
resist the subjectivist ("constructionist") trend in the study of nations and
nationalism see Yuri Slezkine's review of Peter Brock's *Folk Cultures and Little
Peoples: Aspects of National Awakening in East Central Europe*, in *Slavic Review* 52,
no. 4 (1993): 893.

5. See Anthony D. Smith, *Theories of Nationalism*, 2d ed. (New York:
Holmes and Meier, 1983), xxviii–xxx.

6. Cf. Gellner's thesis that "nations, like states, are a contingency" (*Nations and Nationalism*, 6).

7. Roman Szporluk, *Communism and Nationalism: Karl Marx versus Friedrich List* (New York: Oxford University Press, 1988), 164.

8. This was stressed by Szporluk in "Poland and the Rise of the Theory and Practice of Modern Nationality, 1770–1870," *Dialectics and Humanism* 17, no. 21 (1990): 54–55.

9. See Cyprian K. Norwid, *Pisma wszystkie*, ed. Juliusz W. Gomulicki (Warsaw: PIW, 1971–73), 3:465 (the epilogue to *Promethidion*). The conceptions of Polish "national philosophers" of the Romantic epoch are discussed in detail in Andrzej Walicki, *Philosophy and Romantic Nationalism: The Case of Poland* (Oxford: Clarendon Press, 1982), pt. 2.

10. For the distinction between "old continuous nation" (such as Poles) and the "new nations" see Hugh Seton-Watson, *Nations and States* (Boulder, Colo.: Westview, 1977), 6–13.

11. See Tomáš G. Masaryk, *The Meaning of Czech History* (Chapel Hill: University of North Carolina Press, 1974), 138–39.

12. See, for instance Tadeusz Balicki, *Narodowość nowoczesna Studium sociologiczne* (St. Petersburg, 1896); the author of this book, brother of the nationalist theorist, Zygmunt Balicki, interprets modern nationality as a product of capitalist development. For a Marxist interpretation of the role of the petty and landless gentry in the making of modern Polish nations see Hipolit Grynwasser, *Demokracja szlachecka*, 1918.

13. See Andrzej Wierzbicki, *Naród—państwo w polskiej myśli historycznej dwudziestolecia międzywojennego* (Wrocław: Ossolineum, 1978), 78–90.

14. See Konstantin Symmons-Symonolewicz, *National Consciousness in Poland: Origin and Evolution* (Meadville, Pa.: Maplewood Press, 1983), 14.

15. See Roman Grodecki, "Powstanie polskiej świadomości narodowej na przełomie xiii i xiv wieku," *Przegląd Współczesny* 52 (1935): 3–35.

16. Symmons-Symonolewicz, *National Consciousness in Poland*, 20.

17. See Grodecki, "Powstanie polskiej świadomości narodowej" and Konstanty Grzybowski, *Ojczyzna, naród, państwo* (Warsaw: PIW, 1970), 43–45.

18. See Stanisław Orzechowski, *Wybór pism* (Wroclaw: Ossolineum, 1972), 99.

19. See Opaliński's *De officiis* (1659), in *Filozofia i myśl spoleczna xvii wieku*, ed. Zbigniew Ogonowski (Warsaw: PWN, 1979), 1:48–50.

20. It aroused vivid interest in Muscovy and was translated four times, fully or partially, into Russian (1668, 1673, 1682 and 1688). See the chapter written by L. V. Razumovskaia and Boris F. Stakheev in *Istoriia polskoi literatury* (Moscow, Nauka, 1968), 1:29.

21. See Ogonowski, *Filozofia i myśl społeczna*, 32–38; and Józef Ujejski, *Dzieje polskiego mesjanizmu* (Lwów, 1931), 44–48. Dębołęcki's curious work, entitled *Wywód jedynowladnego państwa świata*, was published in 1633.

22. See Janusz Tazbir, "Stosunek do obcych w dobie baroku," in *Swojskość i cudzoziemszczyzna w dziejach kultury polskiej*, ed. Zofia Stefanowska (Warsaw:

PWN, 1973), 80–112. See also J. Tazbir, "Culture of the Baroque in Poland," in *East-Central Europe in Transition,* ed. Antoni Mączak et al. (Cambridge: Cambridge University Press, 1985).

23. See Mateusz Mieses, *Z rodu żydowskiego Zasłużone rodziny polskie krwi niegdyś żydowskiej* (Warsaw, Wema, 1991), 21–24.

24. See Anatol Lieven, *The Baltic Revolution: Estonia, Latvia, Lithuania on the Path to Independence* (New Haven, Conn.: Yale University Press, 1993), 47–48.

Paradoxically, the Lithuanian language was not officially recognized. Lithuanian did not exist by then as a literary language, spoken by the ethnic elite: the Lithuanian boyars used to communicate in the most developed language of the Grand Duchy, that is, in the language of the Kievan Rus.' This shows, by the way, that in the case of the Lithuanian nobility the real alternative of polonization was cultural and linguistic Russification.

25. Maurizio Viroli, *For Love of Country: An Essay on Patriotism and Nationalism* (Oxford: Clarendon Press, 1955), 13.

26. For a detailed presentation of these two national programs see A. Walicki, *The Enlightenment and the Rise of Modern Nationhood: Polish Political Thought from Noble Republicanism to Tadeusz Kościuszko* (Notre Dame, Ind.: University of Notre Dame Press, 1989).

27. See Michał Wielhorski, *O przywróceniu dawnego rządu według pierwiastkowych Rzeczypospolitej ustaw* (On the restoration of the former government according to the original statuses of the republic), 1775. Rousseau wrote his *Considérations sur le gouvernement de Pologne* on the request of the Bar confederates, on the basis of the detailed "Tableau du gouvernement de Pologne," prepared for him by Wielhorski.

28. See Seweryn Rzewuski, *O sukcesji tronu w Polsce* (Warsaw, 1789), 31–33.

29. Adam W. Rzewuski, *O formie republikańskiego rządu myśli* (Warsaw, 1790), 168.

30. The coauthor of this pamphlet was Kościuszko's secretary, Józef Pawlikowski. For a new, critical edition of this important text see Emanuel Halicz, ed., *Czy Polacy mogą się wybic' na niepodległość?* (Warsaw, MON 1967).

31. See Wiktor Sukiennicki, *East Central Europe during World War I: From Foreign Domination to National Independence* (Boulder, Colo.: East European Monographs, New York, 1984), 1:12 and 28.

32. Maurycy Mochnacki, *O literaturze polskiej w wieku XIX* (1830), in Mochnacki, *Pisma Wybrane* (Warsaw: KIW), 215.

33. In Mochnacki's time this program of expressing and shaping subnational regional identities was successfully realized by the so-called Ukrainian school in Polish literature. It seems worthwhile to mention that Mochnacki himself was a son of a polonized Ruthenian family.

34. See Joachim Lelewel, *Mowy i pisma polityczne* (Poznań, 1864), 558.

35. See Stanislaw Pigoń, *Zręby Nowej Polski w publicystyce Wielkiej Emigracji* (Warsaw, 1938). The ethnically Polish peasants of the Kingdom of Poland were no longer serfs, but serfdom still existed in the "Eastern borderlands" (until 1861) and in Galicia (until 1848). In the Kingdom of Poland the emancipation of peasants meant giving them land and abolishing the corvée.

36. See Tadeusz Łepkowski, *Rozważania o losach polskich* (London: Aneks, 1987), 62. Cf. Łepkowski, "Poglądy na jedno-i wieloetniczność narodu w XIX wieku," in Stefanowska, *Swojskość cudzoziemszczyzna*, 232.

37. For a presentation of Kościuszko's views on the relationship between Polish nationhood and Catholicism see Walicki, *Enlightenment and Modern Nationhood*, 98–102. The leader of the Cracow uprising, Edward Dembowski, saw democratic nationalism as negation of the Catholic-feudal period in Polish history and dialectical return to the pre-Christian Slavic communalism (see Walicki, *Philosophy and Romantic Nationalism*, 220–25). Ironically, he was compelled to appeal to the religious feelings of the Galician peasants who, at the instigation of Austrian officials, reacted to the Cracow uprising by massacring the local gentry. Dembowski wanted to placate the riotous peasants by talking to them as the head of a big procession carrying crosses and church banners. He was killed by the Austrians with a cross in his hand.

38. These expectations were based upon the durable phenomenon of the so-called two-level national consciousness among the Polish (or polonized) gentry of the former Grand Duchy of Lithuania. It consisted in seeing oneself as belonging to two national communities at the same time: the broader one (Polish) and the narrower one (Lithuanian), both of them conceived in historico-political terms, not ethnically. See Juliusz Bardach, "O świadomości Narodowej Polaków na Litwie i Białorusi," in *Między Polską etniczną a historyczną*, ed. Wojciech Wrzesiński (Wrocław: Ossolineum, 1988), 232.

39. See Magdalena Opalski and Israel Bartal, *Poles and Jews: A Failed Brotherhood* (London: Brandeis University Press, 1992), 44–47.

40. Opalski and Bartal, *Poles and Jews*, 51–53.

41. See Andrzej Jaszczuk, *Spór pozytywistów z konserwatystami o przyszłość Polski 1870–1903* (Warsaw: PWN, 1986). For an excellent analysis of the earlier phases of the liberal-traditionalist controversy see Jerzy Jedlicki, *Jakiej cywilizacji Polacy potrzebują?* (Warsaw: PWN, 1988).

42. See Jan Ludwik Popławski, *Pisma polityczne* (Cracow-Warsaw, 1910), 1:134–46.

43. According to Peter Brock, this series of articles was written by Adam Zakrzewski but reflected the standpoint of the editor of the *Social Review*, the populist Bolesław Wysłouch. For a detailed analysis see Brock, "Bolesław Wysłouch, Pioneer of Polish Populism," in *Nationalism and Populism in Partitioned Poland* (London: Orbis, 1973), 181–211. Other authors attribute the authorship of these articles directly to Wysłouch.

44. See Kazimiera J. Cottam, *Bolesław Limanowski (1835–1935): A Study in Nationalism and Socialism* (Boulder, Colo.: East European Quarterly, 1978), 91–92.

45. See Bolesław Limanowski, *Naród i państwo* (Cracow, 1906), 98–99.

46. Edward Abramowski, "Pomniejszyciele ojczyzny," *Kurier Warszawski*, March 25–26, 1914, in Abramowski, *Pisma publicystyczne w sprawach robotniczych i chłopskich* (Warsaw, 1938), 268–69.

47. See Adam Próchnik, *Bunt łódzki w roku 1892* (Warsaw, 1932). Ethnic conflicts within the multiethnic working class of the Kingdom of Poland (plus

the upper Silesia) have been skillfully analyzed by Laura Crago in her doctoral dissertation, "Nationalism, Religion, Citizenship, and Work in the Development of the Polish Working Class and the Polish Trade Union Movement, 1815–1929," Department of History, Yale University, 1993.

48. See Ezra Mendelsohn, *The Jews of East Central Europe between the World Wars* (Bloomington: Indiana University Press, 1983), 29–32.

49. See Mendelsohn, *Jews*, 53–55. Mendelsohn rightly remarks that siding openly with territorial minorities, willing to change the borders of the state, was not in the interest of the Polish Jews (54).

50. The openly racist anti-Semitism should be distinguished from the older forms of anti-Semitic sentiment that were religious, cultural, or economic. Acceptance of Jewish assimilation and intermarriage with assimilated Jews are, of course, incompatible with genuine racism.

51. The most recent book based upon this distinction (and the corresponding value judgment) is Liah Greenfeld, *Nationalism: Five Roads to Modernity* (Cambridge, Mass.: Harvard University Press, 1992).

52. See Lord Acton's famous essay "Nationality," in Lord Acton (John Emerich Dalberg-Acton) *Selected Writings*, vol. 1: *Essays in the History of Liberty* (Indianapolis: Liberty Classics, 1985).

53. See Acton, "Nationality," 414.

54. Maurycy Mochnacki, a typical "gentry revolutionary," saw this idea as a specifically Polish way of realizing the ideals of the French Revolution: instead of depriving the gentry of their rights, the Polish revolution would give these rights to all Poles, thus making everybody a noble and covering all Polish lands with coats of arms. See Mochnacki, *Pisma wybrane*, 93–95.

55. See n. 9, in this chapter.

56. The Ukrainian émigré scholar Ivan L. Rudnytsky was right in maintaining that "the entire drift of the historical development in Central and Eastern Europe pointed toward a victory of ethnic self-determination over historical legitimism" (see Rudnytsky, "Polish-Ukrainian Relations: The Burden of History," in *Poland and Ukraine, Past and Present*, ed. Peter J. Potichnyj [Edmonton: Canadian Institute of Ukrainian Studies, 1980], 24). In my view, he was also right in rejecting Adam Bromke's notion that "there was a chance in history for the Poles and Ukrainians to merge into one nation." Individuals and even entire social groups (like the nobility) could cross over the ethnocultural barrier dividing Ukraine from Poland, but this was not possible for the entire Ukrainian people (Rudnytsky, "Polish-Ukrainian Relations," 28).

57. Anderson, *Imagined Communities*, 6.

58. This was obvious to Marx and Engels, who, for that reason, clearly distinguished between the restoration of Poland and ethnic self-determination. In his article "What Have the Working Classes to Do with Poland?" Engels sharply contrasted ethnic *nationalities* with "great European nations," such as Poland; in his view supporting the rights of great historical nations to independent existence was "an old democratic and working-class tenet," which had nothing in common with the reactionary and divisive "principle of national-

ity." The case of Poland was for him a proof that these two principles—*national* independence and the "principle of *nationalities*"—were in fact mutually exclusive, since the restoration of Poland meant "the re-establishment of a state composed of at least four different nationalities" (Karl Marx and Frederick Engels, *The Russian Menace to Europe* [Glencoe, Ill.: Free Press, 1952], 110–11).

Coping with the Problem of Nation in Poland

Telling the story of my life as a story of coping with the problem of nation is not an artificial endeavor. The intense experience of belonging to the Polish nation and thinking of what it means, or should mean, was indeed at the very core of my entire life.

My earliest memories provide arguments for the view that national tradition is not something consciously constructed but rather something "given," inherited, transmitted on a subconscious level. Already at the age of five I felt excited by listening to Polish patriotic songs and by looking on military parades—like the beautiful parade on the occasion of the funeral of Marshal Piłsudski, whom I adored as a national hero. At the same time I began to develop a misty awareness of belonging to a world that was condemned to destruction, or of links with a world that had already passed into history. My grandfather Leon, son of an insurgent of 1863, was a faithful incarnation of the patriotic gentry tradition. My grandmother, Maria (née Manteuffel—from a polonized family of Baltic-German aristocracy) was like a living relic of a lost world—the former "Polish Livonia" (Latgalia), transferred into the new epoch. My father Michal (a historian of art) was born and educated in St. Petersburg but never ceased to be an ardent Polish patriot. When I discovered, as an adult, his youthful poems, written in 1918–19 in Russia, I was struck by the total coincidence with my own emotions in the years when I was a young boy. The symbols of the sword and the cross, the motifs of the old saber and the Uhlan uniform preserved like a holy relic, Russian hooded sledges speeding to Siberia, and birds returning in the spring to their home country—all of these were living parts of my imagination and feelings, despite the fact that this could in no way be my father's personal influence (my parents were divorced and I saw my father only from time to time).

Anyhow, I was not a "nationless" child. When, at the age of six, I began going to school, I discovered that this was rather a rule than an exception *among the children of the intelligentsia: we took for granted that it was best to be Poles, Catholics, and Europeans, and we praised God for being born in independent Poland. The specific feature of my own case was a strong admixture of conservative-romantic values. I vividly remember my first reading, when I was barely nine years old, of Mickiewicz's masterpiece* Pan Tadeusz, *and my childish despair that the colorful world described in it no longer existed. I comforted myself with the thought that certain elements of it had been preserved in the culture of the Polish countryside, and I wanted to defend this agrarian world against the ugliness and rootlessness of the poor Warsaw suburbs. My mother, Anna, who was a left-winger, tried to evoke in me a sympathy to the Bolshevik revolution, but her efforts proved to be counterproductive: I reacted to her stories with a feeling of horror.*

Then came the years of war and the German occupation. From my present perspective I see my experience of this terrible time as somewhat strange, although quite typical for my generation. We were too confident in the victory of the "right cause," identified by us with the cause of Poland, and this made us not sufficiently aware of the mortal dangers, and even not sufficiently sensitive to human tragedies. We saw military defeats, liquidation of all Polish institutions, roundups in the middle of Warsaw, public executions on the streets, and—last, but not least—the extermination of the Jews; nevertheless, prewar Poland continued to exist in the underground schools, the underground press, the underground Boy Scout movement, and this was psychologically most important. I was aware and proud of my father's activity in the underground Home Army. I knew by heart the new patriotic songs, composed under occupation, and expected to hear them at a victorious parade after the war, when the Polish troops fighting in the west return home and join forces with the heroes of guerrilla warfare in Poland.

As is known, these expectations were not to be fulfilled. The Warsaw uprising of August 1944—two months of bloody struggle against the Germans, with the Soviet army passively observing it from the other side of the Vistula River—put an end to the dream of the restoration of a fully independent Poland, a lawful continuation of the prewar Polish state. For accidental reasons I found myself cut off from my Boy Scout unit and did not join the insurgents (who, by the way, had enough unarmed boys in their ranks and did not want to multiply their number). In later years I deplored my lack of resolve to overcome all obstacles and to join the heroic fighters. But when I was leaving the ruins of Warsaw, together with its entire civilian population, I remembered not only the atmosphere of patriotic ecstasy of the first days of the uprising; I took with me also the memory of maimed insurgents, begging for death,

*of old women cursing the patriotic fighters, of children burned alive or suffo-
cated under ruins, of hungry people eating cats and rats, and of other innu-
merable sufferings and horrors.*

*Nevertheless, my youthful romantic nationalism and my loyalty to pre-
war Poland remained unchanged. The new, Communist-dominated "People's
Poland" was for me deeply alien, deprived of the "Polish soul." In the first two
years after the war I regretted sometimes for not being killed in the uprising. In
a youthful poem of 1946 I expressed a longing for a new uprising—an uprising that was to end not with a victory but with a purifying and exalting catastrophe. It ended with the words:*

> *And once again boughs of white roses bloom,
> And gone the fire of dreams long unfulfilled.
> But to overfill the chalice of our bitterness
> We'll go to fight, even though already
> The rosemary for us will not unfold.*

*The "new reality," however, was complex, multidimensional, and chang-
ing; my patriotism was also changing, becoming more complex, more reflective
and many-sided. On the one hand, there were elements of a civil war, people
from the Home Army were repressed. Stanisław Mikołajczyk's peasant party
was brutally harassed, and the elections of 1947 were clearly forged. On the
other hand, there was a universal enthusiasm for reconstruction, and only a
tiny minority wanted another war. An influential part of the intelligentsia
gave the new system a conditional support, endorsing its social reforms, and
seeing the dominant role of the Communists as a necessary price for a separate
Polish statehood in conditions of the postwar division of Europe. There was
also a widespread feeling that the successes of Communism—unlike the successes of Nazism—could not be dismissed as something temporary and short-
lived. Some people felt that Communism was not a senseless disaster but rather
a historical catastrophe, that is, something inevitable and meaningful, signifying the end of the "old world" and the beginning of a new one. I was pushed in
this direction by Sergius Hessen, an émigré Russian philosopher, who was a
close friend of my mother. Conversations with him convinced me that Communism had a historical justification, that we should try to understand its
deeper meaning and to overcome it from within.*

*In 1947–48, when I was still at high school, I developed a strong interest
in history of philosophy. Among my readings of that time were also writings of
Marx and Engels. Thanks to the Polish translations of some works on young*

Marx (H. Lefebvre, A. Cornu), as well as my conversations with Hessen, I soon discovered a "libertarian" Marx, concentrated on the problem of liberating human beings from the degrading effects of alienation. Hence I was well equipped for defending myself against the increasing pressure of official indoctrination in Marxism-Leninism. The general situation, however, was changing rapidly for the worse. The condemnation of Gomułka's "nationalist deviation" in 1948 marked the beginning of full-fledged Stalinism in Poland. The unification of Polish youth organizations into the monolithic Polish Youth League (ZMP) was accompanied by powerful political pressure that combined direct threats with moral intimidation. The new wave of repressions reached also my father, who was arrested and imprisoned for his activities in the Home Army. In these conditions I decided to join the ZMP. There was an element of opportunism in this decision, but no cynicism: I rationalized it mostly as yielding to historical necessity in order to avoid total isolation.

In the year 1949 I began my university studies in Łódź. Because of my bad "social and family background," I was only allowed to take Russian Studies, a department that had been created ad hoc and had a serious shortage of candidates. I had no prejudice against Russian literature; the problem was that studying this subject exposed students to systematic ideological pressure in the worst Zhdanovist form, directly imported from the USSR. At the University of Warsaw, where I moved in the next year, Russian Studies were, naturally enough, the most thoroughly Stalinist department, controlled by party activists with a good Soviet training. My intellectual independence and my interest in prohibited subjects (such as, for instance, the "decadent" Russian poetry of the Silver Age) made me an obvious target for attacks. I did not even try to defend myself on ideological grounds because the language of the attackers was too crude for my capacity to endure. An organized campaign against me took place at the so-called productive sessions (at which the "student collective" criticized me in accordance with the instructions from the Party organization) and at the meetings of the ZMP; it was accompanied by attempts to intimidate me through "private" conversations with the Party activists, or to intimidate my colleagues through warning them that they should keep themselves at a distance from the son of "an enemy of the people." As a result, I fell into a nervous illness and was sent for several months to a sanitarium.

Happily, Stalinism in Poland was not everywhere as consistent as at the department of Russian Studies. Owing to my contacts with people from other departments and outside the university I could write book reviews for cultural weeklies and even a long introduction to a Polish edition of Gogol. With the reputation gained thereby I was offered a research position in the newly estab-

*lished Polish-Soviet Institute. I mention this because I wrote in this institute
my first work on broadly conceived nationalism—a long comparative study
entitled* Vissarion Belinsky and Edward Dembowski as Ideologists of
the Nation-Creating Process *(written in 1953, published in 1954). Its very
title shows that at this stage I saw nations as creations of a historical process
that took place in the nineteenth century and was consciously shaped by progressive intellectuals, such as the Hegelian literary critic, V. Belinsky, in Russia and the Hegelian philosopher E. Dembowski in Poland.*

*This reflected the influence of Marxism on my thinking and, also, my crit-
ical reaction to the Marxist offensive in Polish historiography. Since the First
Methodological Conference of Polish Historians in Otwock (January 1952) militant Marxists had concentrated on the problem of nation building in Poland,
presenting it as a process of the civic emancipation of the masses that had
become completed only in People's Poland. The directly political aspect of this
conception consisted not only in presenting People's Poland as the crowning
achievement of Polish history, but also in an extremely selective approach to
national tradition: the attempt to prove that only radical movements could be
credited with a positive contribution to the creation of a modern Polish nation.
Thus, it was a combination of the classical Marxist conception of the "objective
laws of historical development" (showing modern nations as products of capitalist progress) with a "constructivist" approach, claiming that nations are
consciously created in ideological struggles against conservative forces. The
main target of criticism was, of course, the conservative view of national tradition as something very old, well established, and essentially unchangeable.*

*My study on Belinsky and Dembowski shows that I had internalized
these assumptions to a certain extent. At the same time, however, I had my
own hidden agenda: I wanted to broaden "the criteria of progressiveness," to
vindicate the legacy of the Romantic epoch as a whole, to resist the pressure of
Soviet historians (who, as a rule, treated Polish national movements with suspicion and reduced everything to the problem of agrarian revolution), and so
forth. Ultimately, I wanted to interpret Polish progressive nationalism much
more broadly than official Marxists and to suggest that it should be accepted as
the main ideological tradition of the "new Poland."*

*Soon afterward, at the time of the "thaw" of 1954–56, I elaborated a com-
prehensive life-plan that I summarized for myself in three words: Poland-Rus-
sia-Marxism. It was based on the assumption that the situation of the intelligentsia in East Central Europe was in the first instance determined by three
factors: their own national traditions, Russia and her tradition, and Marxism,
as ideological legitimization of the system. I thought that this was what I*

should concern myself with in my research, for a great deal depended on the kind of patriotism we would have, on the kind of Marxism, and on our understanding of Russia. I even hoped that the Polish "thaw" would enable me to do for Russia what the Russian intellectuals were still unable to do themselves: to liberate the studies of Russian thought from the deadly grip of official ideology and thus to help the Russians to rediscover their genuine traditions and to regain their intellectual freedom.

The victory of the "thaw" in October 1956 brought about a complete change in my life. The ideological pressure almost disappeared, militant Stalinists ceased to influence cultural policy, all doors seemed to be open. I was offered a choice between two positions at the Warsaw University and a position in the Institute of Philosophy of the Academy of Sciences. Scholarly journals wanted my articles, a prestigious publishing house sought my cooperation in publishing Polish editions of Russian thinkers, without demanding from me any conformity with the views of the Soviet scholars. My Ph.D. dissertation, published as a book under the title Personality and History in Russian Nineteenth-Century Thought *(1959), was hailed as a sign of freeing Russian studies in Poland from Soviet ideological tutelage; many people immediately understood that its philosophical content—conflicts between ethical freedom and the alleged "historical necessity"—was directly relevant to our own recent experiences with Stalinism. By choosing to work at the Institute of Philosophy I became associated with the group of influential revisionist Marxists whose undisputed leader was Leszek Kołakowski. I differed from them because I was not a Party member and did not have in my experience a period of commitment to Communism. I shared their hope that the system could be changed from within, but I tended to see the intrasystemic change not only as political "democratization" (let alone democratization within the party) but also as a gradual "nationalization" of the system through deideologization of the state, increased participation of the non-Communist majority, and rehabilitation of mainstream national values, including the patriotic tradition of the prewar state and the Home Army. At the beginning these differences were barely visible and much less important than a common democratic orientation, as well as common methodological assumptions. Hence the entire group came to be seen as representing one current of thought—the so-called Warsaw school in the history of ideas.*

The first half of the sixties was certainly the best period of my life. In 1960 I received a postdoctoral grant from the Ford Foundation and went for an entire year to visit several places in the United States and England. This enabled me to meet several American scholars (such as Richard Pipes, Martin

Malia, James Billington, Nicholas Riasanovsky, and others), as well as a number of important Russian émigrés, like Roman Jacobson, Georges Florovsky, and an entire group of Russian Mensheviks in New York. In England I found a common language with Isaiah Berlin, who was to become my best, always reliable, foreign friend. I returned to Warsaw in an uplifted mood, determined to include into my life-program publications in English. I became an active member of the famous Crooked Circle Club—the only place in the Soviet bloc where intellectuals were free to discuss sensitive political issues. My academic career was undisturbed. In 1964 I defended my habilitation thesis on Russian Slavophilism; it was published in the next year, simultaneously with three other representative works of the "Warsaw school." Soon afterward I was invited to Oxford. I conducted there, under Berlin's auspices, a graduate seminar on Russian populism. Its final product was a book in English. This was a good beginning: in later years I published several other books in English, including a comprehensive history of nineteenth-century Russian thought. But my dream of influencing the ideological situation in Soviet Russia remained, of course, unfulfilled.

Let us return, however, to the problem of nation—the main focus of this autobiographical sketch.

In the middle of the sixties I decided to concentrate my research on the rich legacy of Polish Romantic nationalism. I was motivated by a feeling of deep dissatisfaction with the process of "returning to the best national values," which I nevertheless regarded as absolutely essential for the success of the "Polish road to socialism," proclaimed in 1956. I realized that the revisionist Marxists (including my friends), as well as influential liberal writers, saw it differently—treating national feelings with suspicion and associating the very word nation *with the right-wing nationalism of the 1930s. I thought that this "antinationalist allergy" was the main reason for (what I saw as) their scandalous reluctance in rejecting the artificially narrow criteria of "progressiveness" and in rendering justice to the legacy of the noble, humanitarian nationalism of the Polish thinkers of the Romantic epoch. I was aware that the nationalist faction within the Party was using the nationalist language for antiliberal purposes, but I saw this as an additional argument for the view that liberally minded intellectuals should offer their own interpretation of the national values, and not allow their enemies to monopolize the language of national patriotism. In the concrete situation in post-Stalinist Poland the "antinationalist allergy" was, in my view, a harmful phenomenon: it isolated the intelligentsia from the great majority of society, which was longingly awaiting a rehabilitation of national values, and also from the Party, which, as a mass organization, was becoming increasingly deideologized and more and more susceptible to the influence of traditional Polish patriotism. Progressive intellectuals, I felt, should not shun this spontaneous "nationalization" of Polish socialism; they should rather participate in it, articulating its ideas and giving it a desirable political direction.*

However, the situation did not develop in the way that I would have liked. In March 1968 the antiliberal faction within the Party, headed by General M. Moczar, got the upper hand and launched an openly anti-Semitic campaign, blaming the Jews for all misdeeds of the Communist regime in Poland. Several professors, including my close friends—L. Kołakowski and B. Baczko—were denounced as incorrigible revisionists, deprived of their tenures, and forced to leave the country. At the same time the victorious faction ostentatiously distanced itself from Communist old-believers, pledged commitment to national patriotism and tried to find support among non-Communists. In the social sciences this flirtation with nationalism manifested itself as giving priority to the study of national culture. In our institute, the Section on the History of Modern Philosophy—an institutional base of the Warsaw school—was transformed into the Section on the History of Modern Polish Philosophy and Social Thought. It was given the authority to coordinate research in this field in other scholarly institutions and the appropriate funds for this purpose.

For myself, this turn of events involved dramatic political dilemmas. I resented repressions, I was shocked and ashamed by the wave of anti-Semitism, but I felt at the same time that the nationalist tendency within the Party was much broader than the Moczarist faction and could be used for different purposes. I defined party-nationalists as "barbarians," whom we, the intellectuals, should try to educate, directing their national feeling into lines that would enable it to be expressed as a positive force. I was aware that my acceptance of the position of head of the newly founded section in our institute would create a convenient window-dressing for the regime and even be used for legitimizing the enforced changes. But I knew as well that I was the best candidate for this post from the point of view of my colleagues, that accepting this responsibility would enable me to help many people and to defend the achievements of the Warsaw school. I did not want the new financial and publishing opportunities to be wasted; I was convinced that the very fact of my existence as the official "coordinator" and reviewer of research plans in the history of Polish thought would clip the wings of parvenus of various kinds who, otherwise, would have been delighted to dominate this field and to remake it on the Soviet model, in the spirit of the Zhdanovist "struggle against cosmopolitanism." For all these reasons, I decided to accept this task.

Of course, I had to prove my independence. I did so by publishing an article praising the comparatist approach of the Warsaw school, by protesting against the discriminatory policy of the new editors of the Library of Classics of Philosophy, by publicly distancing myself from various careerists, and so forth. Above all, however, I did my best for the rediscovery and reinterpretation of Polish thought of the Romantic epoch. I wrote a book and a number of articles on Polish Romantic philosophers and messianic poets, prepared new editions of the works of Cieszkowski, Trentowski, and Libelt, as well as a huge, comprehensive anthology of philosophy and political ideas of 1830–64—a part of the monumental edition Seven Hundred Years of Polish Thought, *which was to be the collective work of our section. Romantic nationalism, seeing nations as carriers of universal missions, represented, in my view, the positive model of nationalism, sharply contrasting with the post-Romantic "integral nationalism," which treated the nation as an end in itself and justified ruthless national egoism. I was aware, nevertheless, that Romantic thinkers often indulged in an idealization of national weakness, that their cult of the transcendent "national idea" could entail a lofty indifference to really existing people, and that the Romantic "ethic of imponderables" was so often in conflict with the Weberian "ethic of responsibility." Hence I was very impressed by the ideas of Stanisław Brzozowski, who tried to combine Romantic idealism with "tough-minded realism" in the national question (in the second half of the seventies I published a comprehensive monograph on his views). In 1973, in a letter to Czesław Miłosz (who was, in my view, too critical of all forms of nationalism) I defended my commitments by arguing that a strong national bond was badly needed by Polish society. I wrote: "It is a hereditary bond, and as such is free of the element of contingency, and at the same time is dependent—at a certain level—on conscious choice. It gives us a feeling of roots, and therefore reinforces that feeling of self-respect that we so much need—linking people not only in space, but also in time. In a word, I see more to be gained than lost by awakening national feelings and by consideration of national problems."*

At the beginning of the seventies the situation in Poland seemed to be stabilized. Under the pragmatic leadership of Gomulka's successor, Edward Gierek, the process of nationalization of partocracy took the form of liberalization, opening to the West and almost unconcealed abandonment of the "construction of communism." Most Party members openly despised Marxist indoctrination, looking instead for a kind national legitimization of the system, on the ground of expediency-oriented patriotism. The threat of a "cultural revolution" against intellectuals had subsided; there was no danger that research into Polish thought would be used for political purposes. I decided therefore that I could get rid of my official "coordinating" functions and devote myself fully to my own research. I did so in 1975. Soon afterward I resumed my travels to the West and my plans to write books for the Western readers. During the academic year 1977–78 I wrote in Washington—in the Woodrow Wilson International Center for Scholars—a comprehensive monograph of Polish Romantic nationalism in English.

However, the prospects for relatively smooth systemic changes proved to be more fragile than I had thought. In the middle of the seventies economic conditions began to deteriorate, the authorities resorted to the risky operation of price raising, workers' protest against it took form of a wave of strikes, and in 1976 police forces brutally suppressed popular riots in Radom. A completely new factor in this situation was the emergence of an organized and overt opposition, no longer intrastructural but ostentatiously extrastructural, determined to organize social forces and mobilize them to exert continuous pressure from without *on the Communist rulers. I reacted to this with apprehension: I was convinced that the system could not be overthrown in an open struggle and that an overtly confrontationist stand could only lead to a sharp political polarization, complicating and hindering the evolutionary process of change. Therefore, despite my admiration for the Romantic conception of nation, I warned the leaders of the emerging opposition against "political romanticism."*

This diagnosis proved to be too cautious, underestimating the depth of the systemic crisis. As we know, August 1980 saw the birth of Solidarity and the beginning of sixteen months of nonviolent anti-Communist revolution, followed by the period of martial law. It is impossible, of course, to discuss here all these important events, or even to give a full account of my reactions to them. I have to limit myself to what was most essential for my understanding of the many meanings of nationalism in contemporary Poland.

The Solidarity movement, although prudently nonviolent, was nonetheless a revolutionary movement, that is, a movement using confrontational language and incapable of controlling its own radicalism. Its tactics, elaborated by the extrasystemic opposition, consisted in forcing the authorities to make concessions without saving their faces, thus depriving them of any remaining semblance of credibility. The only convincing argument for moderation was the external threat, but this, of course, delegitimized the system itself, reducing it to a concealed form of Soviet occupation. In this situation there was no need in people who, like myself, tried to "nationalize" the system from within, to reconcile the "new Poland" with the "old Poland," to offer the existing Polish state a national legitimization in exchange for making it dependent on national will and national values.

Second, my knowledge of Soviet Russia did not allow me to cherish an illusion that the Brezhnevite Soviet Union could reconcile itself with the prospect of Solidarity's victory. Hence I could not free myself from the gloomy prediction that the increasing radicalization of Solidarity could bring about either a direct Soviet intervention or something like a state of emergency in which the movement, or at least its radical wing, would be crushed by force. I had no doubts that such an operation, even as mild as possible, would be devastating for the national psyche.

Finally, the movement took the form of a popular crusade, using the language of moral indignation and demanding from intellectuals total commitment rather than critical judgment. This was difficult to bear for someone who valued above all individual freedom and reacted with deep repulsion to all forms of indoctrination.

In 1981 the polarization of political attitudes in Poland reached a stage that excluded the possibility of a genuinely independent stand. Attempts to mediate between the sides of the conflict, or to criticize both of them, were seen as playing into the hands of the Party; even simple silence began to look as silent support for the authorities. This exposed me to intolerable moral tension; the only way of minimizing it was physical absence from the country. Happily, I was offered a research position in the History of Ideas Unit of the Australian National University in Canberra. I left Poland two weeks before the proclamation of martial law, not knowing that my stay abroad would last not for a year or two, but for decades.

The main product of my five years in Australia was a book on the legal philosophies of Russian liberalism, which included a chapter on the Polish-Russian theorist Leon Petrażycki and a chapter on my first teacher, Hessen. But the political and moral situation in Poland was still at the very center of my concerns. I was worried by the fact that the resistance to martial law took the form of intensive anti-Communist self-indoctrination, mythologizing the enemy and interpreting contemporary Poland in terms of the classical totalitarian model, as if nothing had changed since the 1950s. I understood that this Manichaean vision was needed for sustaining the militant spirit; I was afraid, however, that it would arouse too much hatred, divide Polish society too strongly, prevent emergence of influential middle-of-the-road groupings, and thus create unnecessary obstacles to national reconciliation. I expressed my views in the autobiographical book Encounters with Milosz *(in Polish, published in London, 1985), in an article for the Polish émigré quarterly* Aneks *(1984, followed by a vivid discussion), and, from a more detached perspective, in a number of analytical articles in English. I wrote also an essay "Three*

Patriotisms" (published also as a separate brochure in Polish and in English),
trying to distinguish three different types of patriotic loyalty—loyalty to
"national idea," loyalty to "national will," and loyalty to "national interest,"
and showing how they conflicted with one another in recent Polish history.

My political moderation was bound up with advocacy of a consistent sys-
temic change in the direction of market economy. I chose this stand for two sep-
arate reasons: (1) as a liberal, convinced that economic freedom is a necessary
part of individual freedom, and (2) as a patriot, willing to put an end to
destructive forms of political conflict by directing national energy toward the
badly needed economic reform, in which former enemies could constructively
cooperate with each other. In 1987 I visited Poland and was glad to find out
that people calling themselves "liberals" sympathized with my views and
endorsed similar political options.

At the beginning of 1989, when I was working at the University of Notre
Dame and writing a big book on the history of the communist utopia, General
Jaruzelski's government, responding to the changed situation in the Soviet
Union, initiated the so-called roundtable talks with the opposition. This was
for me wonderful news—my dream of a negotiated national compromise was
finally coming true! The events that followed were more and more surprising
and uplifting. In June 1989 the candidates of the ruling party suffered a humil-
iating defeat in semidemocratic elections; the regime recognized its defeat, and
for the first time since World War II Poland had a democratically elected non-
Communist government.

However, it soon turned out that Polish problems with national con-
sciousness, national identity, and continuity of national history were not
solved thereby. The groups of the former opposition that had not been invited
to negotiations and power sharing proclaimed that the roundtable agreements
were in fact a shameful compromise between the "reds" and the "pinks"—if
not an outright betrayal. The president elect, Lech Wałesa, received the
insignia of presidential power from the émigré president, Ryszard Kac-
zorowski, while not inviting the former president, General Jaruzelski, to take
part in his inauguration ceremony. The post-Communist Social Democratic
Party—a small minority of the former Party members who adopted a democ-
ratic, promarket program—was treated by the victors as communists in dis-
guise, subjected to the policy of isolation, and systematically blamed for all
evils of "real socialism" in Poland. Settling accounts with history became
extremely politicized; the increasingly strong right-wingers refused to recog-
nize the importance of evolutionary changes in the history of People's Poland,
presenting the entire postwar period as Soviet occupation and Communist

totalitarianism. It was politically counterproductive because the majority of Poles, who had honestly worked under socialism, wanted to see themselves as patriots, and not as Communists or unconscious (i.e. stupid) tools of foreign occupation. Thus the crudely "anti-Communist" rhetoric of the right helped the "post-Communists" to return to power. This happened in 1993, when the "post-Communists" won parliamentary elections, and in 1995, when their leader, Aleksander Kwaśniewski, was elected for the office of the president of Poland. But the result of this was an outcry of indignation in the entire "post-Solidarity camp," accompanied by open attacks against "procedural democracy" on the right wing of political spectrum. At the moment of writing this text it was widespread in Poland to use liberalism *as a derogatory term, associated with moral relativism and nihilist contempt for "national and Catholic values." The discourse of nation has become dominated by the conception of a single national identity inseparable from "thousand years of Catholicism in Poland," and demanding a full and unequivocally clear rejection of the Communist past. According to this logic it is not enough that the former "communists" actively support market reforms and observe democratic rules of the game: to become accepted in the national community they should repent for their "sins," renounce their "genealogy," abandon all attempt to interpret recent Polish history in their own way; in other words, they should voluntarily marginalize themselves, cease to compete with the legitimate representatives of the nation. Leaders of right-wing parties add to this that only a minority of about 30 percent could be classified as true Poles: other citizens represent "nominal Poles," "sovietized population," or an "accidental society."*

It is difficult for me to observe this situation with detachment, without feelings of bitterness and alienation. I continue to stress the value of nationalism, but only in the broadest meaning of the term. In an article recently published in the Polish monthly Znak *("Sign") I defined my position as* liberal nationalism. *I mean by this the view that nation, in contrast to a tribe, or a sect, is a large, pluralistic community, containing in itself many identities, making room for divided selves; a community created in an evolutionary process of multiple spontaneous adaptations and, therefore, excluding arbitrary definitions of its essence, as well as authoritarian prescriptions for values. My lifelong thinking about the mystery of nation gave me arguments for hoping that a combination of nationalism with liberalism is possible and could be made viable. But hope is only hope, not certainty.*

Andrzej Walicki

Katherine Verdery

Civil Society or Nation? "Europe" in the Symbolism of Romania's Postsocialist Politics

Romania today has two possible directions before it: Bolshevist Asiatism or Western, European standards. Between these, [we] see only one choice: Europe, to which we already belong by all our traditions since 1848.

Charter of the Civic Alliance Party

The temptation of the Common European Home is a utopia every bit as damaging as Communism.

Senator Corneliu Vadim Tudor

Intellectuals have articulated their nations with passion and vigor in many parts of the world, but perhaps nowhere more so than in Eastern Europe.[1] The status accorded intellectuals in these societies combined with their colonial status inside Europe to produce a highly visible and spirited production of national ideas.[2] Often developed in explicit relation to the notion of "Europe," variants of these national ideologies might present their particular nation as part of Europe, as firmly distinct from it, or as a mixture of European and autochthonous traits. So robust were ideas about the nation in this region that antinational or internationalist ideas such as Marxism made headway against them only with difficulty.

Following the collapse of the East European and Soviet Communist parties in 1989, the national idea was turned to the service of legitimating new anti-Communist regimes and building new social orders. "Europe" again played a part in this, serving as the overarching symbol of the end of Party rule and signifying all the Western forms that socialism had suppressed. Among the projects embarked upon in the new contexts was to create democratic polities with strong civil societies— notions closely linked with Europe, for it was seen as their chief exemplar. To build civil society meant to return to Europe—to build a nation of European type. To *talk* of building civil society, like talk of returning to Europe, indicated one's adherence to an entire program of social change (or at least one's opposition to someone else's program). In this sense, "civil society" in post-1989 Eastern Europe is as much a feature of political discourse and symbolism as of societal organization. As such, it collides with other elements of political discourse and symbolism, most particularly "nation."

The present essay examines that collision for the case of Romania during a few critical moments in 1991–93. Unlike some other chapters in this volume, it centers not on "nation" per se but on the relationship of nation to the rhetorical project of building civil society. Nation appears here in two guises: in the idea of Europe, which posits a Romanian nation having specific (European, "civilized") features, and in a more overtly nationalist variant that rejects Europe in favor of a Romania defined independently. Focusing on a small group of politicians and intellectuals who see themselves as partisans of "Europe," I follow their talk about Europe and civil society, noting the counterdiscourse used by some of their political opponents. In Romania during this period, "Europe" meant, for its civil-society advocates, the source of the political and economic forms Romania should adopt; for others, it meant a neoimperialist menace threatening Romania's independence. That is, "Europe" represented either aid and salvation or imperial domination. But for all who used it, to speak of "Europe" was (as has been true for two centuries) at one and the same time a statement of political intentions and a statement of national identity. Democracy, private property, civil society, and Europe: it is around these symbols that "Romanianness"—including policies toward foreign capital, new property regimes, and new political arrangements—was being redefined. The stakes of the redefinition were not only rhetorical: it would shape the very forms and symbols of Romanian politics in the future.

As is clear, for the purposes of this discussion I take Europe, democracy, civil society, and nation as key symbolic operators, elements in ideological fields, rather than as organizational realities. While recognizing that politics is far more than symbolism and discourse, I believe that for the former Soviet bloc these aspects have not yet received the attention they warrant. Therefore, instead of asking (as some would) "Do we have resurgent nationalism in Romania?" or "Is Romania developing civil society?" I ask what a political economy of the symbolism around these notions can reveal about that country's postsocialist politics. I look at how the overwhelming presence of the master-symbol "nation" in Romania's political space limits what opposition intellectuals and politicians can do with symbols like "civil society," "democracy," and "Europe," and I find them compelled to address the national idea despite their aim of constructing, instead, a new political object: a democratic society of European form.

Teleological Elites, Intellectuals, and Moral Capital

In order to link the above symbols with political processes in Romania, I use the notion of moral capital, seen as a type of political capital having special currency in Eastern Europe. Central to rule in modern states are their regimes of legitimation and control;[3] an important ingredient in these is the kind of symbols that rulers and others are able to mobilize. Those symbols, in turn, define and help to build the political capital of the actors who wield them. Efforts to introduce new symbols, redefine old ones, and monopolize their definitions are thus integral both to building political capital by aspirant political elites and to producing new regimes of legitimation where the old ones have collapsed.

The end of Party rule throughout Eastern Europe opened a struggle for relegitimation, while also changing the definition of what count as political resources and undermining prior accumulations of them. To take the most obvious example, position in the Party apparatus ceased to provide political capital once that apparatus was dismantled. Definitions of alternative sources did not emerge *de novo,* however. One of their parameters was a lengthy history in which elite status had been understood in a certain way, a way that paradoxically accommodated Communist elites rather well. Following Ivan Szelényi, I refer to these elites as "teleological elites."[4] For such people, the conduct of politics and intellectual life, as well as their place in these, was defined first and foremost in terms of the pursuit and defense of certain *values,* rather than the mastery and institutionalization of certain *procedures.* This is to invoke, of course, Weber's celebrated distinction between two kinds of rationality—*Wertrationalität* and *Zweckrationalität,* the rationalities of

ends and of means. Although one can never wholly separate ends from
means or create satisfactory ideal types based on them, I nonetheless
find it helpful to see East European elites as having typically privileged
a *wertrational* orientation, one that reached its climax with the teleological elites of the Communist Party. (The hackneyed phrase "The end
justifies the means" says it all.)

Comprising these elites were both producers of culture—"intellectuals"—and politicians, jointly arguing about values, about the knowledge necessary to implementing them, and about the politics appropriate for this. While one might wish to distinguish intellectuals from
politicians, I prefer not to do so, for two reasons. First, for many
decades people of elite status in the eastern part of Europe moved back
and forth between intellectual and political work while participating in
a common discourse; thus, a single individual might hold both roles
several times over.[5] Second, the Communist Party—ostensibly a political formation—blurred the lines further by claiming a monopoly on
truth and knowledge, the standard claim of intellectuals. Throughout
the socialist period a common feature of intellectual/political life was
an ongoing contest as to who was "really" an intellectual as opposed to
a "mere" politician—a division that might also appear as "dissidents"
vs. "Party hacks." People from both groups sought to legitimate themselves with knowledge claims and with teleological pretensions to represent ultimate values better than the others. I take that kind of legitimating practice as defining intellectuals; by this definition, then, it
makes sense to treat intellectuals and politicians in Eastern Europe as
common participants in a single discursive field, rather than to separate
them.[6]

A corollary of these elites' teleological orientation is that certain
kinds of symbolic capital have tended to prevail over other kinds as
political resources: specifically, moral capital—a capital rooted in
defining certain values as correct and upholding them—has held an
edge over what we might call technical or expert capital, rooted in certain competencies and the mastery of procedures and techniques.
Moral capital is present, of course, in the claims of elites in other systems too; differently defined, it often plays a role in U.S. elections, for
instance. In emphasizing moral capital here, I wish merely to underscore that a certain language of claims—moral claims, often intertwined with national values—has had especially great resonance in
Eastern European politics. While Communist Party leaders surely did

not ignore technical questions, their first concern was to establish a monopoly on the definition of virtue, of purity, of social entitlement, and of obligation. These are not chiefly technical or procedural matters (although procedures may be implied in the answers to them).[7] And these concerns established the grounds for social and political action within the societies over which Communist parties ruled.

As time passed and Communist parties found it increasingly difficult to legitimate themselves—that is, as resistant subjects perceived their overbearing elites more and more as "them"—there arose in each socialist country various forms and degrees of organized opposition. This opposition sought to establish its credibility on grounds already set by the past and by Party rule itself: morality. Although some intellectuals sought to challenge the Party on grounds of competence, claiming that as intellectuals, they were better qualified to determine the direction of society, even this claim rested on a teleological foundation: better qualified to *determine fundamental values* for the society.[8] Overall, opposition leaders took their stand on the morality of opposition to the regime, and of opposition as the only morality acceptable.[9] Making morality the only criterion that counts, then, entailed accumulating moral capital with which to challenge the morality of the Party.

How did dissidents accumulate moral capital? That is, how did people with no formal political power acquire politically salient authority—something crucial to their role in politics both before and after the end of Party rule? There were several routes for doing so. Two of them involved elaborating and defending ideas about *civil society* and *national values.* Partisans of "civil society" generally presented it as a sphere free of politics,[10] therefore morally superior to the corrupt politics of the Party and central to any quest for greater democracy. Those who defended "nation" imagined it as a pure value and object of loyalty that the Communists had betrayed; hence moral superiority would lie in restoring it to its rightful place at the center of politics. As concepts, civil society and nation were sometimes coterminous, sometimes developed in tandem, and sometimes set in contrast to one another; the mix differed from case to case.[11] So, too, did the robustness of the idea of civil society, which tended to be stronger in Poland, Czechoslovakia, and Hungary, for example, than in Romania and Bulgaria.

An additional and very important means of accumulating moral capital through resistance was the idea of *suffering.* This might take any number of forms, resulting from the Party's harassment, persecution, imprisonment, or torture of those who claimed to defend civil society or nation against it. Crucial in establishing this form of moral capital during the socialist period was notice by "the West" (West European countries and the United States) in the context of the Cold War. Given Western hostility to Communism, persons who resisted Communist tyranny and suffered for it gained visibility and renown. They might come to the attention of their countrymen, despite censorship, through foreign broadcasts enhancing their moral stature as pioneers of freedom or through appeals from international human rights groups on their behalf. By 1989 it was chiefly dissident intellectuals who gained this kind of renown—people like Václav Havel and Jan Patočka in Czechoslovakia, Doina Cornea in Romania, Jacek Kuroń and Adam Michnik in Poland, György Konrád and Ivan Szelényi in Hungary.

In speaking thus about suffering and moral capital, I do not wish for an instant to diminish the reality and significance of that suffering, which was in many cases terrible and permanently crippling. My aim is only to underscore the way in which otherwise powerless opponents of increasingly unpopular regimes acquired, precisely *because* their powerlessness invited persecution, a kind of political resource. Their persecution, suffering, and consequent moral capital rested on the defense of moral and national values long defended by Eastern Europe's teleological elites; they rested, as well, on the morality claims of the Party itself, which set the agenda for the counterdefinitions its opponents might offer. That the suffering of the latter was real only made more solid the moral capital it built.

The political resource contained in resistance-based suffering was to carry over into the postsocialist period. Doubtless the most stunning instance of the moral-turned-political capital inherent in persecution was Havel's unparalleled ascent from political prisoner to Czechoslovak president. Others who gained political stature from their previous persecution include, of course, Poland's Wałesa; Romania's Ion Iliescu sought to capitalize on this same resource by presenting himself as the victim of his opposition to Ceaușescu's policies, which had led to his demotion and exile to Party posts in the provinces. In the anti-Communist climate of 1990, when widespread euphoria at the end of Party rule accompanied moves to excise the Party and all it stood for from public life, for increasing numbers of people the sufferings it had caused became grounds for visibility and respect. For example, in Romania the suffering of longtime political prisoner Corneliu Coposu helped to constitute his moral authority as head of the resuscitated National Peasant Party, while the persecuted members of the Association of Former Political Prisoners gave that organization considerable clout in the newly forming political opposition. Candidates for political office in such organizations, or participants wanting the microphone at their meetings, might justify themselves with the capital of suffering (expulsion from the workplace, jail, ostracism, etc.) they had accumulated from their refusals to serve the regime.[12] To show that one had suffered under the Communists became in Romania a major claim, entitling one to the *right to be heard* in the political sphere. To argue that one had suffered in this way *for the Romanian nation* or *for a democratic civil order*— that is, to join the two sets of morality arguments, civil society (or nation) with suffering—might strengthen one's moral authority further.[13] This moral authority was not necessarily used to secure political office; rather, it supported a claim to exercise *influence* in defining the new order, one that would presumably exclude Communists. Needless to say, suffering for the Romanian nation was not an argument available to the national minorities,[14] whose main legitimating argument could only be that they had suffered ethnic persecution under the Communists and had resisted it in the name of a more democratic society.

The remainder of this essay illustrates some of these points with specific reference to Romanian political/intellectual discourse between 1991 and early 1993. This was a period in which the mass political movement that had arisen in late December 1989 as the "National Salvation Front" and then become a political party, winning the May 1990 elections, was consolidating its hold on power and clarifying its self-definition. It split into two factions, led respectively by President Iliescu and former prime minister Roman; these later became separate parties, known by their acronyms as FDSN and FSN (they later changed their names again to PDSR and PD).[15] Reflecting a division between older reformist Party apparatchiks and younger technocrats, this schism created room for the further development both of opposition movements and parties[16] and of nationalist ones.[17] The latter were to benefit from the increased vulnerability of the ruling PDSR following the September 1992 elections, when that party could no longer carry a parliamentary vote on its own; it needed allies. Thus, 1991–93 constituted a critical moment in the reconfiguration of Romania's political field.

In assessing what the opposition was able to accomplish in this critical interval, one must bear in mind that there had been little effective opposition in Romania, in contrast with other bloc countries. The idea of civil society had far less purchase there than elsewhere; instead, dissidents had been likely to protest through veiled references to "Europe" and through defending a certain idea of Romania[18]—that is, through the idea of "nation" and the defense of its values. Moreover, an especially vigorous development of Romanian national ideology over the past two hundred years, amid repeated struggles to define and control the symbol "Romanian nation," had endowed that particular symbol with great force.[19] Under Ceauşescu, it had buttressed indigenist (rather than Europeanizing) definitions of Romanian identity: Romanians as autochthons, as sui generis, rather than as Europeans and heirs of Rome. This recent history constrained what one could accomplish politically with ideas about civil society and Europe after 1989.

Romania after the "Events"

In the political field that took shape after Romania's so-called revolution (now generally referred to as the "events" of 1989), initial advantage went, as elsewhere, to the handful of former dissident intellectuals. Party opponents such as Doina Cornea and poet Mircea Dinescu endowed the emerging National Salvation Front with tremendous moral authority, helping to sanctify its other, Party-based aspirants to leadership. The latter included veteran Communists who had signed a letter of protest to Ceauşescu in March 1989, together with a number of second-tier Party bureaucrats claiming (like Iliescu) that their careers had suffered for their refusal to be Ceauşescu's toadies. After December 22, 1989, these variously defined "dissidents" found themselves presidents and presidential councilors, ambassadors, and government ministers. Talk of civil society, democracy, and a return to Europe echoed loudly through the corridors of power, as the newly ascendant opposition imitated the style of speech of their analogues in Poland, Czechoslovakia, and Hungary, empowered shortly before.

But the timing of Romania's revolution had enabled its Party elites to learn from the fates of Party leaders elsewhere, just as the demonstrating crowds in Czechoslovakia and Bulgaria had learned from the encouraging experience of prior demonstrators in East Germany.[20] From the initial chaos of the revolution, members of the former Party apparatus managed to preserve, over the next several years, far more of the structures of rule than was true in the former bloc countries to the northwest. The National Salvation Front and most of its civil-society dissident allies soon came to a parting of the ways (indeed, in February 1993 the government actually brought treason charges against Doina Cornea for undermining the state).[21] In the September 1992 elections, the Front's conservative faction—Iliescu's group of old-time Party bureaucrats—even promoted an *anti*-reform political program and raised questions about the desirability of privatizing agriculture or large state firms. This faction won the largest single bloc of votes. Its political allies in a new governing coalition were several small parties—the Agrarianists and the Socialist Labor Party (the former Communist Party), as well as two nationalist parties, the Greater Romania Party (PRM) and the Party of Romanian National Unity (PUNR).

Given Romanians' dismal experience with "Communism," however, that coalition could not overtly constitute its rule *as Communists.* During two electoral campaigns, Iliescu was repeatedly challenged to explain his relationship to the Party and the doctrines of Marxism-Leninism; he replied that he was no longer a Communist. Thus, in its struggle for relegitimation, Iliescu's party (the PDSR) proceeded along two lines: it insisted on its own definition of democracy, thereby contesting the opposition's use of this symbol, and it placed itself ever more openly on the side of the nationalist PRM and PUNR. That is, it began to stake its legitimacy on defense of "the nation," producing the curious spectacle of an alliance of ex-Communists and nationalists, the "national Communists." This legitimation strategy resulted in part from the opposition's earlier capture of the symbols "democracy" and "civil society" and in part from widespread revulsion at alternative values such as "socialism," but it also accorded well with the political goals of the PDSR.[22]

I should clarify what I mean by the term *opposition.* The word is very imprecise, because the groups that might qualify for it kept changing colors and sides. I use *opposition* as Romanians do, to mean all those Romanian politicians taking a position overtly opposed to that of the party(ies) of government—anyone who regularly criticized Iliescu in the press, for instance. The opposition's unity was far from reliable. Some of the oppositional parties joined the so-called Democratic Convention, an umbrella party formed in hopes of beating the National Salvation Front; these groups nonetheless quarreled often among themselves, as well as with other groups or people (such as the National Liberal Party) who were not part of the Convention but usually voted anti-PDSR. In the space of two years (1991–93), parties divided, disappeared, changed names, and reconfigured their political coalitions; members left their party to join another, disavowed their party program while remaining in parliament as its supposed representatives, and mended fences with former enemies only to split from their closest friends. In such an unstable political landscape, the referent of *opposition* is itself highly unstable. The term therefore refers to a quite miscellaneous collection of personages, orientations, and interests, defined only through their criticism of the ruling coalition.

As the PDSR consolidated its power, the opposition groups lost the advantage they had enjoyed immediately after the revolution.[23] Their inexperience and ineptitude made it easy for the PDSR to diminish their credibility with the public and to undermine their moral capital. Although the Democratic Convention won 27 percent of the 1992 national vote by defining itself as anti-Communist, this was considerably less than expected. Opposition groups remained all too vulnerable to the nationalist accusation that in talking of Europe they were not anti-Communist but antipatriotic, servants of "foreign powers" (i.e., Europe, Hungary), lackeys of the American embassy, and traitors who aim to "sell the country" and who should be expelled from Romania's new democracy. Their disadvantage was not only rhetorical but also institutional, for the balance of electoral forces in parliament meant that they could not carry any vote unless a few in the governing coalition defected.[24] Moreover, the government maintained control over the allocation of radio frequencies, licenses for TV broadcasting, and access to television programming. The opposition's ability to disseminate its ideas was thus increasingly hostage to vertiginous rises in the price of paper—produced under state monopoly.

The coordinates of the field of action discussed in the following pages, then, were these: the governing coalition held most of the cards institutionally speaking and utilized the most powerful rhetorical symbol, while the opposition's rhetoric and its political position were both weak. The illegitimacy of socialist rhetoric (though not of all its ideals) forced the options it might have voiced into other channels of political expression—talk of civil society and nation being the main alternatives. In seeking to show how their political disadvantage compelled opposition groups to modify and even abandon their civil-society discourse, I focus on three groups: members of two civil-society organizations known as the Civic Alliance (AC) and the Group for Social Dialogue

(GDS), which overlapped with a third, the Civic Alliance political party (PAC). These groups, together with members of the National Peasant Party, had formed the core of the Democratic Convention, building its strength by drawing other parties into it; their allies included the party of Romania's Hungarians. Although the various groups included very diverse orientations and interests, all were resolute opponents of both Iliescu's PDSR and its nationalist allies.

The Struggle to Define Central Political Symbols

I begin with some brief examples of the political symbols central to Romanian politics at that time and of the rhetoric defining the field of their use. These symbols include "democracy," "nation" and "the national interest," and "patriotic."[25]

From the very outset, opposition groups defined themselves as the authoritative defenders of "democracy," repeatedly labeling the PDSR and the nationalists "anti-democratic." The PDSR contested both the definition and the label. Shortly after the revolution, Iliescu asserted as his aim the building of "*original* democracy," in which, it soon became clear, opposition was expected to suppress its disagreement for the good of the whole. "Original democracy" was government by consensus, rather than by a process of institutionalized disagreement and compromise, as the opposition defined it. Thus, a contrast emerged between the "original democracy" of the PDSR and what the opposition defended as "true" or "authentic" or "real" democracy. (The opposition's version was far from universally accepted: in brief visits during the summers of 1990–92, I spoke with many Romanians who thought democracy should be consensus and who accused the opposition parties of obstructing the country's forward march by disagreeing with the government, instead of "pitching in and helping to get us out of this impasse.")

In asserting a definition of democracy, people might also claim to defend the "Romanian nation." An example comes from a 1990 letter to the prime minister, in which two nationalist writers well placed under Ceauescu seek permission to start a nationalist magazine:

> We would not have emerged from our self-imposed silence had we not been more and more revolted by the scandalously antinational character of certain publications. . . . [T]hese publications

have become a sort of agent of denunciation, maintaining a climate of tension and terror over the people of good faith of this country. This isn't good. We cannot remain passive before the attempt of these hypocrites, ulcerated with political ambitions for aggrandizement and enrichment, to destabilize the country—and worse—and to enslave it to foreign powers. . . . [W]e see that the most perilous politics (draped in the garb of democracy, naturally!) comes from the [opposition] publications . . . manipulated openly and diabolically by the same old pigsty at Radio Free Europe. All these people were traitors before and still are today.[26]

These writers abjure the so-called democracy of ambitious traitors (namely, anyone who disagrees), and they imply that the national interest would be better served by patriotic consensus.

Such accusations drove opposition groups to offer and defend their own understandings of what constitutes patriotism, anti-Romanian activity, and national interest—preoccupations we might not otherwise expect in people aiming to build civil society. PRM senator C. V. Tudor's chief initiative during the winter of 1993 was to introduce a law punishing "anti-Romanian activity" (meant to include most of what the political opposition was advocating). In a commentary on this initiative, one opposition member listed a number of things *he* would consider to be "anti-Romanian activity," such as injustices committed against the Romanian people, its biological degradation, Romania's drop in living standards during the 1980s to the bottom of the list in Europe, the death of Romanian babies in freezing and underequipped maternity wards, the falsification of the national history, the killing of women from self-induced illegal abortions and of thousands of Romanians from the cold and hunger throughout the Ceauescu period—in a word, the actions of the Romanian Communist Party, which C. V. Tudor and his nationalist friends were busily rehabilitating.[27] In addition, other opposition writings frequently questioned the "patriotism" of those in power and accused them of ruining Romania in all manner of ways—by wrecking the economy, corrupting power, and creating a dismal image of Romania in the eyes of Europe and the world (the epitomal "anti-Romanian act"). And just as the nationalists complained that the opposition wanted to "sell" the country to "foreigners," the president of the Democratic Convention countered that the PDSR was "playing the game of those foreign forces hostile to Romania"[28]—meaning not the Westerners whom nationalists objected to, but Russia.

Besides compelling their opposition enemies to counterdefinitions of "anti-Romanian activity," the government's nationalist allies forced them to elaborate an alternative understanding of the "national interest" and of how this interest related to *foreign* interests. A 1993 editorial in the opposition paper 22, entitled "Are These Our National Interests?" shows this nicely.[29] In it, the author affirms that three years after the so-called Romanian revolution, the original structures and personnel of the former regime have achieved a nearly complete restoration, and its beneficiaries now defend their actions as being in the nation's interests. How can this be, the editorial asks, when they wish to return to the policies that put Romania in last place in Eastern Europe and left the population with grave protein deficits; when the new powerholders are perpetuating the economic disaster and eliminating all opportunity and all hope? "Can this be in the national interests, I wonder?" The author asks the same question concerning the government's use of anti-Americanism and anti-Westernism, which will necessarily force Romania back under the heel of Moscow—"but is this in the national interest of Romanians," when all our greatest misfortunes have come not from the West but from the East? Can it be in the national interest to push the country into the arms of the Russians, "who have never known any relation of 'collaboration' except to subjugate the weaker partner?" Repeating these questions again and again, the author makes plain that the government's definition of the national interest is deeply suspect.

A final example of argument over national symbols shows an opposition paper contesting government spokesman Paul Everac's definition of "national pride." Everac had appeared in a special TV editorial in which he complained that Romanians' sense of national pride was slipping, since everyone seemed only to be motivated by abject cupidity and by chasing after a few pairs of used trousers from foreign aid packets. He decried the contraband in foreign cigarettes as degrading to Romanians. With this, he opened himself to attack from a columnist for 22, who asked,

> Where was our national pride when we were importing collectivization? . . . And when we were importing all the idiot theses of Stalin. . . ? And when we put up with all Ceaușescu's stammerings

and pronounced them words of genius? Where was the national pride when we stood in lines from the crack of dawn for a cup of milk?[30]

Everac had also sought to shore up the national pride by affirming that one of the ancestors of Romanians—the Roman emperor Trajan—was the genitor of Europe itself. To this the same columnist retorted,

> This means either that we have *European* pride—which is more comprehensive—or that we are trying in our way to rediscover our founding father, or more exactly, the European part of our inheritance. Who took it, since we no longer have it, Mr. Everac doesn't bother to tell us. The moment when we lost Europe was placed under erasure just like the moment when we lost Bessarabia and Bucovina.[31]

These lines are reminiscent of the dissident accusation against Ceauşescu, that he was tearing Romanians from their European inheritance and trying to move the country into Africa.[32] To complete the parallel, another news item observed that President Iliescu had expressed criticism of the ancient Romans' "greed and plundering" of other nations; by this he distanced Romania from both its imperialist forebears and "Europe's" similar tendencies of today.[33] These alternative views show us a government defending Romanian "independence" against a pro-Europe opposition, each offering a different image of where Romania's "inheritance" truly lies and who (Europe, Russia) represents the greater danger.

In such company, the opposition did not have the luxury of ignoring the "nation" so as to build up "civil society." They were compelled to respond to the agenda set by those promoting national values. Significantly, however, each time they did so, they further reinforced the idea of nation and left hanging the prospects for the civil society they wished to promote.

The Situational Constraints on "Civil Society": Three Cases

Having shown something of the alternative visions offered for Romania's "democracy" and its "national interest," I will now present three cases to illustrate how the presence of the symbol "nation" dominated the space for symbolic maneuver on the part of those defending a pro-Western vision of Romania's future. In the first case we see how vulnerable is a concept of civil society when defined independently of "the nation." The case concerns the founding congress of the Civic Alliance Party, in June 1991, and involves only members of that group—largely but not exclusively Romanian in membership—in dialogue among themselves. The second case involves (mostly Romanian) members of the Group for Social Dialogue in conversation with members of the Hungarian Democratic Union of Romania, the party supported by virtually all Romania's Hungarians. Since that party was included in the Democratic Convention, for which all members of the Group for Social Dialogue voted, the second case enlarges the field of social allegiances by explicitly engaging Hungarians—who are nonetheless, in broad party terms, political fellow travelers. The third case enlarges the field still further, to include with Civic Alliance/Democratic Convention spokesmen the PDSR and its nationalist allies. In that case, the issue being debated was the composition of the Romanian delegation to the Council of Europe, which was considering Romania's possible membership. In all three cases, "Europe" plays a central role in defining the political options, and the symbol "nation" constrains the efficacy of "civil society."

Civic Front or Ethnic Front? The Congress of the Civic Alliance Party

As described by one of its founders, the group "Civic Alliance" was formed on November 15, 1990, "as a movement to build civil society."[34] Another active member put it thus: "The Civic Alliance is the only group that could constitute a legitimate power in Romania: its principle of action is *alliance* and its basic moving force is *civic consciousness.*" And a third: "The problem of democracy is first of all a *civic* problem—about freedom for one's beliefs, one's ethnic identity, one's politics."[35] The group also claimed to stand for *national reconciliation,* for bringing the country's various ethnic groups together and dispelling the organized confusion and hate sown by the nationalists and PDSR. These statements leave no doubt as to the relative place of civic and ethnic symbols in the group's charter.

In July 1991, this organization held a conference with a view to forming a political party, to be called the Civic Alliance Party, or PAC.[36]

Its aim, in the approximate words of the organizer who read its proposed statute, was to

> contribute to the democratization of Romanian society, and to
> offer a new image of Romania to the world. Romania today has
> two possible directions before it: Bolshevist Asiatism or Western,
> European standards. Between these, the PAC sees only one choice:
> Europe, to which we already belong by all our traditions since
> 1848. All the best periods of our history have been periods of Euro-
> peanizing. The PAC wants to send Europe a Europeanizing mes-
> sage, to offer a credible partner for Romania's neighbors and for
> Europe, and to express our decisive break with the past. We must
> follow our neighbors in breaking down the structures of Soviet
> type; we must break the ties with the Soviet Union that are keeping
> us from Europe—ties like the mutual-assistance treaty President
> Iliescu recently signed with Gorbachev. Among our goals must be
> the separation of powers in the state and an independent judiciary
> that meets European standards.
>
> The stakes of the Civic Alliance Party are not power but Roma-
> nia. We cannot be a party of only one nationality; we must embrace
> all Romania's groups. We cannot work to divide Romanian society
> but must press for a countrywide social dialogue. We must respect
> the right of self-determination, which includes asking people
> where they want to live and then working out any conflicts in this
> by international treaty. [He had said earlier that the nationalities
> issue is a false problem, stirred up by a power that wants to draw
> attention from the real problems it cannot solve.] Our aim must be
> to build a secure Romania, with a law-governed state and a pow-
> erful civil society.[37]

As the conference unfolded, however, it became clear that different people among the organizers and delegates were proposing two
potentially contradictory notions: (1) the PAC must be a *civic* party that
would not be limited to any one nationality and would address the
problem of national-minority rights in a fair-minded way; (2) a vital
element in the party platform must be to re-create the "Greater Romania" of the 1930s, by bringing back into Romania "our brothers" in
newly independent Moldova (a region that between 1918 and 1940 was
Romanian Bessarabia, and thereafter Soviet Moldavia). Among the

opening speeches of the conference were greetings from groups in Moldova, urging the PAC to be a party of "national reintegration."[38] This objective, initially raised by only a few of the Bucharest organizers, came with increasing insistence from the provincial delegates, some of whom even proposed writing into Romania's constitution the intention to reincorporate Moldova. The Moldovan question became still more urgent when a special announcement was made, to great consternation, that there had been severe flooding in Moldova and tens of thousands of people had lost their homes. In response, the congress voted to urge the government to help Moldova, "since we are one people." Nobody mentioned the 35 percent of the population of Moldova who are ethnic Russians, Gagauz, Ukrainians, and others; only "our Romanian brothers" seemed to count.

The Moldovan question raised significant problems for a party claiming to emphasize the civic over the national and to embrace Romania's minorities. That nothing was said about the status of Moldova's non-Romanian 35 percent was sure to be galling to potential non-Romanian minority supporters of PAC (the country's Hungarians, Germans, etc.), concerned at what this national preoccupation implied for their own status in Romania. None of the enthusiasts of reintegration thought to acknowledge the parallel between Moldova and Transylvania, both regions containing sizable ethnic minorities who might prefer to be in some other state or might want guarantees of their civic status in Romania. The Moldovan question showed how feeble were the PAC's civic sentiments, so readily overshadowed by national feeling. As speaker after speaker invoked Moldova, the problems of how to build civil society or integrate minorities into it faded from view.

More was at issue, however, than a groundswell of fraternal feeling in response to natural disaster: the groundswell itself affected the political calculus of the party organizers and the very commitment of some of them to the "civic alliance" inscribed in their name. These effects of the Moldovan question and its consequences for negotiating a definition of "civic" that would not also be "ethnic" came blatantly to the fore during the morning of the second day.[39] Perceiving the drift of comments from the hall, some of the organizers unilaterally decided that it would be wise to scratch a planned reading of the proposed statement on the rights of minorities. They reasoned that if the PAC kept its minorities plank, it would alienate many of the voters who, like the group's own delegates, were sensitive to the national idea; in particular, it would alienate Romanian voters in Transylvania, where ethnic issues were especially acute. Since those were precisely the Romanians most likely to be interested in *other* aspects of the PAC platform, the sticky tactical question now became how far the PAC should go to attract those votes, at the expense of what the party's organizers had initially agreed should be its multiethnic principles—principles in accord with their conception of a European-style civic society. The person who had been chosen to read the minorities statement at the congress was furious and complained (in private) that all the organizers with *ethics* were being pushed out by a new mafia, peddling nationalism and monarchism rather than the moral and civic principles for which the group was supposed to stand.

After heated backstage discussion, it was finally agreed that the statement on minorities would be read after all, but in a very undesirable slot—the time when most people were marking off their ballots to elect leaders of the new party and the hall was buzzing with conversation. Thus, few actually heard a document that was dedicated to Europe, civic life, and the supersession of national differences by these larger values. It spoke of a Romania integrated into Europe and adhering to the Helsinki norms for the protection of minorities; it decried recrudescent xenophobia and chauvinism in Romania, as well as the governing PDSR's complicity in this; it invoked Romanian traditions of cooperation and peaceful cohabitation with other groups. It emphasized that national rights are a fundamental human right and a foundation of democracy, affirming that "no nation can be indifferent to the fate of the minorities with which it lives." While underscoring that minorities had the obligation to be loyal citizens of Romania and to defend its constitution and laws, the statement called for tolerance, the rights of minorities to respect and to equality with all other Romanian citizens (including the right to oppose assimilation, to use their language, etc.), and it granted minorities the right to appeal to international organizations if these guarantees were not observed.

The statement received almost no reaction from a thoroughly inattentive audience.

The problem of the PAC's relations with minorities dogged its footsteps on into the larger political arena. Included among the parties to the Democratic Convention was the UDMR, the party of Romania's Hungarians. It had polled 7 percent in the previous elections and could be expected to do so again—a solid bloc of votes the Convention would surely need if it were to match the voting strength of the PDSR. But the inclusion of the UDMR enabled the PDSR and its allies to accuse the Convention of being "anti-Romanian" and those in the PAC, in particular, of having "sold out to the Hungarians." In Transylvania, the anti-PDSR vote was evenly divided between the Convention (which had expected to sweep that region) and the nationalist PUNR.[40] This greatly diminished the Convention's parliamentary strength and vindicated the calculation of those in the PAC leadership who had wanted to suppress the statement on minorities and, even at the expense of civic values, ride nationalism to victory.

Are Civic Rights Individual or Collective? Relations with the UDMR

Following the national elections in September–October 1992, in which the Convention failed to win the presidency or its expected number of parliamentary seats both despite and because of its electoral alliance with the Hungarian Party, the opposition was unpleasantly surprised by a UDMR declaration in favor of Hungarian autonomy. This document, called the "Cluj Declaration," emerged from a power struggle *within* the UDMR between its radical and moderate factions. The Cluj Declaration angered many among the Hungarians' erstwhile allies, who were unprepared for it, did not know how to interpret it, and saw in it a further erosion of the opposition's political chances. Indeed, the nationalist Romanian parties immediately launched an attack on the Hungarians and their opposition allies.

In this context of anxiety and offense, members of the Group for Social Dialogue (GDS) invited members of the UDMR to a roundtable discussion, later published in the group's newspaper, 22.[41] The Group for Social Dialogue had been the very first civil-society organization founded in late December 1989; most of its members later joined the (much larger) Civic Alliance, some also taking leadership positions in the PAC. In setting up a roundtable with the UDMR, the GDS aimed to discuss what the Hungarians meant by "autonomy" and why they insisted on a definition of "rights" as *collective* rather than individual. This second point revealed fundamental differences between the Hungarians present and their Romanian interlocutors, differences having major implications for their joint effort to build "democracy" and "civil society"—even though the common premise of all was that they *were* building democracy and the PDSR was not. Their differences echoed as well in their invocations of "Europe."

In the Cluj Declaration, Hungarians insisted that they are members not simply of a national *minority* but of a *community;* this entitles them to request autonomy like other communities—religious ones, territorial ones, and so on—allowing them to resolve without external interference any matters relating to their community identity: education, language maintenance, culture, and so on. They also claimed that the jural entities guaranteed equal rights in the constitution should be not just individuals but communities as well. The heart of their disagreement with Romanians from the GDS was that the latter were perplexed as to why Hungarians saw a constitutional guarantee of *individual* rights as insufficient protection: why did there need to be *collective* guarantees? What sort of rights did the Hungarians claim that went beyond the guarantees of individual rights to freedom of expression, of association, and so forth?

Although the long-term implications of the different views include substantially different understandings of such important matters as citizenship, I believe the crux of the disagreement was more immediately strategic: the GDS and other opposition groups would be able to support the Hungarians only if they could do so in the context of a "democratic movement" seeking better definition—and better enforcement—of individual rights under the law. As one Romanian participant put it,

> Your arguments so far refer to shortcomings in the existing legislation. . . . From this it follows that we have to improve the laws and, even more, their enforcement. Why, then, haven't you oriented yourselves to these things that interest you directly and that are also of *general* interest? Why do you think there is another route to your goals than the general route toward democracy?[42]

By the end of the discussion, the Romanian participants were saying outright that the Hungarians' declaration had put obstacles in the path of democratization and had fanned the flames of Romanian nationalism, pushing the PDSR into the arms of the Romanian nationalist parties.[43] Some saw the Hungarians' move as corrupting the proper

definition of democracy, as "introducing into a discussion about democratic rights, about democracy, an extrademocratic criterion, an anthropological criterion—the *ethnie*."[44] Beneath this talk, the Romanians
were saying that if Hungarians insisted on collective rights, to support
them would be politically disastrous.

Two of the many important points that emerged from this discussion concerned how to build civil society and undermine the power of
the governing coalition, and what lessons "Europe" might hold for the
treatment of national-minority problems. First, the Hungarians argued
that their claim to autonomy was significant as a move toward *decentralization*, which would diminish the power of the center. As one of
them put it:

> In our opinion, two political conceptions collide here, two modes
> of seeing things: a political conception whose values emphasize
> decentralization and autonomy, and a political conception accord-
> ing the state a tutelary role that impedes the initiative of the struc-
> tures of civil society. To put forward the idea of autonomy is not a
> problem between Hungarians and Romanians [but between state
> and civil society—K.V.].[45]

To this, one of the Romanians replied that it would be almost impossible to discuss decentralization in Romania because Romanians see this
as imperiling Transylvania's place in a unified Romanian state: any
"local autonomy" might lead to Transylvania's spinning out of Romania's orbit, becoming either an autonomous entity or an annex of Hungary.[46] Therefore, only with great difficulty could Hungarians and
Romanians discuss local autonomy without arousing this fear.[47] Prefer-
able for the Romanian participants was constant pressure on the government for individual civil rights, whose exercise would constrain the
state. We see here two irreconcilable strategies and rationales[48] for
breaking the PDSR's lock on power, with each group seeing its strategy
as central to building "democracy" or "civil society." In both strategies,
however, national concerns distort the space within which civic ones
can be pursued.

Second, while Romanians and non-Romanians in the roundtable
used "Europe" equally to illuminate the political options, they differed
on *how* "Europe" might do this. A non-Romanian position on the mat-

ter came from one of the GDS's own members, an ethnic German, who argued as follows:

> To think of the state as unitary, national, sovereign, etc. is anachronistic. If we think this way, it's only because we're unsure of our identity as Romanians. . . . The underlying question is always, Is Transylvania ours or not. From this flow certain discussions that are in fact old-fashioned, that concern territoriality, which is a deep instinct but doesn't necessarily define humanity's essence. In the world today, especially in Europe, the struggle is for group rights, community rights. This is a reality and we can't exempt ourselves from it. If we bridle at this idea it's because we haven't gotten into Europe yet. We have to get into Europe, and then discuss the problem at a European level.[49]

Thus, to be "European"—a goal to which all participants in the round-table were committed—is to renounce "anachronistic" attachments to territoriality and to defend group rights.

In 1990s Romania, however, this program would be politically suicidal, losing the opposition virtually all its Romanian voters.[50] The Romanian partners to the discussion were thus understandably reluctant to adopt the defense of collective rights. One of them challenged this "argument from Europe" with another argument, also "from Europe."[51]

> [O]ver the past few years, the Council of Europe has been working on an international document about collective rights. But progress has been unimpressive because, it seems, the concept has many complexities that must somehow be resolved. The [Hungarians'] position has surprised us, then, and at least for those of us who occupy ourselves rather more with questions of human rights and the rights of minorities, it raises a lot of problems. To put collective rights above individual ones means to overturn a structure, a whole conceptualization of the relation between individual and community that is fundamental to the new conception of democracy on which post-war Europe was built. In this sense, we would end up giving priority to certain rights of the state, of the "general" collective, even over communal and individual rights. . . . How

does the UDMR conceptually defend this asymmetry between collective and individual rights?[52]

Here Europe is seen as having laid the foundations for democracy with a certain conception of the relation between individual and collective that is not yet quite as anachronistic as the first speaker claims. The second speaker sees democracy as based in individual civil rights, posited as the ongoing legacy of Europe that he thinks Romanian politics should make its own. In these arguments we see how tightly interwoven are "civic" and "national" ideas even within civil-society groups like the GDS. Hungarians claim that their ethnic autonomy will create space for more civil society, but Romanians see it as jeopardizing their own national unity; Romanian civic individualism, in turn, strikes Hungarians as insensitive to Hungarian national concerns.

Absent from the words of the debate but nourishing the strong passions at its heart were also, I believe, feelings about the morality of suffering and the claims it would enfranchise. Several of the Romanians in the debate had suffered persecution as individuals for their opposition to the Party; their consequent moral standing was evident in the respect they enjoyed within the GDS. Arguments for individual civic rights sprang from their courageous individual defense of such rights. Many Hungarians, by contrast, saw the entire Ceauşescu period as a terrible assault on their collective national being: they had felt ever more stringent regulations against their language, schools, publications, and so on as attacks on their very existence as Hungarians (and hence as humans), and they had viewed Ceauşescu's much-publicized village destruction program of 1988–89 as genocide. This collective suffering deserved recognition and redress, as well as guarantees against its recurrence. Given the context of the discussion and the effort of all participants to keep it cordial, the language of justification-by-suffering was almost absent. Even so, however, one Hungarian replied as follows to a Romanian's saying that their aim should be to make the government respect constitutional guarantees for individual and general liberties: "Of course! But don't you agree that we [Hungarians] suffer more, because we live not only in the general context but through what is specific to us."[53] Here relative suffering is used to force a rank-ordering of the desirable civic rights.

The GDS's roundtable highlights, I believe, how difficult it was for the Romanian opposition to consolidate itself as a democratic force in a political field so mined by the national idea and past national conflicts. If the opposition could not contemplate local autonomy as a means of decentralizing and thus of reconfiguring power because to do so would invite charges of treason and national dismemberment, and if there could be no defense of democracy except through *individual* rights— through a set of rights central to building up political subjectivities that may now be obsolescent—then the opposition was sorely constrained in its challenge to the ruling coalition. No defense of individual rights can respond adequately to the homogenizing ideology of nationalism, so closely akin to Party policies that homogenized the social landscape and predisposed people toward homogenizing rather than pluralizing discourses.[54]

On the same playing field as the GDS and UDMR were other groups eager to seize the homogenizing initiative. Consider the following, written in defense of nationalist (PUNR) mayor Gheorghe Funar, of the Transylvanian city of Cluj:

> What would be the consequences if Funar were removed from his post as mayor? . . . The whole of Transylvania would fall into the rapacious and bloody hands of the Horthyists of the UDMR. . . . The UDMR would become the principal political force in Transylvania and would dictate to the overwhelming majority of the population. Statues, monuments, and Romanian cemeteries would be profaned, Horthyism would revive, the Orthodox Church would reel before a Vatican offensive, all Transylvania would tremble. . . . The government can fall, the president can fall, for as it is he is mostly an ornament, but Funar cannot be allowed to fall. . . . Political regimes are ephemeral and pursue only narrow interests. The basis of success must be the union of all Romanians irrespective of their religious faith or political preferences.[55]

For pro-Funar nationalists, the homogenizing discourse of anti-Hungarian Romanian chauvinism proved a potent political resource, gaining them votes and political office in the country's ethnically mixed regions. "Europe" has nothing to offer these people.[56]

Similar if less exaggerated views also came from President Iliescu. He defined Europe's position on the national question thus:

We are criticized in relation to democratic norms concerning national minorities, when the only policy toward minorities in Western countries is to assimilate them, not to assure their rights. Do people in France talk about minorities and their right to use their mother tongue and to organize schools in German? Does anyone suggest creating a [German-language] university in Strasbourg? . . . If we were to follow the example of the West, we would have to promote a politics of assimilating the nationalities, of liquidating all schools in their mother tongues, of prohibiting any language other than the language of state. In France, French is used throughout the administration and system of justice, no? This is what it would mean to follow the Western example.[57]

For Iliescu, Europe indeed provides a model for Romania—one of denying minorities any special status.

To complete the field, here is the opinion of nationalist (PRM) senator C. V. Tudor, staunch critic of "Europe" and advocate of a consensual view of democracy from which Hungarians and their friends should be banned as traitors:[58]

Romanians, Hungarian fascism is attacking us openly. The political paranoia of Budapest has entered its final phase. . . . So we have been right, over the past two years, to sound the alarm against Hungarian terrorism. *In twenty-four hours we must ban by law all anti-Romanian groupings: the UDMR and Soros Foundation* [philanthropic foundation set up by the Hungarian émigré], *as well as their stooges the PAC, GDS,* Literary Romania [opposition literary magazine], *Democratic Convention! Romanians, don't be afraid of the wild beast of Hungarian revisionism, we have put its nose out of joint a few times already, and now we'll crush it decisively and without pity! They want autonomy? Expel them!*[59]

Under circumstances in which writers of lines like these are easily elected, no political opposition to such forces can count on success if it allies with minorities and guarantees their rights. We see, then, the hegemony of "nation" as a political symbol.

The themes of the roundtable between the GDS and UDMR have a coda. In January 1993 the UDMR held its party congress and elected new party leaders, amid a fierce factional struggle. In advance of the congress, observers anticipated that the radical nationalist faction, led by Bishop László Tökés, might take over the UDMR, an outcome that would gravely compromise its place in the opposition coalition. The Romanian groups in the Democratic Convention therefore mobilized themselves, sending their highest-ranking members to the congress. Their speeches all conveyed the message: You are not alone; we share a common struggle to build a more democratic Romania.[60] Not only did the levels of applause for the speeches of the Convention leaders show unexpected support for the moderate line within the UDMR, which went on to win the leadership, but the troubling phrases about "collective rights" were removed (at least for the moment) from the party's program, which mentioned only *local* autonomy and *personal* rights. The opposition's Romanian parties saw the result as a victory for the spirit of interethnic collaboration and a good omen for the Convention's future.[61] (Unfortunately, however, this was not to last, for by late 1994 the UDMR was once again agitating for local autonomy, and the Convention's refusal to back it up led to its leaving the antigovernment coalition in 1995.)

Romania Goes to Europe: Who Will Represent Us?

My third and final case concerns discussions around the parliamentary delegation that was to represent Romania at the Council of Europe. Despite the fulminations of the PDSR and its nationalist allies against "selling the country to foreigners" and "neoimperialism," as of February 1993 the Romanian government was petitioning the Council of Europe for admittance. Maneuvering began in parliament to select the delegates who would travel to Strasbourg to present the case. As Romania's staunchest supporters of the idea of Europe, members of the opposition had somehow expected they would be the delegates. Instead, they found themselves outflanked by the PDSR and its allies. These parties not only managed to secure a disproportionate number of places on the delegation but also gave those places to several nostalgics of the Ceauşescu era, overtly antagonistic to integration with Europe and critical of international organizations. They were people who had often condemned in their writings the "aberrant regulations" of international accords that would have Romania as their victim, a Romania "besieged in the heart of a terrible plot"[62]—in which they saw the opposition as a partner. As one of them put it, "Before our very eyes, these people [the opposition] are selling the country piece by piece."[63]

Some opposition commentators immediately suspected that the maneuvering over the delegation was itself a plot: to *prevent* Romania's acceptance into Europe by sending people who would compromise the country's credibility in Europe's eyes. The resulting denial of membership would then "force" the government into the alliance it actually preferred—with the East. As one journalist summarized this view, "The gravest suspicion that pollutes our political life is that president Iliescu, supported by the former Securitate . . . , intends to alienate Romania from Western Europe and throw it again into the orbit of Slavic imperialism."[64] (The same journalist also believed that the game was in fact more duplicitous, with those in power wanting integration into Europe on terms that would legitimate them and their behavior— that is, integration despite the presence of vociferous nationalists and Ceauşescu nostalgics among the delegates. As sign of its newly "Europeanizing" interest, the PDSR was right then rushing through parliament approval for an EC loan despite that loan's stringent provisions.) Another commentator suggested that the government might think the "love-me-with-all-my-warts" strategy would work because the success of the international boycott of Serbia hinged on Romania's compliance in policing the Danube. For this reason, the PDSR could expect the Europeans to close their eyes to some of Romania's uglier characteristics.[65]

Opposition commentary on the delegation to Europe clearly revealed a battle to shape Europe's image of Romania, with the PDSR and nationalists on one side and various opposition parties on the other. Commenting on one nationalist's view, "We want to offer the West another image of Romania," an opposition journalist worried that the PDSR-stacked delegation "will surely make use of the occasion to tell Europe that in Romania there is no minority problem and no national-Communist current."[66] The president of the Civic Alliance Party, Senator Nicolae Manolescu, nuanced the picture:

The Front [i.e., PDSR] found that it had to choose between sending, let's say, a "correct" delegation to the Council of Europe—one that would enhance our chances of gaining membership—and preserving its problematic parliamentary majority. If the Front chose

Europe, it risked a rupture with [its two nationalist allies], which would wipe out its majority. . . . In these conditions they didn't want to sacrifice a working majority for a possible European membership. . . . We, of course, put the following question: in a matter concerning the national interest, why didn't they accept a consensus across party lines? In both the Senate and the House the opposition proposed a [delegation based on] national consensus. But this consensus was rejected in a way that, in my opinion, shows how an opportunistic political calculation to maintain their political majority is more important to the Front than the national interest. . . . [We are nonetheless not boycotting the delegation] because we can't let those in power claim that the opposition is sabotaging Romania's entry into Europe.[67]

In this comment, the quintessential pro-European party spokesman finds himself compelled to invoke the "national interest" (by which he means international assistance, and which the PDSR has jeopardized in a crassly "antipatriotic gesture)";[68] meanwhile, the government repeatedly accused the *opposition* of sabotaging the "national interest" whenever Romania lost a vote in the U.S. Congress, or in Europe. The issue of the delegation to Europe also reveals, however, some constraints on the behavior of the PDSR itself. Although the government knew it could not survive without loans, it was reluctant to pay the political price of accepting them over the objections of its nationalist allies, who saw integration into Europe as a national catastrophe and the Council of Europe itself as "playing the game of an international conspiracy directed from Budapest."[69] How to win the next elections if Romania's economic situation remained so parlous? And how to improve the economic situation except by Western assistance? At least one observer saw in this dilemma the cause of further fissures in the PDSR itself, between two currents—one choosing European integration and the other resisting it so as to maintain firmer internal dominance.[70] The case shows how complex a symbol "Europe" had become, in the world of Romanian realpolitik.

Conclusions

The above cases illustrate how certain notions—such as Europe, Asia, foreign domination, democracy, national interest, and civil society—

were deployed in Romanian politics from 1991 to 1993. They were deployed as having *moral* significance, based in their implications for the fate of the Romanian nation—an idea seen by all as having ultimate value. Because each of these symbols legitimated a different program and different actors aspiring to power, the different moral claims made by using one or another of them had consequences for the power they helped to consolidate. These various symbols were participating, then, in maintaining or transforming the political, economic, and social structures that have characterized Romania for the past half-century.

In hopes of transforming these structures, some in Romania availed themselves of a global political discourse about rights, democracy, civility, the West, and Europe. This discourse marshals allies in Western Europe and the United States, thereby possibly mobilizing a stream of resources for Romania's transformation. But as was clear from the 1992 election results, it was less successful in marshaling supporters *inside* Romania, especially in the villages, where nearly half the population resides. Analysis of the election results showed that the Democratic Convention's greatest strength was among people with higher education (three times as many voted for the Convention as for the PDSR) and in major urban centers, but that it was weak in rural areas, where six times as many voters preferred the PDSR.[71] It was also weaker than it should have been in the most westernized, developed, "European" part of the country: Transylvania, where long-term co-residence with Hungarians and Germans has both Europeanized Romanians and traumatized them on the ethnic question. There, many who rejected the "Bolshevist Asiatism" of the PDSR voted not for the Convention—too cozy with Hungarians—but, instead, for the Party of Romanian National Unity (Transylvanians elected a full 84 percent of that party's members of parliament).

Aside from the obvious ethnic problem for Transylvanians, why is it that "Europe" and all it implies have been relatively uninteresting to many in the Romanian electorate? This is a complicated question. Its answer involves matters such as the symbolic economy of power, unemployment and the reduced social welfare inherent in Western-style reforms, and the institutional and organizational advantages of the governing coalition. To begin with, "Europe" is an urban intellectuals' conceit; they have not done enough to translate it positively into the life terms of everyone else. Romania's entry into the "civilized" world is important in the self-conception of intellectuals, for whom culture and civilization are of the essence;[72] but these have rather little import for the daily existence of many villagers, for instance, either toiling with rudimentary equipment on tiny patches of land or commuting long hours to work in distant factories. What have Europe and civil society to do with this? For village residents, the defenders of "Europe" have not managed to constitute its symbols as meaningful objects of political action.

Worse still, the effects of Europeanization that villagers have indeed understood are not necessarily an appealing prospect. As several ethnographers have reported, although some East European villagers are eager for privatization of land, others fear that this will divide their communities into rich and poor, make them proprietors without giving them adequate means for producing, possibly subject them to unpayable levels of taxation and force them out of agriculture altogether, and even spell the end of collective farm pensions.[73] In Romania, the PDSR argued convincingly that an electoral victory by the opposition would mean restoring an older era of large estates and landless peasants. More than a few villagers saw the arguments of urban "civil-society" intellectual/politicians as potentially catastrophic—like the previous round of urban-based initiatives toward them: collectivization. By contrast, they saw politicians of ex-Communist or nationalist inclination as "doing something for poor Romanians" and as concerned with those whom full property restitution would disinherit: formerly landless peasants and people who had moved into villages where they had no land and would receive none. The radical restitution programs of the opposition also alienated many urbanites, particularly the residents of nationalized houses who might have nowhere to live if property were returned to the owners. In Transylvania, nationalists benefited too from concern that land, housing, and other property not go to the national minorities but to Romanians, who had suffered so much under Hungarian rule prior to 1918.

Aside from not having managed to create a program appealing to rural residents, the opposition was handicapped by the legacy of socialism's relative homogenization of the social field and its language of equality and unity. Despite people's widespread dissatisfaction with Party rule, some of the Party's moral claims have remained attractive. These include the idea that social solidarity is valuable and that it rests on a shared social condition, to which great differences in wealth are inimical. Many Romanians (to say nothing of others in the region) are deeply suspicious of the differentiation of social interests that is expected to accompany the growth of a democratic polity and market economy.[74] The PDSR's emphasis on egalitarianism plays directly to this feeling. Popular resistance to the possibility of social division has set limits, I believe, to the opposition's civil-society talk, compelling them to present civil society as a *unified* moral realm, separate from politics and the state—just as it was once the unified moral realm of opposition to the Party—rather than as a domain of multiple and competing interests integral to democratic politics.[75] Such an emphasis on unity makes their discourse more consonant not only with popular preferences for equality but also with discourses about the always-unitary "nation." Only if market-based differentiation advances the fortunes of enough Romanians to breed an interest in "pluralism" might the unity and homogenization evoked by the idea of "nation" begin to seem less attractive than symbols of other kinds.

This outcome is not what one might have predicted from the jubilation around ideas of Europe and civil society in December 1989, which suggested that these symbols would now overpower "nation." Given the extent to which Ceauşescu had overused the latter, it was a reasonable calculation that other symbols would have more force in post-Ceauşescu politics; newly empowered anti-Communists would have seen no risks, in 1990, to imitating the democratic and civil-society rhetoric of their analogues in Hungary and Czechoslovakia. As it happened, this calculation proved erroneous. The Romanian Communist Party, in alliance with some of the same nationalists who now support the PDSR, had substantially strengthened the already potent political symbol, "nation," increasing its capacity to structure fields of discourse. In making use of it in post-1989 struggles, the PDSR and their nationalist allies were wielding the most powerful weapon in the symbolic arsenal of Romanian politics.[76] Owing to its force and to continued disquiet over social differentiation, the more closely opposition groups approximate "nation" in elaborating their rhetoric, the greater will be their political success over at least the short to medium run. This would mean less talk of Europe, and a more distant relation with Hungarians—in short, less of what initially made the political opposition an admirable and novel force in Romanian politics, from a certain (North American) point of view.

In a discussion of intellectuals in India, Nicholas Dirks observes that the globalization of the discourses upon which Third World intellectuals draw has the effect of obscuring the conditions of production and the meanings of symbols at their points of origin.[77] Dirks's insight requires that any analysis of the intellectual politics pay special attention to both the local and the global aspects of the conditions of production through which symbols are "processed," as well as of the resources utilized in doing so. This chapter has shown that in 1990s Romanian political discourse, there is a tremendous discrepancy between the local and the global situations and resources of the main participants. The opposition has the more powerful international resources, congealed in their references to Europe and civil society. But within Romania, the "national Communists" monopolize both the institutional resources and the most potent political symbol, and their use of it puts their opponents on the defensive. Their pressure, which is also the pressure of a certain historically constituted discourse and of its master symbol, "nation," compels all other political actors in Romania to "nationalize" their political instruments—and in so doing, to strengthen "nation" as a political symbol even further. The pressure is felt not just at the level of discourse: it affects political strategy also, as my examples have shown. And it requires that for the opposition, "Europe" and the "civil society" it implies must mean first of all something *national*—a conception of Romania as a civilized, European country rather than a backwater of Slavdom. Only secondarily can it mean the forms and practices of a pluralist politics.

EPILOGUE, AUGUST 1997

In the four years since this essay was written, much has changed in Romanian politics—but much has also remained the same. The most significant change is that in the local elections of June 1996 the PDSR took an unexpected beating,[78] as candidates of the Democratic Convention and other opposition groups won the mayoralties of most of the largest cities (among them, despite a huge blitz of PDSR electioneering, the capital city, Bucharest). In the national elections five months later, the PDSR lost its parliamentary majority and the presidency as well. The CD had run on a plainly europeanizing, reformist platform, yet even rural voters—especially in Transylvania—had preferred them to the PDSR. Do these events not contradict my argument in this essay? I don't think so.

Perhaps the most important reason is that among people I interviewed (largely in Transylvania) in summer 1997, many of whom had supported the CD in 1996 in contrast to their vote in previous elections, very few had done so out of a decided preference for the CD platform: rather, they were sick of Iliescu, the PDSR, its rampant corruption scandals, and the economy's failure to improve noticeably. Person after person told me they had voted simply for change, and the CD seemed the group most likely to defeat the PDSR. A CD victory, then, did not mean a rise of public interest in the civic idea at the expense of the national one.

Second, the question of national symbols was by no means absent from the elections. The CD presented its alternative through the rhetoric of "Europe," claiming that closer relations with the West and acceptance of Western reform programs were crucial to Romania's "national interest." This time, however, their Europeanizing patriotism did not set them up as targets for the PDSR. We can see this most clearly through the campaign for Romania's membership in NATO. During 1995, President Iliescu had been persuaded to back that idea, the vociferous opposition of his nationalist allies notwithstanding, and he had taken the risk of signing a reconciliation treaty with Hungary (an essential precondition of NATO membership). This brought him closer to the electoral position of the CD and made it harder for him to defend Romanianness as independent of "Europe." At the eleventh hour, with polls showing him well behind CD presidential candidate Constantinescu, he pulled out all the stops and began decrying the "Hungarian menace" and voicing dire predictions about the fate of Transylvania if the "Magyarophile" CD should win. The blatant hypocrisy of this tactic, however, given the treaty he had recently signed, cost him, rather than winning him, votes. That he imagined he could win by this tactic shows that he considered the national symbol the ultimate certainty.

Third, the CD too had changed its tactics on relations with Hungarians. In the period before the November elections, the CD kept relatively more distance between itself and the Hungarian party (UDMR) (which had formally departed the CD a year before), leaving open until after the elections the question of whether it would form a coalition government that included the UDMR. Moreover, the UDMR leadership had passed from the "radicals" to its more moderate faction, which soft-pedaled the issue of Hungarian autonomy. When the November election results showed that the CD and its main coalition partner (the USD, a new grouping formed shortly before the elections from P. Roman's Democratic Party and the Social Democrats) needed the UDMR to secure a majority, the Hungarians were brought into the government with a ministerial portfolio. Soon, questions of Hungarian-language education were on the agenda; the new government said it must be receptive to Hungarian claims so as to obtain Romania's NATO membership. The manner in which the CD government ran its internal "campaign" for entry into NATO (part of which I witnessed) showed how much they viewed this sign of "Europe" as central to Romania's national identity. That is, the CD still found the symbol "nation" the surest grounds for presenting its goals. We might well expect that in the next elections, the CD's opponents will make even fuller use of its "treacherous" alliance with the Hungarians and its "antipatriotic" pro-Europeanness than they already have in their criticisms of the CD government.

NOTES

This paper was presented at the Ethnopolitics Colloquium, University of Michigan, and at the conference "The Intellectual Roots of European Identity," Harvard University (Michael Herzfeld, organizer), where it benefited from the reactions of the participants. Special thanks to Elizabeth Dunn for lengthy conversations that helped to clarify my argument and to Sorin Antohi, Michael Kennedy, Kirstie McClure, and Ron Suny, for helpful comment.

The paper was published as chapter 5 of my book *What Was Socialism, and What Comes Next?* (Princeton University Press, 1996), and is reprinted here by permission.

1. I mean this term to include the area between the Elbe River and the Urals—thus, European Russia, as well as the narrower Cold War meaning of the term.

2. See, for example, my *National Ideology under Socialism: Identity and Cultural Politics in Ceaușescu's Romania* (Berkeley and Los Angeles: University of California Press, 1991), chap. 1; Robert W. Seton-Watson, *The Historian as a Political Force in Central Europe* (London: School of Slavonic Studies, University of London, 1922); Zygmunt Bauman, "Intellectuals in East-Central Europe: Continuity and Change," *Eastern European Politics and Societies* 1 (1987): 162–86.

3. See my "Theorizing Socialism: A Prologue to the 'Transition,'" *American Ethnologist* 18 (1991): 426–28.

4. See George Konrád and Ivan Szelényi, *The Intellectuals on the Road to Class Power* (Brighton: Harvester Press, 1979), and other works by Szelényi.

5. See Verdery, *National Ideology under Socialism*, 15–19.

6. See further discussion in Verdery, *National Ideology under Socialism*, introduction.

7. The most obvious exception to this way of phrasing things is Hungary, where the defeat of the Party in the 1956 Soviet invasion paved the way for the rise of a counterelite defined in terms of technical competence—the architects of the New Economic Mechanism.

8. See, for example, the discussion in chapter 7 of my *National Ideology under Socialism.*

9. We can see clearly the lengths to which this attitude might go in an example after 1989, the convention of a newly forming opposition party in Romania: after many speakers had proclaimed the new party's high moral standing, someone raised a tiny complaint that the party could not *just* be moral, it must also have a program! (From the Civic Alliance Party's founding convention; see below.)

10. See, for example, Joanna Goven, "Gender Politics in Hungary: Autonomy and Antifeminism," in *Gender Politics and Post-Communism: Reflections from Eastern Europe and the Former Soviet Union,* ed. Nanette Funk and Magda Mueller (New York: Routledge, 1993), 225–26.

11. See the papers in Zbigniew Rau, *The Reemergence of Civil Society in Eastern Europe and the Soviet Union* (Boulder, Colo.: Westview, 1991), for illustration of these combinations.

12. See note 36 below.

13. In political discourse in some East European countries, after 1989 the symbol "civil society" began to float free of the "nation" with which it had sometimes been intertwined earlier, while in other cases building or invoking the one was seen as essential to the health of the other. The separability of the two notions may have been a direct function of the extent to which quasi-autonomous organizations had developed in a given country prior to 1989. (This is a modified form of an idea in László Bruszt and David Stark, "Remaking the Political Field in Hungary: From the Politics of Confrontation to the Politics of Competition," in *Eastern Europe in Revolution,* ed. Ivo Banac [Ithaca, N.Y.: Cornell University Press, 1992], 14–15.) I do not mean that everyone in Hungarian or Polish or Czech politics would now separate "civil society" from "nation" in contrast to Bulgarians and Romanians but, rather, that the *possibility* of separating them in effective political rhetoric became greater in the former countries than in the latter. Wałesa's not-so-covert anti-Semitism in his presidential campaign shows nonetheless how the two symbols could be combined even in the country where a pre-1989 "civil society" was most fully developed.

14. The most important of these are the Hungarians, who form about 7 percent of the population. Roma (Gypsies) comprise a significant (though smaller, and uncertain) percentage but are not politically well organized; the third most important minority, Germans, has declined in recent years to under one hundred thousand.

15. The name of the original FSN, or National Salvation Front, went to the faction of Petre Roman that split off from Iliescu's faction; the latter first called itself the *Democratic* National Salvation Front, subsequently becoming the Party of Romanian Social Democracy, while the Roman faction became the Democratic Party.

16. Among these were the "civil society" movements Civic Alliance and Group for Social Dialogue and the National Peasant, Civic Alliance, and National Liberal parties.

17. The most important of these were the Greater Romania Party (PRM) and Party of Romanian National Unity (PUNR).

18. See Verdery, *National Ideology under Socialism*, chaps. 4–7, for several examples.

19. See Verdery, *National Ideology under Socialism*, chaps. 1 and 3.

20. See Bruszt and Stark, "Remaking the Political Field," 16, where they suggest that the old elites in the later revolutions learned from the earlier ones how better to stay in power.

21. The report on her arraignment in the opposition paper *România liberă* used exactly the terms of my discussion here: "The power gathered in the hands of Ion Iliescu, the same person who, in December 1989, used the moral capital embodied by the dissident Doina Cornea to his own benefit, accuses her today of undermining the state power" (international English edition, February 12, 1993, 2).

22. I mean by this that a "nationalist" strategy preserves the state structures that members of the old *nomenclatura*—the social base of the PDSR, PUNR, and PRM—know how to profit from, whereas an "internationalist" strategy would swamp the country with foreign investors and techniques, destroying the advantage of the former Party apparatus.

23. For excellent illustration of this advantage, see Gail Kligman, "Reclaiming the Public: A Reflection on Recreating Civil Society in Romania," *East European Politics and Societies* 4 (1990): 393–438.

24. This is not a rare event. See, e.g., Anton Uncu, "Anything Wrong with the Voting Machine? It Works According to Programme," *România liberă* (international English edition), February 26, 1993, 7.

25. My sources for these examples are two newspapers central to the political opposition: the daily *România liberă*—I use its international weekly edition, referenced below as *România liberă (IEE)*—and the weekly *22*, put out by the Group for Social Dialogue.

26. Letter of Eugen Barbu and Corneliu Vadim Tudor to Prime Minister Petre Roman, March 2, 1990. Published in full in *22*, December 17–23, 1992, 7.

27. See Florin Iaru, "Extremist Vadim Tudor Claims Communism Trial for 'Anti-Romanian Activities,'" *România liberă*, November 20, 1993, 6.

28. Interview with Emil Constantinescu, summarized in *România liberă*, February 12, 1992, 4.

29. See Ilie Şerbănescu, "Acestea ne sînt interesele naţionale?" *22*, February 11–17, 1993, 5.

30. Tia Şerbănescu, "A reaparut 'Scînteia,'" *22*, February 11–17, 1993, 7.

31. Şerbănescu, "A reaparut 'Scînteia.' "

32. See *National Ideology under Socialism*, 1.

33. Vera Maria Neagu, "Iliescu Censures Roman Imperialism," *România liberă*, November 17, 1992, 11.

34. The social composition of this group was varied—at its maximal extent, it included a fair number of working-class people alongside its primarily urban white-collar base. In the Civic Alliance Party, most of the leaders were intellectuals—university professors, journalists, researchers, teachers, and a handful of others (a trade union leader, a peasant, etc.).

35. These three quotations come from speeches made at the Civic Alliance Party convention, July 5, 1991. All quotations are approximate, inasmuch as I did not tape-record the proceedings but kept only an extended handwritten record of what was said. Translations are my own.

36. Fellow anthropologist Gail Kligman and I witnessed several instances of this at meetings of the civil-society group Civic Alliance in 1991. I am very grateful to Gail Kligman for suggesting that we attend these events and for securing our permission to participate, as well as for many hours of stimulating reflection on what we saw. I wish also to thank the organizers of the Civic Alliance conference for allowing us to attend.

37. Stelian Tanase, speech to the Civic Alliance convention, July 7, 1991. See previous note.

38. The Romanian word is *reîntregire,* which means "making *whole* again." This is something more, it seems to me, than simple "reunification" (making *one* again), which might seem the more natural English translation. The issue of Moldova was fresh in people's minds because Romanian president Ion Iliescu had not long before signed with Gorbachev a treaty accepting the present borders between Romania and the Soviet Union; this treaty, regarded as a "betrayal of the nation" by many at the conference, guaranteed that at least over the short run, the government of Romania would not press for reintegration.

39. This episode was clear to Gail Kligman and me—though not for others present except the organizers, who knew the proposed agenda. The fight went on entirely backstage; our (particularly Gail's) friendships with some of the leaders enabled us to witness what would otherwise have been completely invisible.

40. The Convention polled 19 percent of the vote and the PUNR 18 percent.

41. "Masa rotundă la GDS: Ultimele luări de poziţie ale U.D.M.R. privitor la mínorităţi şi problema naţională," *22*, November 12–18, 1992, 8–11.

42. "Masa rotundă la GDS," 9.

43. This comment referred particularly to the Party of Romanian National Unity, which had expressed certain attitudes favorable to the Convention and was being explicitly courted by the latter, in hopes of breaking the Front's lock on power in parliament.

44. "Masa rotundă la GDS," 11.

45. "Masa rotundă la GDS," 9.

46. This concern of the Romanians is deeply lodged in Transylvania's his-

tory. For many centuries a part of the kingdom of Hungary, the region had a population that was well over half Romanian since at least the 1760s. Romanians struggled for over 150 years to gain civic rights in Hungary, finally succeeding when, in the wake of World War I, the region passed by plebiscite from the Hungarian to the Romanian state. During World War II, however, Hitler gave the northern part of Transylvania back to Hungary, an event many Romanians found personally traumatic. Most Romanians suspect Hungarians both in their country and in neighboring Hungary of incurable irredentism.

47. "Masa rotundă la GDS," 9–10.

48. I say "rationales" because it is quite possible that the principled argument for decentralization as a way to reduce the Front's power was an ex post facto argument from Hungarians who mainly wanted autonomy for their own reasons.

49. "Masa rotundă la GDS," 10.

50. Romania's population is approximately 90 percent Romanian.

51. The immediate response to the above comment was to bring in the example of the United States, where group rights (for Blacks, Asians, women, homosexuals, etc.) have gone so far that one is better off being a "minority"—clearly not an appealing prospect in Romania.

52. "Masa rotundă la GDS," 11.

53. "Masa rotundă la GDS," 9.

54. See my "Nationalism and National Sentiment in Post-Socialist Romania," *Slavic Review* 52 (1993): 179–203.

55. Ilie Neașcu, "Funar și Ardealul," *Europa,* January 18–25, 1993, 1, 3.

56. The writers of these lines also describe the faculty of the University of Cluj (which had put up a fierce resistance to the romanianizing initiatives of mayor Funar) as "judaized internationalist freemasons" aiming to make Cluj a "powerful center of Zionism" (although none of the persons their text names is Jewish). See Emil Ardeleanu, "Inima Transilvaniei, Cluj-Napoca, în vizorul francmasoneriei," *Europa,* January 18–25, 1993, 10.

57. Mircea M. Dabija, "Așa vă vrem, domnule președinte!" *Europa,* January 18–25, 1993, 3.

58. See, for example, report in *România liberă,* January 21, 1993, 11: "Mr. Tudor . . . also reiterated an appeal that a number of purportedly anti-Romanian organizations and publications should be banned"—thus underscoring the appeal quoted in my text. Tudor does not hesitate to use the weapon of expulsion even upon his near associates: a report in the *Romania liberă,* February 12, 1993, 11, reveals that he had expelled from his party a member of parliament who had criticized Tudor's dictatorial tendencies.

59. This quote from Tudor appears in an issue of the opposition paper *22,* February 4–10, 1993, 12; it is from his paper *Greater Romania,* but further details about the source are not given. Emphasis in original.

60. This message was perhaps a reply to an open letter published in *22* by Hungarian Péter Banyai. Banyai had complained that the Civic Alliance's failure to invite Hungarians to speak at its conference in Cluj, following the Cluj

Declaration, was having the effect of radicalizing the HDUR, delivering it into the hands of the populist nationalists who claimed that Hungarians could not count on the Romanian opposition for support. See Péter Banyai, "Scrisoare deschisă congresului Alianţei Civice," 22, December 17–23, 1992, 4. The publication locus of this letter guarantees that it was seen by the Civic Alliance and Convention leaders.

61. See Andrei Cornea, "UDMR—victoria moderaţilor," 22, January 21–27, 1993, 8–10.

62. The words of Greater Romania Party leader C. V. Tudor. Cited in Radu Calin Cristea, "Ruleta rusească," 22, February 4–10, 1993, 4.

63. Cristea, "Ruleta rusească."

64. Horaţiu Pepine, "Viclenie balcanică," 22, February 11–17, 1993, 3. See also Cristea, "Ruleta rusească."

65. Andrei Cornea, "Cine sînt 'aliaţii noştri'?" 22, February 4–10, 1993, 7.

66. Cristea, "Ruleta rusească."

67. Interview with Nicolae Manolescu, 22, February 11–17, 1993, 8–9.

68. Cristea, "Ruleta rusească."

69. See opinions from the nationalists' press cited in Cristea, "Ruleta rusească."

70. Oana Armeanu, "Vrea într-adevăr F.D.S.N. integrarea României în Europa?" 22, February 4–10, 1993, 5.

71. See Pavel Câmpeanu, "După alegeri," 22, November 19–25, 1992, 11. As Câmpeanu shows, the Convention's electorate was also considerably more male than female.

72. Cf. Ladislav Holy, "The End of Socialism in Czechoslovakia," in *Socialism: Ideals, Ideologies, and Local Practice*, ed. C. M. Hann (London: Routledge, 1993), 204–17.

73. See, for example, Gerald Creed, "Civil Society and the Spirit of Capitalism: A Bulgarian Critique," paper presented at the Annual Meeting of the American Anthropological Association, 1991; Christopher Hann, "Property Relations in the New Eastern Europe: The Case of Specialist Cooperatives in Hungary," in *The Curtain Rises: Rethinking Culture, Ideology, and the State in Eastern Europe*, ed. Hermine G. De Soto and David G. Anderson (Atlantic Highlands, N.J.: Humanities Press, 1993), 99–119; David Kideckel, "Peasants and Authority in the New Romania," in *Romania after Tyranny*, ed. Daniel Nelson (Boulder, Colo.: Westview, 1992), 67–83; Peter Skalník, "'Socialism Is Dead' and Very Much Alive in Slovakia: Political Inertia in a Tatra Village," in Hann, *Socialism*, 218–26.

74. See Creed, "Civil Society," who makes this argument for Bulgaria.

75. See Elizabeth Dunn, "Rethinking Civil Society," typescript, 1993, 7–9.

76. See the concluding chapter of Verdery, *National Ideology under Socialism*, for a discussion of how socialism fortified national ideology.

77. Nicholas Dirks, "Subaltern Intellectuals and Postcolonial Politics: India," paper presented at the Annual Meeting of the American Anthropological Association, 1992.

78. In Romania, separate elections are held for the mayoralties of cities and communes ("local" elections) and for parliament and the presidency. In 1996, the former took place in June, the latter in November.

How I Became Nationed
in Transylvania

The story of my "nationing" has two parts: (1) the interest I developed, as a graduate student, in the topic of ethnic identity, and (2) my traumatized reaction to Romanian criticisms of my first book. Both have to do, in different ways, with my being (like Michael Kennedy) relatively "nationless" in my upbringing and initial social consciousness.

From very early, I felt as if I not only had no particular ethnic affiliation (other than WASP), but even my identity as an American was not quite certain. My father, born in California and raised in New York, was several generations away from his French and English immigrant ancestors, so there was no doubt about him. My mother, on the other hand, was born of English and Irish colonials living in the then-British West Indies; she had come to school in the United States in the 1930s, eventually marrying and taking on American citizenship. Even so, she still pronounced some of her words in the English manner and contributed to my having no evident regional dialect in my speech. She also imparted to me some of her sense that England was superior to America. The tenuousness of my identification with the United States was enhanced when my family moved to a provincial town in western Maryland (I was eleven at the time), where many people regarded my mother as a "foreigner" and thus some kind of freak. For the next six years she, my brother, and I felt as if we didn't quite belong.

Such tales are absolutely standard in the biographies of anthropologists: a feeling of not quite belonging to one's home place induces curiosity about, receptiveness to, and greater comfort in places elsewhere. This, added to the proverbial nationlessness of my privileged white background on my father's side of the family, made me doubly unnationed. Was it for this reason that in graduate school I found myself suddenly transfixed by the title of a book my housemate was reading, Ethnic Groups and Boundaries? *Or was it because*

boundaries, separation, and identity were problems for me from early child-
hood and here was a way to get at them indirectly, by another route? Whatever
the reason, I became fascinated with the subject of ethnic identity, completing
my Ph.D. exams in it and making it a central theme of my dissertation, "Eth-
nic Stratification in the European Periphery." As I conceptualized it at this
point, ethnic identity had nothing to do with nationness but meant something
less than that, something more benign. This attitude was doubtless shaped by
the relative homogeneity of my neighborhood and school, then later reinforced
by the toothlessness of most U.S. social science usage of the "ethnic" concept in
the 1970s post-melting-pot age.

As it happened, my lacking both a strong ethnic identification and an
awareness of the passion such identifications can arouse led me straight to the
misstep that was to force my rectifying these two lacks. I had done my research
in Transylvania in a small community inhabited mostly by collective farmers
and factory workers, from whom I had learned something of earlier forms of
strife between Romanians and Hungarians, Romanians and Germans; but
even though I was aware that in the feudal period these groups were known as
nationes, I persisted in thinking of them as "ethnic groups." I had had rela-
tively little contact with those urban intellectuals who regard speaking for and
defending the Romanian nation as their very raison d'être. Thus, when I pref-
aced my first book (Transylvanian Villagers: Three Centuries of Political,
Economic, and Ethnic [sic!] Change) *with two jokes designed to show the*
temporal persistence of certain ethnic stereotypes, I had no idea how upsetting
these would be to many Romanian intellectuals, who read them as an insult to
the Romanian nation. (As I saw it, no group came off particularly well in these
jokes, and it was, after all, Romanians *who had told me one of them. So much*
for failing to realize what it means to belong to a nation whose identity
includes a fair amount of self-deprecation.)

The consequences of my naïveté—bred of having no nation to call my
own—were severe. Among them were lengthy quarrels with close Romanian
friends who felt betrayed, years of feeling mortified by my own insensitivity
and wondering whether I was simply a lousy ethnographer, attacks in the
Romanian press, and the installation of more or less permanent police surveil-
lance: it had now become clear to the authorities that if I could say such nasty
things about Romanians, I must be a Hungarian spy using my research cover
to gather intelligence for the Hungarian government and émigré community.
Strengthening this conclusion was my very name, suspiciously Hungarian in
its first-syllable accent and its -y ending (even top-notch Romanian philolo-

gists sail right past the first five letters that betray my French origins). To this day there are Romanians who are convinced I am a Hungarian and who regard my denials as a case of "methinks the lady doth protest too much." And even in 1996 the police still found me interesting.

I went, then, from having a weak Fr/Anglo non-ethnonational identity to being a "member" of the Hungarian nation, learning—often daily—what national passions mean when one is on the other side of the boundary. Whereas in the United States I am one of those largely invisible ethnics, in Romania I now acquired a stigmatized identity every time I said my name (or even opened my mouth, for native speakers of Romanian sometimes hear my pronunciation of their language as similar to the way Hungarians speak it). A few of my Romanian friends who were prepared to believe that I was not really Hungarian took it upon themselves—repeatedly—to make sure I understood what national sentiment means and why I had gotten into such trouble by not understanding it.

From this emerged my next project, on how Romanian intellectuals had developed a national discourse through which, in their politics and in their scholarly writing (often the same thing), they both produced and defended the Romanian nation. I needed to understand better the sources of the tremendous passion my two jokes had unleashed. A book (National Ideology under Socialism: Identity and Cultural Politics in Ceaușescu's Romania), *numerous articles, and twelve years later, I think I've begun to grasp the subject better. My "constructivist" analytical position, however, is no more to the liking of my Romanian interlocutors than were my ethnic jokes. Often, intellectuals in Romania want to recruit me to amplify their own voices on an international stage. For example, discussions about publishing a Romanian translation of my first book ground to a halt when the translation was made conditional on my adding a new section, in which I would affirm the Roman origins of Romanians and their priority of settlement in Transylvania. I refused, much to the annoyance of those intellectuals who had promoted the proposal thinking their national idea would thus gain the international support of a "neutral" voice; instead, they came to see me as an intellectual who disarticulates their nation even as they themselves strive to articulate it. Once again, my own national origins became suspect. Such experiences have forced me to realize that one cannot shed one's (supposed) national identity at will— something of a blow to my constructivist views!*

My developing a kind of nation-consciousness, then, was the direct result of my nationlessness, colliding with the hyperconscious national sense so prevalent in Eastern Europe. The story of my "nationing" is isomorphic with my intellectual autobiography, and this suggests how much more *powerful the Eastern European experience of nation must be for those born into it.*

Katherine Verdery

Michael D. Kennedy

The Labilities of Liberalism and Nationalism after Communism: Polish Businessmen in the Articulation of the Nation

Liberalism and nationalism have been juxtaposed as fundamental alternatives in defining post-Communism's course. Liberals are individualist, not collectivist. They should favor pluralism, tolerance, and the market economy. Nationalists are collectivist. They should favor statist if not dictatorial solutions to social conflict and economic issues. I think this admittedly simplified but too frequent opposition is a problematic point of departure for analysis. Instead of assuming ideological difference, I propose we reconsider the labilities of liberalism and nationalism.[1] I suggest we focus on the unstable relationship between liberalism and nationalism, as well as on the instability within these broad ideological formations. In this essay, I elaborate such a theory of ideological lability and develop that approach for studying East European liberals and Polish businessmen in the articulation of the nation.

I begin the essay by considering how lability is worked out of liberalism and nationalism. Analysts tend to stabilize these visions by focusing on the articulations of liberal collectivities and more collective nations by their principal spokespersons. This method implicitly reinforces the categorical distinctions between positions. Instead, I propose that we undertake an alternative method in which these labilities are more fully evident.

One of the most important starting points for this alternative method is to treat the articulation of liberalism as critically as post-Communist studies treat nationalism. Drawing on Jerzy Szacki's volume, I describe some of liberalism's instabilities in Polish practice. I turn next to the national formation of the post-Communist liberal subject. I consider the conditions under which the liberal spokesperson articulates the nation, and what formulations of the nation dominate that liberal elaboration.

Labilities are more apparent, however, when one switches from ideological enunciations to everyday life, to the presence of these ideological formations in practice.[2] This approach has certainly been common enough for social histories, but I believe that we should extend it to intellectuals themselves.[3] The everyday life of intellectuals should be as much an object of our analysis as their more public identities. Once we shift our gaze to everyday life, the distinction of intellectuals from nonintellectuals becomes more difficult to render, however. We are more likely, then, to identify other types of actors as intellectuals in function if not in nomenclature.

Businessmen are not traditionally defined as "intellectuals" in Eastern Europe or in the West.[4] I am not suggesting that Polish businessmen are intellectuals in any familiar sense of the term. Rather, intellectuals and the businessmen I analyze in this essay are a subset of a larger category of social actors called *prominenci.*[5] *Prominenci* are those who appear to play a disproportionate role in shaping public opinion, and as a consequence, the articulation of the nation. Polish intellectuals have played that role traditionally,[6] but in post-Communist times, they are "retiring from the stage."[7] With that exit, Polish businessmen become important new voices in the public sphere and in everyday life. Their "rational" and "sophisticated" business practices not only facilitate profit making and European multinational integration, but those practices are also innovative cultural products with public consequence. I suggest that they are transforming the meaning of the Polish nation by extending the principles associated with their business practice to the rearticulation of the nation.

The explicit innovativeness of articulation varies, however, and becomes more pronounced when liberalism's contradictions are more apparent and when the nation's ideological formations intersect with business practice or other putatively liberal spaces. Polish businessmen and women employed in multinational corporations are especially likely to find working conditions conducive to the articulation of a new kind of national liberalism. In this essay, I explore how a few Polish businessmen and women negotiate the contradictions between a necessary nationalism and an ideologically powerful liberalism and in the process generate a new ideological formation for Polish post-Communist capitalism.

In this essay, I do not demonstrate that businessmen have replaced intellectuals in Poland's public sphere. I also do not prove that Polish businessmen are at the center of a new national ideology with business at its core. My primary data—forty-four in-depth interviews with businessmen and women who are themselves involved in multinational business ventures—do not allow that kind of analysis. Instead, I draw upon those interviews to suggest *how* Polish businessmen are rearticulating the meaning of the nation. Before I turn to that more specific reformulation, I begin with an account of labilities.

The Labilities of Nationalism and Liberalism

Both liberalism and nationalism are typically studied in their more "fixed" ideological formations. Focusing on post-Communist Eastern Europe magnifies this tendency.

Analysts typically distinguish nationalisms with reference to its "type," pronounced by its adjective. They stabilize the elusive phenomenon by distinguishing among political and ethnic nationalisms, official and revolutionary nationalisms, or with other categorical differences.[8] This categorical reference begins beyond contexts and typically descends upon a particular set of rhetorics and practices. Official proclamations or symbolic texts, or their carriers—states or social movements—illustrate that nationalism's qualities. As nationalism becomes the new "threat," Western states and international organizations work with indigenous liberals to emphasize the opposition between liberalism and nationalism. Through this collaboration, nationalism is produced as a "dark, elemental, unpredictable force of primordial nature threatening the orderly calm of civilized life."[9] Thus, liberalism and nationalism become the main ideological contestants in the post-Communist world. Nationalisms also contest one another.

One people's nationalism evokes another, which in turn inspires others. Rogers Brubaker has proposed that we move away from comparisons based on dichotomous contests among nations or between a majority nation and its minorities. He suggests that we consider the intersection of nationalizing states, national minorities, and external national homelands as the triadic configuration generating struggles.

Brubaker recommends we study each position in terms of a "field" of activity, of "differentiated and competitive positions or stances." This rethinking encourages us to review contest within fields as much as between them.[10] I find this elaboration quite useful. It certainly invites a conception of nationalism's lability. However, Brubaker's execution pays little heed to the ways in which liberalism is implicated in nationalism or how that implication elevates its lability. This is especially evident in Brubaker's application to the Yugoslav War of Succession, in which he fails to consider how Slovenia's "liberalism" helps to explain the beginning of war.[11] Whatever the application, however, Brubaker's approach is certainly open to considering the mutual implication of liberalism and nationalism.

Liberalism tends to be treated differently than nationalism. Nationalism's ideologists purport to know the core of the nation. Liberalism's spokespersons typically contend that their core is procedural, not substantive. The activities of a plurality of people who accept common liberal rules for action usually define liberalism's core. In this sense, and only if all other things are equal, liberal ideology is closer to everyday life than is nationalism. Its substance is multiple, contradictory and variable. This may be one reason why so many East European intellectuals wound up counterposing "life against ideology" during late Communism. It is also one reason why they are less likely to see liberalism's own ideological power.[12]

In post-Communism, however, liberalism cannot be so fluid. Locked in ideological struggle with Communist rule and later with varieties of nationalism and socialism, liberals must make liberalism more fixed than its ideological project declares ideal. This is especially apparent when its promoters become rulers and attempt to make a liberal economy, if not polity and society. Not only must liberals define the rules of contest, but they also must obviously enter the terrain of other ideological formations. Beyond setting trade policies and forms of property, they must define the nation. They must declare who are citizens and who are not. They must declare the relationship between foreign interests and the national interest. They must establish who may own the land, and who may not. Liberalism, thus, becomes more fixed and stabilized as it enters a cultural fray and moves beyond its commonsensical foundations in developed capitalist societies. Nationalism and liberalism, especially when thus locked in cultural struggle, ought therefore to become more fixed. If we think of ideology as an

increasingly coherent and consistent culture, produced through contest, liberalism and nationalism become more ideological under post-
Communist conditions.[13] Nationalism and liberalism also become
more fixed ideological formations as intellectuals become more central
to the definition of their project.

Intellectuals are central to nationalism in two fundamental ways.
Firstly, nationalism frequently requires the intellectual to articulate
what the nation is because its empirical existence is not what it ought to
be. It may be "repressed" by foreign domination or "immature" due to
economic or social underdevelopment. Nevertheless, that empirical
existence is essential. Intellectuals depend on that ontology to claim the
right to articulate a position based on their own personal identity
embedded in a broader affinity with a larger collective identity.[14] Thus,
intellectuals struggle to fix the nation in their own ideology, reconciling
the expectation of the nation with its current condition.

Second, intellectuals are frequently treated as symbols of the
nation's existence. Intellectual historians and others who research and
write about intellectuals themselves can reproduce those very nationalist aspirations that motivate their subjects. They elaborate their subject's particular articulation of the nation and use that very intellectual
to represent the nation's meaning in social space. By telling individual
life stories of *prominenci* in familiar narrative forms, the labilities of the
nation are thus fixed. For example, we can know nationalism by taking
any particular nation's nationalist exemplar, in Poland perhaps Roman
Dmowski, and study his life and what he has written. One thus can
"know" nationalism by representing a nationalist's coherent life and
ideas. One can make that life even more coherent by emphasizing a
particular period of a person's life that fits with the ideological vision to
be reinforced. Ivan Franko's early years are ideal for those socialist
visionaries of Ukraine, while national democrats tend to focus on his
later years. Few focus on the times and conditions of his mortal illness,
for that contributes little to fixing the nation.

Liberalism, however, depends less on intellectuals. Liberalism
thrives as an invisible ideology, without spokespersons. It does not put
intellectuals in such a central position as nationalism does. Liberalism
may provide a smaller role for intellectuals because liberalism is less
collectivist than nationalism. Perhaps it is because one needs fewer liberal ideologues than nationalist ones because liberalism should be a
less particularist vision that needs only interpreters rather than legisla-

tors.[15] In post-Communist Eastern Europe, however, liberalism is said to oppose both nationalism and socialism. Liberal ideologues and spokespersons are thus necessary to elevate that ideological opposition. To focus on the texts of liberal intellectuals is thus as important as to focus on those of nationalists. At the same time, by focusing on these intellectuals, liberalism's labilities are also likely to be minimized.

Dissecting Liberalism

Nationalism has always been a significant object of inquiry in East European studies, but it has become newly important. In the wake of Communism's collapse and in lieu of terrorism, nationalism is the next threat. Many fewer analysts study liberalism as an ideological formation. Most intellectuals oriented toward the West see it as a virtue rather than a liability and an ally whose dissection could prove troubling. Is it not better to look at the threat that makes one's position superior than to consider whether the ideology grounding hope stands on clay feet?[16] Does one want to offer a critique of liberalism that might create a self-fulfilling prophecy, as some of my Polish sociological colleagues have cautioned me? Fortunately for us, Jerzy Szacki does not recoil from such serious inquiry, and I draw upon his work to offer the following portrait of liberalism's power and tensions.[17]

Many would see liberalism as Communism's legitimate successor. Liberalism most decisively departs from the principles of Communist rule, and at the same time, European liberalism has enjoyed a genuine renaissance through the mid-1990s. Communism's putative antithesis comes at the same time as it enjoys a global heyday. Liberalism's variety is more apparent than any particular essence, however, and the partiality of its success and influence is more apparent than its final victory. Nevertheless, certain tenets of liberalism are hegemonic in post-Communist Poland and the other East Central European countries, even among those former Communists who now call themselves Social Democrats. While liberal ideologues are likely to identify themselves as the true liberals, and others as "false,"[18] much of liberalism has become part of the more general ideological landscape of post-Communist Central Europe.

Szacki cautions that liberalism is not so secure as it appears, however. Post-Communist liberalism shares with other democratic market economies that tension between political and economic liberalism.[19] It also has special problems. For instance, liberals should favor a society in which the rights and responsibilities of individuals are paramount.[20] Such a doctrinaire liberalism seems rather inadequate to the task of rapid economic transformation in which quasi-Bolshevik methods of implementing economic change are widely appreciated among liberals. Finally, liberalism is not an integral element of national cultures in Eastern Europe. Although Polish historiography can place a strong emphasis on the liberal foundations of noblemen's democracy, Szacki is rather skeptical about liberalism's fit with the Polish nation. While it *does* look liberal in comparison to Russian traditions, it is quite different from contemporary emphases on the centrality of the individual and the importance of economic dimensions.[21] As an alternative, Szacki suggests we consider three types of Polish liberalism.

One should understand East European Communism's democratic opposition as *proto*liberal. It elevates civil society over individualism and subordinates the latter to various collectivist impulses from "society" writ large. Any community or social movement could be the empirical expression of this collectivity. This collective society was the agent of social transformation. Solidarity, empowered by workers and its allied intelligentsia, was the best example. Szacki argues that a more *integral* liberalism, one that goes beyond the justification of capitalism, is underdeveloped in Poland. Indeed, the articulation of views on culture and society has remained, among liberals, quite underdeveloped in comparison to their views on economy.[22]

Economic liberalism followed protoliberalism's development in Poland, emerging after the 1980–81 Solidarity movement. It rejected both Communism and the revolutionary means to fight it. This perspective wanted to de-emphasize politics and make economic change central. Before Communism's collapse, Mirosław Dzielski and others looked at the second economy as evidence for Communism's liberal alternative. Departing from Solidarity's vaunting of the working class, this view celebrated the entrepreneur and the middle class. Dzielski wrote, "The person who trades is the pillar of civilization, and in conditions of socialism also its heroic champion."[23] With its simultaneously realist and decentering approach to politics, Szacki identifies three key aspects to economic liberalism: "absolute primacy to the economic system. . . . accepting liberal or neoliberal views on the economy in their orthodox form . . . [and] recognizing these views not only as necessary but also as a sufficient condition of being a liberal."[24]

Although they focus on the economic, liberals also recognize that society itself must change. It is not sufficient to change property laws. Indeed, society must rid itself of economic traditionalism and socialist residues. Like the organic intellectuals in the end of the nineteenth century, today's liberals believe that society must learn that making money is good for the nation. It must learn that socialism is the enemy to the nation that must modernize.[25] Liberals developed this point of view before 1989, but when they took power, its cultural value soared. This societal critique legitimated their attempt to initiate radical systemic change regardless of popular wishes and regardless of liberalism's orthodox interpretation.

Systemic transformation required the rejection of liberal political action. One cannot change a system piecemeal. One could not introduce liberalism as a system with many ways of life. It had to acquire that holistic approach to change which was more characteristic of Communism and nationalism: that there is but one way to construct a system. This introduced, then, the basic contradiction of the post-Communist liberal project, within its own economic formation, as well in relation to its traditional bedfellow, democracy. It had to become, in the words of a former minister of privatization, a "pragmatic liberalism," one that uses the state to shorten the way to the market.[26]

At the same time, that state had to compromise with a society with a "Communist mentality" and preserve some of the welfare provisions that would make continued liberal politics possible.[27] Furthermore, because its social base is so small, pragmatic and democratic liberals (as opposed to pure and authoritarian ones) had to find ways of combining economic liberalism with other Polish values. Szacki has thus posed the right question: "Do the non-economic postulates of today's Polish liberals refer only to the necessity of rooting out the remnants of real socialism from all areas of life, or do they also call for transcending the traditional forms of Polish thinking and Polish life?" (173). This is where the labile relationship between liberalism and the nation emerges.

In most circumstances, liberalism and nationalism are posed as opposing principles. In all its varieties, nationalism's emphasis on the priority of the nation's collective rights overwhelms the individual rights emphasized in liberalism. Szacki argues that their common appearance at any moment is more a matter of historical conjuncture and common enemies than of ideological affinities (53–58). When Communism ceased to be the primary enemy, the allies made in anti-Communism—liberals and nationalists—were opponents again. Those who would emphasize Christian values as the primary concern of Polish politics can find in liberalism an enemy, one that undermines the truth of God's law with its claims to pluralism (177). Economic liberals do not necessarily respond in kind, and rather seek to reconcile Polish and Christian value systems with the new economic liberalism.[28]

Szacki's book, magisterial in its sweep and dedicated in its purpose, nonetheless articulates an implicit hope in the generation of a broader liberalism. He sees many barriers to this in Poland. Liberalism does not have a clear political ancestry in Poland. Polish identity has, with its stateless existence for 123 years, emphasized communitarian values and the centrality of Catholicism. Poland's relative homogeneity means that political tolerance does not appear so necessary as in a more explicitly diverse society. The majority understands its tolerance as benevolence.[29]

Both in his prescriptive conclusion and his historical argument, Szacki identifies both the contradictions of liberalism and its exclusions. It is about economic arguments, and it is difficult to extend its implications to politics and culture. Liberalism is not, after all, a good theory for radical political and cultural change. Too, the religious and the nationalists are hegemonic in the articulation of politics and culture in Poland. In short, the liberal *theory* of politics and culture might be difficult to make effective in post-Communist, and especially Polish, conditions. On the other hand, it is quite possible to see the effect of liberalism in culture as everyday life and in the articulation of national politics. In particular, one can focus on the formation of the liberal subject, and his implication in the nation.

The National Formation of the Post-Communist Liberal Subject

Szacki elaborates Polish liberalism's dilemmas by focusing on its macrocultural and macrosocial contradictions and their expressions in elite pronouncements and political and social conflicts. In this portrait, the clash of cultures and the compromises of elites produce the labilities of liberalism and nationalism. Szacki thus provides the necessary contextual foundation for those who would develop a sociology that focuses on the choices a subject makes among existing alternatives. Sza-cki does not, however, provide the foundation for considering the con-ditions that allow agents to alter the choices before them. In order for that approach to be developed, one must focus as much on the forma-tion of the subject as on that subject's possible choices.[30]

A theory of subject formation is especially important for under-standing the lability of ideological formations. Ideological lability is most apparent when actors reconfigure ideological formations in order to address particular goals. As Bill Sewell describes it, agency is appar-ent in "an actor's capacity to reinterpret and mobilize an array of resources in terms of cultural schemas other than those that initially constituted the array."[31] Sewell identifies five factors that might elevate the conditions of this agency.

1. *The multiplicity of structures:* any social unit is going to be com-posed of a variety of structures which are unlikely to be entirely homologous or in synchrony with one another; this variety of structures can lead to conflicting claims and social conflicts.

2. *The transposability of schemas:* actors are capable of taking schemas or rules learned in one context and applying them to another.

3. *The intersection of structures:* structures with different schemas and different resources overlap and interact in any given set-ting, making their smooth reproduction always potentially problematic given the contradictions that could emerge from their contact.

4. *Unpredictability of resource accumulation:* enactments of schemas can produce quite unforeseen outcomes, and those outcomes, if sufficiently altering the power relations in a given social unit, lead to a transformation of structure.

5. *The polysemy of resources:* the multiplicity of meaning potentially attached to any set of resources means that these resources can be interpreted in different ways, with various consequences for social transformation.

I find the first three factors especially useful for developing a theory of the national formation of the post-Communist liberal subject. One place to begin the empirical elaboration of that theory is with *Business and the Middle Classes,* edited by Jacek Kurczewski and Iwona Jakubowska-Branicka.[32]

This collection exemplifies sociological approaches to such a liberal subject. They focus, above all, on its articulation as a class actor, a middle class. In this particular collection, they find that the new capitalist middle classes ally with socialism's middle classes to construct values that support the development of market society. These middle classes apparently value individualism, private property, and the prestige of financial success more than others in the social structure. The nation, however, appears irrelevant.

There are some places, of course, where the nation does enter the discourse of liberalism. Iwona Krzesak finds that the Business Center Club,[33] arguably the leading business organization in Poland, demands that a member be an exemplary citizen. The club supports the vision of the democratic and competent state based on the rule of law. It expects the businessman to be well informed on political, social, and economic matters in the country. Businessmen, the BCC recommends, should help solve problems and help those weaker than themselves, using their superior organizational skills for the benefit of all.[34] Even in this direct engagement, however, the meaning of the nation remains underelaborated. The liberal's nation is a nation where the rule of law enables pragmatic, well-informed citizens to make intelligent choices. The nation, other than as a site of activity, virtually disappears. The individual subject reigns supreme. Businessmen, as liberalism's carrier, thus tend not to discuss the nation. Their social conditions normally discourage their explicit articulation of the nation. Nevertheless, their political spokespersons do find themselves in that space where the nation must be articulated.

Drawing on in-depth interviews with parliamentary elites, Elżbieta Skotnicka-Illasiewicz and Włodzimierz Wesołowski found Polish liberals from both the post-Communist party and post-Solidarity parties understanding Europe as a "configuration of civil societies."[35] They suggest that liberals view nations as pluralistic sites of interest formation among individuals and groups. Liberals thus tend not to elaborate the nation in ideological terms because *their own nation should not be peculiar.* By contrast, other Polish politicians see Europe as threatening on moral grounds. These deputies, typically from the Christian and Peasant parties, see Europe as a threat to Polish national identity. Europe is debauched, they claim, and Poland retains, or should retain, its traditional moral and spiritual values. These nationalists thus tend to construct nations as particular moral communities with common interests. In such a framework, the elaboration of national distinction becomes quite important. Indeed, it is much more important for the right wing than for the liberals.

Nevertheless, liberals take the schemas associated with liberalism and use them to reconceive the meaning of nations. As political elites negotiating Poland's relationship to Europe, they are obliged to engage the question more seriously than those domestic middle classes with relatively little obligation to define the nation. One might surmise that liberals will typically retreat from articulating the nation, given that the liberal point is to de-emphasize it. National political institutions are composed of a variety of structures in which national claims and liberal claims must intersect, however. Under these conditions, liberal political leaders, distinguished precisely by their claim to *national* leadership, must articulate their vision of the nation. The most liberal and cosmopolitan of actors must somehow define the nation, even as they promote larger regional and global association. For instance, Czech president Václav Havel recently recognized that very point:

> For the first time in the history of mankind, our civilization has become truly global, encompassing the entire world. Yet at the same time, perhaps because of its global character, it is marked by increasingly determined attempts made by various cultures and regions at preserving their distinctiveness.[36]

This need not mean, however, that this national distinction is a threat or barrier. Liberals are at work trying to redefine their own national mission in the context of various liberal integrative projects. According to Slovenia's Milan Kučan,[37] for instance,

> It is very important for us within the framework of European integration in the economic area to also prove capable of evaluating and intensifying our individuality in the area of culture, in the area of spiritual values, and in the area of spiritual forms. The views of the future can be verified only through continuously constructed dialogue.

In this move, Kučan transposes several familiar liberal schemas: (1) He separates the economic from the social and cultural, allowing the nation to develop in the cultural realm while liberalism proceeds apace in the economic; (2) he introduces a spirit of dialogue and compromise, one that presumes, like the contract, the ability for individually rational agents to come to mutually appealing agreements depending on a willingness to compromise and relatively egalitarian conditions of communication.

These articulations of the nation do not imply lability, however. They reflect the liberal and nationalist ideological conflict and the attempt by liberals to articulate a vision of the nation that is compatible with their economic priorities. To consider labilities, we should consider the transformations of visions and their associated practices.

The Labile Engagement of Liberalism and Nationalism

Liberals not only articulate the meaning of liberalism or their own vision of the nation. They also articulate the meaning of nationalism itself.

Nationalists and liberals have uneven access to the global media. Outside their relevant diasporas, nationalists are more poorly known than liberals and are typically mediated by others. For instance, we know that Istvan Csurka is a chauvinist right-wing Hungarian, but he is mostly described for us by others who analyze his threat.[38] By contrast, liberals are more likely to present themselves. György Konrad is a liberal, European Hungarian, and his works are regularly translated and used to illustrate the progressive hope in Eastern Europe.[39] To publish the nationalist in the global media risks endorsing that vision, something most global media will not risk. Hence, the very form in which liberalism and nationalism are presented in global media reinforces the general imagery of liberal definitions looking global, and nationalist ones remaining parochial. The liberal is familiar and unmediated. The nationalist must be explained. Vladimir Tismaneanu's work exemplifies this normative/analytical stance.

Tismaneanu writes a political history of East European transformations around the identification of hope. Hope lies in the virtues of civic culture and pluralism. During the transformations of 1989, he writes, "concepts like popular sovereignty, European consciousness, civil rights and many others reacquired full semantic justification."[40] In this sense, the East European transformations represent not only national liberation, but also the promise of a wider emancipatory hope. Nationalism, however, represents the danger. The new threat is ethnocracy.

Elsewhere, Tismaneanu identifies the basic crisis of post-Communist society to rest in the uncertainty, insecurity, fear, and helplessness characteristic of the change. Radical nationalism, he argues, provides the "myth" that offers "consolation, the bliss of community, a simple way to overcome feelings of humiliation and inferiority and a response to real or imaginary threats."[41] What is more, this is building on the political culture of intolerance and self-righteousness characteristic of Communism itself. It is used by old Communists to preserve their position, but builds upon the unresolved psychological and historical problems of each nation.

In these analytical/normative approaches to the nation, the analysis secures a place from which the nation is simultaneously understood and critiqued. The universal and/or global position afforded by the discourse of human rights or civil society allows the critique of any particular nationalist. Indeed, the general opposition between liberalism and nationalism can be secured by identifying the proper historical and social structural explanations for the particularly labeled nationalism now revived in Communism's wake. Implicit in this account, of course, is that there is an alternative.

Lability can rest not only in altering nationalism's meaning or transforming the meaning of the nation through liberal ideology. Lability also can rest in the transformation of the field in which nationalism is understood. By focusing our intellectual energies on explaining the deviant formation of nationalism, we imply that there ought to, if not could, be an alternative. To the extent that alternative remains unspoken, or embedded in more universalistic hopes of liberalism's virtue, nationalism, through globalization, becomes ever more deviant. And as we multiply adjectives to define the latest nationalist deviation, we embed that innovation in a tradition of nationalism rather than implicate it in liberalism itself. In short, I suggest that explanations of nationalism are problematic to the extent they focus primarily on nationalists themselves. Lability ought to make us more aware of how liberalism structures the explanation of nationalism, even when liberals are hardly evident in that nation.

Of course nationalists are not likely to allow the liberal vision to pass unmarked, but this varies by society. As Katherine Verdery emphasizes in this collection, liberalism in the Romanian context has a much more difficult time than liberalism in the Hungarian or Polish. To be "liberal" in the Romanian context risks not just association with being European, but also with being Hungarian. And to be overly sympathetic to Hungarian discourse might suggest that one sympathizes with that nation, in the Romanian nationalist discourse, which threatens Romanian territorial integrity most. Polish liberals, however, can claim that their westward gaze is simply recognizing a geopolitical choice that Poles must make.[42] Alliance with the West may be the best way to preserve their national independence before a potential Russian threat.

Regardless of nationalist dynamics, the liberal articulation of the nationalist threat and liberal alternative is more effective when it comes from within the nation. National liberals not only indicate the possibility of an indigenous liberalism, but they also provide an example of what it means to be liberal in that context. The liberal thus becomes embodied and signified as a living alternative to the nationalist threat, and the "opposition" between liberal and nationalist is preserved. By recognizing the particular rhetorical move underlying this opposition, however, lability becomes apparent. Without the national liberal in residence, liberalism could never transcend the claim that its opposition to nationalism is based on its own hidden nationalism.

National liberals are also developing their own form of nationalism, however. They are moving beyond the normal civil-society model of the nation that I described earlier. For political reasons, however, this meaning of the nation is better left underelaborated.

Liberals give primacy to the economic system. To the extent they also accept liberal or neoliberal views on the economy in their orthodox form they are also, of necessity, oriented toward a global economy. There is no alternative, in this framework, to reconstructing national economies in order to "fit" with the West. This is a position of liberals in either global or indigenous space.[43] In this very moment of articulation, however, liberals argue that the nation is inadequate, and that economic salvation rests without.[44] Thus, even those liberals who would prefer to avoid the multinational question are somehow implicated in a debate about the relative merits of the nation. And when it comes to economic questions, the nation typically does not fare well before liberals. One of the best illustrations of that can be found in the observations of Jan Krzysztof Bielecki, Poland's most liberal prime minister.[45]

Drawing on his own experience as a director of the consulting firm, Doradca, Bielecki emphasizes his pragmatic orientation. While Bielecki considers his party strongly rooted in a faith around certain ideals with a very Western grounding (especially from the point of view of Moscow),[46] it is based more on reason and common sense rather than ideology. He could develop a clear program, "with our own definition of privatization" (33), based on these ideals and common sense. In order to have this program, however, these ideals depend on a very clear ideology of what is healthy and normal in the world system, and what is aberrant. This liberal ideology allows liberals to look at their own society, their own national identity, with an extremely critical eye, enabling a kind of distance from Polishness itself. For instance, Bielecki says this of Polish culture,

> It is for sure difficult to be a boss in Poland. . . . Poles don't like bosses. In general, Poles don't do well in the position of being a boss, and in my opinion, it is even impossible. We are not a society that has a genetic, built-in formal discipline. . . . In Poland, it is not believed that success is a result of work, knowledge, and exceptional know-how, but a result of a dirty deal. (56, 81)

Bielecki also criticizes society in general for the corruption that he had to deal with as prime minister. For instance, he asks why so many bank cashiers did not concern themselves with these obviously suspicious checks in the famous Art-B scandal. He uses this as evidence of Poles' lack of responsibility, especially in comparison to what would happen in England (77).

Such a liberal critique of the Polish nation would be perfect fodder for nationalist countermobilization if it were mounted from London or New York alone. In this case, however, liberalism comes from within the Polish nation. In that moment, liberalism offers its rebuttal to nationalism. Liberal ideology enables Bielecki to step outside of his "Polishness" to administer the treatment that might cure his nation of its socialist malady.[47] At the same time, because he administered it, he could claim implicitly that he has transcended the problem. And because he is a Pole, the Polish nation, embodied in Bielecki, can become what it is not yet. This implicit liberal rebuttal to the nationalist charge therefore relies on the same nationalist lability identified earlier. The liberal intellectual must be of the nation to make the critique. Proof of that liberal's critique rests in the power of the national ideology, however. If one Pole can do it, all Poles might potentially make it. Liberalism thus enters the nation as an alternative nationalism that claims to be apart from nationalism. Liberalism gains its transformative power by becoming national. Its power also rests on its ability to transcend the national. This is lability.

These two engagements of liberalism and nationalism—the liberal critique of the actually existing nation and the liberal critique of the actually existing nationalist—are both national expressions. Without grounding *within* the nation, the liberal critique cannot escape the nationalist counters. Thus, liberalism must become national in order to become effective and must accept the national claim that national identity matters. Liberalism and nationalism might be distinguished by their relative emphasis on individualism and collectivism in *ideological* terms, but liberalism requires its own nationalism in order to be effective. The labilities of liberalism and nationalism remain, however, underdeveloped precisely because we remain grounded in the liberal *intellectual's* articulation of the nation.

Intellectuals and the Nation in Polish Business

Ideology, by its very contestable nature, is designed to be more packaged, more coherent on a manifest level. Ideological critique might find the labilities, as suggested above, but this is likely to be the work of intellectuals rather than ideologues. Labilities do not live only in deconstructionist lairs, however. Lability is more apparent in everyday life than in the study of elites or ideological expressions. It is more apparent because everyday life typically doesn't encourage the formulation of coherent packages of worldviews. Elites and masses have very different levels of coherence in their belief systems.[48] One might even question whether categories of actors ought to be transformed in the study of the everyday. Businessmen are not, after all, familiar intellectuals in the articulation of the nation.

They are not familiar first of all because they typically don't enunciate the nation. Indeed, as we have explored above, liberalism itself shies away from elaborating that nation because it has relatively little to say, in comparison to nationalists, and what it does have to say is not an elevation of that nation as it already exists. Given the importance, however, of the international qualities of economic reform, Polish business is deeply implicated in the nation's redefinition. Businessmen are also not familiar in this role of articulating nations because they are not typically regarded as intellectuals. Under post-Communist conditions, however, I believe they should be considered as potential intellectuals for two basic reasons.

First, on one empirical level, leading businessmen like to cultivate an image of intellectual accomplishment, a certain *Bildung*. For instance, *Gazeta Wyborcza* published a dictionary of Polish businessmen on May 12, 1993.[49] In this collection of 130 men and twenty women, 68 percent had higher education, and seventeen out of twenty women had this education (in comparison to 7 percent of the general population). Of those with higher education, 40 percent had degrees from the Technical University system and another 43 percent from the university or economic academy. In fact, Małgorzata Fuszara decides that this group might be labeled the "old-new" middle class because it is composed mostly of the intelligentsia who decide to become businessmen.[50] Of course many of the less prominent businessmen do not have such aspirations or credentials. I nevertheless find the businessmen's strategy quite important. They seek to elevate their prestige by *linking it* with the intelligentsia. In these terms of educational background and especially forms of representation, businessmen and women are not distant from traditional images of the intelligentsia.[51] At least businessmen and women are struggling to counteract the negative imagery their newfound profession might imply.

Secondly, businessmen are playing a role akin to what Gramsci described for organic intellectuals.[52] The Business Center Club,[53] for instance, expects its members to influence political and social matters in the country through their example and their argument. Indeed, we might also consider that in the construction of a market economy, the very site of critical intellectual activity in the articulation of the nation changes: away from the publication of texts and the postures of politicians,[54] toward the elaboration of economic activities that are more central to the nation's definition in a market economy.

Regardless of whether Polish businessmen in general, or the ones I consider below in particular, are intellectual, another point deserves to be made here. Lability is more likely to be apparent in the everyday implementation of ideological formations. We are more likely to find intersecting structures and contradictory expectations, and an agency to transpose rules learned in one context to others, in the space of action rather than enunciation. Because everyday life is less intent on preserving ideological integrity than it is in realizing ambitions through the use of ideologies, we are more likely to discover the conditions and ideas generating new ideological formations.

In 1993, 1994, and 1995 research assistants and I conducted interviews with Polish managers, business consultants and private entrepreneurs.[55] In initial research on this cultural encounter between Western business experts and Polish entrepreneurs, we argued that so-called technical assistance is far more than a transmission of expertise, and rather an attempt at profound cultural transformation in business practices. And while our experts might admire the courage of their entrepreneurial employers, or their "instinct" for their market, they found little in the business culture of Poland from which they could learn. They might learn about the evils of Communism or about Polish history, but they wouldn't learn any technique or insight that might even be remotely associated with what American business scholars and students seek when they go to Japan to learn a new approach to business. The only business they learned was a measure of organizational responsibility that the limited sophistication of their enterprise allowed them to assume.[56]

We asked Polish managers and entrepreneurs with whom these experts worked whether the Westerners were in fact mistaken. Wasn't there something Western consultants needed to learn about Polish business culture and/or style in order to advise more effectively? In every interview with top managers of Polish-owned firms, Poles emphasized negative things to me about indigenous capacities and praised certain dimensions of "global" culture. Liberalism clearly provided the cultural schema with which to assess the inadequacies of the Polish nation.

For example, most would agree that there were certain necessary concepts that Polish business simply did not have—cash flow and business plans were among the most commonly identified. Each of these concepts, of course, emphasized a different time frame—business plans indicating the long term, and cash flow the shorter term, day-to-day survival of the firm. But both were equally necessary to the survival of the firm. Businessmen also emphasized that it was absolutely important to change the culture of the Polish firm, to change attitudes toward work and, above all, to the client. One manager called this a "new philosophy" and specifically emphasized *dopieszczanie klienta,* to do more than the client expects, one of the key ingredients to success, and far more difficult to do than "changing the color of one's socks" (no. 131).[57] Indigenous business practices, even if quite ingenious, simply did not build the foundations for good legal business activity. As one person recalled,

> In the beginning, there was no tradition of normal, regular Polish private business. All the business in Poland was, how to say it, corrupt, not in the criminal way, but corrupt in the way that it was not run by profit but by central planning. And . . . private businesses, they had to play by the rules as imposed by the companies' partners, who were more interested in making good connections than making good products. (No. 127)

One of the most common strategies for a private firm was to work with these state companies, as one successful entrepreneur recalled his start.

> There was a big need for computers, but a state company couldn't buy these computers abroad. But the private person could buy them and then sell it for złotys to the state company and then exchange the złotys for dollars on the private market. It was not criminal, but it was not legal. It was great. (No. 134)

In this sense, private business was conducted in opposition to the state and its law. This legacy, recalls another businessman, is a problem. Socialist Poland therefore leaves Poles with no good national tradition of doing business.

> Up to '89, everything was controlled by the state . . . which was by definition against business. So one thing that is very new for us and is a problem is how quickly even as a society we can understand that some public activities, even business activities, . . . really can be assessed and can be judged in a social way, by public judgment. (No. 139)

By the time of the interview, however, this manager finds corruption rampant. He is disappointed with the degree to which the state has taken responsibility for the prosecution of that corruption. Society, thus, is being miseducated by corrupt capitalism. It fails to learn how to act legally and is instead encouraged to maintain the bad practices of the past. It is being encouraged to hide profits, to disrespect authority, and to disobey the law more generally. The liberal transformation, because the state is not strong enough, is making the nation sick.

The liberals resolve the problem, however, by indicting the patient, the society. Poles are not developing a healthy society because they fail to elaborate the proper liberal vision. For instance, one manager recalled with regret how his employees thought of him: as a fellow Pole, rather than as their manager of a multinational firm in a capitalist economy. He recalled the surprise of his employees when he announced that he was closing down one department of the firm. I asked him, with intentional naïveté, why they expected him to defend that department. He said,

> They felt that they, they knew me from the past time [when he was a director thirty years earlier]. That I was, let's say, a patriot of this company. [But] they badly understand what is local patriotism. For me local patriotism is to earn money, for those who want to work, and not to defend those groups and machines that are worthless from the technological point of view. They are good for a museum. They [the employees] are too sentimental. I am *not* sentimental anymore. (No. 952)

I suspect that if these interviews were conducted by Poles, we would have found more positive traits of Polish firms identified and emphasized. But these traits would have been identified in comparison to other Polish firms, minimizing the American comparison. My presence and emphasis on their contact with Western consultants accentuated the American comparison, which in turn undervalued the Polish experience. My presence is not unusual, however. Western know-how is part and parcel of post-Communist liberalism, especially in terms of business. If one examines the interviews and tracts of post-Communist liberalism's leading spokespersons,[58] the West almost always figures as a positive reference point, with the post-Communist country diagnosed as inadequate in some way. In this sense, liberalism in post-

Communist capitalism at most incorporates the entrepreneurial spirit of a select group of leading indigenous capitalists fused with the technical sophistication of a larger world business culture.[59] Indigenous business culture, the cultural soul of the post-Communist capitalist turn, is bankrupt.

We thus find in these interviews the same kind of nationalist liberalism that we found in the more elite statements discussed above. The challenge of liberalism is not just to value individual rights or private property, but to transform the collective identity of a nation, to make it into something that it is not. At the same time, however, these managers display a critique of liberalism that is less commonly found in more political forums. For these managers, liberalism's limitations can often be found in Western presumption. But these limitations are also more typically found where liberalism and nationalism clash: within the multinational firm among managers who have regular contact with West Europeans and Americans.

These managers consider themselves, properly, as relatively sophisticated, given their more or less extensive contact with Western business practices. They are not the "white-socked, corrupt Polish businessmen" who are the object of so much derision. All of them also expressed some distance from the West, however. There were several strategies for that distancing, but nearly all of them had one underlying comment—that the West is at best naive, often insensitive, and frequently arrogant if not downright colonial in its attitude.

The most westernized indigenous manager I have interviewed was a marketing manager in a joint venture. There was nothing intrinsically wrong, she said, with the firm's culture of doing business in Eastern Europe. The company has its own culture that cuts across national boundaries, and the only thing wrong was that sometimes Westerners were too arrogant, talking behind people's backs, snickering at East Europeans as if they were dumb. This, she thought, was a great failing; Westerners should always demonstrate their faith that people can learn (no. 957). Another manager recalled a similar event:

> We employed a Dutch company to develop a management information system for us. . . . After a couple of weeks, they took seven top people from the company for a day, which was really a sacrifice on our part. And we went to a meeting, and they were explaining to us why it is important to have a good management informa-

tion system installed in the company. They were rewording what we told them already, showing us diagrams like input/output or people/other resources/output . . . like they were showing, oh, I don't know, undergraduates or something. . . . The consultants were predisposed . . . that we were dumb, stupid, and incompetent people. (No. 127)

While this kind of consultant arrogance might exist also in the West, in Eastern Europe it is seen to be more than an occupational hazard. It is inevitably implicated in a question of the nation and its membership in a larger global culture of business accomplishment.

Sometimes this arrogance goes beyond insensitivity and produces more than resentment, a hostility, among managers. Another manager recalled a story where the parent company demanded that this manager use his connections to fix standards for the import of some factors of production.

Deliveries to Poland are completely signed that the product has to be delivered according to the Polish rules, Polish standard. And they expect that because I am a previous president [of the regulatory agency], I can have everything [done] like that [as he rubs his hands against each other, like "chip, chop"] So I told them, "Why didn't you sign the contract according to the official standard? I am not responsible for your relation with that agency!" [They tell me,] "Oh well, you have to arrange it somehow." How can I arrange it? How? There are rules, standards. [They say,] "Arrange the meeting with them." Well, I arrange for the dinner with the president of the commission. "You know him! Go ahead, arrange it with him!" You know American officials? You know how to fight for visa in the States? Well it's the same way with the Polish authorities. Apply, for example, valid documentation. Write a letter, attach the documentation, and wait for the approval. How can I arrange it? It's not Bangladesh or any other country in which you can go [slaps the table, as if slapping down a bribe] give the envelope and arrange it. Maybe some envelope maybe would be helpful, but it is impossible to arrange these things without following proper procedures. I told them, I can maybe, *maybe* I can accelerate something. But it is impossible to avoid the necessary actions. They [the multinational managers] don't understand it. It's a colonial attitude. They suppose that they are in the wild countries, in which all the administration is corrupted totally and in which I have friends everywhere and I can arrange it in a way they don't want to, to think about. It makes me crazy sometimes. (No. 952)

This arrogance is not only unseemly, but many East Europeans find that the parent company's arrogance and condescension actually leads them to poor business decisions. Sometimes their point is right out of a business textbook, in a passage familiar to anyone enjoined to "know your customer":

There are many potential marketing possibilities using Polish traditions, using the Polish mentality, using Polish culture, so if you know Polish conditions you can profit, you can really adapt to the needs of the people. . . . The needs cannot be the same because you [speaking to Kennedy] have a quite different experience, quite different history of your own country, so the needs may be the same, but absolutely maybe not. (No. 139)

Sometimes, however, it goes beyond knowing the desires of your customer today, beyond knowing what a focus group or marketing survey might yield. Sometimes it reflects directly on the past, as one manager discussed "employee of the month" awards:

They come up with ideas. They're happy to receive money, this reward. But when you want to put their name and their picture on the board and say, This guy really did something, no. Because it continues to be perceived as something negative, really. Because you are cooperating with authority. Cooperation with authority is not good by definition. Because it's been—and it's not only the Communist system, it's also the history of Poland—you know, when it was partitioned for two hundred years. To defy authority, to fight authority was a good patriotic deed. So now if you, all of a sudden, are recognized by authority, it means—well, who are you? Which side are you on? Even though we try to communicate and explain [that] it's pretty good for all of us. They are very skeptical toward it. In fact if you—I was just amazed myself—when you try to . . . take corporate creeds or mission statements in English, and they make perfect sense, they're sincere and all this, you translate into Polish, it sounds *terrible.* It sounds almost 100 percent like Communist propaganda. (No. 955)

The pragmatic profit-making spirit, at the heart of economic liberalism, thus can critique the global cultural dispositions on which it arrives. At the same time, managers can ingeniously elevate the indigenous culture and link it to liberalism to produce a new Polish nation. They are manufacturing a new Polish nation in which *some* popular sympathies can be sutured to the new nation, while others must be discarded. The fundamental principle of this new liberal nation is that *knowing the nation* is fundamental to good business practice as much as knowing liberalism. And part of knowing the nation involves respecting it as a place filled with people who are capable of learning.

This cultural emphasis is not incompatible with the earlier liberal articulation of the nation as a pluralistic site of law-abiding interest formation. It does, however, incorporate a measure of cultural pride and value of cultural knowledge that the other did not make explicit. This valuation comes, in fact, within liberalism's multinational conditions. It also can be the foundation for more aggressive turns in the nation's articulation. The Polish businessperson might even define himself or herself as part of the national mission: defending the nation's economic interests within liberalism while transforming the society so that the nation can survive. In fact, Poles might even aspire to become the site out of which a more global post-Communist liberalism might be defined.

Managers sometimes identified divergent interests between the parent firm and the indigenous company. One manager spoke of how a company purchased a firm in order to milk it dry (no. 955), and another spoke of how the multinational sought to undermine their capacity to be manufacturers and exporters of finished goods and turn them into suppliers of unfinished manufacturing goods (no. 952).

These critiques of Western practices were not critical of the liberal project itself. Instead, they were critical of the inadequacies of Westerners in a strange land, and in praise of local knowledge. In this fashion, these indigenous managers could embrace the liberalism of economic transformation, urge the adaptation of Western models in Polish reality, and distance the Westerner him- or herself as inadequate to the task of transformation. In this sense, the presence of the Westerner in Polish post-Communist capitalism indicates the inadequacy of the nation, but a temporary inadequacy, one that could be transcended by the creation of a new class of national heroes. The Polish manager is the one, by embodying both the capitalist expertise and knowledge of East European everyday life, that can transform these economies and societies. And at the same time, they can defend Polish business when need be from being ravaged by multinationals, but *not* at the expense of protecting outdated equipment, procedures, or practices. In this sense, they are better than nationalists or socialists, for they have the expertise to protect the nation's economy. But while they protect the nation's economy, they also are obliged to transform the nation.

> Poles still believe that the world owes them something. That Poland is still an important European country, because it was one of the main casualties of World War II, for example. Nobody gives a damn now in the West what happened during the Second World War, and whether Poland was important or not. Poles still think a lot about national boundaries, national states. It's very important for them. It's such a shock to learn that people really travel freely, and that the West is really becoming international. . . . Poland is kind of a nineteenth-century nationalist dream, probably the only one in Europe that has, for all practical purposes, no minorities. . . . Also, I think in this whole business thing, that economies are motivated to run by profit motives. It's a shock. In a way, lots of Polish attitudes, especially in the countryside, are kind of pre-industrialized-world attitudes. Some of them are nice and are not detrimental to progress . . . but some are. . . . Most Poles believe that the most important part is becoming agriculture. They can't understand that Poles might be better off just buying subsidized food from Western Europe. (No. 127)

Even as they transform their nation, Polish businessmen recognize that they have a special identity that they can present in the international field. Poles have long cast themselves as somehow between East and West;[60] now they can claim the same crossroads identity as transmitters of capitalist know-how, understanding better than Westerners the pathological past, but at the same time understanding better than those to their east how to make Western know-how applicable.

One manager recalled how they began working with lawyers from the West in Belarus. One of the experts advised that it was unnecessary to privatize agriculture because it was already private, believing, after all, that *kolkhozy* were private because they were co-ops. Americans, he said, often come in with theoretical knowledge about how supply and demand will solve problems, but East Europeans will rarely believe them. For instance, when shops are privatized, East Europeans believe that only vodka and cigarettes will be sold. But the Polish consultant can convince Eastern neighbors by appealing to the Polish experience and how it really worked (no. 131).

Thus, in a global comparison, East Central European identities can acquire this positive reference in post-Communist capitalism, but only within the post-Communist imagined community. When engaging the Westerner on "European" territory, post-Communist liberalism cannot elevate the Pole or Czech or Hungarian over the European. But when engaging that European on post-Communist space, by understanding the pathology of the nation that endured Communism, the post-Communist liberal can be more effective in its transformation.

In sum, one can find in elite liberal enunciations a clear articulation of the nation. They emphasize that the nation should be normal, not peculiar; it should be like the West.[61] At the same time, underelaborated but pronounced, the nation must be transformed, ridden of its socialist maladies and inappropriate traditionalisms. Polish businessmen share these ideas, but they also go beyond them. They are prepared to assume the new role of national hero. Their rational and sophisticated business practices might enable the nation's salvation, by being able to develop indigenous business competence. They can develop the real patriotism, one that knows how to make money for Poles. They will be in the position to distinguish between good investments and bad investments from abroad. And even more, they might occupy a position that elevates Poland once again to that crossroads identity between East and West, except this time as the interpreter for post-Communist conditions of global liberal visions.

Post-Communist Businessmen Articulating the Nation

The businessmen whose interviews I have recalled here were not intellectuals, in the classical sense. Some of them were once in that position, as teachers in the university, artists, or professionals in other trades. They all certainly had higher education and a breadth of cultivation, *Bildung*, that made them wonderful partners in conversations about intellectual matters far beyond the province of business. But now, their "job" is something quite different.

Now they are challenged by the new intellectual opportunity—taking a global business culture whose stock of knowledge is consequential for developing a firm, and "translating" it into a suitably indigenous practice appropriate to Polish business. While that certainly does not seem to be about articulating the nation, through their practice and example they are also instructing the nation about how they should see themselves. Sometimes it is quite explicit: as one editor put it to me, the mission of his publication was to teach how to look at the world through the lens of money, by highlighting things useful in a market economy, from how a high-flying senator cheated the treasury out of taxes to what elements need to be in a building lease contract in order to be safe in Polish law (no. 125). But it is certainly the case that the nation is not the primary ideological commitment of businessmen.

Unlike intellectual historians of the nation or public intellectuals articulating liberal or illiberal versions of the nation, or even most liberal nationalists, businessmen do not, explicitly, seek to redefine the nation. They certainly have their opinions, as they are Polish citizens, but their job is not to articulate them on the pages of their publications or in advertising for their products. They are not useful, then, for illustrating the alternative types of nationalisms that exist. Through the effect of their practices and their own articulations in everyday life of what the nation is and what it must be, however, they are certainly as influential if not more influential than those who focus on the nation per se. Their effects carry the discursive power of necessity—if economics is the primary basis for identity—and of invisibility—if they speak only practically and not ideologically.

In their view, the Polish nation before the requisites of business is inadequate. It must be transformed by Western business practices. At the same time, Western business practitioners are inadequate before the Polish nation, but not because their general vision is hostile or their general methods inappropriate. They are inadequate only because they don't understand the pathology of what it was to be Polish for the last forty years. Positioning themselves in this fashion, post-Communist businessmen can redefine the nation—dissect it to define its pathology, but at the same time, preserve it by demonstrating that they, as Poles, can do what their critique suggests they must. But this is a different kind of nationalism.

This nationalism does not elevate the nation as superior. Indeed, its superiority only rests in its claim to be able to transcend its past, and to become something it claims as its national right: to be European. Its claim to superiority rests only in recognizing its pathology. But for those in East Central Europe, access to the pathology that was Communism allows them to embrace a kind of superiority that those further to the east do not: they can return to the national identity as bridge between West and East, between the future and the past. And with that, the nation can become superior, only because of the tragedy it had to endure and now moves beyond. Nationalists don't like it, and liberals hardly talk about it, but liberalism, in the hands of Polish businessmen, becomes nationalism. It manages this best, of course, by avoiding the label. Lability.

NOTES

I wish to thank Ron Suny and the volume's anonymous reviewers for their comments on this essay. I also wish to thank the William Davidson Institute and the Center for International Business Education at the University of Michigan for their financial support of the data collection that has enabled this essay.

1. I am building on Nicolae Harsanyi and Michael D. Kennedy, "Between Utopia and Dystopia: The Labilities of Nationalism in Eastern Europe," in *Envisioning Eastern Europe: Postcommunist Cultural Studies*, ed. Kennedy (Ann Arbor: University of Michigan Press, 1994). Niki should be credited with finding the term *lability*, which consolidated and furthered our theoretical work on nationalism in Poland, Hungary, Ukraine, and Romania in that essay.

2. Many of my colleagues have tried to impress on me the significance of everyday life for social analysis, but it was Margaret Foley, Rebecca Friedman, and Naomi Galtz's "Private Life in Russia" conference at the University of Michigan in October 1996 that finally made the mutual importance of everyday life and studies of intellectuals obvious to me. For one important theoretical perspective, see Alf Ludtke, *The History of Everyday Life* (Princeton, N.J.: Princeton University Press, 1993).

3. Geoff Eley, "Intellectuals and the Labor Movement," in *Intellectuals and Public Life: Between Radicalism and Reform*, ed. Leon Fink, Stephen T. Leonard, and Donald M. Reid (Ithaca, N.Y.: Cornell University Press, 1996), 74–96.

4. I use the term *businessmen* to reflect the Polish term *biznesmeny*, as well as to signify the process of masculinization in the elaboration of business and

capitalism in post-Communist Eastern Europe. See for example Peggy Watson, "The Rise of Masculinism in Eastern Europe," *New Left Review* 198 (1993): 71–82.

5. In some ways, this term resembles that classic term of American political science, *influentials*. In *Public Opinion and American Democracy* (New York: Knopf, 1961), 557–58, V. O. Key used the term to describe opinion leaders and activists who disproportionately influence public opinion. I find the connotation of the "prominent" more appealing, however, because it puts the proper emphasis on the *appearance* of influence rather than its actual exercise, as Key's term suggests. Although I first encountered its use in Polish, Janet Hart tells me that *prominenci* has a proper Italian linguistic genealogy. I introduced this term in the context of another project collecting the oral histories of *prominenci* in Estonia, Ukraine, and Uzbekistan (see <http://www.umich.edu/~iinet/crees/fsugrant>).

6. For my previous engagements with intellectuals and intelligentsia as such, see "The Intelligentsia in the Constitution of Civil Societies and Post-Communist Regimes in Hungary and Poland," *Theory and Society* 21, no. 1 (1992): 29–76, "Eastern Europe's Lessons for Critical Intellectuals," in *Intellectuals and Politics: Social Theory in a Changing World*, ed. Charles Lemert (Boulder, Colo.: Sage, 1991), 94–112, and "The Constitution of Critical Intellectuals: Polish Physicians, Peace Activists, and Democratic Civil Society," *Studies in Comparative Communism* 23, nos. 3–4 (1990): 281–304.

7. Joanna Kurczewska, "The Polish Intelligentsia: Retiring from the Stage," in *Democracy, Civil Society, and Pluralism*, ed. Christopher G. A. Bryant and Edmund Mokrzycki (Warsaw: IFiS, 1995), 239–54.

8. For recent reviews, see Geoff Eley and Ronald Grigor Suny, "Introduction: From the Moment of Social History to the Work of Cultural Representation," in *Becoming National: A Reader* (Princeton, N.J.: Princeton University Press, 1996); John A. Hall, "Nationalisms, Classified and Explained," in *Notions of Nationalism*, ed. Sukumar Periwal (Budapest: Central European University Press, 1995), 8–33; Michael D. Kennedy, "What Is the Nation after Communism and Modernity?" *Polish Sociological Review* 105, no. 1 (1994): 47–58.

9. Partha Chatterjee, *The Nation and Its Fragments* (Princeton, N.J.: Princeton University Press, 1993), 4.

10. Rogers Brubaker, *Nationalism Reframed: Nationhood and the National Question in the New Europe* (Cambridge: Cambridge University Press, 1996), 61.

11. For an important demonstration for why omitting liberalism from an explanation of nationalism is problematic, see Susan Woodward, *Balkan Tragedy: Chaos and Dissolution after the Cold War* (Washington, D.C.: Brookings Institution, 1995).

12. See for example Adam Michnik, "The Literary Impact of the American and French Revolutions," *Partisan Review* 59, no. 4 (1992): 621–27. For commentary on this, see Michael D. Kennedy, "An Introduction to Ideology and Identity in Transformation," in Kennedy, *Envisioning Eastern Europe.*

13. Ann Swidler, "Culture in Action: Symbols and Strategies," *American Sociological Review* 51 (1986): 273–86.

14. Homi Bhabha, "DissemiNation: Time, Narrative, and the Margins of the Modern Nation," in *Nation and Narration* (London: Routledge, 1990), 302, 297.

15. Zygmunt Bauman, *Legislators and Interpreters* (Ithaca, N.Y.: Cornell University Press, 1992).

16. Echoing here Slavoj Žižek's ideas about the mirrorlike motive for the enthusiasm over Communism's end. See *Tarrying with the Negative* (Durham, N.C.: Duke University Press, 1993), 200.

17. Jerzy Szacki, *Liberalism after Communism* (Budapest: Central European Press, 1995).

18. Vaclav Klaus and Tomas Jezek, "False Liberalism and Recent Changes in Czechoslovakia," *East European Politics and Societies* 5, no. 1 (1991): 38.

19. Szacki, *Liberalism after Communism*, 31.

20. Szacki, *Liberalism after Communism*, 43–72.

21. Szacki, *Liberalism after Communism*, 173.

22. Szacki, *Liberalism after Communism*, 173.

23. M. Dzielski, "Szefczyk Dratewka ma pomysl," *Duch nadchodzącego Czasu* (Warsaw: Wektory, 1989), 206, cited in Szacki, *Liberalism after Communism*, 131.

24. Szacki, *Liberalism after Communism*, 137–38.

25. Szacki, *Liberalism after Communism*, 143–44.

26. "Liberalizm praktyczy." Danuta Zagrodzka interviews Janusz Lewandowski, Chairman of the Liberal-Democratic Congress and Minister of Ownership Changes, in *Gazeta Wyborcza* 13 April 1991, cited in Szacki, *Liberalism after Communism*, 158.

27. Szacki, *Liberalism after Communism*, 158–59.

28. Szacki finds three basic orientations toward the nation: (1) Christian liberalism, which tended to avoid the basic conflicts between value systems and to believe on that basis that a harmony of beliefs was possible; (2) conservative liberalism, which found basic conflicts, but maintained that cultural matters could be left to religion, and economic and political matters left to liberalism; and (3) that tendency which believes a new civilization is necessary. As one of its main spokesmen, Janusz Lewandowski, asserted, "Only part of the national heritage could enter the new capitalist synthesis. The more sudden the changes of structures, the faster the progress of the market, the more dynamic the adjustment processes have to be and the less room there is for conservatism." See "Czy i jaka centraprawica?" *Przegląd Polityczny* 3 (1992): 16, cited in Szacki, *Liberalism after Communism*, 185. This position does not necessarily mean an attack on the Church. Many, even those in the left liberal tradition, found their own personal reconciliation with the Church, but could nonetheless not resolve those ideological tensions between political liberalism and its view of a many sided truth versus a religious conception of absolute truth, and an economic liberalism that vaunted the market over moral questions of distributive justice. See *Liberalism after Communism*, 192–93.

29. Szacki, *Liberalism after Communism*, 203–4.

30. See William H. Sewell Jr.'s critique of rational-choice theory in "Theory

of Action, Dialectic, and History," *American Journal of Sociology* 93 (1987): 166–71, for one reason why such a focus on subject formation is generally important.

31. See William H. Sewell Jr., "A Theory of Structure: Duality, Agency, and Transformation," *American Journal of Sociology* 98 (1992): 20.

32. Jacek Kurczewski and Iwona Jakubowska-Branicka, eds., *Biznes i Klasy Średnie* (Warsaw: Zakład Socjologii Obyczajów i Prawa, Institut Stosowanych Nauk Społecznych, Uniwersytet Warszawski, 1994).

33. Iwona Krzesak, "Etnografia Business Centre Club," in Kurczewski and Jakubowska-Branicka, *Biznes i Klasy Średnie*, 37–61. See also Pauline Gianoplus's Ph.D. dissertation, "The Business of Identities: Remaking the Polish Bourgeoisie, University of Michigan," 1999.

34. Krzesak, "Etnografia Business Centre Club," 48.

35. Elżbieta Skotnicka-Illasiewicz and Włodzimierz Wesołowski, "The Significance of Preconceptions: Europe of Civil Societies and Europe of Nationalities," in Periwal, *Notions of Nationalism*, 210.

36. Václav Havel, "New Definition—North Atlantic Treaty Unchanged," *Polityka*, June 22, 1996, 13, in FBIS EEU 96 121, June 21, 1996, 6.

37. Milan Kučan, president of Slovenia, and Václav Havel, president of the Czech Republic, "A President Is Primarily a Citizen," interview by Adam Cerny and Martin Ehl, *Prague Tyden*, June 3, 1996, 35, FBIS EEU 96–125, June 27, 1996, 6.

38. For a translation of some of his program, see Harsanyi and Kennedy, "Between Utopia and Dystopia," 164–65.

39. György Konrad, "What Is a Hungarian?" in *The Melancholy of Rebirth: Essays from Postcommunist Central Europe*, trans. Michael Henry Heim (San Diego: Harcourt Brace Jovanovich, 1995), 67–68.

40. Vladimir Tismaneanu, *Reinventing Politics: Eastern Europe from Stalin to Havel* (New York: Free Press, 1992), 285.

41. Vladimir Tismaneanu, "Fantasies of Salvation: Varieties of Nationalism in Postcommunist Eastern Europe," in Kennedy, *Envisioning Eastern Europe*, 104.

42. Skotnicka-Illasiewicz and Wesołowski, "The Significance of Preconceptions," indicate that liberal parliamentarians make this geopolitical point explicitly.

43. Jeffrey Sachs, *Poland's Jump to the Market Economy* (Cambridge, Mass.: MIT Press, 1993), 5; Leszek Balcerowicz, "Gdyby nie Gorbaczow," interview, in *My* ("We," or better rendered in English, "Us"), ed. Teresa Toraska (Warsaw: Oficyna Wydawnicza MOST, 1994), 5–29.

44. Of course this national dependency is manifestly important for smaller nations. As one of the parliamentary elites interviewed by Skotnicka-Illiasiewicz and Wesołowski emphasized, it is a matter of choosing which ally one wants, and which will preserve one's nation best.

45. I use Bielecki's interview with Teresa Torańska, "W świecie poswyższonej schizofrenii," in Torańska, *My*, 30–87, for one text to illustrate

this point. This is a particularly useful text for such an illustration, as it follows Torańska's earlier publication, *Oni* ("Them"), in which she interviewed Communists.

46. Bielecki, interview, in Torańska, *My*, 39, 42.

47. Of course there is ample Polish precedent for such critical takes on Polishness, and thus one need not go to liberalism for this disposition. Witold Gombrowicz, one of Poland's most celebrated writers, eloquently critiqued many expressions of Polish national identity. For example, see Witold Gombrowicz, *Trans-Atlantyk,* tr. Carolyn French and Nina Karsov (New Haven and London: Yale University Press, 1994).

48. Michael Mann, "The Social Cohesion of Liberal Democracy," *American Sociological Review* 35, no. 3 (1970): 423–39; Phillip E. Converse, "The Nature of Belief Systems in Mass Publics," in David Apter, ed., *Ideology and Discontent* (New York: Free Press, 1964).

49. Analysis of which was undertaken by Małgorzata Fuszara, "Styl Życia, Pracy i Konsumpcji Biznesmenów Polskich: Analyza Słownika Businessmenów Polskich, " in Kurczewski and Jakubowska-Branicka, *Biznes i Klasy Średnie,* 21–35.

50. Fuszara, "Styl Życia," 34.

51. Indeed, Joanna Kurczewska argues that the intelligentsia as such are disappearing under post-Communism, to be replaced by more specialized kinds of intellectualities. See "The Polish Intelligentsia: Retiring from the Stage" and Edmund Mokrzycki, "A New Middle Class?" both in *Democracy, Civil Society, and Pluralism,* ed. Christopher G. A. Bryant and Edmund Mokrzycki (Warsaw: IFiS, 1995).

52. Antonio Gramsci, "The Intellectuals," in *Selections from the Prison Notebooks,* ed. and trans. Quintin Hoare and Geoffrey Nowell Smith (London: Lawrence and Wishart, 1971), 5, actually identifies the capitalist entrepreneur as an intellectual, the "organizer of society." For a much greater elaboration of this class's alternative formations and business culture, see Gianoplus, dissertation.

53. Krzesak, "Etnografia Business Centre Club," 37–61. See also Gianoplus, dissertation.

54. Hence it is not surprising that many intellectuals now feel themselves irrelevant. Adam Michnik, for instance, has said that in comparison to the Communist past, the major problem facing intellectuals is that there is now a "cacophony" of voices, and nobody is especially heeded (personal communication, October 1996).

55. In 1993 and 1994, Pauline Gianoplus, Margaret Foley, and Magdalena Szaflarski conducted interviews for this project. Our research was supported by the University of Michigan Center for International Business Education. In 1995, Naomi Galtz joined Foley and Gianoplus to conduct these interviews. Our research in that year was supported by the William Davidson Institute.

56. See Michael D. Kennedy and Pauline Gianoplus, "Entrepreneurs and Expertise: A Cultural Encounter in the Making of Post-Communist Capitalism

in Poland," *East European Politics and Societies* 8, no. 1 (1994): 27–54. One reason we interviewed these managers was to assess whether the same negative assessment of business culture existed among them.

57. The numbers following quotes refer to a particular interview; the identity of each interviewee must, by prior agreement, remain confidential.

58. Torańska's interviews with Balcerowicz and Bielecki, for example.

59. See Kennedy and Gianoplus, "Entrepreneurs and Expertise."

60. See Piotr S. Wandycz, *The Price of Freedom: A History of East Central Europe from the Middle Ages to the Present* (London: Routledge, 1992).

61. For marvelous accounts of different kinds of normalizations, see Daina Stukuls, "Imagining the Nation: Campaign Posters of the First Postcommunist Elections in Latvia," *East European Politics and Societies* 11 (1997): 131–54, and "Transformation, Normalization and Representation in Postcommunism: The Case of Latvia," University of Michigan Ph.D. dissertation, 1998.

Studying Nations, Movements, and Business

The first major subject about which I have written is the Polish Solidarity movement of 1980–81. I have written a bit about other East European social transformations, but I focused on this "independent self-governing trade union" for my dissertation and first book. I began collecting data during field-work in Poland in 1983–84 and then again in the summers of 1987 and 1988. I approached Solidarity and other East European movements for transformation through the lens of Western critical sociology. I focused on power relations, emancipatory praxis, and a normative grounding that played little heed to the significance of nations. I was drawn to Eastern Europe because of the challenge it offered to critical theories inspired by Marxism. I wanted to understand better what went wrong with socialism. And that was the first answer I offered on the Warsaw tram to an older woman who asked this obviously non-Polish American why I was in Poland.

What a jerk. I was being intellectually honest, but I immediately recognized my insensitivity in the expression on her face. After some time, I came upon a more socially acceptable answer. I don't have any Polish ancestry, but I have Irish blood. And then they nodded their heads in approval and understanding. I could invent some reasons why this answer was acceptable, but it has always intrigued me that this served as a good reason for my interest. My Irish ancestry, while a source of some pride, is what American sociologists call a symbolic ethnicity. I grew up with few markers other than as a Catholic, and that produced no privilege or discrimination of which I was aware.

I was raised by my parents, Floyd and Ursula, in mostly white Bethlehem, Pennsylvania. I attended a rural Catholic church and small-town public schools. I was socialized to become a corporate manager or lawyer. My main passion in life, from age eleven to twenty-two, was golf. I was born a little bit late, in 1957, to be connected to the countercultural movements mobilizing

American youth and challenging the sensibilities of American nationality. By the time I reached Davidson College in 1975 North Carolina, the antiwar movements were gone. Even the antifraternity movement had by then disappeared! I was quite distant from the kinds of movements that normally ignite social concern and rearticulations of the nation.

Why then was I driven to read Huey P. Newton's Revolutionary Suicide *in 1973? During the day high school seniors were asked to teach classes, I led Problems of Democracy toward a discussion of when violence was legitimate in movement strategy. The Black Panthers were my example. In college, race relations courses attracted me, but it was Ernest Patterson's courses on labor economics, comparative economic systems, and economic history that led me to C. Wright Mills, my first real intellectual inspiration. I was still in a movement void, however. I was in a place of class, educational, gender, and racial privilege, and without the cohort experience that might have fostered a collective critique. I honestly don't know why I have been interested in questions of domination and resistance since adolescence. Could it have been my childhood fascination with Batman and Spiderman? Was my sense of nationhood informed by the missions of Captain America?*

Perhaps like many others, I decided to go to graduate school to figure out my politics. I went to study sociology at the University of North Carolina at Chapel Hill in 1979. There again I found a movement void. A little bit of organization could easily fill it. One of my teachers, Craig Calhoun, stimulated the organization of a new Democratic Socialists of America chapter, and I helped get it started. I took it into a variety of arenas—anti-condominium-conversion issues, Latin American solidarity work, and city politics. I also became involved in DSA youth section politics, even contemplating an invitation to become a full-time activist. My interest in Eastern Europe, enabled by my teachers already so committed, Gerhard Lenski and Tony Jones, prevailed nevertheless. My fellowship to Poland proved to be the final pull. Nevertheless, I was leading a double intellectual life.

Quite by chance, I decided shortly before entering graduate school that studying the USSR would be the best way for an American on the left to figure out his politics. Few people thought that way, either on the left or in the field of Soviet studies, however. Solidarity of course changed that. It remained nonetheless difficult to combine a commitment to activism with my East European scholarship. One American colleague had already been kicked out of the Polish People's Republic for his work with Solidarity.

Officially, I focused on the safe question of the occupational structure of Poland's professions, with an implicit concern to assess, in Poland, Konrád and Szelényi's thesis of an intelligentsia on the road to class power. I really wanted to see how this thesis worked within Solidarity; I wanted to see how the movement managed to translate class differences into class alliances. Once I hit the right networks, clandestine snowball sampling methods led me from one physician activist to the next, and I developed my project empirically. I also became integrated with some parts of Poland's great social movement. While there, however, I ignored how the nation structured the movement.

Of course I knew that Poles drew on a history of collective behavior in opposition to foreign domination. I thought these explanations were too obvious to be interesting. They didn't fit with my politics either. I wasn't interested in seeing nations as the dramatis personae of history. I used other lenses— movement, class and occupational sociologies, and above all, a critical sociology that made little room for the nation. Already that says a great deal about how American my sociology was.

When I came back from Poland, I focused on writing my dissertation and getting a job. After a year in South Carolina, Liz and I married and moved to Michigan, where we found, for the first time in my life, a vital movement sector in the United States. I became involved right away with a progressive's congressional campaign, but for the most part became an academic. Liz's involvement with Women's Action for Nuclear Disarmament, however, connected me with the local movement community, and it was this peace work that moved us to contact peace activists (Freedom and Peace) in Poland in 1987, enabling my most direct connection between social movements and scholarship. I felt at last that research in Poland could make a difference in movement politics. I could help American progressives understand why their own good intentions could seem so naive if not dangerous to those who "felt Communism on the skin."

My linkage of American and Polish peace activists elevated the significance of the nation for me. I remain convinced that my focus on the class alliance underlying 1980–81 Solidarity is proper. I found, however, that the American peace movement's view of Eastern Europe through its nationed lenses was a problem. It was inconsistent with the global aspirations it set out for itself. I found, then, a newly appealing role: as an "interpreter" for the critical academic dialogue between Poland and the United States. I did not know how to engage that national identity, however.

Fortunately, the University of Michigan was an incredible place for me to begin making up that loss. The Center for Russian and East European Studies was especially committed to studying the nation, with Geoff Eley, Zvi Gitelman, Janet Hart, Ron Suny, and Roman Szporluk providing inspiration and guidance. I also was fortunate to be able to work for a term at the Institute for the Humanities with Nicolae Harsanyi, on a fellowship from Timisoara. We compared national identity formation in Poland, Ukraine, Hungary, and Romania. That encounter enabled me to understand better my own peculiar nationing.

Niki spoke about the nation as a lived experience. I spoke about it as a matter of academic concern. My nation is virtually invisible to me, while his nations, and my nation, were explicitly shaping his life chances. I could elevate, or deflate, the significance of the nation by altering my foci. While Niki's good spirit enabled him to go along with me, nations and their states pervaded most of what he could do.

Being a white male American means enjoying substantial privilege. English has been hegemonic in the world system. Many nation theorists regard the United States as one of the most inclusive and an exemplar of liberal nations. Its nationalism is supposed to be more constitutional or political than most. After the end to the Vietnam War and maybe the Cold War, the places I travel seem to find my American status to be positive. Thus, I could ignore my national identity. When I began interviewing American business experts offering technical assistance in Eastern Europe, they found the same thing: to be American was another credential of expertise. Given the profound misunderstanding in the American peace movement about Eastern Europe, however, I found it hard to believe that American businessmen and women knew the region better.

The article I have written here completes the circle. The process of global capital is restructuring nations profoundly. Businessmen certainly articulate the nation, but these East European businessmen are rearticulating the nation to fit with a global capitalism previously denied by state socialism. Once again, I could afford, as many of my colleagues do, to ignore the nation. Instead, I want to know how intellectuals manage to diminish the explicit significance of the nation.

Finally, it is clear from this that I have no commitment to the nation as theory or to any particular nation as the barrier to, or solution for, problems. In this sense, I remain quite motivated by those less national Enlightenment ideals, and some of that postmodern hubris, both of which enable privileged distance from the explicit influence of the nation. At the same time, however, I am aware that this distance must be a product of my own nationnessless.

Michael D. Kennedy

Ronald Grigor Suny and Michael D. Kennedy

Toward a Theory of National Intellectual Practice

The fusion of a modernist, constructivist approach to nation making with attention to the role of human agents in that construction has guided researchers to a new set of analytical problems and a heightened (some would say excessive) attention to the position and contribution of intellectuals in the gestation and elaboration of nations. Beginning with modernization theory (here Karl Deutsch and Ernest Gellner were the paradigmatic examples), social theorists connected the processes and institutions of social communication, education, and the production of intellectuals to the generation of nationness. Gellner in particular emphasized the shift from structure to culture with the move to the modern. But even more impressively, with the turn toward discursive and culturalist analyses, scholars have elevated the actively creative, imaginative, and constitutive activities of nation-making intellectuals. To take but one species of intellectual, Eric J. Hobsbawm writes of his own profession, "Historians are to nationalism what poppy-growers in Pakistan are to heroin addicts; we supply the essential raw material for the market. Nations without a past are a contradiction in terms; what makes the nation *is* a past; what justifies one nation against another is the past and historians are the people who produce it."[1]

Neither national past nor national language exists before the hard intellectual work of appropriation, selection, distinction, and articulation takes place. That creativity (in many ways an act of creation, *pace* Motyl) is neither completely arbitrary nor fatally determined; it is not fabrication from nothing, but from the elements and experiences available to be remembered, recombined, and reorganized into a narrative of a continuous subject, the nation. A single poet, like the unknown author of *Ter Getzo*, or a veritable army of scholar-priests, like the Mekhitarists in Venice, may contribute essential threads to a new national tapestry (in this case, the Armenian), sometimes quite accidentally, but more often, in the wake of already-existing ethnic communities or prenational dynastic or imperial states, quite consciously reacting to and accommodating to patterns given by others who are then historically privileged as forerunners. The essays in this collection illustrate the varieties of practices of national intellectuals. Our task in this conclusion is to elaborate our own views on a theory of national intellectual practice, and in carrying out that task we will both borrow from and contest some of the ideas put forth in our contributors' chapters.

Norms, Theory, and Their Object

When we work toward a theory of national intellectual practice, we are nominally doing the same as our other contributors. But as the previous pieces suggest, and especially what is to follow indicates, we all do not share the same theoretical assumptions and goals, even if our conversations with other theorists help refine our ambitions.[2] The pieces by Alex Motyl and Janet Hart in our collection are more self-consciously "theoretical" than the others and represent the poles of inquiry available in the academy. Both of them explore general problems of intellectuals in the articulation of the nation more than offer particular historical explanations. But Hart and Motyl suggest very different analytical stances.

Motyl argues that the constructivists are, if logically consistent, empirically inadequate and if they are empirically adequate, they are theoretically trivial. We agree with Motyl that the articulation between lifeworld and national identity is very important and believe that ideology and identity are analytically distinct concepts, capturing different parts of national identity formation. As does Motyl, we believe that intellectuals refashion cultural stocks and do not invent nations ex nihilo. Indeed, without stocks of culture and compelling and resonant stories of origins and danger, nations cannot be invented. For that, it is also useful to consider both intellectual and nonintellectual contributions to the articulation of the nation. But we also need to problematize the category *intellectual* and, following Gramsci, locate intellectuality in those who do not claim the term. We agree that it would be misleading to think only of conscious intellectual work as the basis for nation making, but we also think that we need to move beyond such categorical distinctions as elite and nonelite, conscious and unconscious, voluntary and coercive, structural and cultural. Although both Motyl and we recognize that these are merely analytical distinctions, we find other concepts more useful to clarify and explain social processes, if not generate abstract theory.

Motyl seeks a logically pure theory, one without fuzzy concepts and retaining only the precise ones. For example, although he never defines elites, their action must be conscious (and not habitual) for their contribution to nation making to be "constructivist." Also, elites must visibly construct nations with arguments. To enforce those arguments with resource-laden penalizing rules turns intellectuals into bureaucrats. In this sense, he shares much with positivists, who treat concept formation as only the means to the explanatory end. By contrast, we seek not only to explain the relationship among phenomena, but also to problematize the concepts themselves that purport to illuminate the social processes we seek to explain. Hence, in contrast to treating elites as self-evident, or resolved by operationalization, we are trying to elaborate how intellectuality is itself expressed in the nation's articulation and where it is located. In addition, instead of considering how elites consciously invent nations, we inquire into how their practice contributes to the reproduction and transformation of various elements of national identity and ideology. Hegemony, rather than coercion, intellectual practice rather than elites, are signposts for our different conceptual tastes.

These differences also extend to propositional thinking. For Motyl, propositions about nation formation ought to be generalizable and conditional, not conjunctural. He seeks an abstracted theory, one that can imagine what nations are ("groups of people who believe in two things: that their group, as a group, comes from somewhere, and that their group differs from other groups in other ways besides origins as well" [68]) and what conscious elites do, or do not, accomplish, in general. This approach can yield generalizable propositions, like, "a nation . . . exists, or comes into being, when people sharing a lifeworld believe in a set of logically complementary propositions regarding origins and otherness" (69). This also reflects something important for Motyl: the question, as he put it, is "what are the conditions that make national identity possible?" (67). The answer, if generalizable, conditional, and based on large-scale comparative work, must minimize differences among nations, and among elites, and among the alternative formations of nations and elites, for this theory to become possible. This approach to theory building comes out of a very strong tradition in the social sciences, especially sociology and political science. But in our effort here we prefer to build theory into historical explanation, and history into theory, and not to rip theory and history apart.[3] We see concepts as inevitably bound up with the processes we seek to untangle. As such, it does matter to us when and how people use the nation category. Indeed, the nation is not just a nominal term, but it is a resource used in a world of nations. To identify it as perennial means that the concept itself is not consequential. While the distinction between national identity and nationalism is very appealing, it is not clear what theoretical advantage one obtains by insisting on such a loose definition of nation that most of its qualities as a peoplehood are lost in the search to generalize. Indeed, the search for generalizations, it seems to us, might be better sought by holding social environment relatively constant.[4] To compare nations in periods with and without nationalisms is to compare apples and oranges without an obvious compote in mind.

In light of our critique of Motyl, it would appear that we share Janet Hart's theoretical ambitions. Hart self-consciously adopts a feminist and postmodernist stance but at the same time admires and seeks to recuperate the confidence and commitment evinced by two socialist intellectuals facing interwar fascism: Antonio Gramsci and Dimitris Glinos. Although she is also interested in how intellectuals articulate the nation, she does not seek, as Motyl does, to decide whether they do or do not, based on comparison with nonintellectuals. She also does not assess all intellectuals but is specifically interested in radical intellectuals and the paralanguages that undergird their praxis. She is not interested in modeling the relationship between these intellectuals and their nations, but rather in using their experiences to "clarify the dilemmas of radical selfhood and nation building in the modern era" (172). As in her book, *New Voices in the Nation,* she seeks to open up "new worlds of conversation about the shape of the past" in order, simultaneously, to enable us to rethink our own constraints and possibilities. Much like the intellectuals she engages, she scours "the historical record for analogous moments, comparable in terms of scene, emplotment, and protagonists; and maintaining a critical consciousness in reading and receiving transmitted wisdoms about past events" in order to craft future praxis (194).

Gramsci and Glinos suffered the wrath of repressive regimes and gained an authority through their conscientious commitment, maintained despite its devastating effects on their health and lives. They were intellectuals in the Foucauldian sense of thinking actors who disrupted existing cultures, shook up habitual ways of acting and thinking, dispelled commonsensical beliefs, and participated in the making of a new political will. These were intellectuals as revolutionary citizens unable to coexist with tyranny and willing to engage in politics to reconstitute their national civil societies along the lines of justice and freedom. Here the making of the modern nation was a revolutionary project articulated by oppositional intellectuals against the visions of those in power. Fascism presented an urgency to the socialist intellectual faced by a life-and-death struggle, not primarily for personal power, but for popular empowerment. With that kind of threat, it is hard to imagine Gramsci and Glinos as part of a new class, even one *in statu nascendi*, antagonistic to the popular classes.

Hart focuses on how Gramsci and Glinos articulate new visions of the nation within the constraints their authority establishes. Theoretical consequence is to be found in analogy and the inspiration of new imaginations about comparable circumstances for intellectuals today. Here she shares something with Tololyan's method, who examines the poem, "Ter Getzo," to examine how it negotiates the contradictions of the moment and of history to project its own national future.

Hart's essay does not focus on the particularities of the Greek or Italian nation very much, but rather on how commonly Glinos and Gramsci engaged the nation, both with a degree of commitment that found them prisoners of conscience. They both focused on generativity, finding in future generations the freshness and innovation that they sought in remaking the nation according to their radical visions. They approached youth as a group to be enlightened and educated, approached with tenderness but also reproach. Youth were in a sense foundational, but age was not exclusive. Indeed, their common emphasis on continuing mass education meant to transform and expand the citizenry of the nation by providing people the means to realize those visions while simultaneously transforming the intellectuals themselves through their immersion in the everyday life of the masses. Through their political activity and their own intellectual example, Gramsci and

Glinos sought to transform the meaning of the intellectual as they sought to transform the nation.

For Gramsci, Glinos, and Hart, the nation was hardly something perennial. Rather, history was but a resource in the elaboration of praxis. How, but through "lived emotion" (191), might the people be transformed intensively and aesthetically? How might the nation fit the foundational agendas of the modern political era" as they envisioned them? Instead of theorizing enduring objects, Hart finds that Glinos and Gramsci engaged in a "nonstatic, contingent, proactive theorizing resulting in the practical resolution of communal problems" (181). Thus, here we find something profoundly important about the way in which Hart, Gramsci, and Glinos approach the problem of intellectuals in the articulation of the nation. The nation is not the principal object of engagement, but one of the communal levels through which the solution of practical problems is realized, much as the Polish businessmen treated the nation in Kennedy's essay.

If one theorizes only nationalist intellectuals in developing a theory of national intellectuals, the nation is portrayed as a rather clearer object, centered in intellectuality both as subject and object of history. But if the ideology is as powerful as we believe, it affects not only nationalists, who make the nation the "key signifier" in their intellectual practice, but also affects those whose aims, whether socialism or capitalism, subordinate the nation to other principles. And in such a subordination, the nation becomes even more contingent than one would imagine in a constructionist account of a nationalist. Hence, by decentering the *nationalist* intellectual from our analysis and introducing others, we can more effectively see how intellectuals help to "fix" the nation. By considering nonnationalist intellectuals, and those conventionally not included in a narrower understanding of the intellectual, we can see more clearly the nation's lability, as Kennedy illustrates.

Although Hart helps us explore the ambiguities of the nation and especially the intellectual, for our theory of national intellectual practice Hart does not elaborate as fully as she might how these intellectuals themselves became national. Indeed, even as they transform the categories and imperatives of intellectuals, they seem to be the ultimate political intellectuals, remarkably if not omnisciently aware of the national conditions structuring their action and seeking ever greater capacities to produce those intellectual products, through publication and education, that might realize their transformative ambitions. They inspire, much as Hart intends. But how are they constrained? Through Hart's footnotes we can see how their ideas are gendered and raced, but, in this work at least, the nation appears mostly as an object to be transformed, rather than a structure that empowers and constrains.

In Kennedy's essay, the Polish businessman, while clearly not the "pure" intellectual typified by Glinos and Gramsci, nevertheless finds himself trapped by his nationing, even as he seeks to escape it. Working out of the tradition of structuration theory, which seeks to explain not only how agents transform structures but how structures form agents, Kennedy's approach allows us to inquire into the conditions of agency more clearly. Consider the following as a working proposition: to the extent intellectuals are dependent on national resources, the constraints of their activity will also be more national. Hence socialist intellectuals dependent on popular empowerment of a single nation are likely to have to congeal socialist and national visions. Businessmen who are dependent on international trade are likely to be obliged to diminish the significance of the nation in their work, but might, through other structures of life, whether at the kitchen table or in the governmental ministry, find the contradictions of the nation and the global more palpable than the socialist intellectual. The overlap between structures of the nation and other ideological or more material structures therefore vary depending on the location, and practice, of intellectuals.

Methods of case selection, and not only theory, alter how we approach intellectuals in the articulation of the nation. By focusing on businessmen, Kennedy maximizes the contradictoriness of the nation in its structuring of intellectuals. He cannot identify the consequence of these businessmen's rethinking the nation and can only suggest that an alternative vision of the nation is in the making. By focusing on those who seek the radical transformation of both of our foundational categories, Hart stabilized the actor, and finding exemplary actors, she makes the nation disappear as a structuring object, even as she transforms our very subjects of inquiry, intellectuals and nation.

Yuri Slezkine's contribution is, in method, very similar to Hart's. He also stabilizes the problem of intellectuals articulating the nation by focusing on another "exemplary" intellectual. But for Slezkine, the intention of the case is radically different. Although Slezkine's article is less explicitly "theoretical," the mood and tone of his article challenge Hart's specific theoretical arguments and inclinations. As told in

Slezkine's ironic style, Nikolai Marr's "nationing" shaped, from the womb, his intellectual direction. The offspring of parents who literally did not speak the same language, Marr sought the languages that transcended apparent divisions, even while seeking to elaborate the foundationalism of Georgian. Marr was, in some ways, the ultimate intellectual for Slezkine, being simultaneously a "linguist, archaeologist, historian, folklorist, and ethnographer" (218). But while his claims to intellectual capital were considerable, Slezkine compromises Marr's status throughout the essay.

Marr's role as a "minor celebrity and a powerful academic entrepreneur" (217) is hardly portrayed in the words used to elevate intellectuals, as Bourdieu's analysis reminds us.[5] Throughout the text, Slezkine engages in a subtle, and sometimes not so subtle, mockery of Marr's theoretical transformations and ambitions, calling the Japhetic thesis an epidemic, for instance (221), and elaborating in considerable detail its empirical and logical inadequacies. The intellectual distinction of the products, too, are called into question by invoking the well-known story of Party arbitrariness, and at the end, Stalin's supremacy. If Marrism gained influence, it did so not as a consequence of intellectual work per se, but because of its use by the Party. Rather than being the fount of creativity and potential consequence, as Glinos and Gramsci were for Hart, Marr becomes the symbol of Communism's absurdity and its wild inconsistency before nations and other ethnographic and linguistic groupings.

Particularly ironic (and paradoxical) is Marr's support for primordialist notions of the nation in an intellectual context in which an argument from contingency and constructivism would have conformed better with the official ideology's deepest historicist impulses. Marr helped "make" nations in a huge multinational "nonnation" that over time resembled for more and more people the epitome of that ubiquitous prenational state form, empire. In this sense, intellectuality became victim to the empire state.

These portraits of intellectual victims, radical intellectuals, and businessmen in the articulation of the nation produce very different effects and images concerning the nation. In part, a matter of selection, they are also a consequence of theoretical orientation and normative grounding.[6] Kennedy, being the unmarked white American man, having a socialist background but also a newfound admiration for the power of business practice in remaking Eastern Europe, stands ambivalently before business intellectuals articulating the nation. By contrast, Hart seeks the possibilities of radical selfhood, inspired not only by the examples of women resisting fascism and intellectuals rearticulating nations, but also reflecting the lifeworlds of African American women. To appreciate the initiative and motivation of such revolutionary intellectuals in our own postrevolutionary, post-Communist age takes its own kind of act of imagination. Hart reminds us that *Communist* can mean Gramsci in his cell, exercising the brain that Mussolini tried to stop, just as it has come to mean Ceaușescu turning off the heat. Slezkine's essay is grounded in an ironic detachment, an understandable response to conditions shaping intellectuals in the articulation of nations under Stalinist rule.

Tololyan's essay is marked, by contrast, with a kind of familiarity and sympathetic position vis-à-vis a broadly conceived Armenian national project of diaspora intellectuals. More than any other author in this collection, Tololyan makes discourse his object of inquiry, which he argues is situated midway in the subjective-objective continuum. He writes of how discourse originates in "real" events, perpetuated and made accessible by material and social practices, and acquires consequence by speaking to the subjectivity of individuals and larger audiences, which in turn initiates a new consciousness that subsequently produces new texts and a politics unimaginable without the prior work (95). By focusing on a single work, its "agency" in history can thus be explored. He finds that the poem "Ter Getzo" can both intentionally and unintentionally articulate the relationship between various forces in order to recruit people to new ideas and practices that create the subject position of the nationalist. Tololyan is not, then, interested in assessing whether intellectuals are necessary, or in articulating the conditions under which they might be. His and Motyl's concerns are radically discontinuous, but his discursive interest means that Tololyan's theory fits well with our ambitions of clarifying the intellectual in the articulation of the nation.

Verdery's theoretical orientation also fits rather well with the theory we seek to develop. While focusing less on any particular text, Verdery does focus on the rhetoric of civil-society intellectuals and the political economy of symbolism that enables them to succeed or structures their failure. But more than the text itself, Verdery assesses the producers of texts. Their capital influences how texts are read and what they can accomplish. In *National Ideology under Socialism*, Verdery focused on the capital intellectuals acquired through a politics of complicity with the state that in turn helped to reproduce the nation as a master symbol. The moral capital associated with civil-society intellectuals is a resource acquired "in opposition" to those structures of domination. These forms of capital might, therefore, augment the power of argument, but at the same time, she is quick to point out, they do not guarantee success, as the fate of civil-society discourse indicates.

One's choice of theory clearly influences, then, how one views intellectuals and the articulation of the nation. We seek to develop a textured theory, grounded in historical and cultural analysis, assuming the pervasiveness of power relations, the constructedness of social life, and the inevitability of normative influence. Rather than providing the skeleton with which we might go out and test propositions, we enter the cases, and juxtapose them in order to provide variable accounts of intellectuals in the articulation of the nation. We seek anomalies, as much as consistencies, in order to refine our understandings not only of the variations in the relationship between intellectuals and nations, but also in the construction of each of the concepts themselves.[7] This is theory building of the first order, where we not only try to refine our propositions about the world, but the conceptual tool kit we bring to study it.

This is a profoundly social theory as well, for we are not only looking at those mythical actors who are conscious and autonomous imposers of values, but at real historical beings who are formed by social, political, historical, and cultural forces[8] (evident in Kennedy and Slezkine) and then attempt to reshape those worlds sometimes by virtue of their direct political activity (evident in Hart and Verdery), or by the intellectual products they leave behind (as in Tololyan). We are working in a tradition of structuration theory, where the multiplicity of structures and their contradictions give variable opportunities to those who have experience across these structures and can transpose rules, with adequate resources, across sites of action to express their agency.[9] In the words of one metatheorist, Jonathan Turner, we are developing "sensitizing analytical schemes" that allow us to explain historical processes in ever more refined theoretical categories.[10]

Distinguishing the Nation

Whether one sees the imagination of a national political community as a modern, elite-driven process or the generation of "national propositions" by ordinary people depends on what one understands by "national." A sense of kinship or cultural community, what might be called ethnicity, is produced daily and through time by lived experience of people in proximity to one another, and here elites as well as ordinary people actively develop traditions, institutionalize customs, and define sameness with one another and difference from an other. Motyl equates this generation of ethnic culture and community with the national, which while perfectly defensible as a heuristic choice, has the unfortunate effect of conflating all cultural communities through time into "nations." Our preference, consistent with the recent work of most scholars of nationalism and the majority of the authors in this collection, is to reserve the concept of nation to that form of "imagined political community" which was constituted from the late eighteenth century to the present with its distinctive imaginative style, discourse, and structures.

Our argument in this book is more than what Motyl calls the "soft constructivist" approach—that everything in history is made by humans and is therefore "constructed"—and closer to his "hard constructivist" position that emphasizes the pivotal, though not exclusive, role of elites in nation making. For us, nations, like the mobilized, cohesive, "conscious" working class of Lenin's imagination, are particular formations that may grow out of ethnic (or civic/territorial) communities, but that come together and understand themselves as a nation only with the efforts of intellectuals and political elites that bind disparate social and cultural pieces together, dissolve differences within the community as much as possible (at least on the discursive level), and elaborate the differences with those outside the community, the "other." The relative significance of intellectual practice varies, of course, historically and culturally, and it is the task of a theory of national intellectual practice to offer the conceptual tools with which such an explanation can work in a comparative and historical framework.

This nation formation first took place historically as a universal "discourse of the nation" was being constituted, which involved notions of the "naturalness" of the nation, its apposition to other "nations" in a world in which the "natural" division of the human race was into nations. Ethnocultural and linguistic distinctions, or civil cultural differences (even in the same ethnolinguistic community, as in eighteenth-century America's rupture with England) separated one people from another and made possible, in this new discursive environment, claims to territory, political self-representation, and statehood. Rapidly included in this new discursive formation were ideas of popular sovereignty and the requirement that for states to be legitimate they must represent nations. As a hegemonic political universe was established through the nineteenth and twentieth centuries in which states existed in a multistate environment, legitimized themselves through appeals to the nation, and implicitly and explicitly challenged the remaining "nonmodern" polities that were not nation-states, state legitimation flowing from the nation and its people (in both the sense of the population and of the national community) worked powerfully to undermine more multiethnic, cosmopolitan polities like empires. Intellectual activity was absolutely central to this transformative project because of its disproportionately significant role in formulating the discourse of the nation.

Nations in this modern sense could not exist before there was a discourse of the nation, that is, before there was an understanding, a language, and a practice of nationness in this modern sense. This does not mean that before nations there were not other forms of political communities, other styles of imagining community (even some called *natio* or "nation" in another sense), but they are usefully distinguished from what has become in our own century, especially with the demise of the last colonial and contiguous empires, the hegemonic, nearly uncontested state form.[11]

As Andrzej Walicki demonstrates, a particular use of "nation" already existed in the Polish-Lithuanian *Rzecz Pospolita* of the sixteenth and seventeenth centuries, where "will of the nation" meant the sovereign will of the gentry. This precocious nation imagined its political community as a cosmopolitan cultural unity defined, not by ethnicity or language, but by membership in a social estate. To be a Pole meant being a member of the gentry independently of religion, ethnicity, or language. In the late eighteenth century, and under the influence of the French Enlightenment and Revolution, a "republic view of the nation," which involved inclusion of nonnoble property owners and a notion of popular sovereignty, supplanted gentry republicanism. This rationalist, civic nationalism, really a kind of patriotism, was still-born, as the partitions of Poland eliminated the Polish state, and was in the nineteenth century replaced, first, by a national ideal based in Polish literary culture and embodying an historic mission of freedom and brotherhood for all nations. Still later, after the defeat of the 1863 insurrection, nationalist intellectuals decisively moved to include the peasantry into a new concept of an ethnolinguistic nation.

The problem for Poland through most of the next century was the bad fit between the ethnographic Polish nation and the historic Polish state that existed in the visions of some Polish nationalists. A variety of ideas of the Polish nation competed for the loyalties of peasants and workers, and the independent Polish republic of the interwar years was a hybrid polity that was at one and the same time a polonizing, nationalizing state (in Rogers Brubaker's formulation) and a multinational state with indigestible national minorities, some of which had "homelands" across the eastern and western borders.[12]

Part of the problem for assessing the significance of intellectuals in the articulation of the nation depends on the degree to which the imagination of a people as a nation (Motyl's Armenians), or the transformation of that nation into a different form (Gramsci's Italians or Glinos's Greeks), is assessed in terms of (a) the degree of intentionality of the actors, and (b) the exclusivity with which that construction is made by those arguably "intellectual." In other words, to what extent must national consciousness be articulated and discursive, rather than merely "practical" and unarticulated?[13] Nationalist intellectuals and socialist intellectuals symbolize this radical and conscious elaboration of an explicit ideology. But at the same time, to distinguish discursive from practical, conscious from habitual, is to miss one of the important points of the profoundly national intellectual. As Tololyan and Hart suggest, deeply national intellectuals find in their identities the collective as well as the individual, in which their individual self is immersed into a nation or the popular.

Intellectuals, in the narrow sense, are not so important when identities are imposed by legislative fiat. In this case, it is state authority and their elites that matter. But even as the Polish state is legislating the Polish nation anew, the businessmen on whom Kennedy focuses are anticipating, and expressing a tension in, an identity that the ideologically liberal nation state cannot recognize. In this case, and in contrast to the nationalists and socialists perhaps, identity is less coherent than ideology. But it is, perhaps, in the struggle over the contradictions between nationness and liberalism in the businessman's lifeworld that a new vision could be produced, one that reconciles those tensions and restructures states to articulate the nation differently. But that, as far as Kennedy is able to see, has not yet happened, although it is in process of formation among elites.[14]

In short, we ought to recognize that to explain the intellectual's articulation of the nation, we should elaborate the different kinds of national identities that might emerge. We should look at the nation's initial "formation" as well as its various alternatives in relation to ethnic inclusiveness, political economy, gender politics, and so forth. Finally, one might consider whether the nation's significance might in the future be diminished. A single dependent variable of initial nation formation will not do.

Strategy, Resources, and Constructed versus Objective Nations

Walicki is particularly convincing when he distinguishes between the different paths to the nation of different peoples. He writes, "The relative weight of the subjective and objective factors in the making of nations is different in different countries and in different historical periods" (261). He shows that the transition to modernity opens up opportunities for transformations of the historical nation through intellectual interventions. The noble nation of the Rzecz Pospolita exemplified the power of intellectual politics in defining a nation. Even the initial post-partition politics shows the power of this intellectual politics, in both its accomplishments (survival and redefinition of the Polish nation) and its failures, which Walicki attributes to the "underestimation of the 'objective' aspects of nationalism" (280). The power of ethnicity seems to thwart those modern nations that aim to construct themselves as purely political nations.[15] But, as the Himka essay demonstrates, ethnicity itself is also constructed.

As Himka emphasizes, the Ruthenians of Galicia cannot be understood as "basically the same as other Ukrainians, albeit with certain local variations" (140). While it is true that literary Ukrainian did resonate with the vernaculars of Galicia, and while Ukrainophile constructions of the nation did accommodate more elements of preexisting culture than Russophile constructions, it was in the political constellation of available alternatives that the Ukrainian orientation gained precedence over a number of alternative definitions of ethnicity that were available to that population. In contrast, perhaps, to the Polish, this sense of alternativity in ethnicity, and hence constructivism as a theoretical option, is apparent because of the oppositional position of Ukrainian national identity. Where hegemonic, a national identity can appear more "objective" because, all other things being equal, it is more difficult to transform it.

Thus, we might challenge the language of invention and imagination because it leaves little room for the variable degrees to which nations are transformable. We need a language that allows us to recognize that nations are made out of a combination of more enduring and more constructed factors, or in Walicki's terms, more objective and more subjective factors. Here the range of views remains great. Anthony Smith remains far more objectivist, looking, like Walicki, for the prior ethnic core around which the future nation was constructed. On the other hand, Brubaker pushes the limits of contingency.[16] But we might reorient this problem and change it away from a theoretical position to one that is the subject of empirical inquiry based on comparative analysis.[17] Our own view is that one needs to employ the kind of sensitivity to context, time and space, that historians, even better than other social scientists, exemplify. One ought to consider how embedded various national identities are at different times and under what conditions they are most malleable and least malleable. Or to put it in the terms Roman Szporluk uses,[18] does it always matter in the same degree what a nation imagines itself to be?

Speaking in terms of objective and subjective may not be the most effective distinction. Perhaps if these terms referred less to categories and rather pointed toward a more continuous spectrum that indicated the relative structuration of a process, they would be more useful. In some ways, objective factors are also subjective. They are also the consequence of some kind of intellectual politics. For example, as Walicki indicates, without the historical classes, national consciousness was delayed. When it came, it came as a consequence of modernization, but included in that modernization package was not only ethnic competition but also the education of a part of the budding nation's stratum, who in turn revealed to others the nature of their conflict. After all, Poles in Łódź could recognize perhaps that Jews and Germans were their oppressors, but they chose to emphasize these distinctions rather than other distinctions, like their position in the hierarchy of the enter-

prise. Here they drew upon an available discourse, an intellectual politics of ethnic distinction that linked their oppression in Łódź to that
which was happening in Poznań or elsewhere.[19]

When Katherine Verdery describes the challenges and failures of a
politics of civil society in Romania, the "objective" quality of Romanian
nationalism seems to come up against the failed subjectivity and intellectual articulations of Romanian liberals. The objective qualities, too,
of a political system meant alliances with Hungarians were less valuable to the liberals than distancing that sympathy for a politics of inclusion. The nation was, thus, hegemonic, the master symbol, as Verdery
calls it. But Verdery avoids the language of objective versus subjective.
While she indicates the problems that peasants and villagers must face
and that the discourse of civil society fails to resonate, she does not
deploy a language of inevitability, but of failure. It was not that the liberals could not; rather, they did not do enough to "translate it positively into the life terms of everyone else" (329). The nation endures in
part because the discourse of its alternative can neither address the
needs of everyday life, nor mobilize the indigenous constituencies that
might challenge the nation's dominance as the key symbol in post-
Communist politics. This distinction is even more apparent in Ukraine,
where the contest between Russophile and Ukrainophile imaginations
of their peoplehood was above all the consequence of intellectual politics, itself also a reflection of the manipulations of intellectuals and their
communities by state powers.

Instead of reserving to intellectual elites the subjective role, and
assigning to social history the objective, we propose that while the
social construction of any phenomenon, especially the nation, goes on
everywhere, the relative power of any actor to reconstruct preexisting
patterns in a new way varies with the conditions of their action (the
particular conjuncture) and the strategies and resources the actor has at
his or her disposal to transform existing discourses. There are several
examples in these papers we can use to illustrate this problem.

For those who like to emphasize the "organic" quality of nations,
the articulation of the nation with the people must be emphasized, and
there the conditions of the articulation can differ profoundly. One contrast that might work well in this regard is to compare the ability of
Poles and of Ukrainians to link national emancipation with peasant
emancipation. Here we can see that the "objective" process of national
awakening actually depended in part on mobilization by Ukrainian

organic intellectuals in Galicia, a kind of mobilization that Polish intellectuals could not realize because of the organization of Polish class relations. The fit between class and ethnic relations is absolutely central to defining the "social" resources of intellectuals articulating the nation.[20]

"National" depictions of the process, however, sometimes can lead to accounts that underemphasize the role of external agents. This theme, a familiar one in the social-movements literature,[21] certainly involves a measure of intellectual politics within the analytical community. To emphasize the external, one calls into question the nationalist assumption that nations are simply realizing who they "ought" to be. To suggest that nations are themselves tools in great-power politics undermines the rhetoric of self-realization. Clearly, Himka's identification of the significance of the Vatican and Austrian state in making the Ukrainophile tendency is an illustration of the potential importance of the external. An even greater illustration of the delicate political nature of the problem is in Himka's depiction of the intimate relationship of Polish politics and its state with Ukrainian movements. Properly treated, any nation should not be simply the object of great-power designs; but to leave out geopolitics in a nation's making is to attribute a greater degree of "objectivity" to the nation than empirical conditions, and critical theory, would suggest. Such an emphasis on "external" actors invites us, as Himka illustrates, to consider how nationalists themselves attempt to construct relatively distant peoples as their own. The Ukrainophiles' attempt to transform the Subcarpathian Rusyns into more proper Ukrainians was also an intervention by an "external" actor in some sense. Such a formulation may be intolerable to most nationalists, but the borders between the "national" community and the "other" are never simply given but are themselves part of the intellectual (and social) construction that brings forth the nation.

A theory of national intellectual practice suggests that the articulation of a nation by the leading lights of one's own nation is not that different from the articulation of that nation by those formally "external" to the nation. But one should not discount the nationalist position either. One should explain it. What are the social processes that make boundaries between internal and external self-evident in nationalism? Rather than take that as a given, as nationalism would demand, we must investigate the social processes that make it obvious. And to do that, we must ask how the nation's field of legitimation acquires the power of the obvious. What better place to begin that investigation than in a place where the qualities of the nation are less than obvious?

Himka is thus extraordinarily helpful. While the Ukrainophiles do command a powerful position for claiming national leadership by suggesting their literary language connects better with the vernacular, the Russophiles also have a significant claim: they are better connected with the region's tradition of using a "foreign" tongue for high culture. The Ukrainophiles ultimately win the status of "authentic" national intellectuals not because of the greater authenticity of their argument but because of their greater resonance with the ideological frame of a global nationalism. Part of that global ideology was that each nation must have its own high culture. If the "authentic" Ukrainian nation lacked one, it had to be made in order for that nation to become the equal of other nations. Intellectuals had to make that argument; it was not something embedded in the nation. And that suggests a power for intellectuals that ideologies of nationalism tend to undermine, especially since that power also implies a potential divergence of interests.

As we argued in the introduction, new-class theory is quite accustomed to articulating the potentially different interests of intellectuals, whereas nationalist theory is loathe to suggest that intellectuals and the nations they articulate might have different interests in that articulation. In our volume, although Himka opens the question, Verdery more clearly than others expresses the potential of that new-class theory not only with her explicit embrace of Szelényi's thesis on the potential hegemony of teleological intellectuals in post-Communist and Communist systems, but especially in her identification of the intellectual's problem: civil-society theory fails, in part, because the popular life-worlds and articulations of intellectuals are radically different. What an intellectual from Bucharest knows about peasant needs is likely minimal, she suggests. Nationalists too might well elevate the significance of the peasantry, but this itself can be more of an ideological celebration than it is an awareness of their life conditions.

One's normative politics influences the object of analysis, of course. To demonstrate the significance of the nation, many a nationalist points out that the intellectual merely brings to explicit awareness the conditions of a people's history and life. The intellectual's brilliance is embedded in the nation's virtue. To advance the new-class thesis, one must move beyond the nation as a field of reference. One must demonstrate that the intellectual's own lifeworld is apart from the nation that she/he released. To identify a nationalist project as a new-class project one should show how the intellectual's position is or would be improved with nationalism's successes. But to pose the question of a new class establishes a critical distance from the movement under investigation, and the analyst might well decide that the power relations enveloping that movement are more noxious than the hierarchies within it.

By questioning the boundaries of the nation and the possibility of intellectuals becoming a new class, we take issue with a basic assumption of nationalism. There is no alien intervention in nation making, just as there is no authentic expression of the nation.[22] At least there should not be in analytical terms. We seek to construct a conceptual framework that subverts the implication of authentic and inauthentic that resides in the perennialist versus constructionist opposition. Rather, we compare how those with various kinds and degrees of resources attempt to construct nations out of various cultural stocks. It allows us to compare, for instance, the resources and strategies of Ukrainian nationalists and Communists in Subcarpathia, and the resources and strategies of the Austrian government and Vatican in Galicia. It also allows us to question how the strategies and resources available for making a people translate into the elevation of that individual's or his or her group's status and conditions, and how such an elevation articulates with the popular ideologies that make a nation.

The Distinction of Intellectuals in Making Nations

As we have mentioned above, one definition of the intellectual refers to actors by virtue of their products, which are in some way construed as the formulation or manipulation of symbols of national meaning. This understanding, however, slips easily into making intellectuals and other political elites relatively interchangeable, since political elites use symbols in their own legitimation. In these terms, one could argue that Kościuszko was an intellectual-activist, moving beyond the legislation associated with modern intellectuals toward mobilization of these ideas in the popular imagination and social action. He in many ways developed a *better* intellectual politics as he elaborated a more powerful politics of emancipation that included the normatively superior position of extending the whole of Polishness to any estate and any ethnicity. To exclude someone like Kościuszko from the imagination of intellectuals articulating the nation would miss a powerful example of an important transformation of symbols of national meaning with potentially great social consequence.

After partition, Polish patriots managed to retain the national sense, relying more exclusively on intellectual, or cultural, means that simultaneously elevated literary culture and the significance of intellectuals in the nation's making. This intellectual strategy was ideologically consequential, too, as it provided a protomodern vision within old formulations of political legitimacy. But it had unintended consequences. The literary definition of Polishness moved the sense of the nation away from its political definition toward an ethnic definition. This ethnic definition then undermined the capacity of intellectuals to define who was and who was not Polish. The practice of intellectuals also shifted away from the high intellectual toward more organic intellectuals in Gramsci's sense. Organic work, especially in education, if not in industry, was a key form of intellectuality in this period. But the ease of distinguishing intellectual from nonintellectual also declines. Organic intellectuals are more embedded in everyday life. In short, in moments of political definition, when future possibilities are open, such as the initial periods of nation formation, intellectuals play an apparently heightened role in the nation's articulation. That role seems to decline as the intellectual becomes more organic and the nation is based ever more on the everyday sense of what it means to be of the people.

The problem is exacerbated in the post-Communist scenario. While Communism managed to preserve the distinction of an intelligentsia, the post-Communist scene threatens to undermine it.[23] Indeed, those who are easily identified as business intellectuals are influencing the nation's imagination of itself more than its writers or philosophers, as Kennedy argues. In this sense, not only might we be witnessing the declining influence of the intellectual over the nation's articulation, but we might also be witnessing the decline of the intellectual as a recognizable actor, even if intellectuality remains fundamentally important.

One might propose the following: a national intellectual is a social actor whose claim to distinction rests primarily on his/her claim to cultural competence and whose social consequence is indirect, through the use of their symbolic products as resources in other activities constructing the nation, whether through histories, poetry, or organizing pamphlets. Intellectuals may organize themselves in different ways—through associations, through coffeehouses, through political parties. They might even deny the category and claim that they are really something else—an entrepreneur, a man of the people. But these modes of distinction are themselves part of the definition of intellectuals: they define their own distinctions. And thus we are in a terrible quandary for stabilizing our unit of analysis.

We resolve the problem by moving away from focusing on intellectuals as such, to focus on intellectual practice that may, or may not, be done by those who claim themselves, or are designated by others, to be intellectuals. Verdery deals with this problem by discussing "the global and local aspects of the conditions of production through which symbols are processed as well as of the resources utilized in doing so" (332). To be more specific, we can say that we are interested in *(a)* the formation of intellectuals—that is, the basis for their claims of superior knowledge; *(b)* the activity of intellectuals—that is, what they do in the name of their superior knowledge, whether organizing social movements or writing poetry; and *(c)* the products of intellectuals—those various discourses that carry the effects of the intellectual beyond his or her ordinary milieu, whether in the oral repetition of the intellectual's speech, the reproduction and consumption of her poetry, or the mobilization of a movement around the cultural frame the intellectual articulated.

There are some activities and products that are more "obviously" intellectual than others: the creation of a standard literary language and its promotion through literature and poetry are, above all, the product of intellectuals, requiring a degree of linguistic sophistication that mandates some intellectual claim. Ethnographic work, detailing the cultural properties of various peoples, is another illustration of significant "intellectual" activity, as we see in Slezkine's discussion of Marr. Writing history might be less exclusively intellectual—consider, for instance, the number of "histories" being produced to explain the Yugoslav War of Succession (most by journalists with the authority of being eyewitnesses), and how many of them are not regarded highly by professional historians[24]—but it clearly is one of those activities and products normally associated with intellectual practice. To the extent any of these things is done well, the intellectual category is more easily applied. That distinguishes, after all, the propagandist from the intellectual in most discourses. But when one returns to Hobsbawm's claim of the centrality of history to nation making and notes how histories are actually manufactured—in daily reportage, official commemorations, publicly sanctioned textbooks—the work of professional historians can be seen as far less influential in the generation of nationalism than more popular productions of historical remembering.

Clearly, some intellectual products are critical resources for the making of the nation. Himka has illustrated, and Walicki more or less assumes for Poland, given its earlier construction, how important these products of intellectual work are for the making of a nation. Without a high culture, one cannot claim the rights of nations (Himka, 140–42). Making a high culture is most important in the "early" stages of nation making, and indeed an essential one for many nationalisms. Yet even the most purely "intellectual" of activities requires additional resources to be consequential. Sometimes consequence is realized by being the "servant" of state interests or populist imaginings. Then the "independent" intellectual may attempt to delegitimize the dependent intellectual by denying her the intellectual distinction. This is the last strategy of intellectuals after all: to define not only their own distinction, but who belongs to it. Hence, the category intellectual remains as important in the nation's construction as the nation remains important to the intellectual's making.

As historians, or historical sociologists, or historically minded political scientists, we must be sensitive when similar phenomena, even those described in the same terms, are different. Walicki compares the Polish ethnolinguistic community at two very different stages of existence: in the thirteenth century and at the end of the nineteenth. Though more research is required to substantiate this point, it can be argued that the former was much more an imagined community based on intellectual politics and elite ideologies, while the latter was much more the product of long and deep social processes. In the latter, the imagining of the national community is in this way more dispersed, that is, more popular and egalitarian, and intellectual politics less concentrated. Both intellectuality and nationness seem fundamentally different in these two periods and, we believe, should not be collapsed into one another.[25]

Himka's discussion of the alternatives in the Ukrainian nation reinforces this point about the historical variations in intellectual consequence. While the direction of Galicia might have been imagined in many different ways in the nineteenth century, by June 1915, the Russophile tendency, despite Russian military aid, could not suppress the Ukrainian movement and convert the population to orthodoxy. This sedimentation of the Ukrainophile position was constructed earlier, however, by state action and intellectual articulations, as when the Austrian government reconstructed the ecclesiastical boundaries and monastic orders that were pro-Russian.

In short, our essays seem to demonstrate that the centrality and visibility of the intellectuals' creative construction of the national in the earliest phases of nation making dissipates with the acceptance of the national framework by broader layers of the population. As the national processes over time become ever more "social," as a process of "social layering" occurs, the intellectuality involved in the nation's reproduction is dispersed ever more widely. Whereas earlier intellectuals had freer range to act upon the incipient nation, once the nation becomes the naturalized form of political community, intellectuals lose that freedom to act "arbitrarily" in disarticulation with the social, that is, to legislate with impunity in Bauman's sense. Likewise, it becomes increasingly difficult to identify a distinct intellectual articulation of the nation, as intellectuality itself is more widely dispersed, and national consciousness becomes ever more practical, rather than discursive. To illustrate that, let us return to Walicki and Tololyan.

While the Polish intellectual elite was on the verge of defining an ethnolinguistic nation in the medieval period, the social processes were not there to reinforce it. Here the "subjective" vision of the elite played the principal constitutive role, but it did not have great reach. Because the elite imagined a common language to coincide with the boundaries of state does not mean that such a language yet existed both among the ruling elites and the lower estates. Language use may have varied among the lower classes significantly. The Góraly and the Kaszubs are the most obvious distinctions from the standard Polish, but might linguistic ideologies themselves be responsible for our assumptions of linguistic homogeneity?[26]

However grounded in linguistic expertise, ideas about language communities might diverge from the "subjective" perception on the ground. The differences between Eastern and Western Armenian (or the many dialects of modern Armenian that were not mutually intelligible) served to divide Armenians, but linguists can demonstrate that they are part of the same language. Whoever, then, defines these Armenians to be part of the same ethnolinguistic community establishes the community. Is Serbo-Croatian a single language or two languages? What about Bosnian? The arguments over Macedonian and its relationship to Bulgarian, just like the debate in the United States about Ebonics, and the deeply politicized question of whether a given speech practice is a dialect or language, all are powerful examples of how intellectual power contributes to the making of the nation and how contingent is the nation's making.

Walicki's discussion of the Nation of Nobles illuminates important contributions of elites and intellectuals to nation formation. An ideological construction by intellectuals (Sarmatism) facilitated the polonization of non-Polish ethnic gentry, and by this embrace of Sarmatian theory by Lithuanian and Ruthenian gentry the non-Polish masses were effectively deprived of their "historical classes." Without this elite, the masses were delayed in the development of their national consciousness, as the particular cross-ethnic formation of the gentry nation undermined the previous foundations of the ethnolinguistic Polish nation in formation in the fourteenth century. Whatever view one might have about the medieval ethnic Polish nation, Walicki's argument about the gentry nation attests to the importance of the character of the intellectual articulation of the nation and its very existence as a precondition for nation formation, at least in the transition to modernity.

In Romania the post-Communist regime employed the "nation" to legitimize its rule, just as oppositional parties and movements tried to enlist it in their causes. Those who attempted to link Romania with Europe, the path of "civilization," or with civil society found that an existing discourse and symbolization around the nation limited the range of political imagination. Romanian elites, particularly under the Communists, desperately needed this kind of normative legitimation, for, in Verdery's terms, they were "teleological elites" defined by their pursuit and defense of certain *values* rather than elites empowered by competence and the mastery of certain *procedures*. Dissidents as well as rulers fought for this moral high ground, and once the Communists were displaced, those that had suffered under the old regime could use their accumulated moral capital to make a claim to power. Not only Iliescu in Romania, but Havel in Czechoslovakia and Wałesa in Poland, were able to build a political claim on their oppositional role and persecution. But in Romania, where dissidence had been relatively weak and the anti-Communist "revolution" relatively late, rather than real oppositional dissidents coming to power, refurbished "reform" Communists took over and managed to legitimize themselves through anti-Communist postures and nationalism.

Although the advocates of civil society gained more power in 1996, Verdery's main story illustrates the limits of intellectual consequence in redefining the Romanian nation. One might make an even stronger case that the main articulation by intellectuals today is toward the diminishment of the nation. Indeed, the post-Communist world promises a different kind of nation than any other previous period. More than before, the world is globalized; circuits of capital, both financial and intellectual, are more extensive and more rapidly flowing than ever before. Forms of international organization are better developed than ever before, and at least based on different principles than the old imperial orders. States have less ability, or are said to have less ability, to control the conditions of their own reproduction, undermining the nation's claim to sovereignty and supremacy in the world system. Might intellectuals in fact be implicated in the articulation of globalization in the same way that they articulated nations?

The case is good: consider their work as interpreters and communicators of information across the globe (the significance of the Internet in redefining the Chinese nation, or calling attention to the plight of East Timor under Indonesian attack),[27] legislating the architecture and terms of their entry into larger supranational organizations and doing the lobbying in international bodies that at one time might have required organic intellectuals protesting in the streets with the masses.[28] Are they not the principal advocates of an international politics of human rights intellectuals? Or might we not consider that intellectuals, precisely by their status as those best able to "interpret" for their nations in a globalized community, are situated to acquire a kind of status that allows them to legislate anew? And with globalization, has the local not been elevated, enhancing the very possibility that a new formation of organic intellectual can emerge, in the Gramscian sense, but at levels in which the nation is less statist, and more local in its wish to control education but not economies and state sovereignty?

This final paragraph is certainly speculative, but suggests the value and importance of seeing just how the categories of our inquiry, whether nation or intellectual, are mutating before our eyes.

The National Process of Making Intellectuals

Focusing on the intellectuals' articulation of the nation is more than simply noting the ways in which elite ideology inflects social processes. It also exposes the ways in which social processes inflect the subject position of intellectuals. By looking at the ideology and identity formation of intellectuals, states, and the peoples on which they have an effect and by which they are affected, an investigator can attempt to judge the relative weight of various factors in defining the nation. In John-Paul Himka's rich and nuanced essay examining the complex context of cultures, structures, and social processes in which national imagining operates (and is operated upon), historical determinations never fatally dictate futures, for human interventions and state politics affect the degree of a nation's contingency at particular moments and places. Himka shows that the denaturalizing of the nation-making process among scholars has brought forth questions and avenues of research seldom imagined in a more organic narrative. Galician Ruthenians end up as Ukrainians by the twentieth century, but once scholars have problematized that result, the exploration of alternative streams that eventually ran out into the sand offer new insights into choices made.

One of Himka's most important contributions is to show that intellectuals do have autonomy, but that their ideas do not always have consequence, much less win hegemony. By introducing the intellectual who breaks from dominant social determinations—the revolutionary Ruthenian Assembly supporting leftist Poles, for example—Himka demonstrates that intellectuals must have resources beyond their ideas to realize their intentions. But certain kinds of resources may undermine the claim to being a good intellectual or a good nationalist. Some definitions of the intellectual even rely on their resource poverty. Becoming a political leader, for instance, could mean compromising one's intellectual status. Or, for example, when Poles emphasized the confessional basis for Ukrainian ethnicity, the Ukrainian nationalist had to minimize the confessional distinction and elevate language and culture, thus refusing Polish resources for their movement.

For many peoples in the prenational period, elites often assimilated to the dominant culture of the state or empire in which they lived, as in Himka's story where Ruthenian nobles adopted Polish language and the Catholic religion. Distinguished by their ethnocultural differences from the people, as well as other marks of material and social distinctions, elite cohesion was maintained in acts of separation from those below. Class distinction and privilege often took on ethnic or religious coloration. Baltic German aristocrats and bourgeois looked down on Estonian peasants and artisans from separate, higher parts of town, or ruled over Latvian farmers from grand manor houses. Often it was from these "foreign" elites that the first interest in the "people" came, but once "native" intellectuals began to explore the past and customs of their own people, distance became a disadvantage and connectedness an integral part of the new national imaginary.

In the Ruthenian case the ethnic elite were clerics, who accentuated the religious differences with the fellow Catholic Poles, emphasizing the difference between the Greek and Latin rites. Married Greek Catholic priests could not adopt Latin Polish Catholicism that did not recognized married priests. Religious barriers were great enough to encourage the development of a separate Ruthenian higher culture, but, Himka argues, religious distinctions alone offer only part of the answer to the move toward separate nationality. In other cases, like the Polonophile Ruthenians of Chełm or the Catholic Armenians of Lviv, people of different rites assimilated into Polish culture quite willingly. With the Galicians the larger discourse of nationality of the mid–nineteenth century provided a context that placed folk culture on a positive historical trajectory. The year 1848 gave a new political clout to nationality, and Ruthenian intellectuals had to choose between joining one of the dominant nations, the Poles or Russians, or develop their own distinct nationality. Himka shows how state patronage and repression aided and undermined the fortunes of Ukrainophiles and Russophiles.

Whatever the vicissitudes of identification, by the 1920s a Ukrainian orientation dominated the Galician population—not to be reversed in the twentieth century. The physical presence in Galicia of key Ukrainophile intellectuals, many of them immigrants from Russian Ukraine, contrasted with the relative absence on the ground of Russophile intellectuals, the most prominent of which emigrated to the Russian empire. The shared language intelligible to readers on both sides of the Austro-Russian border consolidated identification with Ukraine, despite the religious differences between Galician Greek

Catholicism and Ukrainian Russian Orthodoxy. Ultimately, Himka concludes, "the Ukrainian construction could accommodate more elements of the preexisting culture(s) of Ruthenian Galicia than could the all-Russian construction" (140). Rather than borrow a language appropriate to "industrial culture," like Polish or Russian, Galicians joined Russian Ukrainians in the harder task of transforming a vernacular into a language of higher culture.

Himka clearly challenges the portrait of nation making based on a primordial, perennial, or foreordained emergence of a national essence. Indeed, this view, while continuing its popularity within nationalist ideology, is no longer plausible. But what is contestable is the relative place and importance of different features. For Himka, the major determinant of the construction of a national culture was political (145), by which he means political struggles within empires and contests among empires themselves. Intellectuals in the articulation of the nation were formed within this nexus. Although they played generative roles in formulating literary languages and alternative histories, the conjuncture of their demographic and class position with occupational mobility within Galicia produced the blocked opportunity that so often leads intellectuals to articulate the grievances of the grass roots. This is not inevitable, as the assimilators indicate, but it increases the likelihood of their opposition to authority. The concentration of Ukrainophile intellectuals in Galicia, and the insignificant numbers of Russophile intellectuals there, suggests that a substantial number of intellectuals is necessary for a national movement to emerge (136). To determine how general this rule might be, one would need to focus more on those cases where intellectuals have appeared relatively unimportant. Few such cases exist, and this suggests that intellectuals are necessary, though, as Verdery's case of the initially failed civil-society project illustrates, they are clearly not sufficient.

Conclusion

We have sought in this volume to elaborate a theory of intellectual practice affecting and affected by the nation. From the different contributions of our authors, and the discussion in our introductory and final chapter, we offer the following theses and diagram on intellectuals in the articulation of the nation.

Figure 1 indicates the complete set of factors we have discussed throughout this book. No one works at every different level with the same measure of attention, although Himka and Verdery are the most balanced across these different levels. Both discuss how intellectual practices are constituted, which intellectual practices articulate with the nation, alternative images of what the nation means, and which intellectual practices are consequential. Alexander Motyl and Andrzej Walicki limit the degree to which they investigate the formation of intellectuals and rather establish conditions under which the intellectual articulation of the nation is consequential. They also, perhaps not accidentally, limit the variations with which we might consider alternative nations within the same ethnolinguistic community and rather focus on nation formation. Khachig Tololyan also does not investigate as extensively as Verdery or Himka the formation of intellectuals but does focus on the formation of that text which he identifies to be history's agent and suggests is consequential in the very initial formation of the modern Armenian nation.

Michael Kennedy cannot explain how the articulation of the nation by businessmen affects the nation independently of state power, but does spend more time than others on examining how the various structures, including that of the nation, influence the formation of business intellectual practice. Janet Hart spends, by contrast, relatively little time indicating the formation of Gramsci and Glinos, but rather focuses on their effects. Yuri Slezkine devotes little of his discussion to effects, or rather indicates that the intellectual, apart from the state, has little effect. Instead, he for the most part indicates how Marr's intellectual practice shifts with state power behind it.

Though each nation's evolution travels its own path, the focus on intellectuals in this volume reveals many of the broader, common features that nationalisms share. Empirical studies of intellectuals and nations in various parts of the world have already (and will continue to) amplify the varied and shifting relationship of intellectuals to the nation. To take but one example, a recent study of the complex history of Jewish intellectuals illustrates their extraordinary odyssey from initial acts of Zionist imagining to the empowerment of part of the intelligentsia in the state of Israel. The traditional stance of influential Jewish intellectuals, from Moses Mendelsohn in the Enlightenment to the "critical humanists" like George Stein in the present, has been one of distance from nationalism and a dedicated loyalty to a cosmopolitan ideal of learning and emancipation. The limits on Jewish integration in

Analyst's Normative and Theoretical Priorities Establish Object
and Mode of Analysis within This Larger Set of Issues

THE NATION
(in its Manifestations
through History, Language, etc.)

OTHER STRUCTURES
(Economy, State, Everday Life, etc.)

constructs in various ways, through socialization, construction of interests, etc.:

INTELLECTUAL PRACTICE
understood as a combination of

Intellectual Resources
Cultural Capital, Sophistication of Intellectuality, Autonomy of Activity, Prestige,
and Articulation with other Kinds of Power

Forms of Intellectual Activity
Organization of More Exclusively Intellectual Associations, Implication in State Power,
Mobilization of Popular Movements,
Cultivation of New Readerships, etc.

Kinds of Intellectual Products
Social Movements, State Action, Exemplary Performances, Literature, etc.

which influences, both intentionally and unintentionally, singly and in conjunction with
other social forces, various manifestations of the nation:

↓

THE NATION

Other
National   Its formation   Its alternatives   Its decline
Actors

Social and Ideological Environment, Geopolitical Strategies

Fig. 1.   A Theory of National Intellectual Practice

Europe inspired a small number of Jewish intellectuals, most notably Theodor Herzl, to elaborate one of the most daring projects of imagined nation-making, the founding of a Jewish state in Palestine. But the anti-nationalist position, articulated by Julien Benda, Franz Rosenzweig, and others, remained strong, and even after the triumph of Zionism in the late 1940s, committed nationalist intellectuals, who had long attempted to marry nationalism and critical reason, despaired at the gap between the ideals of their national vision and the bitter, embattled reality of the new state. In the history of Zionism intellectuals originated the idea of the return to Palestine, the foundational idea of a religio-secular Jewish nation. They fostered the revival of the Hebrew language, most importantly in the years before World War I, and taught it to the migrants to the "new land." They organized and led the nationalist movement in its various phases, transforming themselves from scholars and journalists into strategists and military commanders, and, finally, rulers of the state.[29] From emancipators they also became the oppressors of the indigenous non-Jewish population.

These phases through which intellectuals passed occurred in a variety of nationalist trajectories, not always all of them, and not necessarily in the same sequence. But this range of intellectual activity and articulation needs to be specified. It is not simply that intellectuals followed their cold rational self-interests and sought good jobs in a new polity, as one might vulgarize (though not by much) the position of some analysts. They were also the "revivers" of cultures that had been forgotten, or, in many cases, not yet constituted. They were the discoverers of the folk, the people, whom they defined and delimited. In an increasingly democratic age they were the political philosophers who shaped the new universal discourse of the nation, linking people, power, and territory to notions of representation, self-determination, and popular sovereignty. Intellectuals transformed inchoate peoples into mobilizable nationalities and modern nations in ways similar to the homogenization of populations carried out by bureaucratic states. They spread the national message, wrote the articles and published the newspapers, edited the grammars and dictionaries, taught the classes and wrote the laws that bounded the people and determined the citizenry. And in many cases they came to power, took control of the instruments of the state, and used that awesome power to promote their nation's welfare and security as they saw it, its advancement and expansion, in a dangerous world of national competition.

NOTES

As with the introduction and the editing of the collection, both authors have written and rewritten this concluding essay. The ordering of names is not designed to mark the measure of contribution. We thank Geoff Eley and Yaroslav Hrytsak for their readings, as well as the comments of the anonymous reviewers for the press.

1. Eric J. Hobsbawm, "Ethnicity and Nationalism in Europe Today," *Anthropology Today* 8, no. 1 (1992): 81; the essay has been reprinted in *Mapping the Nation*, ed. Gopal Balakrishnan (London: Verso, 1996), 255–66.

2. In this sense, this collection, while more focused on the intersection of nationalities with intellectuals than Alexander J. Motyl's *Thinking Theoretically about Soviet Nationalities* (New York: Columbia University Press, 1992), is also more epistemologically and disciplinarily diverse, with postmodernists and positivists, anthropologists, sociologists, historians, literary theorists, and political scientists participating.

3. For one good example of the value of this disposition, see Margaret Somers, "Narrating and Naturalizing Civil Society and Citizenship Theory: The Place of Political Culture and the Public Sphere," *Sociological Theory* 13, no. 3 (1995): 229–74.

4. Here, we derive the point from Gerhard Lenski, Patrick Nolan, and Jean Lenski, *Human Societies* (New York: McGraw-Hill, 1995), where the distinction between agrarian societies in an industrial social environment, and agrarian societies in an agrarian one, is fundamental to assessing their structure and dynamics of change.

5. Pierre Bourdieu, *Homo Academicus* (Stanford, Calif.: Stanford University Press, 1988), contrasts intellectuals possessing scientific capital with those possessing administrative capital. In the discourse of intellectual status, it is not difficult to see what kind of intellectual is awarded more status, if status is based on normative foundations elevating the power of arguments over the argument from power.

6. Normative grounding, of course, influences all intellectual practices. For how it has affected work in Polish studies of stratification, see Michael D. Kennedy, "Transformations of Normative Foundations and Empirical Sociologies: Class, Stratification, and Democracy in Poland," in *The Polish Road from Socialism*, ed. W. D. Connor and P. Płoszajski (Armonk, N.Y.: M. E. Sharpe, 1992), 283–312.

7. For elaborations of theoretical orientations we find stimulating, see Michael Burawoy, "Marxism as Science: Historical Challenges and Theoretical Growth," *American Sociological Review* 55 (1990): 775–93, and "Two Methods in Search of Science: Trotsky vs. Skocpol," *Theory and Society* 18 (1989): 759–805; and William H. Sewell Jr., "A Theory of Structure: Duality, Agency, and Transformation," *American Journal of Sociology* 98 (1992): 1–29.

8. William Sewell's critique of James Coleman is especially illustrative of that emphasis. See James Coleman, "Social Theory, Social Research, and a The-

ory of Action," *American Journal of Sociology* 91 (1986): 1309–35; and Sewell's response, "Theory of Action, Dialectic, and History," *American Journal of Sociology* 93 (1987): 166–71.

9. Sewell, "A Theory of Structure."

10. Jonathan Turner, *The Structure of Sociological Theory* (Belmont, Mass.: Wadsworth, 1991), 9–11.

11. These themes have been developed in Ronald Grigor Suny, *The Revenge of the Past: Nationalism, Revolution, and the Collapse of the Soviet Union* (Stanford, Calif.: Stanford University Press, 1993), and "Ambiguities of Empire: States, Empires, and Nations," *Post-Soviet Affairs* 11, no. 2 (1995): 185–96; and Geoff Eley and Ronald Grigor Suny, "Introduction: From the Moment of Social History to the Work of Cultural Representation," in *Becoming National: A Reader*, ed. Eley and Suny (New York: Oxford University Press, 1996), 3–37.

12. Rogers Brubaker, *Nationalism Reframed* (Cambridge: Cambridge University Press, 1996).

13. The distinction between discursive and practical consciousness is from Anthony Giddens, *The Constitution of Society* (Berkeley and Los Angeles: University of California Press, 1984).

14. Elżbieta Skotnicka-Illasiewicz and Włodzimierz Wesołowski, "The Significance of Preconceptions: Europe of Civil Societies and Europe of Nationalities," in *Notions of Nationalism*, ed. Sukumar Periwal (Budapest: Central European University Press, 1995), 208–27.

15. Walicki's argument here contributes substantially to those authors who wish to emphasize the deeply embedded and necessarily ethnied or raced qualities of the most political nations. Consider, for instance, not only how Anthony Smith indicates that even the most territorial or political of nationalism draws upon some ethnic core to legitimate claims (*The Ethnic Origins of Nations* [Oxford: Blackwell, 1986], 216), but also how the whiteness of American national identity is raced (See David Roediger, *Toward the Abolition of Whiteness* [London: Verso, 1994]). Contrast this with Liah Greenfeld's optimistic image of American political nationalism that finds racism and sexism in its midst an aberration (*Nationalism: Five Roads to Modernity* [Cambridge, Mass.: Harvard University Press, 1992], 456–59).

16. Rogers Brubaker, "Rethinking Nationhood: Nation as Institutionalized Form, Practical Category, Contingent Event," *Contention* 4, no. 1 (1994): 3–14; also in *Nationalism Reframed.*

17. As Walicki points out, the idea of nations as constructed goes back at least to the Austro-Marxists of the last century (one might also see a similar idea in the famous address of Ernst Renan). But the theorization of the implications of constructivism is relatively recent, and it has spilled over into the study of other social categories, most importantly class and gender. In part because objectivist- or realist-inclined scholars tend to focus more on classes than on nations, classes remain more defined in realist terms than nations do. But those who emphasize the constructedness of nations, if pushed about classes, usually make similar claims about classes. While some Marxists still claim class to be a

more "objective" social entity than nations or races (see, for example, Barbara J. Fields on race: "Ideology and Race in American History," in *Region, Race, and Reconstruction: Essays in Honor of C. Vann Woodward*, ed. J. Morgan Kousser and James M. McPherson [New York, Oxford University Press, 1982], and "Slavery, Race, and Ideology in the United States of America," *New Left Review* 181 [May–June 1990]: 95–118), a number of other writers have argued for the historical contingency of class (see Suny and Eley, introduction to *Becoming National*). While never divorced completely from processes and structures outside the sway of individuals, the meanings and experiences attached to class, like those attached to gender, nation, or race, are not simply subjective in the sense of what "I" experience, but more importantly what is understood and endured intersubjectively, between and among individuals and social groups.

18. See Roman Szporluk, *Communism and Nationalism: Karl Marx vs. Friedrich List* (New York: Oxford University Press, 1988).

19. See Brian Porter, *When Nationalism Began to Hate: Imagining Modern Politics in 19th Century Poland*, forthcoming, Oxford University Press.

20. For the national problem among the Polish peasantry, see Keely Stauter-Hausted, "The Nation in the Village: The Genesis of Rural National Identity in Austrian Poland, 1848–1914, typescript, "Peasant Nationalism in Galician Poland: The Centennial of the Kościuszko Uprising and the Rise of the Kościuszko Cult in Galician Villages," *Austrian History Yearbook* 25 (1994): 79–95, and "The Moral Community and Peasant Nationalism in Nineteenth-Century Poland," in *Transforming Peasants: Society, State and the Peasantry, 1861–1930*, ed. Judith Pallot (London: Macmillan Press, and New York: St. Martin's Press), 73–89.

21. See, for instance, Aldon Morris's work, *The Origins of the Civil Rights Movement* (New York: Free Press, 1984) for a critique of the resource mobilization perspective's emphasize on external resources.

22. Julie Skurski, "The Ambiguities of Authenticity in Latin America: *Dona Barbara* and the Construction of National Identity," in Eley and Suny, *Becoming National*, 371–402.

23. Joanna Kurczewska, "The Polish Intelligentsia: Retiring from the Stage," in *Democracy, Civil Society, and Pluralism*, ed. Christopher G. A. Bryant and Edmund Mokrzycki (Warsaw: IFiS, 1995), 239–54.

24. This came out very clearly in a workshop called "Doing History in the Shadow of the Balkan Wars," organized by the Working Group on Southeast European Studies at the University of Michigan, January 17, 1997.

25. But obviously, to argue contrarily and emphasize the continuity of the Polish nation is to privilege certain elements of national identity formation over other more social forms. That in itself is an important strategy in the nation's articulation.

26. For an elaboration of these ideas around contemporary Ukraine, see Laada Bilaniuk, "The Politics of Language and Identity in Post-Soviet Ukraine," University of Michigan unpublished doctoral dissertation, 1997.

27. Henry Park, "The Views, Movements, and Social Backgrounds of Stu-

dents from the People's Republic of China in Ann Arbor," Ph.D. diss., University of Michigan, 1992; Benedict Anderson, "Long Distance Nationalism," in *The Spectre of Comparisons: Nationalism, Southeast Asia and the World* (London: Verso, 1998), 58–77.

28. See Dieter Rucht, "Limits to Mobilization: Environmental Policy for the European Union," in Jackie Smith, Charles Chatfield, and Ron Pagnucco, eds, *Transnational Social Movements and Global Politics: Solidarity Beyond the State* (Syracuse: Syracuse University Press, 1997), 195–213.

29. Michael Keren, *The Pen and the Sword: Israeli Intellectuals and the Making of the Nation-State* (Boulder, Colo.: Westview, 1989).

Contributors

Janet Hart is Associate Professor of Anthropology at the University of Michigan. Her work on women, nationalism, and revolution is reflected in her book *New Voices in the Nation: Women and the Greek Resistance, 1941–1964* (1996).

John-Paul Himka is Professor of History and Culture at the University of Alberta. A specialist in East European and Ukrainian history, he is the author of *Socialism in Galicia: The Emergence of Polish Social Democracy and Ukrainian Radicalism, 1860–1890* (1983) and *Galician Villagers and the Ukrainian National Movement in the Nineteenth Century* (1987).

Michael D. Kennedy is Associate Professor of Sociology and Director of the Center for Russian and East European Studies at the University of Michigan. He has worked on problems of intellectuals, professions, civil society, and the nation in East Central Europe, particularly Poland. He has more recently turned to a comparative project on identity formation and social problems in Estonia, Ukraine, and Uzbekistan. His publications include *Professionals, Power, and Solidarity in Poland: A Critical Sociology of Soviet-Type Society* (1991) and the edited volume *Envisioning Eastern Europe: Postcommunist Cultural Studies* (1994).

Alexander J. Motyl is Associate Director of the Harriman Institute of Columbia University. A scholar of nationalism and Ukraine, Motyl has brought empirical research together with theoretical insights in his works, which include *Will the Non-Russians Rebel? State, Ethnicity, and Stability in the USSR* (1987); *Sovietology, Rationality, Nationality: Coming to Grips with Nationalism in the USSR* (1990); *Thinking Theoretically about Soviet Nationalities: History and Comparison in the Study of the USSR* (1992); and *Dilemmas of Independence: Ukraine and the Politics of Post-Totalitarianism* (1993).

419

Yuri Slezkine is Associate Professor of History at the University of California, Berkeley. His interests in both ethnic Russians and the non-Russian peoples of the czarist empire and the Soviet Union are represented in the coedited volume *Between Heaven and Hell: The Myth of Siberia in Russian Culture* (1993) and his monograph *Arctic Mirrors: Russia and the Small Peoples of the North* (1994).

Ronald Grigor Suny is Professor of Political Science at the University of Chicago. The first holder of the Alex Manoogian Chair in Modern Armenian History at the University of Michigan, he writes on Russian/Soviet, Armenian, Georgian, and Azerbaijani history and politics. His publications include *The Baku Commune, 1917–1918: Class and Nationality in the Russian Revolution* (1972); *The Making of the Georgian Nation* (1988, 1994); *Looking toward Ararat: Armenia in Modern History* (1993); *The Revenge of the Past: Nationalism, Revolution, and the Collapse of the Soviet Union* (1993); and *The Soviet Experiment: Russia, the Soviet Union, and the Successor States* (1998).

Khachig Tololyan is Professor of English at Wesleyan University. The founder and editor of the journal *Diaspora*, Tololyan has written widely on Thomas Pynchon, Armenian politics and culture, and political terrorism. Among his publications is *Spiurki mech* (In the diaspora) (1980).

Katherine Verdery is Eric Wolf Professor of Anthropology at the University of Michigan. Her extensive fieldwork and archival research on ethnic identity, politics, and change in modern Romania is reflected in her major works: *Transylvanian Villages: Three Centuries of Political, Economic, and Ethnic Change* (1983); *National Ideology under Socialism: Identity and Cultural Politics in Ceauşescu's Romania* (1991); and *What Was Socialism and What Comes Next?* (1996).

Andrzej Walicki is the O'Neill Professor of History at the University of Notre Dame. An intellectual historian of Poland and Russia, his numerous publications include *The Controversy over Capitalism: Studies in the Social Philosophy of the Russian Populists* (1969); *The Slavophile Controversy* (1975); *A History of Russian Thought from the Enlightenment to Marxism* (1979); *Russia, Poland, and Universal Regeneration: Studies on Russian and Polish Political Thought of the Romantic Epoch* (1991); and *Marxism and the Leap to the Kingdom of Freedom: The Rise and Fall of the Communist Utopia* (1995).

Name Index

Subject Index